GOD

IN HIS

PROVIDENCE:

A COMPREHENSIVE VIEW OF THE PRINCIPLES AND PARTICULARS OF AN ACTIVE DIVINE PROVIDENCE OVER MAN, — HIS FORTUNES, CHANGES, TRIALS, ENTIRE DISCIPLINE AS A SPIRITUAL BEING, FROM BIRTH TO ETERNITY.

BY WOODBURY M. FERNALD.

"The very hairs of your head are all numbered." — *Matt.* 10:30.

"Thou hast beset me behind and before, and laid thine hand upon me." — *Psalm*, 139:5.

BOSTON:
OTIS CLAPP, No. 3, BEACON STREET.
CROSBY, NICHOLS, & CO., 117 WASHINGTON ST.
NEW YORK:
D. APPLETON & CO.
1859.

Entered, according to Act of Congress, in the year 1859, by
WOODBURY M. FERNALD,
In the Clerk's Office of the District Court of the District of Massachusetts.

LITHOTYPED BY COWLES AND COMPANY,
17 WASHINGTON STREET, BOSTON.

Printed by
GEO. C. RAND & AVERY.

To

MY WIFE:

WHO, BY THE MERCY OF THE DIVINE PROVIDENCE,
WAS GIVEN TO ME FOR A COMPANION AND HELP,
AND WHO HAS LABORED SO CHEERFULLY THROUGH ALL —
THROUGH GOOD REPORT AND THROUGH EVIL REPORT,
THROUGH PRIVATION, SUFFERING, AND AFFLICTION,
AND WITHOUT WHOM I NEVER SHOULD HAVE BEEN ABLE TO
ACCOMPLISH SO MUCH,

This Book

IS AFFECTIONATELY DEDICATED,

WITH DEVOUT GRATITUDE,

BY HER HUSBAND,

THE AUTHOR.

PREFACE.

We write our book for "the wide, wide world." Not that we expect to have the world for readers, but that we do humbly hope to gain some audience with the Church Universal. Long and drearily have we heard of the "Eclipse of Faith," and sadly have we contemplated the chaotic state of the Christian Church. If this book will do any thing to remove the shade which gathers so heavily around many souls, to inform the understanding, and to pour sunlight upon eyes so darkened, our labors will be more than amply rewarded. We have written in the love of it. We have not sought merely to add another book to the many now in the world: this work is the fruit of more than twenty years' professional thought and reading, and labor and observation among men, and we have honestly felt that it is now called for. We think we have heard the Lord's voice, and that we understand something of his Providence. We do not, of course, claim that every idea in it is exactly correct, and we shall be more desirous than any one else to unlearn our errors.

One word more for the Church. While we hold ourself in strong sympathy with the Church Universal, we believe also that God is at this day forming, out of the good of all the various sects, a New Church answering to John's description of the "New Jerusalem." We would not therefore be understood as writing for any sect, or organization, or particular body of men. We are heart-sick of sectarianism in all its forms. We hope we shall not be caught with the least remnant of it upon our garments.

But it will be seen that we have made much use of a favorite and highly illumined author; that author is Swedenborg. And although we do not accept him, or any other man, as an infallible teacher, and believe that he saw only in part, yet we do believe that he was the great providential man of the Church, raised up and qualified in a time of great darkness, and that he was the first, in an eminent manner, to begin the "New Jerusalem," or a true and more spiritual church upon this earth. We have quoted from him liberally. But with all our partiality, we *know*, better than any one can tell us, that we are not in slavery to him, and do not blindly follow him.

Again we say, we write for "the wide, wide world." We have endeavored to popularize certain truths, to clear up certain spiritual, philosophical, and theological problems, and to present the great theme of the Divine Providence in an attracting and profitable form. How well we have succeeded, futurity will most assuredly tell.

So saying, we have not another anxious thought about it; it goes from our hands most freely; and with feelings deep and indescribable, it is now humbly and trustfully committed to the care of the Divine Providence.

W. M. F.

BOSTON, Mass., Sept. 1859.

CONTENTS.

PART I.

NATURE OF THE DIVINE PROVIDENCE.

CHAPTER I.

PRELIMINARY REMARKS.

CHAPTER II.

PROVIDENCE AND NECESSITY — WITH FREE-WILL.

CHAPTER III.

THE NATURE AND ORIGIN OF EVIL.

CHAPTER IV.

ABSOLUTE DIVINE SOVEREIGNTY.

CHAPTER V.

THE CONNECTION OF GOD WITH NATURE.

CHAPTER VI.

THE DIVINE ESSENCE IN THE INMOSTS AND ULTIMATES OF ALL THINGS.

CHAPTER VII.

CONNECTION OF RELIGION WITH PHILOSOPHY.

CHAPTER VIII.

GENERAL AND SPECIAL PROVIDENCES.

CHAPTER IX.

THE NATURE AND MINISTRY OF ANGELS.

CHAPTER X.

ILLUSTRATIONS AND INSTANCES OF THE ANGELIC MINISTRY.

CHAPTER XI.

DIRECT AND INDIRECT PROVIDENCES.

CHAPTER XII.

DESIGNS AND PERMISSIONS.

CHAPTER XIII.

PART II.

ENDS AND OPERATIONS OF THE DIVINE PROVIDENCE.

CHAPTER I.

A HEAVEN FROM THE HUMAN RACE.

CHAPTER II.

THE ETERNAL MEMORY OF THE SOUL.

CHAPTER III.

DIVINE PROVIDENCE IN THE REGENERATE LIFE.

CHAPTER IV.

NATURE AND OPERATION OF THE NEW BIRTH.

CHAPTER V.

SPIRITUAL WARFARE.

CHAPTER VI.

TEMPTATIONS OF THE REGENERATING LIFE.

CHAPTER VII.

FLUCTUATIONS.

CHAPTER VIII.

THE WINDING WAY.

CHAPTER IX.

THE UNKNOWN PATHS.

CHAPTER X.

VIEW FROM MOUNT PISGAH.

CHAPTER XI.

FINAL REST.

CHAPTER XII.

CHAPTER XIII.

DIVINE PROVIDENCE IN THE MODERATION OF THE HUMAN WILL.

CHAPTER XIV.

DIVINE PROVIDENCE AND HUMAN PRUDENCE.

CHAPTER XV.

DIVINE PROVIDENCE WITH DIVINE FORESIGHT.

CHAPTER XVI.

DIVINE PROVIDENCE IN THE PERMISSION OF PARTICULAR EVILS.

CHAPTER XVII.

DIVINE PROVIDENCE EQUALLY TO THE GOOD AND TO THE EVIL.

CHAPTER XVIII.

DIVINE PROVIDENCE IN EARTHLY AND HEAVENLY RICHES.

CHAPTER XIX.

DIVINE PROVIDENCE IN ANSWER TO PRAYER.

CHAPTER XX.

DIVINE PROVIDENCE CONCERNING FORTUNE, CHANCE, AND ACCIDENTS.

CHAPTER XXI.

DIVINE PROVIDENCE IN SORROW AND AFFLICTION.

CHAPTER XXII.

DIVINE PROVIDENCE IN REGARD TO LITTLE CHILDREN.

CHAPTER XXIII.

DIVINE PROVIDENCE IN MARRIAGES.

CHAPTER XXIV.

DIVINE PROVIDENCE IN THE TIME OF ONE'S DEATH.

CHAPTER XXV.

TRUST IN DIVINE PROVIDENCE: ITS NATURE AND EFFECTS.

PART I.

NATURE OF THE DIVINE PROVIDENCE.

———"Beholding, in the sacred light
Of his essential reason, all the shapes
Of swift contingence, all successive ties
Of action, propagated through the sum
Of possible existence,—He at once,
Down the long series of eventful time,
So fixed the dates of being—so disposed,
To every living soul of every kind,
The field of motion and the hour of rest,
That all conspired to his supreme design,—
To UNIVERSAL GOOD."

CHAPTER I.

PRELIMINARY REMARKS.

"A mighty maze, but not without a plan."

THE Divine Providence may be said to be, in general, the government of the Divine Being, by his infinite Love, Wisdom, and Power, of the whole universe which He has created, so that every thing which transpires shall not only be the best that can possibly be, up to the time of its occurrence, but shall tend, without waste or hindrance, to still increasing good forever: so much so indeed, that nothing can happen, ever so small or unfavorable, and to the obscurest creature, which does not have this tendency. There is probably no one truth, which, were it susceptible of clear demonstration, and could it be received into the heart as well as into the understanding, that would have so great an effect to reconcile man to his present condition, to subdue his fears, and make him contented and happy in his lot, as this one. What a familiar truth it appears to be, and how large a place does it occupy in all theology, and how frequently is it uttered, both by the religious and the irreligious! The very *proverbs* of mankind, that "every thing is for the best," and that "whatever is, is right," are a confirmatory evidence of the great truth herein contained; for the proverbs and common sayings of men have not originated from that more indiscriminate mass of truth and falsehood which composes the great bulk of their learning, but are rather the effect of a truer and more universal influx from God into the minds of humanity. Hence the Latin proverb, "*Quod semper, quod ubique, quod ab omnibus est verum.*" What is believed always, everywhere, and by all, must be true. But this is a truth which needs to be demonstrated, and illustrated, and made clear to the unfolded reason.

In the first place, then, let us ask, What is it that *obstructs* our faith? Why do we ever have doubts and misgivings, and why do questionings arise in our minds? In reply, we say that there are two reasons for this: first, the confusion which we see around us in the shape of dire evils and injustice, and the apparent hap-hazardness of so large a part of the great world's movement; and second, a certain *necessity* which seems to reign through every thing, which, despite the utmost allowance for the free-will of man, presents a prospect more akin to the Fate of the ancients, than to any providence of a personal God. There is, on the darker side of this subject, so much that oppresses us, — that confounds and bewilders us, — so much entanglement, deceit, and treachery, and so many things that it seems impossible, for the time being, to admit into any really divine government, that the natural mind succumbs — shrinks away into dark and discouraging states, and the spiritual is overpowered by the present disorder. For the time being, it loses its control, and heavy shadows concerning the Divine Providence pass over the mind. It may not lose its faith entirely, but it cannot see, and in the darkness of the present occasion, it asks despairingly, Why is it? and How is it? In fact, with almost every Christian, there are moments of scepticism; and scepticism, be it observed, is not a thing which pertains to faith in God, or to immortality merely; the belief in these two fundamental truths may be most firm, and impossible to be shaken; but at the same time, what God is, and how He acts, or whether his providence, after all, is so different from a certain necessity more or less allied to the ancient Fate,—here is room for a scepticism quite at one with an unshaken faith in God, in immortality, and the final well-being of the universe. And there are many religious persons who are sorely tried on these things. The human heart—these poor, sympathetic, and intensely susceptible natures, cannot bear every thing; and when its hopes are rudely stricken down, or too long and too painfully deferred, what wonder if it sink, betimes, not only into inconsolable grief or settled melancholy, but into religious distrust — into philosophic questionings of the Divine Providence? And when giant evils burst forth in the nature of accidents, — when the evil triumph over the good, — when, by merest hap, as it were, the simple and the uncalculating have fortune thrust upon them, and the worthy and sagacious are doomed to disappointment, — when intrigue and cunning carry it over plain-dealing and honesty, — when crimes abound, and the simple are entrapped, and a thousand things are daily occurring, so confused and bewildering to one who attempts to give any rational account of them, — when there is so much evident free-will on the part of man, and withal, so much fatality in human movements and human experience, — so much to lament and grieve over, or else to sink under in hopeless apathy and stoical indifference, — what wonder is it if all thoughts of Providence momentarily flee the mind, or it has its hours and days of sceptical and tempting distrust?

Let a man stand, for instance, in the heart of a great city; and only for a few minutes let him cast his eye upon the vast concourse of life and activity going on around him. What stir of human passion and interest! What driving and pursuit of a common object, though variously estimated as to its nature, and power to confer the happiness sought; and what dark crowds of complicated thoughts, of evil desires, of covetous longings and vain ambitions, flit by him in a single hour! And within all the piles of brick and stone that stretch abroad on every side, how much of calculation, and of what character, either for success or disappointment, is going on there! Or, look at the records of a single newspaper, and see the wretched list of casualties and crimes, — robberies, burglaries, arsons, rapes, murders, forgeries, suicides, and terrible outbreaks, which is furnished in the history of a single day. "Merciful heavens!"

might not one exclaim, "and is there a *particular providence* in all this? if so, of what kind and nature? Has *God* any thing to do with it, and to do with the *whole* of it, and for particular purposes in regard to man's nature and destiny?" The prospect is utterly bewildering. It does not seem to be governed by any intelligent will, either of design or permission. A carriage wheel breaks and a man is killed; another falls and maims himself for life; a destructive fire breaks out and sweeps down all before it with remorseless disregard; a man was just a moment too late to save a human being from the flames; a boat is upset in the harbor; the lightning strikes some one's dwelling; a child is devoured by a ravenous beast; three thousand persons, as has just happened in a foreign country, break through the ice and are drowned;—such is the aspect, confused, uncertain, criminal and accidental, which even everyday life presents for contemplation. And when we rise from this fleeting, transitory scene, and extend our thoughts to the nations and ages which have rolled by us in the murky past, and are still rolling on, amid warfare, carnage, detestable hate, and monstrous outrage;—when we read even what is called "*church* history," and see the deeds that humanity is capable of committing, and think still that there is a human soul under all this terrible demonism,—that here are the materials of an angel world,—the contemplation becomes almost too strange to speak of. Instead of providence—any thing from God, or controlled by Him, the prospect seems rather of a wild, tumultuous, and boundless ocean, where the surges of humanity rise and fall, and drift to and fro, and break in confusion against each other, and upon the rocks and shores of the solemn coasts that enclose it.

To be sure, there is one way of viewing all this, to save the idea of Providence. And that is, to speak of it generally, and not particularly, or to speak of the particulars as included *in* the general; and this, indeed, as far as it goes, is a *true* way of contemplating the mighty scene. There can be no universal providence which does *not* include all the particulars, but the convinced understanding would like to know how these occurrences *are* providence, or how they are in *any* way connected with the Divine Being, who rules and governs with absolute power.

CHAPTER II.

PROVIDENCE AND NECESSITY — WITH FREE-WILL.

"Though God is a most perfect free-Agent, yet He cannot but do what is best and wisest in the whole. The reason is evident; because perfect wisdom and goodness are as steady and certain principles of action, as Necessity itself; and an infinitely wise and good Being, indued with the most perfect liberty, can no more choose to act in contradiction to wisdom and goodness, than a necessary agent can act contrary to the Necessity by which it is acted; it being as great an absurdity and impossibility in choice, for Infinite Wisdom to choose to act unwisely, or Infinite Goodness to choose what is not good, as it would be in nature, for absolute Necessity to fail of producing its necessary effect. It is the beauty of this Necessity that it is strong as fate itself, with all the advantage of reason and goodness." — *Clark's Demonstration of the Being and Attributes of God.*

"Philosophically speaking, there is no such thing as free-will; practically speaking, there is." — *Dr. Hartley.*

We come now to the consideration which has perplexed the minds of men in all ages, and which will explain, in part, the existence of the aforesaid confusion. The resort to Philosophical Necessity has ever been the short and compendious way of relief from the whole burden which presses so heavily upon the mind. But *is* there any such thing? And if so, does not this at once deny free-will, and remove God from the universe? Or, at least, does it not merge God, and man, and nature, into one indistinguishable system of inevitability, and throw us back to inexorable Fate? We reply, there is such a thing as universal and inevitable necessity; but this does not deny free-will, nor remove God from the universe, nor merge the whole of being into indistinguishable fatality. There is a great distinction to be made between the destiny of blind, unintelligent fate, and that which is made so by the certain operation of the laws of a personal God. In the one case, a man has a loving Father to look to, whom he knows has consulted his highest good in every thing, — who, by will, and design, and mental calculation, has done it; in the other, he has nothing to contemplate but blind, unconscious laws, and he is the sport of these cold laws forever. These may indeed, must, from their very necessity and fixedness, insure him a destiny undisturbed by any chance, or fluctuation of interfering evil, but they do not meet and respond to his own spiritual and personal nature; they do not touch his soul with affection, and with that complete assurance which springs from the recognition of an infinitely good, wise, and powerful God. In the *certainty* of such a destiny there is indeed no difference; for "known unto God are all his works from the beginning of the world."

But is not this admitting the only essential point in the controversy? For though we refer such a necessity to the Divinity, and to the laws which He has established, and which man obeys or disobeys, it only changes its motive character, it does not change its certainty or inevitability. Yes, we answer, it is admitting the necessity of the whole movement of the universe. And that is precisely what we mean to admit, in all its entireness — in its whole length, breadth, and depth, and in all its particulars. There is no escape. But we also say that the free-will of man is a truth consistent *with* this, in equal entireness, so far as all consciousness and all practical purposes are concerned. What is the free-will of man? Without perplexing ourselves here with any metaphysical questions, is it not sufficient to say, that if a man has *conscious* and *practical* freedom, it is all that is necessary? Suppose there is discoverable, by the aid of the intellect, an inevitable train of causation, by which man's will, in every instance in which it is executed, is seen to be involved in a certain kind of necessity. And yet it is also seen and *felt* too (which is the more powerful seeing), that there is no *mechanical* acting, that a man is not forced, that he is most certainly in the wrong when he does a bad act, that he condemns himself righteously and wisely, that he truly says he ought not to have done it, that he realizes all the consequences of its wrong—pain, remorse, chagrin, outward troubles, for an indefinite period, in fact so long as the wrong spirit continues; and that, spite of all the necessity of the action, there is an equal necessity for all this moral judgment and suffering. Then, I say, the will is free enough. And we here see the truth of Dr. Hartley's statement, which is a complete *multum in parvo.* "Philosophically speaking, there is no such thing as free-will; practically speaking, there is." But now, what is meant here by philosophically speaking, as he uses the term ? It is *intellectually* speaking. But this is only *half* speaking. Man has a moral and spiritual nature, as well as an intellectual. And I say, *morally* and *practically* speaking, he is *absolutely* and *entirely* free. For by the above brief showing, every rational man has so decided it, and will continue to forever. Here, then, we rest our argument, for the present, on the peculiar freedom of the will. We prefer to be practical. We can most thoroughly *afford* to be, having the true theory. We prefer the wisdom of a sound moral understanding, to the subtleties of the metaphysician.

We will remark, here, however, in accordance with the above presentation, and for the further clarification of the subject, that *neither* of these things — neither free-will nor necessity, in their absolute and universal sense, is a whole truth in itself, but that taken both together, they make a complete truth. They are indeed but two halves of one whole. They are both true, and both *equally* true, but either, separately considered, is a falsity. It is the freedom of necessity, and the necessity of freedom. Or, it is free necessity, and necessary freedom. This truth must be felt by all parts of the mind, in order to be comprehended. A man may reason on it forever, and he will not know it, because it does not pertain to the reason alone, but to the will also. Women in general believe more in free-will than men do, because they have more *of* will. A man must have a perfectly balanced mind to see and feel the great truth that there is here. If he is all head, or predominantly given to reason and the law-side of things, he will decide in favor of philosophical necessity; if he is predominantly a man of heart, or a practical man, he will decide for free-will as commonly understood. But if he has a well-balanced mind, disposed to see into the laws and connections of the universe, the union of God with Nature, Spirit with Matter, the spiritual world with the natural world, and intellect with affection, or truth with good, he will then both see and feel the truth in both of these things; and, gratefully acknowledging the stupendous force and mechanism of the universe, and the power of God through all, will at the same time act in accordance with those higher *moral* and *spiritual* laws which equally reign therein, and make a part of the wonderful unity. In short, he will not only think, but feel; not only reason, but act; not only say this or that, but go to and *make* it an actual and practical necessity.

To return now, for illustration of the Divine Providence in this view of it, let us begin at the foundations. What greater necessity than the very existence of God? His whole substance — his very ground of being and motion — and all his glorious attributes and qualities, are eternal and absolute necessities. He had no choice in his existence; He was and is; the I AM, the ETERNAL. In the next place, all the laws which grow out of such a necessary existence must be equally as necessary, and in their operations as inevitable as fate. But as before said, not *blind* fate, but the enlightened operations of a willing and intelligent God. The Divine Will itself, in fact, or at least the Divine Wisdom, which is the rule of that Will, in this view of it may be contemplated as Law. It *is* law, if we make the proper discriminations, and consider it with reference to internal and external, personal and impersonal. And all the laws which operate in nature, such as gravitation, chemical affinity, etc., are but the operations of the Divine Will in the ultimates of existence. We must come to a simpler philosophy of law and will, or God-force and Nature-force. One is as much law as the other. There is not a law in the whole material universe which acts with a more fixed and determinate method, or within more prescribed limits or conditions of action, than the Divine Essence itself. In order more fully to be convinced of this, let us seek precisely the best definition of the term "Law." And it has been well remarked that "law, as it is understood by the best authorities, means simply a rule of action, or a definite mode or method in which force and motion proceed toward the accomplishment of an end. It is not, therefore, of itself, either force or motion, but only the *rule* of action which these, in their operations, are made to observe.

"Now it may be safely asserted that there is no force or motion, either in the universe of matter or the universe of mind, which, in its operations, does not observe *some* rule, *some* method, and hence *some law*. If, indeed, there could be any action or motion *without* method or law, that action or motion would necessarily be chaotic, and would tend directly to the subversion of all law and order, and thus to reduce all things to chaos. It is impossible for a man to conceive a thought, except in accordance with some law of thought. Nay, it is evidently impossible even for the Infinite Mind to conceive a thought, or put forth an action, except in connection with some definite mode or form, and hence law of procedure, which that thought or action spontaneously assumes. In the Infinite Mind, therefore, Law, in its spiritual sense, is self-existent and eternal. Thence it proceeds, by volition, into outer creations, and assumes the forms of what are termed the 'laws of nature.'" *

In other words, it may be said that God is a law unto and in Himself. He is the essence and form of *all* law, and is, in the operations of his Divine Wisdom, more *truly* and *absolutely* law, than any law which operates in the natural universe.

* "Fishbough's Macrocosm and Microcosm," pp. 234, 235.

These are only outbirths and correspondences of the *inmost* and *Divine* Law. Therefore they are not so real and essential. All the necessity which we see in material nature — in the movements of the planets, etc., is *nothing* compared to that primal and eternal necessity of the Divine Nature. It is all law, then, in one sense, whether we speak of God or Nature, distinguished only by internal and external, or inmost and outmost. How the internal laws assume the nature of personal effort, and overcome the external at particular times and places, we shall speak of presently. The Divine Will or Love, indeed, is not so properly law as the Divine Wisdom by which that Love acts: one is the force or motion, the other the rule by which that force acts. But with this sole distinction, and speaking of the Divinity in his own Eternal and Essential Wisdom, which is the external or Form of the Love, it is all law from beginning to end. And so there is a truly *Divine* Necessity — a *primal, absolute* necessity, in and from God throughout the universe. And this, it will be perceived, in perfect consistency with the Divine Free-Will. For the freedom, as in man, is necessary freedom and free necessity. Two halves of one whole. A complete flowing of the Divine Spirit, in its own infinite voluntary, by its own infinite rule. For example, Love and Wisdom *could* not feel hatred, or act foolishly. Its very nature requires that it should *necessarily* act with the most perfect goodness and accuracy. It must, then, to a hair, control and work out the destinies of men, in all particulars, for time and eternity.

I am thus particular to speak of the *necessity* of the Divine Love and Wisdom, because it is so essential to the doing away of that secret and transient scepticism which results, perhaps, as often from an unphilosophical view of the whole matter, as from any *evils* with which the understanding may be blinded. The truth is, we are frequently expecting *too much* of the Divine Providence; we look to it for impossibilities; for things which are as inevitably excluded from the sphere of the Divine action, as certain imaginary results are excluded from the operations of the laws of nature. The Divine necessity will not allow of them any more than the natural necessity. In fact, the one is included and involved in the other. And yet, because of a necessity in the Divine Nature and action, that is no reason for any heart-failings, or cheerless, inconsolable conclusions concerning the Divine Providence. This point may be illustrated by appealing to the very fixedness and necessity of Nature. Take the Pantheist's creed, or the Atheist's, and suppose there was nothing in existence but Nature,—no God, and no intelligent and living controller of human destinies. And yet things operate with a most wonderful exactness; Nature is ever true, ever the same, and her laws and forces are such as may be calculated on with the most unfailing precision. In fact, even the sheer naturalist may say with entire truth that every thing is for the best, and the best possibly that can be, up to every moment of time. Why? Because they can be no otherwise, — because of this very necessity that we are speaking of, by which the constitution of Nature embraces every thing in inevitable and mutual adaptation. Consider how much is included in this proposition. How vast is Nature! —how almost infinite! How good it all is, (if goodness may be predicated of unconscious nature,) and how well it operates! Far, far from earth, and all that meets our vision from this little point of the universe,—even to other systems circling other suns, — and if we consider them inhabited, as they undoubtedly are, what a field of mighty contemplation — I had almost said, for the *devout* mind, but I will only say the humane and natural mind! Who doubts? Where is the sceptic? Is not every thing for the best? Who would alter it, or change it in one of its least particulars? What nicety of balance, what admirable circulation, what almost miraculous exactness of organism and adaptation, through all the animated and unanimated parts of it, and what a tide of joy flowing through all its life and being! If evils, or what are called evils, happen under such a system, they are not really evil, but good, or at least the best that can be. All natural evils, such as earthquakes, storms, and outbreaks in physical nature, our naturalist finds to be good and necessary; and as to all moral evils, social, political, etc., these are only a consequence of the same fixed and necessary system, and are held to be a part of it.

Here, then, even upon this low plane, is a ground for trust,—trust in an infinitude, as it were, of blind, unconscious, but systematic laws. But now behold the more wonderful and beautiful truth still. The truth is, this outward or material nature is but a correspondent and outbirth of the interior and Divine Nature. And the necessity that reigns in one is but the effect of the necessity that exists in the other. It operates in the same way—just as philosophically, only more interiorly. God and Nature are connected most intimately, and separated only by "discrete" degrees. We shall explain this term presently. Love and Wisdom, in their substance and form, are the internal; Matter, the external, of an absolute Unity of all existence. But inasmuch as Love and Wisdom are higher than mere laws and forces of matter, so is the trust higher, and every sentiment and feeling of the heart higher, for the simple reason that now there is recognized, discretely existing interior to Nature, yet substantially connected with it, an Intelligence—a Conscious Mind like our own, only infinite and perfect.. And if *Nature* is exact, to a particular and to a hair, how much more must the *God* of Nature exercise a providence thus wonderfully particular! The Providence is *necessary*, and for that reason is to be believed in. It is the same exactness and regularity, only on an immensely higher plane, and to all eternity! Instead of being any reason for cheerlessness and discomfort, it is the reverse, if we will only view it aright. It is the *not* recognizing this element of necessity in the Divine Will, and the looking for things impossible to be performed, because not within the sphere of Divine Power, that causes the depression and gloom which are sometimes felt. It is a scepticism which comes from an unenlightened understanding as frequently perhaps as from the evils of the heart. Only recognize the *mentality* of the Divine Being, his Love and Wisdom, in distinction from mere natural forces, and we may be in no doubt or gloom about the particularity of the Divine Providence; it *must* be particular, as Nature is particular; universal, as Nature is universal; necessary, as Nature is necessary. Only, it is a Divine necessity, instead of a mere natural necessity. It is Love and Wisdom instead of Gravitation, Chemical Affinity, etc. But the latter, be it most particularly observed, is but an effect, correspondent, and representative of the former. *All attractions, affinities, and forces, of whatever kind, exist originally in the Divine Spirit, and thence in the ultimates of material nature. And when we speak of gravitation, chemical affinity, etc., in material nature, we must remember that there is a like and correspondent necessity in the Divine Will.*

But it must not be concluded from this, that the Divine Necessity is such that it must rush right on, regardless of the varying states of man, and newly occurring exigencies in the universe, to immovable and inexorable destiny. This would be little better than the old Fate. Of course man's various states are consulted, with the utmost particularity and carefulness; and sometimes there are *higher* laws called into requisition, and operated by spiritual beings, which, for particular purposes, are brought to bear upon the lower, overcoming them for the time being and in particular localities, but not violating, or suspending them otherwheres, and thus producing effects which the ordinary flow of nature is incapable of causing. There are many wonderful events which have occurred and are still occurring, where the evidence is all-sufficient, that a high angelic agency, directed of course by the Divine, has intervened, to accomplish in mystery what the ordinary operation of nature could not accomplish. Even the spiritual phenomena of the present day are sufficient to prove a power over matter itself, to cause it to move in opposition to gravitation, and every other known law of nature. And the miracles of the Lord are certainly sufficient to show that no such necessity as the Pantheist would imagine, be he ever so spiritual, can possibly limit the Divine Being. Indeed, it may be said that the Divine Being may even make some *immediate* applications of Himself, without the mediation of any angel or spirit, which are specific, and to the case existing. It must ever be recognized as a distinct truth, that influx is twofold, immediate from the Lord Himself, and mediate through the angelic world. But then it must be remembered that even these immediate applications do not exist without law, which law, as before said, is the veriest and most essential of *all* law, from which all other law, in the outmosts of nature, had its origin, by which it continually lives and acts, and which, in fact, is only the exterior and ultimate of what exists in God. Whatever immediate and specific influences, then, may proceed from the Divine Being in accommodation to man's varying states, or whatever mediate and angelic influences for a like specific end, it must be remembered that there is equally a law and a kind of necessity in them, and indeed, that *from eternity all these varying states must have been known* — must have been seen as certainties which would grow out of the existing constitution of things, and therefore, must have been eternally consulted and provided for. So that God the Infinite still remains immutable and unchangeable. Even the freedom of man — all the freedom he has, by which these varying states were brought about, was also known and consulted, and thus these more immediate and specific providences, so far as they seem to vary from the common and general, are in fact nothing but *appearances to our minds;* they are as truly a part of the great and orderly whole as the most natural occurrence in the universe, and do not imply any more variation on the part of God. Still, as divine providences they are beautiful to contemplate, and are no less timely, opportune, and beneficial to man, than though they were absolute departures from the eternal and inevitable laws to meet an exigency not before contemplated. Thus we see again, how the religious and the philosophical, the needful and the necessary, will-force and law-force, the timal and the eternal, meet and harmonize.

There is a passage in Swedenborg which speaks well to the point under consideration: —

"While I was discoursing with the angels, concerning the Divine Providence of the Lord, there were spirits also present who impressed on themselves some idea concerning fate, or absolute necessity; they supposed that the Lord acted from that necessity, because he cannot otherwise proceed than according to things most essential, thus according to those things which are of the most perfect order. But it was shown them that man has freedom, and if he has freedom, it is not from necessity: this was illustrated from the case of houses which are to be built, in that the bricks, the mortar, the sand, the stones serving for pedestals and pillars, also the timbers and beams, and several things of the like nature, are brought together not in that order in which the house is to be constructed, but according to pleasure, and that the Lord alone knows what sort of a house may thence be built; all these things which are from the Lord are most essential, but they do not follow in order from necessity, but in application to the freedom of man." A. C. 6487.

The idea is, or may be, that all the materials of the house are brought together freely by man, according to his own best judgment and pleasure, and yet that the Lord's essential and necessary will, which is in some respects different from the man's intention, is so applied that the man acts freely, even in the variations from his original intent, in the accomplishment of the *Supreme* Will.

Here, then, is a great truth, in all the operations of the Divine Providence. Events are *in application to the freedom of man.* Of course, then, his varying states are consulted, and every possible emergency into which he may come. And to accommodate himself to *some* of these emergencies, there are absolutely higher laws, and higher personal agencies put in requisition, than the ordinary regular course of nature can possibly comprehend. Because they break forth in time, and opportunely to existing cases, that makes nothing against their eternal and inevitable necessity, and, so to speak, germinal movement in the Divine Mind from the very first. But it is not *fate*-like, *pantheistic* necessity, but only such as is essential to the Divine Order, and to the very being and nature of God Himself. A man, for instance, *cannot* be all head, or all feet. So heaven cannot be all sameness, or all one degree, but there must be first, second, and third, and innumerable varieties within each of these. And the like with every thing. Concerning *all* these variations, then, of the states and circumstances of men, and the most miraculous interpositions of God, still the Divine *Providence* does not vary; it only varies to *our experience*, not in the everlasting, predetermined method. The great eternal movement proceeds straight on, for from eternity it was seen what states were to be embraced in the Divine Plan, and from eternity all these variations were included.

Here it may be remarked, for the satisfaction of those who would stumble at terms, and make more of these than their meaning would imply, that there is indeed what may be called *relative* non-necessity, that is to say, a freedom of action and personal application on the part of God and angels, which, compared with the lower and more stated movements of material nature, are *not* necessities. Gravitation, for instance, may be called a necessary and involuntary movement, and the divine or angelic will that acts upon it to overcome it in particular localities and for the time being, *not* such a movement. And this is true. This is what supplies satisfaction to the religious nature, and is indeed essential to it, and is what Dr. Bushnell would call a realm of powers above nature acting upon nature. Thus there is a relative non-necessity. Of course we should not deny so plain and fundamental a truth as this. But take that angelic will itself, in reference to another will that is above *it*, which moves it, and another above *it*, and so on to the Divine, which from eternity is the most necessary Fact in all existence, inclusive of *all* necessities, and the truth still remains, of the absolute inevitability of all things. *Relative* non-necessity there indeed is, — relative of one thing, or one power, in reference to another, — but take *all things together*, God and his universe, and the truth remains in all its force, of universal Freedom and Necessity blended into one complex and wonderful unity.

And as to man's free agency, to which all events are in some sense applied, it is not *possible* that it can be such as to interfere permanently with the Divine necessities. Man is a part of nature — a part of the great Unity. To be sure he is of a *spiritual* nature, but that does not take him out of the great system. Is not the whole of creation one consistent and connected work? Are there not mutual dependencies and interblendings of all laws and existences, from God to lowest nature? Strike the line of absolute division anywhere, and you break the universe and destroy order.

> "In nature's chain, whatever link you strike,
> Tenth, or ten thousandth, breaks the chain alike."

Now, then, can one part of nature be different, except in its degree, from another part? Can human nature be freer than *any* nature, only as it is spiritual and rational? And must not this spiritual and rational partake of as inevitable laws and necessities as the clod of the valley, or the tree upon the mountain top? In short, we lay down this proposition as invincible. Every thing has freedom equally — one thing as much as another — *in proportion to its nature.* Man, for instance, has no more freedom in proportion to his nature, than the planets which whirl round the sun. But man has reason. Therefore he has freedom *according to that reason.* But even that reason has its own laws. We cannot escape from this necessity at all. It is not true, therefore, to say —

"And binding nature fast in fate,
Left free the human will."

The human will is not an exception. The universe is a consistent unity. Man *appears* more free than the rest of nature, but that is only because he is so high *above* all the rest. But he is not a jot freer in proportion. Nay, even stones and animals, have as much free agency, in proportion to their nature, as man has in proportion to his. The same reasoning applies here that was used before in reference to spiritual and material necessities; *viz.*, that the laws of gravitation, chemical affinity, etc., are only outbirths, correspondences, and effects, of similar necessities that exist in the Divine Will. So of free agency. This *mimic* choice, selection and rejection, which we see in chemical affinities, is only the external and ultimate of the choice which exists in the Divine Mind; one is both as *free* and as *necessary* as the other. In man we see it more perfectly, because he is higher up in the scale of nature, and has reason and forethought. Hear what the great Seer before quoted says on this subject.

"Unless there were some free-agency in *all created things, both animate and inanimate,* there could not have been any creation. For without free-agency in natural things, as to beasts, there would not be any power of choosing food conducive to their nourishment, nor any power of procreating and preserving their offspring, thus no beast. If the fishes of the sea, and the shell-fish at its bottom, had not such freedom, there would be no fish or shell-fish. * * * If there were not something analogous to free-agency in every metal, and in every stone, precious and common, there would not be a metal nor a stone, yea, not even a particle of sand; for this freely imbibes the ether, exhales its native properties, rejects what is obsolete, and renews itself with fresh substances. * * * Since, therefore, *freedom has been given to all created subjects,* to each *according to its nature,* why not free-agency to man, according to *his* nature, which is, that he may be spiritual?" T. C. R. 499.

To be sure, and of the same kind, too, varying only in the

proportion of his nature, which is immense. In short, free-agency in man is nothing but a conscious, *willing affinity*, exerted according to reason; in the stone, it is unconscious, unwilling, and irrational. In both there is a similar necessity. Even the reason of man has its own laws of inevitable and immutable action.

As we have quoted Swedenborg thus far, and as the character of this book will partake somewhat of the profound philosophy which is unfolded in the writings of the illustrious Seer, we desire to give here one or two other quotations concerning what he says of the freedom of the human will.

"To these things I will add an angelic sentiment concerning will and intelligence with man: the sentiment is this, that *there is not given a grain* of his own will and his own prudence with any man; saying, if there was given a *grain* with any one whatever, heaven would not hold together, nor hell; and the whole human race would perish." D. P. 293.

Again, observe how well he pronounces all the free-will that man has, only an *apparent* truth.

"It is a law of the Divine Providence, that every thing which man wills, thinks, speaks, and does, should *appear* to him *as of himself*, and that without that appearance, no man would have his own, or be his own man. The operation of the Divine Providence of the Lord to lead man from evils is continual; if any one perceived and was sensible of this continual operation, and still was not *led as one bound*, would he not continually withstand, and then either quarrel with God, or intermingle himself with the Divine Providence?" D. P. 176, 177.

"Let it therefore be known, that these goods are no otherwise appropriated to man, than that they are constantly of the Lord with man; and that as far as man acknowledges this, so far the Lord gives that good may *appear* to man as his; that is, that it may *appear* to man that he loves his neighbor, or has charity *as of himself*, believes or has faith *as of himself*, does good, and understands truth, thus is wise, *as of himself;* from which one illustrated can see of what quality and *how strong the appearance is*, in which the Lord wills that man should be; and the Lord wills this for the sake of his salvation, for no one can be saved without that *appearance.*" D. P. 79.

"The case with man as to his affections and as to his thoughts is this; no person whatever, whether man, or spirit, or angel, can will and think from himself, but from others, nor these others from themselves, but all again from others, and so forth, and thus each from the first life, which is the Lord; that which is unconnected does not exist."

"I know, however, that fallacy will prevail with many, and that they will believe that they will of themselves, and think of themselves, when yet *nothing is less true.*" A. C. 2886, 2888.

From this it will be perceived that man has *conscious* and *practical* freedom, and that is all. That is enough. He wills and acts *as of himself;* and if he does it *as* of himself, it is the same, for all practical purposes, as if it were really *of* himself. But as we are writing now for the *philosophy* of this subject — to convince certain minds who do more thinking than practicing, and are hence made sceptical concerning the Divine Providence to a degree which does not sufficiently admit the freedom of man and the application of events *to* that freedom, we wish to admit the law side of this subject, the necessity which there is in it, *in all its force,* for the purpose of showing the freedom which is in *consistency* with this necessity; nay, for the stronger argument that even this very kind of providence, which so regards the will of man, is still as necessary as the existence of God. We will acknowledge no half-way — no scepticism at all, but show both the philosophy and the religion of the matter, the theory and the practice. For it may be said of this subject, as emphatically as of any subject whatever, that there are two sides to it, and that both sides are triumphantly and wonderfully true.

Here, then, we approach somewhat to a rational conclusion. We see the necessity, — we see the everlasting chain of causation by which every act of the will is as fixed and certain as the movement of a planet or the ticking of a clock, but not so mechanically, and yet man cannot divest himself of this ever-present consciousness and appearance of freedom. He is so free, that when he wills or acts, he does not, unless he is inwardly experimenting on the nature of his volitions, stop to think and reason whether he is free or not, or how free he is, but he starts right off and does the work, or makes the decision, just as though there was no philosophical necessity about it. He has a conscience, and it approves or condemns him; affections, and they animate him; reason, and it presides for him. If he does badly, he knows it is wrong; he suffers, and acknowledges the justice. If he has not seared and brunted his conscience all over, he is fearfully plagued and tormented, and he plunges himself in bitter misery. He *ought* not; that is the sentiment of his heart, and it weighs upon him like an incubus. Now why is this, if man is not absolutely free? We will speak first with regard to the good, and not to the evil. And we say, *this is the individualizing law of his existence.* This is the way in which he becomes a man at all, unconfounded with the Divinity. If man did not *appear* to will and act of himself, if he had not this strong *consciousness* of freedom and individuality, he would not have any separate existence from the Creator who formed him. He would not enjoy, nor suffer, nor be any thing but an irrational and unconscious thing. But now, being so far separated from the Divine, and yet being moved and acted upon *by* the Divine, with a self-hood that appears as his own, and *is* his own so far as all his individuality is concerned, he can think, reason, feel, decide, act, in that self-hood, and enjoy moral approbation, thus become happy and blessed as a noble human creature, while at the same time, as all religion testifies and philosophy confirms, *all* this power is derived from God, and he has not any thing, and cannot do any thing, of himself alone. It is only *as* of himself, after all. And this "as of himself," is such a strong appearance, and such a living, real consciousness, that a man cannot, while acting, divest himself of the thought that it *is* him: and this answers all the purposes of accountability, responsibility, joy and satisfaction in well-doing. If they exist, they exist; and that is enough. Accountability only represents the fact that a man ought to use his powers to the very best advantage, as under the law and authority of another. And this he can do with the powers so connected.

Some may think we are talking enigmas here, but to show that we are not, to show the entire truthfulness of the whole representation, it is only necessary to advert to some real facts and illustrations of common occurrence. We may thus see how these appearances of freedom, without any absolute and entire freedom, (except practically,) follow us all along. Take an animal, for instance, — a dog, or a horse. Let him be quietly at rest from all exertion, or attraction to any foreign object, and by and by let some man approach him with something to arouse his desire — his hunger, or some other of his animal propensities, and see how quickly he will start for the object held out to him, "as of himself." To be sure, he did have the power to will and go, but who aroused it? who wrought upon it till it was made active? Man; was it not? Again, the *man* sits, quietly musing on some cherished project, or else in vacancy and listlessness, and by and by a thought comes to his mind, it is quickened, his feelings are enlisted, and off he starts for a new object. The man thinks, or rather does *not* think — is totally thoughtless about the philosophy of the movement — and feels that he wills and acts of himself. And so he does, practically, but there is an angel over him who approaches him with the very first impulse of movement, and who has been, perhaps, long watching for the opportunity. He silently drops the thought into the man's mind, and stimulates his will to action. If he acts not with the first effort, the angel will increase the power, — will add a little more, and a little more, till by and by the mandate is obeyed, and the object accomplished. The will is never violated, never forced, in orderly states; it is always in co-operation with the man's reason; but what cannot be rationally done at one time, may be and is so done after a sufficient preparation. But again, there is a higher angel over this one, and a still higher over him, and so on till we reach the Lord Himself, who sways the whole intelligent creation by his own sovereign Will. But it must be observed here, that it is not by *particular* influx, as from one or more angels, that the will of man is always swayed, but by *general* influx of the whole society of spiritual beings with which the man is in association, and the power on both sides, of heaven and of hell, by which he is also in equilibrium: it is thus that his will is governed, and his true and proper freedom kept intact and inviolate through the whole procedure. If Swedenborg has done any thing in exposition of this subject of the freedom of the human will, it is, different from all other authors, in showing how the *balance of forces* is kept in the spiritual world, in the mid region between heaven and hell, by which man is plied on both sides with good and evil, and so his freedom kept in equilibrium. So far, so good. But even in this exact and wonderful equilibrium, man is not *absolutely* free; he has no self-motion; if by these means he is enabled to look on both sides of him, and calculate the evil and the good, and submit it all to an enlightened reason, even then, when he acts, he does not wholly act of himself; he cannot; only God can do this; and when man does will and act, it is only because, in these perfectly free and fair conditions, somewhat of the divine influx, mediate or immediate, or both, insinuates itself into his mind, and produces a determination which he *adopts as his own.* He is free, as free as he can be, to *adopt* it; but even this is by no means self-motion, such as God has, but only *as* of himself, which God in mercy gives him to feel. The human will, in fact, may be said to be *relatively* free—free within a certain sphere with relation to another sphere, as man is proportionally freer than an animal, and an animal freer than a vegetable, but that is all. The connection is perfect with God and all the heavens and the whole spiritual universe, so that, taken all in all, there is nothing but universal necessity and universal freedom united.

So beautiful a truth is this, and so entirely at one with the highest religion and the most thorough practice, that it is worthy of still further illustration from a high point of the regenerate life. Man is ever boasting of his liberty, and the natural mind little mistrusts how completely his very highest freedom consists in renouncing his own will, and being led entirely by the Lord. Let this point be illustrated somewhat from first principles. It being a recognized truth that all life is from the Lord, and in man only as a receptacle and by derivation, it is at once perceived that a perfectly accordant state of unition *with* the Lord, is most favorable to the divine influx. And all the will that man has — this proprium, or self-hood — this strong *apparent* self-life and action, is conferred upon him for the very purpose that he may feel the Divine Life as his own, when yet it is not his own, that he may have thereby all the greater joy as a being filled with the Divinity, while at the same time he is unconfounded *with* the Divinity. In other words, God loves his rational creatures so well, that he wills to impart as much as possible of *Himself* to them. Hence it is that those angels who are in closest conjunction with the Lord, who have the least sense of their own will, and are in deepest conviction and acknowledgment that all they feel and will is from the Divine, have invariably the most life, and the most will as of themselves. They are the most perfect receptacles and instruments of the Divine influx. While not doing their own will, but the will of Him in whom they live and move, the will which they *feel* as their own is mercifully quickened in them, and made susceptible of a thousand delights which could not flow from any other source, in any other way. Thus they have at the same time the most self-consciousness, and are most truly free. And they become continually more and more so. For this heavenly proprium increases by virtue of this very influx of the Divine Life, which, while it makes them feel more and more their life in the Lord, at the same time convinces them of their own individuality, as beings whom He has thus largely endowed.

And so it is with man in the world who is *becoming* an angel. In short, these extremes do all meet. He who feels least life of his own has most life; he who has least will of his own has most freedom; he who feels least power in himself has most power from the Divine Omnipotence. He who is *nothing*, in himself, and is most sensibly convinced of it, has most of all things properly belonging to man, for this emptiness of his own self is the very condition which opens all his resources, and turns him to the Fountain of all being, and draws most largely upon all the powers and capacities of the Infinite. The Lord can come where there is room for Him; not into those souls whose self-importance excludes all thought of extraneous help, and presents a form and a sphere of opposition and repulsion. To be in this condition is to be in the veriest bondage to evil and false spirits; for they are all stated in this conception of life from one's self.

It is a beautiful thought here, that by this self-abnegation, which is the condition of true freedom, we do not lose one particle of our *real* self, which so many are afraid of — our proper, conscious individuality, but only our *conceited* self, which must die in order that we may truly live. For the *heavenly* proprium — the sense of life — the serene joy of the angels, as they move on in their eternal spheres of activity and usefulness, doing only the Divine Will, is as much more complete and self-satisfying than the apparent freedom of those who are only in the delight of their own self-love, as the blessedness of God is superior to the care and solicitude of man. For while diligently working — continually submitting their own wills to the Divine Will, and desiring nothing else, they have no care nor anxiety, but the "daily bread" of the spirit is given every day, and being in the stream of the Divine Providence, they are thus in a state of peace.

CHAPTER III.

THE NATURE AND ORIGIN OF EVIL.

"Inquire no longer, man! who is the author of evil; behold him in yourself. — Take away every thing that is the work of man, and all the rest is good."— *Rousseau.*

"'Twas man himself
Brought death into the world: and man himself
Gave keenness to his darts, quickened his pace,
And multiplied destruction on mankind."— *Bishop Porteus.*

It will be expected, undoubtedly, with the foregoing view of the Divine Providence in regard to good, that we should say something on the more difficult subject of evil. If the will of man is as we have represented it, — if with regard to the production of good it is only apparently of himself, but really of the Divine Being from whom all good is, how is it with regard to evil? Does this, too, come from the Divinity? If it does not, then it must be either that there is an eternal Devil who inspires all the evil, or that man himself has a power to will and do evil different from that with which he wills and does good: that is to say, more independent, more self-originated, more absolutely of himself. And this, particularly with regard to the *origin* and *first starting* of evil, we shall find, without any inconsistency, to be the case.

Let us in the first place consider what evil is. It is not positive and essential; there is but one original and eternal essence; that is the Divine Good. Evil is that essence perverted and inverted by man. It becomes so in man by the receptive forms or spiritual vesicles of his mind. When these forms are in order, and upright, then the Divine influx is in him for good. When they are turned or twisted away from their proper order, and turned up-side-down, as they frequently are when evil is entire, then the Divine influx is received accordingly. What before was good, is now changed into evil. This may be illustrated from things in the material world. It is the same heat and light which flows into thistles, as flows into roses; — into all poisonous and noxious plants, as into good and useful vegetables. But the receptive forms make all the difference. Just so it is with man, when he becomes inverted to the Divine celestial influences. This is so true, that, in the *spiritual* world, persons actually *appear* inverted to each other; — opposite as two men feet to feet, with their respective heads upwards and downwards. Such is the aspect of the whole heavens and hells. They are vast, organic, opposite relations. They have that appearance because the wicked have inverted true order, by making self-love uppermost or chief in the mind, and love to the Lord and the neighbor underneath all, or denying it altogether. Thus it is written — "The way of the wicked He turneth *up-side-down.*" (*Psalm* 146 : 9.) The whole Word has respect to appearances in the spiritual world. And so the heavens and hells are not only inverted and opposite to each other, but comparatively speaking, one is positive and the other negative. The hells have no power but what the heavens, or the Lord through the heavens, can control. "Thus far, and no farther, and here shall thy proud waves be stayed."

Here, however, let it be observed, that although evil has no *absolute* positive existence, yet it frequently becomes *relatively* positive, so as to overcome, for the time being, good itself. How often is it the case! But in the end, it is destined, we believe, to defeat. Good must eventually triumph over all evil, and God be glorified in all.

Evil is sometimes said to be "undeveloped good," or "unripe good," or "good in the making:" there is indeed a truth concealed even in these expressions; but it is only true that while a certain spiritual good *was* making, evil came into existence.

Not that the good was made out of the evil, but that the evil started up as an opposition to the process. The subject dates back to the creation of man. It was the natural, animal mind of man, that objected to being made spiritual, or objected to that *greater choice* of good which was involved in the exaltation of his being from the childlike, infantile state, and instead thereof chose the evil.

Here let it be understood that man originally, as he came from the hands of his Creator, was a merely natural creature. He had a human soul — an internal and external man, and the *capacity* of becoming spiritual. But he was as yet only natural or unregenerate. Regeneration, according to this theory, or rather, *re-creation*, took place before the Fall; and it was necessary that it should so take place, for man at the first was only *without evil*, or in natural, not spiritual good. His regeneration, therefore, before the Fall, differed from that after the Fall, only in the sense that it was then without conflict; and if he had not fallen into evil, he might have proceeded straight on, as the Most Ancient Men did, with all pleasantness and facility, accomplishing his regeneration in the most orderly and agreeable manner. But he fell into evil, and hence the process is now so difficult, and of the nature of a warfare. It is impossible to tell how low man was at the first, or how long he remained in this condition; but it suffices to say that he was gradually educated out of this state, by the Lord through the ministry of angels, and raised to the complete height of a spiritual and celestial man. This was the *apex* of the first re-creation. This process is what is described in the spiritual sense of the first chapters of Genesis. It has no reference to the material creation, except so far as the processes of nature in the physical universe are correspondentially woven into this spiritual narrative. It is an account of the first re-creation of man from a purely natural to a purely spiritual state. From that state he fell; not suddenly, but gradually, and here commenced the origin of evil.* Be it observed, then, that the calamity here contemplated did not begin in evil, but in less good. Man at first began to diminish in his amount of good. This may be called a negative evil, but not a positive one. It was only the absence of so much of the divine life. But how came man to grow less good? Because of his immense distance from the great Creator, and the freedom which thus necessarily entered into his constitution as a man.

Let it be observed here that all freedom consists in this *proprium* or self-hood of man. Man would not be man without this. And as all goodness consists in the harmonious unition of this self-hood with the Divinity, so all evil consists in the *non*-unity, or separation of man from God. In the progress of this life of the self-hood, man comes to feel his own will too much. He begins to think he is something in himself alone. He puts on airs of self-conceit, and like a fool, unlearns his dependence. This is the primal sin, which "brought death into the world and all our woe." It is this which closes up the receptacles of true life in man, so that the Divine Life cannot enter. This was the serpent in the Garden of Eden. Hence it was that the greatest care and solicitude were manifest towards man in his state of innocence, lest he should eat of "the

---

* In this account of the origin of evil we do not forget another account given in that remarkable book — "Arcana of Christianity," by Rev. T. L. Harris. It is a statement which certainly has the merit of startling novelty, with a strong tinge of tradition in it, and is worthy of serious consideration. It is there affirmed that evil commenced on another planet, contiguous to our own, and that the hell of that planet extended its invasions into our world. But if this be even so, it does not essentially conflict with the spiritual causes here assigned for the same evil, and it varies from it only as to the whereabouts of its commencement, and some other particulars which need not here be named. The account which we give here regards the psychology and laws of evil as it exists in our own world, and does not pretend to any knowledge of pre-existent orbs, nor material ultimates in the Garden of Eden.

tree of knowledge of good and evil," and afterwards also of "the tree of life." The tree of knowledge in *itself* considered, is a divine gift and blessing to man. It signifies the perception of truth from the Lord. But the sin is in *eating* of that tree. To eat signifies to *appropriate*, as physical food is appropriated and becomes a part of the body. An *orderly* appropriation is not forbidden; but to appropriate divine truths in such a way as to think they are of ourselves — of our own intelligence, is the sin here prohibited. For by this means, all such truth becomes perverted into forms of selfishness, the Lord is shut out, and the healthy influx of the Divine Life obstructed. This is the source of death. "In the day," or state, "thou eatest thereof, thou shalt surely die." All thy wisdom and perception and life shall perish. It was called the tree in the "midst of the garden," because it was the very *central principle* of life.

But, we say, all this began, not in positive evil, but in becoming less good. A little less thought of the Divine Creative Source that perpetually sustained him, and a little more, and still a little more, of himself. Thus his good gradually diminished, till by and by it all ran out, and man in his *natural* mind became nothing but evil, — became entirely selfish. For all this, he needed no tempter, no Devil, but the serpent in himself, — the sensual principle of his own natural mind. This was continually suggesting — "Ye shall not surely die, for God doth know that in the day ye eat thereof, then your eyes shall be opened, and ye shall be as gods, knowing good and evil." That is, ye shall be like God himself — shall have wisdom of yourself, and life of yourself, and not be led by another. O man, the deceiver!

But still the question recurs — Why should man *begin* to allow this? Why should he take the very first initiatory step in all the series, to turn away from God, and turn unto himself? — especially if he had no real, absolute and entire will of his own, but only an apparent one, as in the will of goodness, and if in this state of high spiritual re-creation he was so entirely good. This is the very question.

And we answer in the first place, that good as he was, and dependent as he was, there was necessarily an imperfection entering into his nature by the very act of creation. God *could* not create a being so perfect as Himself, without imparting *all* of Himself, which is a contradiction. Secondly, He must create man at an immense *remove* from Himself; for notwithstanding he is in his "image and likeness," yet being clothed in flesh, and ultimated in the natural and material world, he is necessarily a weak and puny creature, subject to vanity from the very first. And thirdly, he must be made to *choose* good. He must, in order to the highest possible enjoyment as a man, have *moral* enjoyment, which consists in a choice between good and evil.*

All this could not be without necessarily being involved in many imperfections which the Divinity itself could not prevent. These imperfections lay chiefly or altogether in his sensual or external mind, which was nearest to earth, and most likely to be deceived by appearances of things instead of the reality. Yet it was very necessary that man should have such a mind; it is the basis on which the interiors rest. It is very necessary too, to have it cultivated to the outermost possible region. Herein lay all the danger, and herein, when fully done, will be given the finishing stroke of the Divine Artist, in the complete ultimation of a rounded human character. Nothing is perfect till ultimated in exteriors. The men before the Fall did not know evil, nor could they have known that great good which will be experienced by redemptive man, when he

* It is not indeed asserted, as is sometimes understood, that evil is necessary in order to the existence of any good at all, for it is not. Man could have been preserved in good, and in a distinct knowledge of it, without this terrible contrast of evil; but still the *ability* to choose an opposite was necessary to his perfect freedom, and enjoyment of the higher good.

shall have passed through this evil experience, and come fully to the joys of deliverance. The men before the Fall were a good, docile, tender, innocent, unsophisticated, spiritual, infantile people, and had, by their purity, open communication with the angels of heaven. But they had not that peculiar power and experience — that wondrous susceptibility to good and enjoyment — that filling out of the whole being, even to the extremest parts of the natural mind, with wisdom, knowledge, and variety, that man will attain to by passing *through* the Fall, and coming to the state of the progressed man of the future. For be it known here, that the Fall of man, through thousands of years, is not inconsistent with a *general* law of *progression.* Like a sinless infant passing into corrupt manhood, the very Fall, in this sense, is a progression. For it was necessary that man should pass out of this state of infancy, and through the various periods of manhood, even at the risk of sin and defilement, that he might come fully into the most external state of his sensual and intellectual nature, and thus purify even these by the interior life flowing out and ultimating itself in the whole man. Then he is no longer an infant, but a strong man, able to battle with the opposing elements of nature, to subdue and beautify the outward world, and press it into his service by all the art and science of experienced manhood. When this is done, or when man by regeneration becomes purified again, it will be seen that even the Fall of man was a part of the progression. *But not an orderly part.* It was not orderly for man to sin, and so to lose his pristine glory; but *having* lost it in the effort to exert and cultivate his sensuous and external nature, when he regains it, it will come with a greater power, with a more enlarged expansion of all the faculties of the natural mind, and be in reality a Golden Age of the future surpassing all the glory of the past. Thus, although this kind of progression is not orderly, yet like every thing else, the Fall of man is overruled for good, — a good more glorious than can be imagined.

It is to be particularly observed here, that it was not necessary that man should *sin*, but it *was* necessary that he should pass out of this state of infancy. Man at the first was a being of a different order.* He was a mere child from the hands of his Maker, and received intuitionally, and by angelic influences, all the knowledge that was requisite for him. He rested on the bosom of the Father's love, without any desire for the things of the outward world and of mere intellectual science such as men now have and turn to so much usefulness. Would it not have been a greater evil for the human race to have remained forever in that state? And how could they ever be brought out of it but by coming into a different life — by exerting their own reason and senses, and endeavoring to find out truth themselves? In short, how could the rational faculty ever be cultivated without using it? But with the use, came the abuse. As soon as they began to reason, they fell. The Fall consisted in the gradual closing up of their interior, spiritual minds, their spiritual senses also, with all their powers of heavenly perception, and the sensualizing and materializing of their whole better nature. But it was all seen and calculated from the beginning, and mercifully permitted them, notwithstanding it would lead them so far away from the Lord of all life, and be the means of their terrible ruin. It was permitted them as a means of strengthening their whole nature, internal and external: that is, speaking of their posterity largely, and at the same time not excluding them from a share in the Divine Mercy. By such a permission, a new and still better race will be introduced upon the earth.

It might have been done otherwise, without the Fall, if man would have allowed it. And we have no hesitation in saying it would have been *better*, thus effected, and that man had free-will enough to have prevented this whole catastrophe, and to have improved and spiritualized his external nature without sinning, *if he had chosen to do so.* He was no more

* For particulars, see the first volume of Swedenborg's Arcana.

obliged to do it then than now. He was not any more compelled to take the first step in iniquity, than he is now compelled to murder, or to do any other abomination. He *could* have abstained from it, and *ought* to. But he *would* not, and that is the whole story. And thus this very faculty of our nature — this whole sensual and external mind which might have been *orderly* turned to so much use and proficiency, and so much happiness, became the means of a downfall which has drenched the world in wickedness and misery for ages upon ages, and peopled the vast abysses of hell.

Here it should be observed that this first life, so beautiful, *could not be sustained* without their loving it more freely and outwardly as of themselves. This is manifest from the New Church idea of *proprium* — in Adam's finding it not good to be alone, that is, under the Divine guidance exclusively, and desiring some other aid, which was called a *woman*, and which was *taken out of man*, that is, a self-hood which could be loved most dearly. Here, then, a greater freedom, because more external, more apparently of one's own self, was to be established in the human constitution, which in time should become equally at one with the inmost celestial life, and sustain it in greater fulness. And it was in their learning to acquire this that the stronger power of choice between good and evil came into play. Before, they only knew good by the simple, unmixed enjoyment of the heavenly influx into their tender and celestial minds. Now they were to know it more thoroughly, at least their posterity were, but attended with tremendous dangers. And God the Creator would not shrink from the work, but would follow them in the whole experience, lead them through it, and out of it, and bring a greater joy from this very scene of trial and suffering.

Here then we see what kind of a *necessity* it was that man should pass through this evil experience. It was not any thing in God which made evil a necessity of his own choosing. The only necessity which existed in God was a necessity to

4

make man free; that is, as free as he could be, for a being so utterly dependent. This the Divine Being *could not help* choosing. The paradox, in its highest sense, is consistent. Man must be free in order to the enjoyment of the greatest amount and highest kind of good. This good involves choice. He must choose it in order to enjoy it. It cannot be forced upon him. He must will it most freely, and *love* it, for all delight is in love. But this could not be without an ability to choose evil. The very choice of good involves the rejection of evil. A man might indeed choose between two goods — a greater and a lesser, without any *ability* to choose evil, but this was not so consistent with the high and noble nature which was to be bestowed upon man. He must be made to choose good, and to indicate his high and decided preference for it, by refusing the evil. This gives him a deeper and quicker sense of it. He must, in short, either find his life in God, or in himself. There was no other alternative. This is the necessity on the part of God, and although He foresees the evil — foresees how man will abuse this freedom by setting up his own little conceited will into an authority against the Divine, yet *this* was no necessity with God. Man was made free enough to avoid it. He could have chosen the upright path of good from the very first. If we cannot say thus much, then we cannot say that man can *now* abstain from any sin or crime which he commits. God, too, saw all the *lineal consequences* of the first sin, — how it would go on, by a law of hereditary descent, from generation to generation, till the whole world should groan in evil, and sigh in bitter bondage. But it would not do to meddle with this law of hereditary descent. I have heard men complain that they should suffer so much from hereditary entailments which they were not at all accountable for, and which have plagued them through a long life; — perhaps been an insurmountable barrier to success or prosperity in any thing. But here is a divine simplicity again — an excellent necessity. It is only one law that passes down all the evil and all the good. By my obedience to the laws of God and nature, I not only secure to *myself* good habits and results, but hand them down constitutionally to my children — and they to theirs — and they to theirs. It is, then, by this law of hereditary descent, that all the *good* is secured, and treasured up, and passed on: and to cut off the law, or arrest its operation, in order to prevent the evil, would be to arrest it and prevent the good. Therefore it must remain; and therefore, from the very first motion of evil in the Garden of Eden, which represents the unfallen, celestial state of man, has rolled on this flood of iniquity over all the world. It has gathered weight and momentum in its passage, each individual adding his own actual evils to the amount of his hereditary, and is only broken by the strong arm of the Lord Jehovah, in the descent and incarnation of Himself in our humanity.

Such, then, is the nature of evil. It is not by any means an undeveloped good, nor any kind of rudimental righteousness. Evil, in short, is no more a lower degree of good, than a lie, an utter falsity, is a lower degree of truth; or theft is a lower degree of honesty; or adultery is a low degree of chastity; or hatred and murder, low degrees of love and the works of love. But these things are all *opposites*, good and truth turned out of their proper position, and when fully consummated, "turned up-side-down." If it had been said that evil is *rotten* good, instead of "unripe" good, it would have been nearer the truth.

But it must be observed here, without which the subject would be very imperfect, that after evil is once introduced and has obtained such sway in the world, and after it has created also the hells in the spiritual world, it flows back from thence in almost resistless torrents upon the human race with whom it originated. Thus that the most grievous temptations exist from the hells with which we are surrounded, and man is led by them into all sorts of iniquity. It is all influx, first into man's own proprium, and afterwards from the spiritual world. Man to be sure consents, as in the first place; but as in the origin, so here, his free-will is not absolute and entire, except practically, while he is involved in an everlasting chain of Divine necessities and human freedoms. Praise God who holds the balance equal! We are not tempted above that we are able, and God who suffereth the temptation, makes a way of escape that we may be able to bear it.

Notwithstanding, then, the malignant nature of evil, it is held in control by Him who permitted it, and made subservient to final good. It is not of course said that a still greater good would not have resulted had man not sinned. For unless we take this position, where is all our every-day morality? Where is the wisdom of obedience — the preference for virtue over vice? The mind is inadequate to conceive how much more glorious would have been the scene, had man kept on in an orderly manner, and spiritualized and enlarged his whole natural mind without ever consenting to evil. Nor can we tell how much further in advance of all present attainments the human race would have this day been; — what splendid virtues would have adorned mankind, what angel qualities, graces, and refinements, would have possessed and filled out the whole natural humanity, which the Fall has only retarded perhaps for millions of years, and now made possible only through the tremendous experience of a blasted and sin-smitten world! But it is an evil which cannot last: in the long run it must lessen its awful shadow forever and ever. To all eternity it is destined to defeat. God never would have permitted it — never *could* have permitted it, without this end. In his dominions no Devil can arise but who hath beforehand decreed for him the end of his rope, and all whose machinations are made to play into the hands of the Divine Providence. "As for you," says Joseph to his brethren, "ye thought evil against me; but God meant it unto good, to bring to pass as it is this day, to save much people alive." (*Gen.* 50: 20.) Or, God *thought* it for good, according to his own order from eternity. How beautiful is this truth! — that man has no *absolute, unconnected, independent* will for *any thing* — not even for the production of evil; — *surely* not to defeat the Divine purposes; — but that it had its origin in a necessity which could not be prevented without the incurring of a still greater evil — the evil of no choice — and that it is continually overruled for good by the Divine Providence forever!

And if it is not finally and utterly destroyed, and the entire universe purified from all corruption, then it must be because of a defect in the Divine Being and economy which we cannot believe exists, and which is a still greater mystery than the origin of evil itself. It cannot be. Every thing is superficial and perishes but love and truth only, and these eventually must triumph over all.

It may indeed be admitted here, as a doubt, or as a possibility, that evil will continue to exist through all eternity, or all time, by breaking out on new planets, and among new races of men continually to be created: the very fact that it has *once* appeared, here upon our earth, may perhaps warrant the probability that it may in like manner appear somewhere again — and again. It may be a possibility thus forever existing. But not with the same individuals. It is bound to come to an end, we believe, with all who experience it, else there is no satisfaction, no consistency, no God-given theology at all, that is full and fair and perfect.

CHAPTER IV.

ABSOLUTE DIVINE SOVEREIGNTY.

"And all the inhabitants of the earth are reputed as nothing; and He doeth according to his will in the army of heaven, and among the inhabitants of the earth; and none can stay his hand, or say unto him, What doest thou?" — *Daniel* 4 : 35.

Having now seen the origin and nature of evil, as well as the nature of human free-will, we are prepared to recognize the Divine Providence more fully in all things — evil as well as good. God is Sovereign. Man's will in the case may be temporarily divergent, but there is a divine hand and curb upon it, in the worst of its irregularities. "Calvinism, in its essential features," says Mrs. Stowe, in her "Sunny Memories," "will never cease from the earth, because the great fundamental facts of nature are Calvinistic, and men with strong minds and wills always discover it. The predestination of a Sovereign will is written over all things. The old Greek tragedians read it and expressed it. So did Mahomet, Napoleon, Cromwell. Why? They found it so by their own experience; they tried the forces of nature enough to find their strength. The strong swimmer who breasts the Rhine is certain of its current. But Ranke well said, that in those days when the whole earth was in arms against those reformers, they had no refuge but in exalting God's sovereignty above all other causes. To him who strives in vain with the giant forces of evil, what calm in the thought of an overpowering will, so that will be crowned with goodness! However grim to the distrusting, looks this fortress of sovereignty in times of flowery ease, yet in times when 'the waters roar and are troubled, and the mountains shake with the swelling thereof,' it has been always the refuge of God's people. All this I say, while I fully sympathize with the causes which incline many fine and beautiful minds against the system."

There is indeed great truth in this; the pity is, that the spiritual truth in Calvinism could not be dissociated from its stern and arbitrary features, and seen more perfectly in connection with the good Lord's gentle influences, and the proper freedom of man. "No wonder," says another writer, "that predestinations, absolute decrees, and sovereignty, were so prominently thrown up in the petrified exhumations, revivified by the sternest of the Reformers, in those days of fiery trial. *And now again will this great moving power be called into requisition, in deeper trials and more fiery ordeals than human souls have ever passed through upon earth.* But it will be upon a plane of life that has been so long closed upon earth, that its very existence has been denied by the church generally; and is now practically denied by even those who acknowledge the scientific truths of the New Jerusalem. The truths of God's absolute Power over all the destinies of human beings, both in time and eternity, will now become so inwoven with all the heart experiences that belong to a spiritual plane of feeling and of thought, that no appearances will have power to divert the mind from the realities of eternal life." *

Ah yes, the Lord reigneth, let the earth rejoice. Men and devils are nothing before Him. Preposterous! that man, the finite creature, should be endowed with a power which all confess is wholly derived, which will enable him finally and eternally to defeat that very Power from which all power is derived! Surely he can never do it. He cannot do it even for a single moment, looked at interiorly. Man may *delay* God's purposes, which is synonymous with protracting his own sinful state, but he cannot finally and utterly defeat them. God

---

* *Conflict of Ages Ended,* pp. 298, 299.

only lent him that power, thereby to accomplish his own purposes more fully and completely. And yet He will never violate man's free will — never force it, but by continually following man as a Father his own child, will ply him gently and wisely with a thousand myriad influences; and by throwing different motives around him, and changing and modifying those motives according as man can bear them; by causing him to feel the pains of punishment as well as the joys of goodness, He will eventually deliver him from the evil, and advance him to as high a state of goodness and happiness as he has any power or susceptibility to enjoy.

All this is spoken, not with the same meaning for those in the hells, for of them we fear another process, yet have faith in the end of evil. But before this end can be obtained, these resolutely wicked, lost and abandoned spirits, will have to pass through pains and horrors inconceivable and impossible to utter. Ages on ages will roll away, in the dim, dark regions of eternity, and yet to millions will there no deliverance come. "Verily I say unto thee, thou shalt by no means come out thence till thou hast paid the uttermost farthing." (*Matt.* 5 : 26.) And when deliverance does come, is it the man — the sinner, that can thus more properly be said to be delivered? I do not see how it can be. When once a man has really and persistently taken the downward life that leads to hell, and has passed through the World of Spirits, or intermediate state, and taken up his abode *in* hell, I see no process of deliverance for the conscious sinner. The law of destruction seems to hold here, as in all other departments of nature. It is just like an infected tree; when it has passed beyond a certain point in the progress of decay, there is no salvation for it. It must all run out. So, I believe, of the sinner in hell. He passes to destruction. Not annihilation of his entire being, for there is still a divine germ—perhaps a human germ, so transcendently high and pure within him, that it cannot be destroyed, though it may never come into consciousness with him as a man.* This may remain as the foundation of a new life and existence. Somehow or other, by a process which we cannot here elaborate, but which may form the subject of a future treatise, this inmost germ of undying good may find its ultimation again in natural life. It is no more unreasonable to think it can, than that it found a beginning *at first* in natural life. It may grow up into a new man — into an angel. The general principle of this is what I believe. But the destiny of the sinner is thus horrible to think of. "Destruction of soul and body in hell"— "second death"— "burnt up root and branch"—"utterly consumed"—"everlastingly damned." May God deliver us from the awful destiny — set our feet *here in this world* heavenward, and spare us the penalty of the second death. For it is the word of his Truth which we cannot doubt — "He that is filthy let him be filthy still; he that is holy, let him be holy still." †

But before we speak any further of this grand and final result in the Divine Government, let us proceed to consider these intermediate evils through which the world is now passing, and in which it groans and travails in pain, waiting for deliverance. These evils, I say, *all* of them, have come into existence by a certain necessity which there is for them, not in the Divine Constitution, but in that peculiar freedom and imperfection which was all that could be bestowed upon the creature man, but which nevertheless were sufficient to keep him upright if he had chosen to remain so. Let there be no quibbling with this statement. Because God *could* do no more, that is no reason why it was not sufficient to maintain man in his integrity, if man had so chosen. If it is asked — could he

---

* See pages 364, 365.

† This conclusion is somewhat different from that expressed in a pamphlet previously published by the author, on the "Eternity of Heaven and Hell," but it is to him now the better conclusion and the higher theology, and more consistent with the inmost sense of the Divine Word throughout.

so have chosen? I answer yes; but if, from a chain of causes through all past eternity, there was a certain necessity (not compulsory) in the very choice itself, what is that against the choice? Who feels it any thing now? Who does not feel both sides of a truth so double? We acknowledge the necessity, and we acknowledge the free-will. They are both true, and it is a truth of such delicacy, and of such demand upon our whole nature, that it must be felt and perceived equally, if possible, by the affections and the intellect. But we cannot go over this ground again. What we insist upon here is, that the Divine Providence is absolute, universal, thorough and complete, as much in the evil, or with *regard* to the evil, as in the good of the world. As to the evil, instead of saying providence, we should say *pre*vidence. God provides the good, and prevides for the evil. But to make this still clearer, one other division of the subject is necessary, which is fundamental and vital.

CHAPTER V.

THE CONNECTION OF GOD WITH NATURE.

> "O Adam, One Almighty is, from whom
> All things proceed, and up to him return,
> If not depraved from good; created all
> Such to perfection, *one first matter all,*
> Indued with various forms, various degrees
> Of substance, and, in things that live, of life:
> But more refined, more spirituous, and pure,
> As nearer to him placed, or nearer tending,
> Each in their several active spheres assigned,
> *Till body up to spirit work,* in bounds
> Proportioned to each kind." — *Milton.*

Our ideas of the Divine Providence are densely and darkly obscured to many minds, by the confused speculations of philosophers and theologians concerning the *mode of the Divine existence*, or what, for clearness' sake, we may call *the manner of God's connection with the spiritual and material universe.* We have heard so much of matter and spirit as two distinct and separate entities, having no kind of appreciable relation or connection with each other, that the whole of theology rests in a fog from that consideration alone. Once make the distinction and separation that is made, — that spirit and matter have nothing in common, — that one is the perfect and complete negation of all the other, — that spirit is something without form, parts, divisibility, extension, color, or any of the properties that are usually recognized in a veritable, substantial entity, and that still it is *something*, — that it is best defined by what it is not, rather than what it is, — once set up this definition, and we have very nearly, as to all definite conception, either removed God from the universe, or admitted a Phantom into it which is the plague of theology during the whole of its adoption. It is the Will-with-o'-wisp of all fruitless speculation. It does worse than the changeful, passionate gods of heathenism,

> "Who set at odds heaven's jarring attributes,
> And with one excellence another wound,"

for it sets confusion at the very threshold of Christian reason, and removes all real faith from the mind. It is beyond all doubt, that this nondescript denial or ignoring of all the essential properties of spirit has produced more scepticism, both with regard to God and a future life, than any other one cause apart from the evils and corruptions of the heart. If there *is* a God who acts upon the universe, it is demanded by common sense and reason that He be something. That which has no form, parts, or extension, is nothing. God is a substance. He is an Essence, all admit. Of course then, He is substantial. Not material, but substantial. And now the question arises, whether there can be more than *one* eternal and original Essence? If we admit two, we introduce confusion and rivalry into the Eternal Being. We admit two equally self-existent, co-eternal, and different Essences. Manifestly, there can be but one. This is the highest intuition and reason—the simplest faith. Whence, then, came Matter? It could not be created from nothing; what, then, can it be, but a creation or formation from the Divine Essence? Creation is formation—not origination from nothing. God created matter from Himself. The whole universe is but an outbirth from Him, similarly as a man sends out from him and around him the whole invisible sphere of his being. So it is with God, only on a grander and more perfect scale, in the surrounding creations of the spiritual and material universe. The following from Swedenborg expresses the truth in an appropriate form:—

"There are two suns, by which all things were created from

the Lord, the sun of the spiritual world and the sun of the natural world. The sun of the spiritual world, from which all spiritual things issue as from their fountain, is pure love, [the first of all substance in intense activity,] proceeding from Jehovah God who is in the midst of it. That sun itself is not God, but is from God, and is the proximate sphere about Him, from Him. It is the first proceeding of the Divine Love and Wisdom. The sun of the natural world is pure fire, [which corresponds to love, love itself being spiritual fire,] and is created from the spiritual sun. From this spiritual sun, as a great centre, proceed circles around it, one after another, even to the last, where their end is, subsisting in rest: and these circles are spiritual atmospheres which the light and heat from that sun fill, and by which they propagate themselves to the ultimate circle: and in the last, by means of the atmospheres, and afterwards by means of the natural atmospheres which are from the sun of the world, was effected the creation of the earth.

"That substances or matters, like these on the earth, were produced from the sun by its atmospheres, is affirmed by all who think that there are perpetual intermediations from the first to the last, and that nothing can exist but from a prior self, and at length from the First: and the First is the sun of the spiritual world, and the First of that sun is God-Man, or the Lord. Now, as the atmospheres are the prior things, by which that sun presents itself in ultimates, and as these prior things continually decrease in activity and expansion, to ultimates, it follows, that when their activity and expansion cease in ultimates, they become substances and matters like those on the earth.

"In the substances and matters of which the earth consists, there is indeed nothing of the Divine in itself, for they are deprived of all that, being the ends and terminations of the atmospheres, whose heat has ended in cold, their light in darkness, and their activity in inertness; but still they have brought with them, by continuation from the substance of the spiritual sun, that which was there from the Divine, which was a sphere surrounding God-Man, or the Lord; from this sphere, by continuation from the sun, proceeded, by means of the atmospheres, the substances and matters of which the earths consist."

What can be plainer? From hence it will be seen that there is but one primary and essential substance, and that there can be but one. We do not quote the above passages from

Swedenborg, nor any other passage, as authority, to be received without the concurrence of the understanding; but only as preeminent wisdom from divine illumination, which it would be folly to pass by or conceal, when it expresses so well what every rational mind, it would seem, will most gladly assent to. "Let every man be fully persuaded in his own mind."

Now, therefore, we have got rid, by this brief philosophy, of one of the most formidable and monstrous chimeras that ever entered into the imagination of man;—that of a God, who is Spirit, who is Essence or Substance, and yet who has no appreciable connection with any other substance;—who is without form, parts, extension, and every attribute or quality by which a distinct entity can be made of him at all. No wonder that men have become Materialists. In the conception of such men there is at least *something;* in the popular notion of God there is *nothing* rational, receivable, nor definite. It presents a universe cut utterly in twain, the union only existing in a vain imagination, or a blind faith.

Let us fix our minds, then, intently upon this one, only, eternal and original Substance. We shall find in it the secret of all things. With such a conception, it is just as easy to understand how *God* can act upon the universe, as it is to conceive how one part of nature can act upon another part. God and Nature are as much a substantial unity as air and water; or earth, atmosphere, and electricity; or soul and body.

> "All are but parts of one stupendous whole,
> Whose body Nature is, and God the soul."

Spirit and Matter are but the *two extremes* of one united and indissoluble Essence. Not that "spirit is a refinement of matter," as some say, and as the great poet quoted at the head of the chapter would seem to say, but rather that matter is the sediment or precipitate of spirit. Spirit is first, or most interior; matter is the outmost expression of it.

But here comes in a most important distinction, of "discrete " degrees. It is only this that saves us from Pantheism. God and Nature are by no means confounded, but one is as absolutely and clearly distinct from the other, as a man from the house he builds. Only, man builds artificially, God naturally. How great is the distinction, for instance, between the Spiritual Sun and the natural Sun! How great the distinction between the spiritual and natural worlds! and between God and man, in their separate personalities! It is only necessary to distinguish properly between the *kinds of degrees* existing in all being, to preserve every essential feature of a true theology, with the advantage of a philosophy which makes it dearer far, and more intimate with the expanded reason of man.

The distinction then, is between *continuous* and *discrete* degrees. That all things, all matters and existences, are *from the Divinity*, and in one sense *continued* from Him by successive degrees from inmost God to outmost nature, is a truth of the first importance. But there are two kinds of continuity, simple and compound, or natural and super-natural, or self-propagating (so to speak) and divinely begotten.

These degrees may be seen first in the kingdoms of nature. These have not been developed, one out of the other, by a simple process of transmutation, or continuation of one into the other. It is true indeed that the progress of creation has been gradual, has proceeded in regular steps from the lowest to the highest, and that man could not have existed *before* the animal, nor the animal before the vegetable, nor the vegetable before the mineral. Each previous creation was necessary as a groundwork for the next, as well the separate kingdoms as each species in a kingdom. But there were certain processes performed at the *beginning* of each separate species and kingdom, which destroy altogether the natural development theory, and introduce us to what we may designate as *specific acts of the Divine Creator*, distinguished by discrete degrees of continuity. Science has demonstrated nothing more clearly than that one species of animals is not transmuted into another, but that whole species have been created at once, by a distinct and separate act. This is very properly called a discreting process, where the present order of nature is discontinued, except so far as propagation from its own is concerned, and a new order commenced; or where the Divine influx insinuates itself by a new way into the prepared substances of Nature, and a new species of creatures, not from the wombs of the old ones, are introduced into existence.

But let us take, for greater clearness and distinction, the separate kingdoms of nature. The mineral kingdom, then, was not continued up as high as it could be, and then imperceptibly transmuted into vegetable, although the precise line of demarcation may be very difficult to indicate. There was no power in nature itself — no force, spirit, or energy, as mineral, to pass that line, and lift creation to its new ascent; but after the mineral world had reached its utmost height, then another degree of the Divine vitalizing essence came out from the Fountain of Life, and, uniting itself with the advanced condition of the previous creation, evolved a new and *vegetable* existence. So, after this vegetable creation had ascended to its very highest point, it did not pass on by imperceptible degrees of transmutation into the animal, but another and distinct degree of the Divine creative influx came out, and took effect in the advanced and prepared stages of the present series, and a new and *animal* existence was introduced into the world. So also with man. He is not a simple continuation of the oyster, or monkey, but when he made his appearance, the Spirit of God again brooded upon the earth, and an entirely new and distinct degree of the Divine vitalizing essence came down to meet the previous conditions, and man was thus discreted into being.

This is not mere theory, but is supported by the facts of science. Nothing is more contradicted by nature than the transmutation theory, and nothing more fully confirmed than the other. It may be impossible to tell precisely *how* the process was performed upon the previous materials, and the new order in each instance particularly commenced; we cannot enter into all the *modus operandi* of the divine creation; but of the correctness of these *principles*, there can be no rational or scientific doubt.

But it may be asked what we gain by this view, — how it affects the *theology* of the subject. And we answer, we are saved from Pantheism by it. It is only this view of a *discreted* creation that delivers us from such a theory of mere continuity of the divine Substance into all things of nature, as makes them identical *with* nature. And yet there is a truth, even in Pantheism. Nothing, for instance, could be more pantheistic, in its first indiscriminate view, than one only primal Substance, out of which all things have been created. And if there was nothing but a simple continuity of that substance into the natural creation, then all things *would* be God, and God all things. But if there is another process — a discreting process as herein explained, then we gain a distinct idea of the Divine influx *separate* from nature. For nature is now seen to be, not merely continued on, from one degree of it to another — as it were, the Deity spun out into Himself; but nature stands distinct in her several kingdoms, (saying nothing now of any minuter divisions,) as material productions from the Divine Spirit. And when another kingdom or division is required, it is not *nature* — not any power inherent in matter itself, which keeps right on, but God, who now comes with another degree of his own Divine influx *into* nature, by a new and distinct way, and produces the next birth.

Matter itself has been discreted from the Divine Spirit — not simply continued from Him. It is continuous in one sense, as before explained, — in the sense that all substances and matters are from the Divine Essence; but it is by discrete-continuity, or supernatural instead of mere natural; God added to nature, and conceived in it, instead of nature giving birth of herself.

It may occur to some minds, how such a process would

affect the Deity, — whether by these continual procedures from Himself to go into the countless formations of material worlds, his own proper Divine Essence would not thereby become diminished, and whether this is not an absurdity sufficient for its own rejection. In reply we say, that to us the subject is preserved by its very infinity, and by the dwelling of God *in* all matter, even after it is created from Him. God is infinite. What can lessen infinity? May not countless millions of creations pass off from Him, through eternal ages, He himself being in those creations, in a lower degree, and yet his own resources be infinite? I cannot think, therefore, that the subject is at all embarrassed by this view, but that it is preserved in all its strength and consistency. We lose *ourselves* in the infinite theme — our own natural and finite minds, but we do not lose the idea of God.

It might as well be said that his Divine Essence is lessened by impartation of it to man. And yet who does not know that man was created from God, and that we are constantly receiving the Holy Spirit from Him? Surely, we were neither created, nor do we subsist, from nothing.

The Divine Spirit does indeed change its *form* when it passes into material creations; but there is no substance lost or annihilated; and God is still the very life of all that matter, and dwells in it.

But again, we offer it only as a suggestion, it is not perhaps unreasonable that the matter of the universe may in some way *return* to the spiritual Fount from whence it emanated. If not to the very person of God, still to that Spiritual Sun which surrounds Him; — thus that there may be complete *circles* of creation, from God into matter, and back into spiritual substance again, from everlasting to everlasting. Refining and beautifying, perhaps, at each successive revolution. "For of Him, and through Him, and to Him are all things, to whom be glory forever."

To return now more particularly to the subject of discrete

degrees. These degrees may be seen in some of their lesser manifestations, in the smaller divisions of nature. Continuous degrees, for instance, are continuations of one thing into different degrees of the *same* thing; as light into less light, into shade, into greater obscurity; or as thick into thin, gross into fine, hard into soft. Discrete degrees are *new settings out* of the Divine principle in nature. They may be illustrated on a very small scale, from what we see, for instance, in an egg;— in the yolk, white, and shell. The yolk is not continued into less and less yolk, till finally it begins to be the white, albuminous matter; nor does the white become less and less albumen, till finally it begins to be shell. But these things are discreted one from the other. Again, in an orange,—in the seeds, pulp, and peel. In a nut,—in the germ, meat, and shell. And in earth, water, and air. And so in many other things.

But the distinction here insisted on becomes more sublimely apparent when we pass upward from material things, and think of the whole material world as discreted from the spiritual world; and the whole spiritual world from God the Creator of it. And in all the distinctions between the several heavens, and the heavens from the earth, we see the same great law prevailing, by which, from the one only Divine Substance, creation has gone forth in majestic continuity, but not in simple, natural continuity. This it is that saves us from Pantheism. There is indeed, as before said, a great truth in Pantheism, and we see now what it is, and why it has captivated so many minds. It comes from the one substance. But like every other truth, it has been abused, and perverted, and made ministrative to a false theology and to no theology, running even into Atheism, for the want of a correct and discriminating philosophy. We may now believe and reason too. We may now see the distinct God flowing into the distinct nature, united and yet separated, as they ever should be. All things are *from* God, even as to their substance, but all things are not

God. After they have passed from Him and entered into their separate creations, they have an existence distinctly their own. It may be illustrated from the solar system. Enlightened science now universally recognizes that the planets were created from the sun. Nebulous rings have been thrown off, which have broken and separated, and formed into distinct planets. But those planets are not now parts of the sun. They came from the sun, but they are now no longer to be confounded with it. So of man — of his spiritual soul. It *came* from God, even as to its very substance; but it is now no longer a part of Him. But if there was nothing but simple continuity, all creation would simply be a spinning out of God, or rather of Nature, undistinguished and confounded, whereas now it is a sublime and orderly creation, with nature entirely distinct, and the degrees of the Divine existence and influx conspicuously marked.

We have thus gone over at some length, the subject of the two kinds of degrees existing in all being, for the purpose of illustrating more clearly the great subject of the Divine Providence. We may now see how that in *every thing* there is a definite Divine Providence. Not only by a certain divine necessity, and by evil as well as good, but by the intimate connection of God with Nature, — the essential unity of Spirit and Matter. It is by *universal influx* into all things, as well for creation as for preservation. Providence only means the provision and care of God, of all things which He has made. And we see now, without any chimerical notions of a Phantom God separate from all nature, how that God *is* in every thing to provide and care for it. He could not *be* in it, if He were such a Spiritual Non-descript as is involved in the common definition of his Being. He would thus have no appreciable relation or connection with the material universe at all. He might indeed be in the human soul, but there are many possibilities of divine action, and many wonderful providences, where control over *material* things is requisite, and where without some definite and clear philosophy, we cannot appreciate how the Divine Being can act at all, or how there can be *any thing* worthy of the name of a divine providence. Some of these instances are altogether surprising and wonderful. But now we understand how God is connected not only with the human soul, but with all nature; and how, interiorly, He is the life of every thing, because every thing is only a more or less discrete continuation from Himself, and has forever a more or less discrete connection with Him. Behold the marriage of philosophy and faith! Behold the unity, and still the separation, of all things.

But let it now be particularly observed, in order to the repelling of any, the very last remains, of Pantheism connected with this subject, that God is not to be contemplated merely as a great Focus, or Sun, in the centre of creation, but as altogether and distinctly MAN. He is an organic Being, the finite image of which is man as we see him in his human or angelic form, and whose personal appearance was itself revealed to us in the Lord Jesus Christ. He indeed extends throughout the universe, both spiritual and material, by his radiating and all-penetrative sphere, and is the life and energy of all things: but He is seen in the spiritual world not only as a Divine Sun, shedding spiritual heat and light through all the regions of it, but, to those whose perceptions admit of it, as a Divine Man *in* that Sun, the Sun itself being but the proximate procedure of the Divine Love and Wisdom. How transcendent and beautiful the conception! And when, therefore, we speak of matter as emanated and discreted from Him, we do not think, most highly, of a mere Focus of almighty energy and glory, but the spiritual mind rejoices in the perception of the Divine Man *within* that glory, whom we can love, honor, and obey, and before whom all the hosts of heaven fall down and worship.

CHAPTER VI.

THE DIVINE ESSENCE IN THE INMOSTS AND ULTIMATES OF ALL THINGS.

———" And I have felt
A presence that disturbed me with the joy
Of elevated thoughts; a sense sublime
Of something far more deeply interfused,
Whose dwelling is the light of setting suns,
And the round ocean and the living air,
And the blue sky, and in the mind of man:
A motion and a spirit, that impels
All thinking things, all objects of all thought,
And rolls through all things." —*Wordsworth.*

WE are now prepared to speak still more pertinently to the *confusion* and *disorder* of the world, in connection with those evils, both moral and intellectual, which so desolate the earth, and make it a scene of strife and misery.

First, then, let it be observed, that all these occurrences have had their origin, substantially speaking, in the one only eternal Divine Essence. First the spiritual creations, and then the material creations, have proceeded from the great Divine Sun, which is the first procedure of the Divine Love and Wisdom. And if every thing had maintained its *orderly* procedure, we should have had *nothing*, either in material or spiritual experience, contrary to our best ideas of the Divine Providence in every thing. But because they have in part proceeded disorderly, does that cut them off from the Divine Source? Certainly not; except so far as the free-will of man comes in to arrest, at certain points, the line of orderly procedure, and turn it into that which is disorderly. It is precisely like the flowing of a river, which might flow on in regular and beauteous directness to a certain point, and thence be diverted into irregularity, and even opposite directions. But the *source* is the same, and the essence and substance are the same; in like manner, all events of the spiritual and material universe. Their first cause, without regard either to good or evil, is *substantially in God:* for there is but one original and eternal substance. Thus, then, we are able with the utmost clearness to put our finger upon the point of connection between God and all occurrences in the natural and spiritual universe. Because man has perverted the line of procedure, it does not, we say, cut off the connection; and we can plainly begin to perceive how, this being the case, a providence can be instituted, rather *is* instituted, over every thing that exists. The Divine has a hold upon every thing, being in the inmost, invariably, even where the utmost perversion and confusion reign in the exterior.

This is well illustrated by a passage from Swedenborg's Diary. There was a multitude of spirits, he says, around him, whose influx was inordinate and tumultuous, there being nothing of unity among them, but each at variance with his fellow, so that the whole threatened destruction. "But in the midst of these spirits," he says, "I perceived and heard a gentle sound, thus angelic and sweet, wherein was nothing but what bespoke order; those from whom it proceeded were within, while the disorderly spirits were without. This angelic flowing [as it were] continued for a time; it was often repeated, and it was told me that the Lord governs, in this manner, all those things that are discomposed or disorderly, and inordinate, etc., which are circumfluent or exist around. For the Lord acts from a pacific principle, thus peacefully, wherefore the things which exist without, or in the circumference, are necessarily reduced to order; each thing [is reduced] according to the error of its acquired nature; consequently the human race and their external principles, which are their fantasies, by which at the present day their actions and their conversation are governed. As I was thinking about this subject, I compared the disorderly states of the said multitude of spirits to a tempest in the air, and to the stormy clouds, and the dust flying at that time through the atmosphere, all of which are then out of their equilibrium; but in the mean time the purer atmosphere, or ether, remains in a tranquil state, and acting by its latent and silent power of equilibrium, is continually operating upon the turbulent state of the atmosphere, until it reduces it into equilibrium and rest. A similar state exists also in man, when his external emotions disturb him, and his internal states are pacific. The case is analogous in very many instances." (S. D. 1175, 1176½.) So also we say of the whole confusion and disorder of the outward world. A Divine Providence can be instituted over it, because, having proceeded from the Divine, the Divine itself is in the inmost of the whole of it; and it can be done in the above-mentioned way. Truth to say, how often it is done, when men know nothing of the power that is operating, by this silent and invisible influx from the spiritual world! It is thus that outbreaks are quelled, rebellions subdued, the evil dispersed, and much of public and domestic strife reduced to quietness and order.

But now, in the second place, it must be observed, that all that exists in exteriors, in the natural universe or in human society, whether orderly or disorderly, has not only had its origin substantially in God, but is in fact an ultimate of the Divine Essence, either in true order, or in perversion. Or rather, instead of saying an ultimate of the Divine Essence, let us say an ultimate *from* the Divine Essence. For the things so ultimated are not the Divine Essence, but from it. Thus, all that we see, in the confusion that reigns around us, whether criminal or accidental, — the whole drive and stir of the city, and the busy movement of the whole world, — is but an ultimate existence, substantially connected all the way, from the Great Divine Interior Cause. And every man, when he walks the streets, or contemplates the subject at all, ought to feel it so.

He may then be delivered from one great cause of scepticism. He sees the confusion; that is only a perverted ultimate. He sees crime, and villany, and hap-hazardness through all human operations; frightful accidents occurring at every hand, and distressing casualties, and a reign, as it were, of human free-will and mystical fatality the least like providence that can possibly be imagined; let him know that the Divine must be in the whole of it, and controlling the whole of it, because there is, in the first place, but one original divine Substance, and not two, and it is that alone which is here ultimated into externals, either in true order or in perversion. It is not, in the language before explained, "continuous" from the Divine, but "discretely" from the Divine, and that is continuous in one sense. All the substance is from God. And although the evil originates with man, yet he could not have originated even the evil had there not been a Divine Essence for him to pervert. It was not, substantially, self-created by man; it was only perverted by man. And in still further reflection, even the confusion, seen from a Divine, interior standpoint, in reference to its necessity, and its instrumentality for higher good, and its constant tendency and overruling *for* that end, prompts us to a partial recognition of the poet's truthfulness: —

> "All nature is but art unknown to thee;
> All chance, direction which thou canst not see;
> All discord, harmony not understood
> All partial evil, universal good."

Thus, then, we come to the most satisfactory conclusions. When looking abroad upon this vast scene of earthly confusion, — its crimes, its villanies, its terrible strifes, its fearful accidents and apparent misrule, we can, without abating one jot from the real Divine Will in the case, see how, philosophically, there is a necessary Divine Providence in every thing. If we do not, however, hold on to this element of necessity, rightly and divinely considered, we cannot solve the problem. We cannot explain human society. We cannot account for the terrible confusion which reigns around. Oh! how many fatal things there are that grate upon the reason and the heart, which are only eternal necessities of the Divine Love and Wisdom, growing out of a Divine Order which we cannot comprehend, and that order perverted by man. Can it be *providence?* says one, — this amazing complication of city life, — the whirl, and drive, and iniquity, and hap-hazard of all this world? Yes, we answer, *necessary* providence. From out the one eternal Substance the world and all its substances and motions came, and in the most superficial view that meets the eye, whether of crime, or accident, or vanity, or passing folly, we recognize the ultimates of that existence which is first or substantially in the eternal Cause, and which man has really nothing to do with, only so far as he abuses it, from the first to the last motion of it. Practically and qualitively, it is he that turns it into evil. And it is he that most righteously and tremendously suffers. But the Divine Being is necessarily in and over the whole of it, controlling and regulating every particle of it. And furthermore, as the Divinity is necessarily eternal, and necessarily infinite, as well as good and wise, so it is absolute and necessary truth, that each one of these incidents, though trifling in itself, is connected with infinity and eternity; — that the chain and complication of events extends through the soul's eternal experience; — that nothing *can* happen which does not more or less affect the spirit of man, and that the most trivial thing may be, as it is sometimes *seen* to be, the necessary link in a chain of events which reaches to the most momentous results, involving many individuals in its providential occurrence. And thus, in the language of the Scriptures, that "the very hairs of our heads are all numbered," and in the language of the Seer of Stockholm, that "the Divine Providence, in all that it does, regards the infinite and eternal, especially in man's salvation."

CHAPTER VII.

CONNECTION OF RELIGION WITH PHILOSOPHY.

"It is a maxim, we think, which should rule in the hearts of Christian men, and

> 'Most of all in man that ministers,
> And serves the altar,'

that the world is to be convinced *that Christians are not of necessity fools.* And in doing this, we care not how much of sound reason, and true philosophy, and the analogies of nature, are brought into the sacred desk. The truth is, that religion sets up its jurisdiction over all the operations of the mind. And the truth is, also, that those who have done most to vilify and abuse the use of reason, have been the very men who have incorporated the most of false philosophy into their own systems of divinity."—*Rev. Albert Barnes.*

WE confess, in the development of the subject thus far, to a certain externality or naturalness which will not be fully agreeable to the most religious minds. That is to say, we own a predominance of the law side of things, in distinction from what may be called the will side; and certain philosophical necessities which *seem* to remove the idea of a willing and intelligent God too far from the mind. But in answer to this we have only to say that we have *purposely* commenced our work with this train of thought. We are fully aware of the perversion which some of our remarks and positions are liable to, and we are also aware of the extreme tendency of the natural mind to find a law for every thing, — even, sometimes, to reduce the very being and action of God to such a combination of laws and forces as is little better than downright Pantheism. But so we also know that there is a *good* and *truthful* natural mind; a preponderating reason in the human nature which *rightfully demands* the philosophy of every thing. Surely, there can be nothing theologically true which is *not* philosophically true, although we are sometimes unable, from the yet undeveloped state of our faculties, to discover that philosophy. Now, it has been our object thus far, to administer to this natural mind. We are aware of the immense scepticism and downright unbelief which results from this mind. We find men everywhere, in the church and out of it, in a state of bewildering doubt and confusion, just from the preponderance of the natural reason, which perpetually seeks the law of things and cannot find it, and who yet, from the glimmerings of the spiritual which they cannot quench, sometimes believing against reason, and sometimes reasoning against belief. That takes place here in the intellectuals, which so often exists in the morals,— a warfare and conflict between the superior and the inferior principles. It is our object, as far a possible, to deliver from this warfare. Therefore we have commenced our work upon a broad and solid foundation of nature. Some might choose to begin the other way, with the most spiritual and religious faculties first; we have chosen to begin this way; and by all the admissions which can be made to the common reason, and common intuition and sense of man, administer to those wants in the human soul which its disbelieving and perishing state so urgently requires.

But we must not forget, in the above allusions, that there is a spiritual reason as well as a natural reason — a spiritual philosophy as well as a natural one; and that this cry of the natural for the law and the reason of every thing comes in part from the spiritual nature. The truth is, the natural and the spiritual are to be harmonized; and the natural *itself* is to be made spiritual. It will never occur, in man's most advanced state of the regenerate life, that he will believe without reason: on the contrary, in proportion as he ascends, by the Divine Spirit, into regions and states of the angelic life, in that proportion will the Great God's infinite Reason be imparted unto him, and he will see every thing in the light of that supernal day. So that, in making this progress with the natural, and from the natural, we are only pushing our way more and more into the regions of heavenly light, where, when it is full day, all three degrees of the mind will harmonize, and man will be a complete unity of celestial, spiritual, and natural perfection.

Again it should be observed, that the most religious persons, before alluded to, who may not find full satisfaction in the views hitherto expressed of the Divine Providence, are frequently, and almost without exception, not the most philosophical or rational persons. They are developed disproportionally in one region of the mind. They run up high in the organs of veneration, marvellousness, and spirituality, but the reflective and perceptive faculties are wanting. Such has been the character of the "old saints," almost without exception. A fire from heaven has warmed and illuminated the apex of their minds, and many times played wonderfully through them. The Holy Ghost has descended and rested upon them, even to the impartation of the gift of vision. They have lived continually in this "Mountain of the Lord." They partook largely of the will element, and of the affections, and of that piety which looks continually straight up to God; but not so much, sometimes very little, of that intellectual sight which looks out and around upon objects of the visible, or the forms, connections, and laws of the invisible world. They were religionists, frequently, but not theologians; and many times theologians without any tendency to philosophy, either true or false, as the old and rickety creed-world abundantly testifies. They wanted nothing of the kind. They felt the *need* of nothing of the kind.

———"Enough," say they,
"To press the lips of God, and feed for aye,
On constant influx streaming from his breast."

"I know," says one, writing very sensibly on this difference, "that it has very much vexed men belonging to other classes of mind, that some writers and speakers have claimed the pre-eminence for this class; but oh, when will we learn that this is such a solemn universe,—it is such an earnest thing to be alive in it,— that all this comparing of ourselves among ourselves is one of the saddest human insanities. It is no matter of ours who we are greater than, or who we are less than. The question we have to ask each day, is, what is the work which I have to do this day, and how may I most intensify my energies for the doing of it? But let us also remember that if there is any class which may properly claim the pre-eminence among men, they are but babes and pigmies when compared with the untold myriads of beings in the upper spiritual spheres, and in the orderly earths of the Universe.*

Let us be thankful that we are coming into a new age, when, without any affectation, the most religious may be also the most intellectual, and the most intellectual the most religious. All hail the breaking morn of such a day! We would fain contribute our part to its shining. And now, having spoken hitherto predominantly of the law-side of things, we gladly pass on to the more interior regions, where we hope to find abundant comfort for the religious mind, without sacrificing one particle of the strong and sturdy philosophy which ought ever to characterize the full and perfect man. "The Christian," it has been well enough said, "is the highest style of man;" and let us be abundantly thankful that in the soul of the Christian are contained such wonderful capacities for the most refined and interior joy, and the most cultivated and intellectual religion.

---

* *Samuel Leavitt, Herald of Light,* vol. 1, p. 263.

CHAPTER VIII.

GENERAL AND SPECIAL PROVIDENCES.

"Stilling's guidance was always systematic; or rather, the plan according to which he was led was always so manifest, that every acute observer perceived it. He himself likewise felt this perceptibly, and it humbled him in the dust; but it gave him also courage and boldness to struggle forward in the path of conflict; and it may easily be supposed how such a guidance promotes true Christianity, and faith in the Redeemer of the world." — *Autobiography of Heinrich Jung Stilling.*

In general, but two theories have prevailed concerning the Divine Providence, and these two, as is always the case with the great and governing thoughts of mankind so far as there is any truth in them, harmonize into one. Men have so deeply felt God in application to their particular wants, and in moments of distress and suffering, when sudden relief has sometimes come in so many unexpected ways; and the greater affairs of nations and people have presented so many instances of a marked and timely providence, that it has been impossible to remove from the mind some sense of interference or interposition, quite distinct from the natural and usual routine of things, by which the Divine Being himself has interceded in behalf of man. Nor would we by any means seek to remove this feeling. It is founded in the deepest truths of the Divine Nature, and in the infinite abyss of subordinate being.

So strong indeed has been this feeling, that the only question of doubt or difference has been in the matter of "special," as distinguished from "general" or "universal" providence; some contending that God the Creator, having produced the universe, is in it by law or force of his own nature, — in it as the vegetative life principle is in a tree; — not interfering, not departing from regular laws, and not by any special or personal agency, except what is included *in* law: thus making providence identical with existence and preservation; which does not differ much from nature; differing in nothing except in the recognition of a Deity who is spiritual, — who is Love, Wisdom, and Power, instead of mere material nature. Others have contended for a Divine agency and interference as special and distinct as man's; which puts forth the right act at the right time; which exercises a watchfulness, and comes in at the crisis, and is, in fact, a special, personal, constant superintendence over all the affairs of individuals and nations.

It is not too much to say that this latter hypothesis, at its very first presentation, makes a stronger appeal to man's spiritual mind, and has altogether a higher theological element in it. And for that reason it undoubtedly contains the most truth. There is truth, however, in both hypotheses, and the latter is more worthy of the name of a theory. It is a grand point to *reconcile* these views of the Divine operation, and so to put reason and faith, philosophy and theology, at one. And the truth is, it is only owing to our limited and imperfect conceptions of the Divine Being, that there is any difference of opinion on the subject. It is supposed to be contrary to the most exalted and divine conceptions of the Deity, to suppose Him to be interfering with his works and operations as man does: and it undoubtedly is so, in respect to not foreseeing the future, and not knowing how to act till the crisis comes: but in respect to special and timely agency, and personal interference at the right moment, impressing an individual mind, or a thousand or million minds, to one end, or many ends, here is a vast truth not to be lost sight of. It would be strange indeed, if God had not as much special action and application as man! But in the first place, in all discussions of this nature, it is of immense importance to settle well the use of terms. What do we mean by *special* providences? These of course must all be included in the orderly operation of laws, or consistent with them, and yet we must not lose the idea of a distinct personality, and personal, timely agency, on the part of the Divine Being. That God is personal, there can be no doubt, for man is created in his image and likeness, and Jesus Christ was God manifest in the flesh. That He is infinite and universal, acting at once in all and through all, is also a truth. What, then, is a special act of his? We answer, it is not a departure from the regular round of things, but it is just so much of the universal as is more prominent to our perceptions, or more important, as affecting an individual, or many individuals, and also, as taking place by a higher law than the merely natural, and likewise involving more spiritual agencies. Every thing that transpires is of Providence, because, as before shown, it is some ultimate from the Divine Essence, either orderly or disorderly; and by the very necessity and correctness of the infinite procedure, it is either provided or arranged for, designed or permitted, by the Infinite Being. But some things are more manifestly so to our perceptions, as we see the wonderful divine means which have led to them. There is, therefore, *no speciality at all*, in respect to their taking place without law, or contrary to law; but when we come to see, in many particular and more prominent instances, how very wonderful the providence is, and how it has manifestly occurred by the operation of some higher laws than pertain merely to earth or nature, even the agency of spiritual beings being used for the production of it, then it becomes what we call special: but it is special, not as taken out of the universal, but as included in it; yet as projecting out of it *to our view*, so as to convince us of more than mere laws, and of personal and divine agencies working with those laws.

Laws, indeed, as has been observed before, are sometimes suspended in their operation in a particular locality, for the time being, and with reference to a particular performance there, and new laws brought to bear in their place, as in the case of miracles; but they are never violated.

One great reason why we have no clearer views of this subject, is that we confuse ourselves with contemplations of the infinite. We are not at all fitted to contemplate clearly the abstract infinite, simply because we are finite. And indeed, in reference to the Divine Providence connected with so vast an infinity, we are situated similarly as a fly would be, who should undertake to speculate upon the machinery and extent of the steam-ship that he alights upon in the Atlantic. Says the fly — "This is certainly a matter of no special, personal agency at all; it is all a stupendous natural operation." And yet he could not see even the main-wheel of such a structure; much less the chief engineer, and the intelligent will that put it all in motion. And how much like the fly is man, wheeling through infinity on a little planet like this!

Another reason for obscurity on this subject, is our views of eternity. We find it difficult to conceive of any *timely* providence on the part of God, because, connected with a false idea of special, we cannot imagine God to come or act at one time more than another. And He does not, strictly speaking. God is not as man. Man does not know how to act frequently till the crisis comes, and does not act till then; he has not foresight in the case. God has even better than infinite foresight. All things are in a distinct sense ever present to his omniscient eye. The Infinite embraces from first to last, and from centre to circumference, all the finite, which are only so many possibilities and complications of existence, all included in the original Substance, and their breaking forth in time is only their occurrence in the extremes or ultimates of nature. The Omniscient Eye must have seen these, and the infinite wisdom provided for them. The same as God's own appearance in the incarnate form of the Humanity. This was no new thing to Him, only in act and in ultimation. So with every individual soul's existence, which must, from eternity, have been embraced in germal distinctiveness separate from every other soul. When born into the natural world, it was but the ultimation of an eternal divine conception, and, as it were, birth from Him. And so of all the experience which each soul is called to undergo, through time and eternity. It is all, as it were, previsioned and pre-enacted — all but the evil, and even that is presubstantiated, (not as evil) in the Divine Mind from eternity. How else could they be foretold, if not seen, and in a certain sense existing, from eternity? And how are many things in human experience previsioned even to the eye of man, with such wonderful accuracy and particularity, sometimes months and years before they have happened, — things impossible to be imagined, and most unlikely to occur, if the very tissues and substances of them, in the natural and spiritual worlds, were not woven into a fatal pre-existence? There can be no *sight* without *substantial connection*, or a fine medium like the light and atmosphere, through which to convey the impressions to the optic nerve and the retina. And this substantial connection, we may be assured exists, from eternity with the omniscient God. And all, as before explained, not contrary to, but accordant with, the entire practical free-will of man.

Such is the sense, then, and even more than we can possibly comprehend, in which all things are ever present to the eye and mind of God. Therefore, what He does in his providence, is done in the Divine Mind from eternity. Although things transpire in the most orderly manner, and at the moment when needed, and never a moment before, and this is called a coming in at the crisis, and is in fact so, yet it is not that God at that moment does a new act to meet the exigency. The act was ordered and done from eternity in the Divine Mind, but not yet ultimated into nature; and it was seen that just at that moment, that day or year, it would most infallibly transpire. Now this is *timely* providence. And it may be, must be, very particular. It must involve certain persons, where no others would answer, and certain moments, and what appear to us as accidents. Indeed, providence must be particular, to the smallest iota, because the *universal* is made up of nothing but all the particulars. And if one single particular, ever so small, were left out, there could be no universal providence. But here it is, timely, particular, exact, wonderful.

But now for all these difficulties, there is one most happy and philosophical relief. The truth is, the infinite and the eternal, so far as we can conceive of them, which is but faintly, afford us a lesson of the *greatness* and *majesty* of God, but no distinctive lesson of his providence. For a proper conception of his providence and personal agency, we must shrink up into certain limited spheres accommodated to our capacity. Thus it will be observed, we may preserve all the *proportions* of truth, and in our inferences concerning the infinite and the eternal, lose none of its correctness and fitness. And within these spheres, there is proof enough, and illustration enough, of this most interesting subject.

First, we have the grand and infinite truth of God himself accommodated to us, in the personal manifestation of the Lord Jesus Christ. For however much we may speculate on the nature and origin of Christ, the simple truth will be found to be, that He was "God manifest in the flesh," — that the Divine Essence took form and humanity, above all the operations of human generation, yet not without law, showing us how much of God, how much of personality, is comprehended in that infinite Essence which prevades all nature, but which is only clearly revealed to us in Jesus Christ. And can any one who admits this truth doubt the personal agency and providence of God now? — now that He has revealed Himself — stood out to us as one of us — unveiled the infinite glory, and without the violation of a single law, made known to us that God is personal, and can assume that Form of the Only Begotten, to teach us what could not be taught by all the blazing suns of the firmament. In the simple language of the Scriptures — "No man hath seen God at any time: ye have neither heard his voice at any time, nor seen his shape: the only begotten

Son, who is in the bosom of the Father, he hath brought him forth to view." (*John*, 1: 18; 5: 37.) Here then, is the *first* relief to our thoughts. We *can* look upon Jesus Christ as the *manifested* God, and no longer doubt the divine personal providence.

But, again, there is another relief for us; and that is, in the multitudinous *angelic* ministry. "He shall give," saith the Psalmist, "his angels charge over thee, to keep thee in all thy ways." (91: 11.) Here again we may perceive that the same accommodating *principle* of reasoning is preserved,—which is, that by shrinking up into certain limited spheres, we thereby preserve all the *proportions* of truth, and lose none of its correctness in our inferences concerning infinity and eternity.

Here also is *personal* providence. The angels of God encamp around them that fear Him, and are continually in the habitations of men. In the primeval ages of the world, when men lived in greater simplicity and purity,—in the *Golden* age, which is no mere fable, we have the evidences of an open and common communication with heaven. The men of those times, says Swedenborg, "enjoyed immediate revelation in consequence of their consociation with spirits and angels, and also by means of visions and dreams from the Lord."

Again, the whole heathen mythology is profuse in its recognitions of the ministry of spiritual beings. The great sages of antiquity were by no means strangers to a theme like this. The great truth gleams all athwart the history of man.

The Sacred Scriptures are most full upon the subject. The patriarchs and prophets were cheered and guided on their way by these bright messengers of God: Abraham, and Jacob, and Elijah, and Daniel, and Zechariah; in fact, almost all who form a part of that magnificent drama of the Israelites, show their acquaintance with these heavenly messengers. They came to the infirm humanity of Jesus, in his temptation and his agony,—to Paul, in his fear of the shipwreck,—to Cornelius, who was directed in his vision to send to Peter,—and to many others mentioned in the Scriptures; and there can be no doubt, these spiritual beings form an immense and very particular part in the all-embracing providence of God.

There are also evidences, and always have been, among private Christians, of the approach and interposition of these heavenly guides, impressing the right thought at the right time, weakening the power of temptation, suggesting noble resolutions, and interposing their friendly care in the more difficult and trying straits of human existence. And how often has the bed of death been cheered by the open vision of these celestial messengers!

These, then, are the *agencies* of a divine, personal providence. It is not all law, as that word is usually understood; we do not live in a staid and mechanical universe, given up to fate and nature; there are thousands upon thousands of watchful and untiring eyes upon us; yea, in strictest truth may it be said with the poet Milton—

> "Millions of spiritual beings walk the earth
> Unseen, both when we wake and when we sleep."

And now, in the light of this truth, we can see something more of the propriety and meaning of the term "special." It is manifestly more special for an angel to approach and influence me, or any friend for me, than for me to be blessed with the common air of heaven, or the sight of the green grass, or the light of the sun. The regulations of the atmosphere, of light, and the growth of vegetation, come under the head of *natural* law. Yet we should not forget that the Divine Person established even *these* laws, and works in them. But do not the angelic ministrations come under the head of *spiritual* law? For, behold the analogy. An angel is not moved to come from his high abode to relieve the distresses of a suffering mortal, or to minister to his spiritual good, by any less of law, than that by which a stone falls to the ground. The stone falls by the law of gravitation. The angel comes by the strong law of *sympathy*, by which, in a certain degree, he is *impelled* to draw near to a suffering mortal, and to impart the needed relief. He comes *because he cannot help it;* just as a good man cannot refuse to give a loaf of bread to a starving beggar. It is the law of his *goodness* that prompts and urges him on. Or, in other words, it is spiritual attraction of soul to soul, instead of material attraction of earth to earth. But surely, there is something in the contemplation of *angelic* performance — help from the heavens — and in that personal *will* and *effort* which an angel, like a man, puts forth in our behalf, which takes the occurrence out of the common order of nature, and invests it with a divine speciality and importance. These, then, although in a high sense special providences, yet are no more out of the sphere of law and order, than the growth of the grass or the falling of the rain. They are special with man, but not with God. Highly opportune and timely, but with God they were always so! They come under the operation of a *higher* law, and of personal agencies acting *by* those laws, and that is all the difference. Yet this is a difference which wonderfully affects the heart of man. It touches more peculiarly his *religious* nature, and causes him to look up.

Here, then, is a great central truth. The truth is, it is only the *infinity* of the subject that confuses us. As before said, the contemplation of an abstract infinity is overpowering and embarrassing. It is the fly upon the steam-ship. When we once take this whole subject, and do with it as our finite natures require — shrink up into certain limited spheres, in which we may preserve all the *proportions* of truth, and in our inferences concerning infinity lose none of its correctness, then we shall grow wise. When once we see the true God in his Divine Humanity, and so accommodated to human senses and faculties; and when we recognize the spheres of angelic being hid from mortal sight, and ranging up and down with their bright ministries, then the whole contemplation gleams with beauty and brightness, and is in fact a system of truth far more correct and beautiful than the most magnificent system of material astronomy that enriches the heavens, or adorns the pages of scientific truth. It is *divine* philosophy; it is the philosophy of spiritual things. It is that *theology*, too, for which the heart of man craves, and for which his reason is now hungering and thirsting. The universe of existence thus contemplated becomes a connected *chain* of being and operation, from inmost God to outmost nature; and as the impulses of divine love and care first stir in the heart of the infinite Father, so they are communicated to the angels nearest Him, or nearest the Divine Centre of being, and thus on, out and down through the vast ranks of glorified spirits, till they reach to earth, and protect the merest child from injury and danger. They also have the highest and most constant reference to the *regeneration* of man, and to his place in the heavens for eternity. But this is a branch of the subject which falls to another division of the volume.

CHAPTER IX.

THE NATURE AND MINISTRY OF ANGELS.

"Oh, never rudely will I blame his faith
In the might of stars and angels! 'Tis not merely
The human being's Pride, that peoples space
With life and mystical predominance;
Since likewise for the stricken heart of Love,
This visible nature and this common world
Is all too narrow! Yea, a deeper import
Lurks in the legend told my infant years,
Than lies upon that truth we live to learn." — *Coleridge.*

In the further pursuance of this subject, it were well to gain some clearer idea of the *nature* of angelic beings, and the particular part they play in the great movement of the universe. If we have not a right conception of the true nature of these heavenly beings, we shall fail to appreciate the dear and familiar truth conveyed to us by the contemplation. The word angel suggests to most people an intermediate order of beings between God and man. And the poetry and painting current in Christian literature and art convey frequently no other truth than the winged cherubs and seraphs which people the imaginary heavens. But this is both to unhumanize and undeify the truth. There is nothing in the Scriptures to justify this view of the heavenly beings; or, if there appear to be passages which speak of cherubim and seraphim with wings, the word is used in a correspondential or spiritual sense, to signify that power of elevation of which material wings are the proper emblems. But when the angels appeared to the patriarchs and prophets, and to Jesus Christ and the apostles, they were in human form, and were frequently recognized as the same beings who had once departed from the earth. Of the three angels that Abraham entertained, it is said, "three *men* stood by him." (*Gen.* 18 : 2.) Of the angel that wrestled with Jacob, it is said, "And there wrestled a *man* with him until the breaking of the day." (32 : 24.) Of the angel that came to Daniel, it is said, "I lifted up mine eyes, and looked, and behold a certain *man*, clothed in linen, whose loins were girded with fine gold of Uphaz : his body also was like the beryl, and his face as the appearance of lightning," etc. (*Dan.* 10: 5, 6.) This angel is also said to have been "one like the similitude of the *sons of men*." (16.) Also in Zechariah, the angel that talked with him is said to have been a "*man*." (1 : 10 ; 2: 1.) To Jesus also their appeared angels, and on the Mount of Transfiguration, it is expressly said that *Moses* and *Elias* appeared. And in the revelation, when John would have fallen down to worship before the feet of the angel, the angel himself declares unto him, "See thou do it not; for I am thy *fellow-servant, and of thy brethren the prophets*." (*Rev.* 22: 9.) From all which it is manifest that the angels are spirits of glorified human beings. They are united to us by a tie of kindred nature. Herein is the strong reason for their sympathy. They have all been born, and lived, upon some earth; those who are appointed to watch over us, undoubtedly for the most part are from our own earth, having passed through the same trials and the same sorrows, and thus, with a kindred nature and experience, are altogether the fit ministrants to our weakness, and the fit guardians of our peace.*

* A reason may here be given why all angelic beings must first be formed and born on some material earth. It is that the ultimate or most natural plane in their being could not be formed without it. All divine influx is from first principles to last. And in the last, or ultimate, the Divine exists in its fulness. There is thence acquired a *foundation* and *continent* for the superior degrees to rest in. Hence all creation is effected in ultimates, and all divine operation proceeds to ultimates. Thus also

The term "angel" signifies in general a *messenger*, or *one sent*, and though applied both by Hebrews and Greeks, to messengers from the spirit-world, there is nothing in the term itself, when thus used, which implies so much the nature as the *office* of the being so commissioned. In some places, indeed, the human nature of the being is expressly implied, as in the Revelation, 21 : 17, where the wall of the new Jerusalem is spoken of, "an hundred and forty and four cubits, according to the measure of a *man*, that is, of the *angel*;" where, of course, the quality of the church is referred to, as to its human perfections.

It is, then, both according to nature and reason, and to highest revelation on this point, that all spirits and angels were once the inhabitants of human bodies on some one or more of the planets. We will not say how much those bodies may have differed, and do still differ, — how great may be the refinement and purity, and almost spirituality, of the creations far beyond our gaze, where the Divine Being may have ultimated himself in forms of beauty and glory in the unsinning humanities. But we confine ourselves to essential principles pertaining to our own earth. And how refreshing and beautiful is the contemplation! The bright invisible hosts around us are "our fellow-servants and of our brethren." They were born in the flesh, they ascended as we ascend, from mortality to immortality, from corruption to incorruption. And they exist in the surrounding spheres in a form as human and as perfect, by a nature as beautiful and orderly, as that by which the material earths were first peopled by the Spirit of the living God. Some are higher and some lower, some cherubim and some seraphim, angel

---

the material universe, though not first in importance, is the natural foundation of the spiritual universe, and the angelic minds formed here in the world, are most full and complete, and prepared for the higher degrees of heavenly life. Hence also the importance and necessity of the *regenerate* mind being formed or begun here in the world, as it cannot be formed if the first foundation is neglected.

and archangel, and for those who were born in the ages long past, how great must be their progression, their superiority and refinement! But they cannot forget us; they cannot so progress as to pass beyond the sphere of sympathy; on the contrary, they must realize more and more, as they unfold and purify their own natures, the wondrous gift of human perfectability, and yearn to lead *us* up also to the sun-bright summits of their own beautiful and celestial home. Nay, their own progress is more or less identified with this effort for ours; for it is not a selfish glory which they can enjoy, but only that existence which is most replete with the Divine Love, and the whole intellectual of which is brightened and made more exalted by this baptism into the waters of charity. Hence it is that one of the loudest and most jubilant strains of joy among the angels is that occasioned by the gleam from this dark earth, of "one sinner that repenteth."

Is not this enough? Why need we return to myths and fables, to find credence for beings that only exist in the imagination, occupying a place between us and God, when He himself is only Infinite Man, and all are in his image and likeness?

Thus much for the *nature* of angels. Let us now observe how full is the Bible of this truth of the angelic ministry. The very first mention of distinct angelic appearance, in Genesis, 16, in connection with the wanderings of Hagar in the wilderness, is spoken of as the presence of God. "And she called the name of the *Lord* that spake unto her, Thou God seest me." It should be remarked here, that the reason why so frequent mention is made of the "angel of the Lord," in the Old Testament theophanies, is because the Lord took so full hold and possession of the angel thus used, that he became infilled with the divine presence, and was thus in a peculiar manner the Lord's messenger. It is stated by Swedenborg that the possession or infilling was so complete, that the angel, for the time being, frequently knew no other than that he *was* the Lord. And the men of the Most Ancient Church, called Adam, frequently saw the Lord in this way. *See Arcana,* Vol. 2, No. 1925.

The story of Hagar is touching and beautiful. She wandered with her child in the wilderness of Beersheba, and fainting and thirsting, withdrew a little distance from the object of her love, for "she would not see the death of the child, and she lifted up her voice and wept. And God heard the voice of the lad, and the angel of God called to Hagar out of heaven." (Gen. 21 : 17.)

And thus it ever is, and ever has been, whether or not we have enjoyed the open vision of the truth, that in seasons of distress, when the subject admitted of it, the appointed aid from the heavens has been given.

How beautiful was this truth figured forth to the patriarch Jacob! In a dream of the night, he saw the ladder extending from earth to heaven, symbol of this very connection that exists between the two, and upon it were the angels of God ascending and descending;—raising the thoughts and affections of man to God, and bringing down thence the gifts of heaven to man.

How often was the prophet Elijah ministered to in his wanderings, in his fatigues and distresses, by the same angelic guidance! On one occasion he lay sleeping under a juniper tree, to all outward appearance as one forsaken, and like the disciples in Gethsemane, "sleeping for sorrow." Yet a divine watch was kept over him, and a sensible demonstration was given of the ministry of the elect angels about them that fear God, sent forth to minister to the heirs of salvation. An angel "touched him, and said unto him, Arise and eat. And he looked, and behold, there was a cake baken on the coals, and a cruise of water at his head. And he did eat and drink, and laid him down again." (1 Kings 19 : 4–8.) Here in this gloomy wilderness, where the prophet had sank to refresh his weary limbs in sleep, he is thus made sensible of the heavenly and divine care of beings of a kindred nature. Yet this bodily weariness and sleep, and this material food which was furnished on the occasion, was intended to be illustrative of that spiritual sleep which is sometimes suffered to pass over the soul, and that spiritual food which is more properly the refreshment of the soul.

It was in the danger of shipwreck, as before alluded to, that Paul was approached and comforted by angelic assurance of safety. "For there stood by me this night," says Paul, "the angel of God, whose I am, and whom I serve, saying, fear not, Paul, thou must be brought before Cesar, and lo, God hath given thee all them that sail with thee." (*Acts*, 27 : 23, 24.) Also on his way to Damascus, at the time of his conversion, he was approached by Jesus himself, or by some angelic messenger from Him, with the thrilling question—"Saul, Saul, why persecutest thou me?" (*Acts*, 9 : 4.)

To Peter also, there occurred a like heavenly procedure, when he fell into a trance, and saw heaven opened, and heard the voice, and experienced the vision, which, together with the vision of Cornelius, formed the interesting co-incidence of the meeting with the three men, and resulted in the grand discovery that God was no respecter of persons, but that the gentiles also were included in his purposes of grace, and that Peter was to be made a powerful instrument in that work of God. (*Acts*, 10.)

Again, for a more manifest exhibition of the heavenly power over the gross obstructions of matter, and the workings of the Divine Providence in such supposed hindrances, take the case of Peter's deliverance from prison. How simple and affecting is the account! "Peter was sleeping between two soldiers, bound between two chains; and the keepers before the door kept the prison. And behold, the angel of the Lord came upon him, and a light shined in the prison: and he smote Peter on the side, and raised him up, saying, arise up quickly. And his chains fell off from his hands. And the angel said unto him, Gird thyself and bind on thy sandals. And so he did. And he saith unto him, Cast thy garment about thee, and follow me. And he went out and followed him; and wist not that it was true which was done by the angel, but thought he saw a vision. When they were past the first and the second ward, they came unto the iron gate that leadeth unto the city; which opened to them of its own accord; and they went out, and passed on through one street; and forthwith the angel departed from him. And when Peter was come to himself, he said, Now I know of a surety, that the Lord hath sent his angel, and delivered me out of the hand of Herod, and from all the expectation of the people of the Jews." (*Acts,* 12: 6–11.)

It has been well remarked on this passage — "Who can read this narration, and doubt that angels can even act upon matter? Or that they bend their high intelligence, through love, to the trivial wants and necessities of our outer life? It seems very wonderful, that so powerful an angel, whose mere presence filled the dark prison with light, should bid Peter *gird himself,* and *bind on his sandals,* and *cast his garment upon him;* and even Peter thought it a dream or vision; but the ponderous iron gate that had opened before the will of his bright attendant, and the free, open street, in which he found himself, were tangible proofs of the material actuality of his presence."

But it was not that the angel had a material body. To such a poor, ineffectual presence, the iron gate would have presented a more formidable barrier. But it was that the angel acted from a sphere *within* and *above* matter, by a more substantial organism. So also was the stone rolled away from the door of the sepulchre. So were the foundations of the prison shaken, and the doors opened, for the release of Paul and Silas. (*Acts,* 16: 26.) The operation of the angel upon the body of Peter, in causing him to arise and walk, may indeed have been through the *spirit* of Peter; but the operation upon the iron gate not so. Here was a power exerted directly upon the strong barriers of materiality, which were swept away by the angelic will like a feather before the blast.

How perfectly such accounts set at naught the vague theory that the spirit of man is a flamy vapor or ether, floating somewhere in space, or in limbo, without form or vitality, awaiting its final re-union with matter!

Such are some of the evidences which the Bible affords of the distinct and efficient ministry of angelic beings. Other evidences and illustrations might be cited to almost any extent.

CHAPTER X.

ILLUSTRATIONS AND INSTANCES OF THE ANGELIC MINISTRY.

"Far above the glances
Of our eager eyes,
Listen, we are loving!
Listen, through man's ignorances,
Listen through God's mysteries,
Listen down the heart of things,—
Ye shall hear our mystic wings
Murmurous with loving."—*Mrs. E. B. Browning.*

THROUGHOUT all the works of God, there is a perfect analogy and harmony. The higher everywhere ministers to the lower. In human life, where that life is not perverted, the helpless infant finds its natural guardian in its mother's love; and watchful and constant as an angel's eye, is this kindly providence extended. The good parent is guardian to his children; the learned to the ignorant; greatness, everywhere, is not given to be ministered unto, but to minister. They that are strong are to bear the infirmities of the weak. In a righteous government, the higher always protects and guards the lower. The good king is the friend, not the oppressor of his subjects; and in that perfect state of society which is yet to bless and save this world,—in that day of days when the church and the world shall be one—one grand harmonious unity, corresponding to the man of whom the apostle speaks, composed of the head and all the members, how will all human governments as they now appear, sink and dwindle into insignificance before that order and form of heavenly wisdom which shall observe a regular chain and series of protection, blessing, and mutual help, from the centre and highest, to the farthest off and lowest down of all the members of that divine Association!

Now, inasmuch as it is so on earth, so is it according to nature and reason to suppose it in the connection between earth and heaven. "It is this system of existence which the ancient mythology represented by a *chain*, which, fastened to the throne of God, fell in perpetual folds, embraced the earth, encircled with one or other of its golden links, every created being, and then returned to Him from whom it descended. Or, to refer to another and more appropriate symbol, the laws of existence thus understood, realize the ladder of the patriarch's dream. It rests upon the earth, and its top is in the heaven; and upon every step of its infinite length, the angels of God are descending and ascending forever and ever." *

Thus, by this beautiful law of connection and affinity, each individual has his or her spiritual friend, who is near when no other is near; whose vigilant eyes, in moments of danger, sleep not nor slumber; whose nature and delight it is to guard its kindred from danger and from evil, and by the spirit of a loving God, to carry it through this scene of earthly trial, and lead it up to virtue and to heaven.

I confess myself surprised, when I look over the ancient records of the Hebrew and Christian faith, and see the almost endless recognition of spiritual and angelic agency, that no more account of it is made by those who profess to be guided by them. It is all, or nearly all, in our day, a theology of the immediate agency of the Deity, while in truth scarcely any can form a worthy conception of what the Deity in his great infinity is, or how He personally operates, while here, in the agency of the Lord Jesus Christ, and the angels who are his ministers, is a familiar, interesting, definite theology, dear to every human heart, and such as the understanding can intelligibly receive.

* *Parson's Essays,* first series, p. 35.

Even the heathen had a much better faith than many of us have. Confucius, the Chinese philosopher, taught that the spirits of the departed frequently returned to the halls of their ancestors. Zoroaster, the founder of the Persian religion, claimed, and we have no doubt truthfully, to have intercourse with the spiritual world. Pythagoras and Plato both taught distinctly the doctrine of guardian spirits. Socrates, the wisest and best of all the heathen philosophers, always declared himself to be sensible of the guidance of a superior being, who warned him of danger, and directed him aright. The ancient Egyptians are full of the same faith, and the evidence is, that, cleared from ignorance and superstition, and unobstructed by sense and materiality, it is the faith of human nature. It has been the powerful support of all fiction, and the highest element of romance is indeed missing when this feature of it is not present.

The early ages of the Christian Church also furnish the most direct evidence that what was vouchsafed to the Prophets and Apostles was also, in a degree, continued to many private members of the church. It is matter of well-authenticated Christian history, that, so late as the middle of the third century, but especially in the age of the Apostles, many spiritual gifts, such as prophecy, speaking with divers tongues, working of miracles so called, healing of the sick, discerning of spirits, vision and revelation, and other divine influences connected more or less with powers and intercourse of the spiritual world, existed and were multiplied everywhere. And it is well known, that such works as the Epistles of St. Barnabas, St. Clement, St. Ignatius, St. Polycarp, and the Shepherd of Hermas, written immediately after the apostolic age, or perhaps one or two of them just before the death of St. John, recognize the existence of such extraordinary gifts and privileges as properly belonging to the church at that time; and these epistles were for a long time publicly read in the churches, as having an authority little inferior to the apostolic writings.* And why has not the church *now* this sensible intercourse and these crowning gifts? Is it any thing but our want of a living, active, affectionate faith, and a greater purity and spirituality, that prevents it? Nothing else in the world.

There is indeed getting to be, at this day, some better recognition of spiritual agency, but for the most part it is crude and low; it is not Christian; it pertains not prominently to the regeneration of man and to eternal salvation, but chiefly, to spirituality in distinction from materiality, and to heterogeneous communications from promiscuous spirits. We are glad to see the world progress in any direction; there is need enough for the thorough renovation of the Christian temple; but if we forsake the Divine Word, if we deny the central truths of Christianity; especially if we look not to Him, the Lord of all hosts, and the Almighty Saviour, in vain do we resort to any spiritual agencies to deliver us from the errors and evils of a faithless and impure life.

But the great truth of spiritual and angelic agency must be admitted as conspicuous. It occupies a very prominent part in the foreground of the Christian revelation, and the providence of God in this respect is immense. No mind can conceive, or imagination form, an adequate idea of the constant, universal, complicated agency of these spiritual beings, in the care and government of this world. They come in moments of danger when we see them not, and prompt the thoughts to safety and to peace; they come in sorrow, to infuse the balm of comfort and the strength of cheerfulness into the mind; they come in temptation, to avert the soul from its purposes of wickedness; they stand by the couch of sickness and the bed of death, and, having themselves passed through the same scenes of mortality, they minister to every human frailty and

* See an article on Christian Spiritualism, in the *Herald of Light*, by William Fishbough.

weakness, and shed the light and strength of heaven through the soul ready to despair. Oh! could we but realize it! Could we but see all the reality, and the parting circumstance of the dying bed, how would death be robbed of its sting, and the grave of its victory!

But they stop not here. They are with us when we are awake, and when we sleep. They are abroad upon the whole world, and they rule the nations more than men. They are limited in their power; they cannot do every thing for us; they are necessarily limited to the general conditions of human progress, and to human organization and susceptibility. There may be a multitude of circumstances which they cannot and are not permitted to control. But they roll on the great car of human improvement more than we do. They urge the proper ones to their proper work. They stimulate the reformer to his hard but glorious task, and lead him by a way that he knows not, and, seeing the end from the beginning, sustain him in his trials and carry him onward in his triumphs. We are not alone in this mighty movement of a progressing world. Hosts of purified spirits, who have passed through the same battles with the wrong, and stood out for freedom and truth, are looking down upon our efforts, and assisting us in the work they love. Thus also do the Scriptures assure us of "a great cloud of witnesses." The strength of every good cause has more of heaven in it than of earth. There is more of Peace, Freedom, Temperance, and the advocates of a better world and church, among the guardians of our world in heaven, than is to be found on earth. Every solitary thinker, every lonely man and woman, who, in retirement, or in the midst of persecution, is engaged in the work of human improvement, is, after all, not alone, but in a glorious company strong and bright for the same great movement. And in this respect, when we are tempted to despair, or in weakness and discouragement would look round upon the fearful odds against us, we may say as Elisha said, when suddenly surrounded with the hosts of the

Syrian army. "*Fear thou not*, for they that be with us are more than they that be with them." It was said in reference to a divine vision which was given to his servant, when the Lord opened the spiritual eyes of the young man, and lo! "the mountain was full of horses and chariots of fire round about Elisha." (2 Kings, 6: 15–17.) So it has always been. The spiritual hosts outnumber the carnal hosts. Heaven is always on the side of the right.

In looking for illustrations of this subject in actual life, the Bible evidences are of course the most impressive, because they come with a higher authority, and have invariably in them some lesson of a deeper and more spiritual import, connected with the regeneration and salvation of men. But there are plenty of other instances. The common, every-day history of humanity is indeed full of evidences of the same divine and guardian care, more than most people imagine. Our literature of this character lies for the most part out of sight of the common gaze of the world, chiefly because of a dread of superstition, and because frequently such occurrences are held too sacred for the frivolous converse of mortals who have no faith and no sympathy for any thing of the kind. But the record is very full for those whose attractions lead them to seek it, and we are moved here to present one or two instances without the pale of Scriptural relation, for the further confirmation and illustration of the subject. The first which we select is from a work entitled "Guardian Spirits," by H. Werner, Doctor of Philosophy, Stuttgart and Tubingen, Germany. The whole work is of the most interesting character, and has the impress of the high literary standing and sacred office of the author. It is translated into English by Rev. A. E. Ford, minister of the New Jerusalem Church, in this country. It is chiefly the account of a young lady who was prostrated by sickness, and who, in a somnambulic state, sent for Dr. Werner, whose presence, she declared, would contribute essentially to her restoration. The Doctor followed the advices which she received in that state, and by these means the cure was effected. The particular case which we now refer to is all the more convincing of the presence and agency of guardian spirits, because the fact set forth was first announced by the patient from the interior or somnambulic state, which event was then occurring at a distance, and letters were afterward received confirmatory of the whole account. The occurrence is as follows: —

On the 19th of May, 1834, between the hours of two and five, P. M., the subject of this spiritual influence, while giving directions for another person, suddenly broke from the train of her remark with anxious and trembling exclamation. She called on her guardian spirit for aid immediately, for her Emily, as she called her, a sister in a distant town, she said "would fall into the street." After a short pause, she commenced a strain of praise and thankfulness that help had already come. "Thou faithful guide and friend," she exclaimed, "even before I knew the danger, and could ask, you had prepared aid." To all this, the Doctor in attendance inquired, "What has so startled you?" "Alas, alas," she replied, "my little sister! She was in the upper story of the house, while they were raising wood up by means of a windlass from the street. She tried to seize the rope by which the weight was swinging, and the vibration would have drawn her out, as there is no balustrade above, if her father had not seized her at the moment and drawn her in." After a long pause, lasting more than an hour, during which she lay quite motionless like one exhausted, she raised her arms and exclaimed, "Thou faithful God and Father, how do I thank thee that thou hast saved my sister from death! Yes, she also shall thank thee, and acknowledge thy mercy." To this the Doctor again inquired, for he was himself somewhat sceptical of her accounts, "How is it possible for you to be with your guardian angel at so great a distance, to be speaking with us at the same time, and just now to look at your sister?" To this she replied, "That seems strange to you, but it is not so. It was all by the contrivance of my guardian spirit. Without him, I should not have seen my sister. He knew and foresaw the threatening disaster, and prevented it. In what way, I cannot see in him. This, however, I did see in him, that he had Emily in his eye, and thus I was compelled to see her also. He chose to have it so, and I could not prevent it. But this took place with a rapidity you cannot imagine."

All this took place on the 19th of May, between the hours of two and five, P. M. Now, on the 20th of May, (next day,) says the Doctor, "We did not fail to make inquiries in the town where the sister lived, if any thing unusual had taken place with her on the day preceding. We soon received the following, to us very surprising account: 'On the afternoon of the 19th, some time after four o'clock, some persons were employed on the upper floor of the house, in raising stuff from the street by means of a windlass. The little Emily had a mind to have a hand in the work, and incautiously laid hold of the rope by which the weight was swinging, without considering that the opening at which she stood had no balustrade. As it, together with its load, was in continual vibration, and the child of course had not strength to control its momentum, she was on the point of being carried out by it. She had already lost her balance, and had uttered one cry. At this moment, her father, who came behind her, seized her by her clothes, and drew her in. Terror so overpowered the child, that she lost all consciousness, and they were obliged to carry her down in a swoon into the sitting-room, where, however, she soon recovered her senses.'

"To these accounts the following very remarkable fact was added. So early as half-past three o'clock, her father, who was writing in the chancery, at some distance from his residence, felt a restlessness he could not account for, which increased at last into an impulse, equally inexplicable, to go home. For a long time he resisted it, as his business was not yet finished, and he was compelled to say to himself that he had nothing to do there; but at last, the attraction homeward had become so imperative, that, to relieve the feeling, he seized his papers with the intention of finishing them at home. When he reached the house he directed his steps forthwith to the upper floor, without depositing the papers, which formed a considerable bundle, in the sitting-room, close by the door of which he had to pass, and came just in time to save his child from the certain death of a fall from the gable of the house into the street. A moment later, and help would have been impossible." (Pp. 68–71.)

Now, the *rationale* of this occurrence is most plainly indicated. It was undoubtedly the guardian spirit of both the sisters, that saw the danger first, and the father was selected as the most suitable person whose mind to impress in that direction. This was the cause of the uneasiness. The spirit said to the father, in mental language as plain as it could be said, "*go home.*" It might not, perhaps, have been able to impress the reason. The father's understanding, so immersed in business, and not perhaps believing in these influences, was not susceptible of any thing more than was done. But when he reached home, it said to him — "*delay not; go into the upper story of the house.*" He obeyed, as he thought, the suggestion of his own mind. But when he got there, God had a use for him which he very quickly saw. And how opportunely was it all done! A moment later would have been too late. If it had been so, it would not have been the fault of the guardian care, but of the father, whose spiritual nature did not admit of a more powerful or seasonable impression. Oh, if our natures were not so sensualized, and fallen from their pristine purity, how much more might be done for us than is done, in the way of guarding and directing us through this scene of earthly danger! This is what we should generally call "a hairbreadth escape" — "a fortunate occurrence:" alas! how many such there are, not by any means accidental, but the sure ordering of Him who hath "given his angels charge over us, to direct us in all our ways," and who "suffereth not a sparrow to fall to the ground without his notice!" There may be thousands of such providences going on at this very moment!

Should it be questioned here why there are not more of such *successful* guardianships, or why many who do fall, and injure themselves in various ways, are not saved in like manner, we reply, no man can tell how many such providences there are; often, when we ascribe it all to luck and chance, the providence is even more complicated and wonderful than this; and we are saved, all unawares to ourselves, from the most fearful calamities.

"When in the slippery paths of youth,
With heedless steps I ran,
Thine arm unseen conveyed me safe,
And led me up to man."

But if there are many cases which are not provided for in this way, it is because they are better provided for in another way; or it is because it is best, on the whole, that the accident should occur: one may be saved, by a sudden death, from a life much more hazardous and painful; and often, when we know it not, there are permissions, and arrangements for those permissions, which illuminate the dark side of this subject with a light equally glorious, if we only had the eye to pierce its many foldings and to recognize the connection of all occurrences in one wonderful complexity.

How extensive and complicated is this subject! Looked at from some of its more ordinary aspects, in those every-day occurrences where we have equal reason to believe the Divine Providence is so carried on, how interesting does it become! Two or three men, for instance, are brought together from what to them seem the merest incidents of every-day life. Some angel who has arranged the meeting, drops a thought into the mind of one of them, it is talked of, reconsidered, considered again, and the result is, some movement or institution far in the future, which was at that moment seen and designed by the superior powers.

Not only in the activity of the daytime, but in the stillness and slumber of the night, is the same never-ceasing vigilance and work going on. We close our eyes in sleep, the divine messengers frequently come more distinctly. "For God speaketh once, yea, twice, yet man perceiveth it not. In a dream, in a vision of the night, when deep sleep falleth upon men, in slumberings upon the bed, *then He openeth the ears of men, and sealeth their instruction, that He may withdraw man from his purpose, and hide pride from man. He keepeth back his soul from the pit, and his life from perishing by the sword.*" (*Job*, 33: 15–18.) How many have been saved, by warnings given in this way, from the dangers which beset them! The angels can come to a man in sleep, frequently, when they cannot approach to influence him so powerfully in the hours of wakefulness, for the simple reason that at such a time, all his external senses are quieted, the things of the material world shut out, and he is then altogether in a more passive and susceptible state to receive definite views and teachings from the interior world. Take the following well-authenticated instance from the "Church's Companion." We condense the account for the sake of brevity.

"A poor and innocent criminal is condemned to death on the charge of murder. A farmer in one of the Western counties of England is awakened one night with an irresistible impression, not a dream exactly, that he must start off immediately to a county town thirty or forty miles distant. Why he must do so, does not appear. It is unaccountable, but it is irresistible. He endeavors to shake it off, and composes himself to sleep again. He is awakened the second time with the conviction that he must start that instant. He summons his horse, takes the midnight journey, arrives in town the next morning, but now that he has got there, he has not the slightest knowledge of any business to be transacted there, and so amuses himself by sauntering about town, and at length enters the court where the assizes are being held. The prisoner at the bar had just been to all appearance proved guilty by circumstantial evidence, of murder, and was then asked if he had any witnesses to call in his behalf. He replied that he had no friend there, but on looking around the court amongst the spectators, he recognized the farmer, who almost immediately recognized in him the man who had applied to him for work, on the very day and hour, in one part of the country, that he was charged with committing murder in another part. The farmer was summoned to the witness-box, and the prisoner acquitted."

He found then that he had not taken his midnight journey without some purpose. And how faithfully he was influenced and led by that invisible hand, about the town and into the court room! How evident it is, from the foregoing principles and illustrations, that the spiritual guardian of this poor but innocent man saw the danger, and saw too the only person who could be of any service to him, and so, hurrying on the wings of love to the sleeping farmer, suggested a journey to the scene of interest and danger, reiterating the impression with a dictate of imperative authority! And what joy ran through the echoing aisles of heaven, at the redemption of the innocent from so terrible a fate! Thus—

" Heaven encircles all. The blest immortals
Near us, divine with love's pure beauty stand;
Alluring us, through Faith's translucent portals,
Into the better land.

The friends we mourn as lost have not departed;
They have but laid aside Earth's frail disguise;
On your dark way they pour, O lonely hearted!
The light of loving eyes.

The saints and seers who made the old time glorious,
Dwell beautiful within our human sphere:
Serene they move, o'er doubt and pain victorious;
Paul, Plato, John, are here.

There lives no man, however crushed and lowly,
Bound with the gyves — immured in darkest cell,
But with him, ministrant of influence holy,
Some Seraph Friend doth dwell.

Each wondrous thought of Truth, or Love, or Duty,
  Flooding with sunrise beams through Mind and Heart,
Inspiring us with Wisdom and with Beauty,
            Some Angel Guest imparts.

No curtain hides from view the Spheres Elysian,
  But this poor shell of half-transparent dust,
And all that blinds our spiritual vision,
            Is pride, and hate, and lust."

—*Rev. T. L. Harris.*

CHAPTER XI.

DIRECT AND INDIRECT PROVIDENCES.

"God moves in a mysterious way in grace as well as nature, concealing his operations under an imperceptible succession of events, and thus keeps us always in the darkness of faith. He not only accomplishes his designs gradually, but by means that seem the most simple, and the most competent to the end, in order that human wisdom may attribute the success to the means, and thus his own working be less manifest; otherwise every act of God would seem to be a miracle, and the state of faith, wherein it is the will of God that we should live, would come to an end."—*Fenelon.*

As before stated, the whole of the Divine Providence is by influx from the Divinity into all that is beneath Him. But influx is of two kinds; mediate, through the spiritual world, and immediate from God. We are not so entirely dependent upon angels and spirits for divine influences that the Divine Being may not make some immediate applications of Himself; were it so, we could not feel that intimate connection with God which it is necessary to feel, and which the deepest and strongest intuitions assure us ought to exist between man and his Maker. But on a subject so confessedly high and interior as this, we trust that no apology is necessary for introducing again the words of one who evidently enjoyed in greater fulness than any other man, a spiritual and divine illumination, and whose great fame and experience entitle him to the utmost respect. Says Swedenborg —

"The influx of the Lord is also immediate with every one, for without immediate influx, the mediate is of no effect. * * * What proceeds immediately, is above all the understanding of the angels; but what proceeds mediately, is adequate to the angels in the heavens, and also to men, for it passes through heaven, and hence puts on angelic quality and human quality. For all and single things are from the First Esse, and the order is so instituted, that the First Esse may be present in the derivatives both mediately and immediately, thus alike in the ultimate of order and the first of order. 11 A. C., 9683.

"That many things on earth are effected immediately from the Lord, is evident from the case of the apostles, who sometimes, when they spake, were inspired by the Holy Spirit, and the words which they should speak were given to them, which was immediate inspiration."—*Spiritual Diary*, 1509.

This last assertion we find no difficulty in crediting. We can readily believe, not only that angels of a high order approached to influence the prophets and apostles, but that the Lord Himself, in a more direct manner, also comes into the interiors of men, and did so come in many cases of divine inspiration. That the Lord when in the world received into his humanity the Divine Spirit "without measure," and this immediately from the Father, or principle of Divine Good, is presumptive evidence that He can impart of it in the same way to others. And that many did receive of the "Holy Spirit," and were said to be "full" of it; also that Jesus himself "breathed on them, and said, Receive ye the Holy Spirit," (*John* 20: 22;) is evidence enough, we should think, that the Divine Influx can thus be imparted from God to man, without the medium of angelic agency. At the same time we are constrained to confess, that the instances with man at the present day, when he can receive such direct application and prompting from the Divinity, seem of necessity rare and unfrequent. Of the *common* immediate influx, such as is required to give effect to the mediate, and such as "flows into all things," we do not now speak: but of that other immediate, or rather what Swedenborg calls the conjunction of the two, this he says "is not effected unless in the case of those who have perception of truth from good; for they with whom immediate divine influx is conjoined with mediate, suffer themselves to be led by the Lord, but they with whom those influxes are not conjoined, lead themselves, and this they love." (A. C. 7055.)

So with regard to all the providences of God. Some of them may be direct or immediate, some indirect or mediate, and others more or less so. But while on this subject, we cannot refrain from the following liberal quotation from the "Macrocosm and Microcosm," before referred to. After stating that "God orders even his providences according to laws, or, it may almost be said, has made them *synonymous with* laws," the writer remarks:—

"It may safely be believed that the present order and plan of creation is the best that could have been devised by the Divine Mind; for otherwise the present plan would not have been adopted. But if it is the best, then it requires no fundamental changes, and not even any modifications, except such as may comport with a constant *general progression* on the basis of the original plan. But while all progression in each department is dependent upon an influx or inhalation (hence free bestowment by the Divine Being) of *additional degrees* of the Divine vitalizing influence which is specifically suitable to itself, and while all progression is in this sense providential, God cannot, either in causing a progressional or any other change, and without deranging the established and hence best possible order of things, act providentially and *directly* upon any department of creation, except *through the medium of that particular kind of force or vitality of which the thing acted upon is a suitable receptacle.*

"Thus, considering the universe in its most general aspect as one grand whole, God cannot act *directly* upon it, or modify its existing activities and tendencies, except through the medium of those forces and laws of Expansion, Contraction, Circulation, Aggregation, etc., in the degree in which they apply to the universe as a whole. He cannot act *directly* upon solar systems and worlds, except through the medium of the same laws and forces in their higher degrees of unfolding as applicable to solar systems and worlds; God cannot act *directly* upon Mineral creations, except through the forces and laws of *chemical affinities;* He cannot act *directly* upon Vegetable Kingdoms, except through the forces and laws of vegetable life; He cannot act *directly* on the Animal Kingdom, or any of its forms, except through the forces and laws of animal, sensational, and semi-intellectual life; He cannot act directly on selfish and sinful human nature, only by those isolated and disjointed motive forces which are adapted to reach and affect the disjointed mental and moral constitutions of selfish and sinful human beings; while God can act *directly* and *fully as God*, in all his affectional, intellectual, and moral nature, only upon a perfectly pure and sinless intelligence — a being fitted for the harmonious influx of all the affectional, intellectual, and voluntative principles of the Divine Soul — a being, hence, who stands in the perfect image of God, and who, in principle, is *one* with Him. Hence, when such a being acts (and there never was but *one* such a being), it may be said that God acts *with* him, *in* him, and *through* him, and that his every act is in the fullest and most Divine sense, a *providence*.

"But as the infinite Divine, personal, volitional Intelligence is above all things, and over all things, and is the inexhaustible Source of all streams of vitality and motive force which flow into the various departments of His creation, it may be rationally conceived, that by withholding his inflowings into the universal system as a whole, He could cause universal stagnation and dissolution to ensue; or that by increasing those inflowings, He could stimulate all firmamental developments and solar and planetary motions, to unwonted activity; or that by diminishing his influence in one portion of space, and increasing it in another, He could cause the dissolution of some worlds, and the absorption of their materials by others; or that by modifying his influences upon the electric, ærial, and subterranean forces of a particular planet (such as our own), He could cause floods to deluge the earth, or subterranean fires to overwhelm cities, and destroy such human beings as must otherwise stand as obstructions to true progress; or that in a similar way, He might cause a rarification of the atmosphere in one locality, and a condensation in another, and thus cause a current of wind sufficiently violent to cleave the waters of a gulf, and afford a dry passage for a particular people through whom he designed to effect great purposes.

"It will doubtless still be argued that such occurrences, if they ever do take place, are results simply of the forces and laws of nature. In a qualified sense, this is granted, as we have shown before that *all* action, whether physical or spiritual, is according to some laws; but we insist that it is an exceedingly superficial view of the laws of nature, which supposes that they are self-generative and self-active, or that they can exist for a moment as separate from that Divine vitalizing and spiritual Principle which, in an earlier stage of this work, we showed was necessarily self-existent and eternal.*

"But if this self-existent, all-generative, and vitalizing Divine principle may operate upon mundane forces and developments in the way just described, He may, in a similar way, control, modify, and direct chemical and mineral, or vegetable, animal, and spiritual forces and developments, by a voluntary gradation of those influences proceeding from himself, as adapted to either of these departments of his creation. And all such operations would be instances of *direct* providences.

"But while it would be impossible for God, consistently with the fundamental, which we have presumed to be the best possible plan of creation, to act *directly* upon any *one* department of being, by forces specifically adapted only to *another*, (as, for instance, to act directly upon mind, by that Degree of attractive force known as 'gravitation,' or to directly control planets by the motive forces of moral and rational convictions,) it is none the less conceivable that each department of existence may be *indirectly* influenced through the medium of some other department, which is made the receptacle of *direct* influence. Thus it may be conceived as possible for God, by special and designed action upon a particular planet, to change the orbit of such planet, and thus *mediately* change the orbits of all the planets with which it may be associated, and thus to change their seasons, and thus their inhabitants, if they have any, and thus even to produce an endless concatenation of *spiritual* changes; or, that by action upon one particular department of the Mineral, Vegetable, or Animal Kingdom, He might change other departments of the same kingdom, and thus indefinitely change the relations existing between them all.

* Operations upon the atmosphere, and upon the physical globe, even to the production of storms, and other like occurrences, such as are here referred to by our author, are no doubt effected when wanted, by the mediation of spirits and angels. By working upon the electric elements of nature, they are thus probably enabled to control to a great degree, when permitted, the material conditions of our earth. The Scriptures also speak of whole armies given to destruction; and of a pestilence of which seventy thousand men died, effected by the destroying angel. 2 *Samuel*, 24: 15–17.

"Similar remarks are especially applicable to the Divine government of the *human* world. Notwithstanding every human being, and the whole race as one grand Man, was designed to reflect the image of the Creator, human nature in its present state is undeniably more or less depraved, selfish, and inharmonious, and hence is not receptive of the Divine influence in its pure and harmonious state. The Divine spiritual influence therefore, coming *directly* and *immediately* into the human world without the medium of a perfect human personage to harmoniously reflect, truly define, and correctly apply, its principles, would necessarily take a form of manifestation more or less characterized by the imperfections of degenerate humanity as its *receptacle*—in the same way as the Divine operative influence, flowing into animal or still lower creations, takes a form of manifestation peculiar to these creations. On this principle, and this principle alone, it is conceived, we may account for the imperfection of the *impressions* which the Divine inspiration gave to Moses, and David, and the prophets, and the imperfections of the code of ethics, principles of government, and policy in respect to other nations, which grew out of these impressions; for all these were evidently imperfect when judged by a *Christian* standard.* Still, by means of such

---

* If our author means, as he may, that Moses and the prophets were instruments only for the *preliminary*, and *thence* imperfect, dispensations of God to the Hebrew and Jewish people, he is right; but if he means, as his language might imply more or less, that the inspired servants of those times only wrote as they could receive into their own imperfect mental *organisms*, and *hence* were the medium of errors and falsities, we shall have to demur. This would be to overlook the fact which we believe to be essential to the understanding of the whole subject of Divine inspiration; *viz.*, that the *self-hood* of the writers was in such cases so entirely taken away, or subdued by a Divine power, that they could be made to write, and did write, not altogether what flowed into their understandings, for they had no interior, spiritual understanding, but what was dictated to them by the Divine Spirit, and what they were moved to write with a more or less strong afflatus, and some conviction of its truth and importance. They also wrote automatically, and sometimes the very words were dictated into their ears. They understood in general enough to know that what they wrote was a message from the Lord, but they *could* not understand its systematic, internal meaning, in all its relations to the glorification of the Lord's Humanity on earth, and

inflowings as the psychical and mental constitutions of these mediums rendered possible, God, without immediately obliterating existing evil, pressed these evils into the service of ultimate good; and by arraying one nation against another, subjecting some to utter extermination, humbling others by long disciplinary chastisements, etc., so directed the general course of human events as to provide for the influx of more and more light, and for the final coming of Him who was emphatically 'the Light of the world.' And now that that Light has come, a similar course of indirect Divine providences is continued with reference to nations and individuals, evidently with the view to the ultimate bringing of all under the full influence of its life-giving beams, and to the establishment of that Divine Kingdom in the world which 'shall break to pieces and consume all other Kingdoms, and stand forever.'

"But if in this disjointed and degenerate state of the human faculties, God can discharge the highest functions of his Divine Government only by bringing the appropriate forces of one human faculty, one person, one society, or one nation, to bear upon another, it is equally true that in the *perfect* man, God rules *directly*, *personally*, and absolutely *as* God, in all his harmonially consociated affectional, moral, and intellectual attributes, in the same way as he rules mechanical, chemical, or vegeta-

---

the consequent Regeneration of man. The internal sense is most perfect; at least as perfect as any thing of the kind can be, when rendered into writing; and both the principles of the Jewish code and government, and their policy in respect to other nations, were so directed and overruled of God in his wonderful providence, as to represent, by correspondence, spiritual things concerning the church and heaven. It was, therefore, *Christian truth*, concealed in the letter of the Old Testament, but perfectly harmonizing in its internal sense with all that exists in the New, and all that is now revealed for the New Jerusalem. To be sure, we have *fuller* revealings now, but Moses and the prophets were true as far as they went. They were imperfect only in the sense of short-coming, and in not fully understanding their own message. The great distinction, indeed, to be made in this matter of the Bible writers, is between the inspiration of the *writer*, and the inspiration of the *thing written;* the former being frequently very dark, and the latter all-illumined. We have thought proper to say thus much, merely to guard against misapprehension, at the same time knowing our author so well as that he himself would probably assent to the generality of the truth here expressed.

tive Force, in different departments of nature without. Nay, in such a being, as the ultimate and harmonious embodiment of *all* the principles of his Love and Wisdom, God absolutely *dwells*, in his integral and *personal* capacity, as in a temple; and therefore such a being *is* God, in his focalized capacity, as adapted to a direct conjunction with humanity. All that authentic history informs us of the character, actions, and teachings of Jesus, goes to justify the belief that he was such a divinely human and humanly divine personage.

"It should be observed, that a perfectly pure and sinless intelligence, such as is here conceived, must, as viewed in a *human* aspect, stand at the very *apex* of visible creation, or at that point in a grand seven-fold circle of existence at which *endings* merge into *beginnings*. Hence, the Divine Soul, focalizing in all its harmoniously combined principles, in such a being, would maintain the same relations to inferior physical constitutions, and to all outer physical substances which lie within its sphere, as the Divine Being in his whole infinitude sustains to the physical universe as a whole. Hence the Divinity, in this *focalized* capacity, would maintain toward all things within its sphere, the relations of a New Beginning Principle; and if God in his *infinitude*, as the Beginning Principle of the universe as a *whole*, could, from his free volition, make and unmake laws to govern the present system of things, then God, in the condescended form of his personal Being as manifested through a suitable human organism at the end of the old and the beginning of a new creation, may, in equal consistency with the rules of Divine order, establish new laws, or rather enact immensely higher degrees of old ones, as relating to such existences within his sphere as need such interference. There is nothing irrational in the supposition, therefore, that the Divinely human, or humanly Divine Principle (which are one and the same), could, by volition through the outer organism which served as its medium, concentrate its vital energies upon the diseased bodies of men, and even the inorganic elements of the outer world, and produce such effects as are commonly designated by the word 'miraculous,' and that, too, simply according to that *higher degree* of laws specifically adapted to such operations, and unfolded for such specific purposes. Such would be instances of the highest manifestations of *indirect* providence.

"But if God dwells and rules, with a perfect and harmonious display of all the principles of his nature *as* God, in a being such as we have supposed, then it follows that the more any man is *like* such a being, the more fully God 'works within him, to will and to do according to his own pleasure,' the more he is under the *direct* operation of the highest order of Divine Providences, the more he is raised, as it were, above the sphere of mere material things and their laws, and the more he becomes a medium through which the Divine Being, in his affectional, intellectual, and volitional nature *as* such, acts upon beings and conditions *below* him, to bring them up to the true standard of healthfulness, harmony, and perfection! And when all human beings shall be fully united to God — shall fully 'dwell in Him, and He in them,' then all human beings, with their outer conditions, and even the whole *physical* world, divinely acted upon through their mediation, will undoubtedly be spiritualized, and elevated one Discrete Degree, and peace and plenty, and that universal harmony and love, which may be considered as the uncontaminated and unperverted outflowings from the Divine Fountain of Infinite Harmony and Love, will take the place of the corroding selfishness, the distracting animosities, and the physical, as well as moral, diseases and sufferings which now roll their desolating waves over the earth." M. & M. pp. 250–256.

The main drift of the foregoing extract we believe to be correct. Some allowance should be made for the stand-point from which the author writes, and for the minds which he seeks to reach and influence. Indeed, it is professedly given as "a rational deduction of *philosophy*, aside from the teachings of Scripture." And as its aim is to reach and convince such minds as *demand* the philosophy, and for the want of which cannot believe in the Scripture, we consider it able and illustrative.

We must here conclude what we have to say of direct and indirect providences. We have already referred to such providences as are brought about in roundabout ways, by complicated connections of many incidents and many persons; indeed, of almost every providence it may be said thus much; for what a train of connection is that which begins in God, and extends through all time, involving all persons, and stretching to eternity! There are no accidents, in the common acceptation of the term; there are no little things; each occurrence is as the grain of sand which makes part of the mountain; each movement a part of the whole movement; and in much mercy is the connection hidden from our eyes. For, if we could see only a small part of the infinite dependences of things, we should not only interfere with the Divine Providence by our own rebellious wills, resisting the unappreciated good, and demurring at the way in which we are led, but we could not even stir in the smallest act, without being overwhelmed with such a sense of responsibility as would be paralyzing and fearful. How terrible and overwhelming would it be, could man see how his every act was the initiatory to a universe! And yet that connection exists, and, directly or indirectly, every individual is involved, in the smallest thought, feeling, and action, in infinite and eternal consequences! The prayer should ever be with the Psalmist — "Lead me in a plain path, because of mine enemies."

CHAPTER XII.

DESIGNS AND PERMISSIONS.

"For either thy command or thy permission
Lay hands on all: they are thy right and left
The first puts on with speed and expedition;
The other curbes sinnes stealing pace and theft.

"Nothing escapes them both: all must appeare,
And be dispos'd, and dress'd, and tun'd by thee,
Who sweetly temper'st all. If we could heare
Thy skill and art, what musick would it be!"—*Herbert.*

ONE of the most important distinctions to be made in the subject of the Divine Providence, is that relating to what is designed and what is only permitted. Sometimes this distinction is summarily ignored by those who profess to view most deeply the ways of the Infinite; and where it is acknowledged, it is frequently the least apprehended, for it is not easily seen how any thing can be permitted by the Divine Being, which is not so involved in the councils of eternity and the foreseen course of events, as to amount to a thorough willingness that it should so transpire. And if a *thorough* willingness, why not a design? why not an equal reconciliation to it in the Divine Mind? Does it not, in fact, amount to a division and conflict in the Deity, if some things are only permitted, which, on the whole, He would rather not have exist?

These are certainly very serious questions. They strike at the foundation of the Divine Nature, and bring us again in direct contact with the "vexed question" of the sovereignty of God and the freedom of man. Let us inquire, then, into the precise nature of a divine permission. What is meant by it?

Is it to be understood that God permits simply because He is obliged to, or compelled to, — that is to say, because of any necessity in the Divine Nature by which He *cannot prevent* what is thus permitted? Or, is it to be understood that He has full power to prevent, but will not, because the freedom of the creature must not be violated? We answer, if the former only is understood, the term permission loses its significancy. It is not permission, but compulsion, or impulsion impossible to be withstood, which in effect amounts to the same thing. And however much the element of Necessity must be admitted into the Divine Nature, it cannot so be admitted as to deny the power of choice. As before said, it is the necessity of freedom and the freedom of necessity. Or, it is infinite will, acting according to infinite wisdom, which is its law. And although it may be said that God in a *certain sense* cannot prevent what is permitted, yet it is only in the sense that He has first chosen to make man free, because his greatest good is only consistent with that freedom. *After such a choice*, (the terms before and after, when applied to the Divinity, being only used in an accommodated sense, adapted to man's finite conception of eternity,) then it can no longer be said that God can prevent any thing that transpires. He could prevent it, if from eternity He had determined upon another plan or system of Divine Government: that is to say, He could have prevented it if in the first place He had chosen a system into which it could not enter; but having freely chosen this one, or this having of necessity existed in the Infinite Wisdom from eternity, then there is no possibility, or even power, on the part of God, to prevent the most grievous evil that is suffered to exist. Man might prevent it, if he would, but God cannot. Why? Simply because the system chosen is the best possible that can be, and as man *would* sin, it was best that he should be allowed to. God permits evil because man wills it, not because *He* wills it. He permits for the sake of the *end*, which is salvation. And the evils permitted cannot be prevented without violence offered to that freedom which must be preserved at all events: for as before said, man's freedom to choose good involves an equal freedom to choose evil, that he may choose the one by *rejecting* the other. And it is this one thing—the freedom of the human will, that the Lord guards as the apple of the eye; it is watched on all sides, in the spiritual and natural worlds, and attended to by angels placed over man for the purpose, to remove any preponderance of evil, or any influence which may exist to destroy or infringe upon that freedom, by destroying the equilibrium in which it consists. God therefore permits many things which are not in themselves good, for the simple reason that they are the best that can be under the present system, and the present system is best. And when it is considered that all these evils are overruled for good, and end in good, of some kind or other, we have not the least possible reason to object to the established order.

There is a very vicious mode of reasoning which is sometimes indulged in, by which it is supposed that the Divine Being has power to prevent certain evils, by the employment of extraordinary means, influencing man so powerfully in his spirit as that he must and shall freely desist from them. It is a kind of reasoning all the more specious and imposing, and readily adopted, because of the undoubted and appreciable existence of those very powers which it is supposed might be employed in such a work. For instance, it were very easy for the Divine Ruler to command his angels, or any company of spirits in the spiritual world, to flow into man on earth, and take possession of his affections, thoughts, and inclinations, and control his reason, in such a manner as to cause him to pause in his evil career, and forego the mischief which he was bent upon performing. No doubt that almost any one could be so arrested, as some have been, and thus the evil be prevented, which in so many cases is not, but freely permitted. But where evils are *not* prevented in this way, it is only because, all things considered, it is best that they should not be, and therefore they *cannot* be. The Power is at one with the Goodness. It cannot be separate. Divine Power, in fact, is nothing *but* Goodness, in actuation. And as the Divine Being has seen and comprehended from eternity every possible combination of existence, and so established irrevocably the present order, embracing each individual case in all its particulars, such suppositions as the above mentioned are not admissible. God *could* not so come to man. He could with mere Power, if He were not so *good* as He is, but as He is He cannot. It would not be consistent with the creature's highest freedom, or his best good, or the pre-established order and wisdom of the Infinite. Where it *can* be done, it *is* done — done gently and imperceptibly. Sometimes, in cases admissible, it is done more manifestly. But in general, no such extraordinary means can be employed. The virtue that might be made to appear by such instrumentality, or the evil that might be desisted from, would not so exist when the unnatural force was withdrawn. A continual strain must be kept up by the unseen agencies in order to preserve it, which in the end, instead of permanently reforming or regenerating man, would destroy him. His freedom would be overborne and crushed out of him, and he reduced to an unhappy and inane creature, tending to nothing. Therefore, the evil that is permitted *could* not be prevented. It is contrary to the Divine Goodness, and *thus* to the Power. And therefore God's permissions, though *different* from his designs, are still in the most perfect harmony with them so far as the *end* is concerned, but the evil of man cannot be said *in any way* to accord with the design of God. It was not embraced in his plan of government. It was only foreseen as a necessity which would grow from the freedom of the creature. We object, therefore, to the phraseology — "Will of design and *will* of permission." God only *wills* the *good*, and permits the evil. He is willing that evil should exist, but for the end only — not for itself. If there appear, therefore, to be two wills in the Divine Being, his will of design and his will of permission, in reality it is not so. There is but one will, and that is the will of good. Still He has the most perfect *control* over the evil, and in the end will not allow it to defeat his purposes at all. It is only in this sense that I can understand the passage — "And all the inhabitants of the earth are reputed as nothing: and He doeth according to His will in the army of heaven, and among the inhabitants of the earth; and none can stay his hand, or say unto Him what doest thou?" (*Dan.* 4: 35). He causeth "the wrath of man to praise Him, and the remainder of the wrath will He restrain." That is to say, there are *bounds* and *limits* set to the perverse power of man, and to all evil angels. "Thus far shalt thou go, and no farther, and here shall thy proud waves be stayed." It is seen from eternity that man can only go a certain distance in his evil career; and this is permitted him in regard to his freedom. But he has *not* power to overthrow the Divine Government, in one single iota of its being, here or hereafter.

We have thus far only spoken of those evils which are of a *moral* or *spiritual* nature. We need not enlarge, in this general department of the subject, upon other evils of a physical nature. The disorders which are usually recognized as natural evils are capable indeed of a presentation from a spiritual point of view. This, in fact, is the true point of view from which to look most profoundly at any thing. We can make no progress in the just comprehension of the various disorders which afflict our earthly dwelling-place, without an interior and spiritual standpoint. All external confusion is to be viewed as an effect and outbirth from an interior cause. The internal always gets out of order first. It does not always appear so, in many superficial and physical aspects, but trace it back to its cause, and it will be found to be in the spiritual nature. Inasmuch as the whole material world is an outbirth *from* the spiritual, in creation and in historic procedure, so it is that no confusion or outbreak can exist in the material which has not somewhere a connection with spiritual causes — which has not, in fact, *invariably* a spiritual cause, for its origin and whole procedure. Just the same as the body of man, in respect to its diseases and disturbances, and its whole outward contour and condition, is a production from a disordered spirit; and if no spiritual discord had ever existed, health, and harmony, and unimpaired beauty would have continued to characterize the human organism. So also the great body of nature. It has throes and violence, and calamitous outbreaks from the earth and atmosphere, and although we would not pretend that *sin* is the cause of the whole of it, for we honestly confess we can not see it so, yet we may see that it has had very much more to do with it than is commonly imagined or allowed. The truth exists in the *correspondence*, which is nothing more than the relation of cause and effect,—spiritual causes and natural effects. And though it may be impossible to trace the correspondence in all its fullness, we may be sure that it exists, and operates most thoroughly. The idea of the old theology, that man sinned, and nature, " sighing, through all her works gave signs of woe that all was lost," is not by any means destitute of truth. If we cannot see the whole truth, we can at least see a part, and it needs only that we consider how human spirits fell from their pristine state, and passed into the spiritual world in congregated hosts of wild humanity, creating the hells of direst confusion there,— of fiercest passion, most tumultuous rage, and all the seething elements of hate, and violence, and dread disunity, to comprehend how from the close proximity of that spiritual world to this, the influx rushed back upon us, sweeping violently through the souls of a fallen humanity, infecting the electrical and more spiritual parts of the material atmosphere, and the very earth upon which we tread, and creating, by the ever-operative law of correspondence, confusion and uproar in the elements of physical nature. First the storms and outbreaks of the spiritual creation, and then, as an ultimate, the material disorder of a broken and degenerate world.

Here, then, without any further enlargement, we come to see

the providence of these physical calamities. They are only permissive; they pertain not to true order; and most of them, to say the least, originating in spiritual disorders, the same argument applies to them which applies to the sins of men. Storms, pestilence, famine, the destructive earthquake and devouring heat, blight and blast, and killing cold, and all the "fierce extremes" of physical nature; we cannot, I say, without a wider range of knowledge than we now have, see how they are *all* connected with moral evil as their origin, but we can see how very much of it; most perhaps that we now suffer with, is the effect and outbirth of deranged spiritual conditions in the wills of a sinning humanity. Buried up here in flesh and sense, with the spiritual world entirely shut out from our eyes, the mass of men have little idea of the stormy and violent seasons that rage beyond this visible sphere, nor of the correspondential calm and beauty which pervade the earths and atmospheres of the higher heavens. And we have the utmost reason to believe, that when our world is restored to *moral* and *spiritual* order, much more than the anticipation of the poets will be realized to the earth. It will then also be restored to *physical* order, by a law of correspondence as sure and certain in its operation as any law of the more familiar nature. Storms will not be necessary to purify the atmosphere when that atmosphere itself partakes of the qualities of a pure and regenerate world. What will become of all foul and pestiferous things in an age of cleanliness and sweetness? The fierce cold of winter, the extreme heat of summer, will give way to a more mild and even temperature; tranquillity and pleasantness will be restored to the material globe in precise proportion as the Garden of Eden becomes fruitful in the souls of men, and the smile of God in all human affections is the sunshine and glory of the world.

CHAPTER XIII.

GENERAL SUMMARY.

"Let us hear the conclusion of the whole matter."

We have now taken a condensed view of the *nature* of the Divine Providence. Imperfect, I allow, and no doubt containing some minor errors which have escaped the notice of our own vision. We have seen how all true Providence is founded in the very necessity of the Divine Nature, — that the free-will of man is no obstruction to the Divine Government, although it is an obstruction to his own advancement, when used, as in his power to do so, contrary to the designs of God. The origin of evil was not a necessity in the Divine Economy, although foreseen as a certainty, and provided for: but having entered the world, it is continually overruled for good, and will finally terminate in good to all who are involved in it, and in the end be utterly destroyed forever.

The Divine Sovereignty is absolute and entire. Not such as to violate in the least iota the will of man, but to control it perpetually, and keep the reins of government in the hands of the Almighty Ruler, who cannot suffer Himself in the least thing to be defeated. The connection of God with Nature is most perfect. The one only Substance secures and perpetuates all unities and relationships, not by simple continuity, but by discrete continuity, and establishes the Divine Essence in the inmosts and ultimates of all things. Hence we have a religion and philosophy which harmonize most perfectly. The mind may unloose itself for the most adventurous flight; it can discover nothing but what has proceeded from the infinite Reason; and while it returns with the riches of incomputable value from every quarter of the universe, its every fact and principle become consecrated as a free-will offering to Him who hath built the mighty Temple, and who only asks, and can only accept most fully from his creatures, the intelligent worship of a devout and philosophic mind. There are also what may be called general and special providences; but the chain is so unbroken which connects the universe of things and regulates all movements, that at last the great truth breaks upon us, that it is only with man that any thing is special, not by any means with God, who ever worketh all in all: but still, that our wants and circumstances are so minutely cared for, and seen and provided for from eternity, as to time, place, and particulars, that nothing could be more wise, more beneficent, or more admirable, and in *effect* more special and impressive to man. And while the upper world so closes in around us, and the angels of God, from a kindred and sympathetic nature, are so diligent in their ministry, to keep and to guard us from danger, and lead us to all safety and peace; while Providence, both mediately and immediately, directly and indirectly, is thus forever leading us on, from one degree of perfection to another; and both in its designs and permissions, is so all-embracing, beneficent, and kind, what have we to do but to place ourselves more readily and immediately under the Divine Protecting Hand, renounce forever our petty cares, anxieties, and harrowing solicitudes, and trust forever in the Lord Jehovah, in whom is everlasting strength? It is only thus that we can best honor the truth which beams so brightly from all points of the clear, high heavens which are over us, to which the ladder set upon the earth reaches and is lost in the great infinity, and upon every step of which, in degrees and orders of divine beauty and glory, the angels of God are descending and ascending forever and ever.

PART II.

ENDS AND OPERATIONS OF THE DIVINE PROVIDENCE.

"O sacred Providence, who from end to end
Strongly and sweetly movest! shall I write,
And not of Thee, through whom my fingers bend
To hold my quill; shall they not do Thee right?

"Of all thy creatures both in sea and land,
Only to man thou hast made known thy wayes,
And put the penne alone into his hand,
And made him Secretarie of thy praise." — *George Herbert.*

CHAPTER I.

A HEAVEN FROM THE HUMAN RACE.

"Supremely happy in Himself alone,
Out from his vast infinity were rolled
Yon mighty orbs, and peopled every one,
With wonders upon wonders of a life
So strangely beautiful, so greatly full,
So bright with intellect and rosy love,
Godlike and God-derived, that shine afar,
In every altitude and every star,
That even creature glory might attain
To God's eternal joy." — *Landerf.*

THERE is one great end to which all the dispensations of the Divine Providence tend perpetually, and where every line, however dark or bending, in the life of man, meets and converges to a common centre. It is the production of a heaven from the human race. This *must* be. We are created immortal, we are introduced into this world without our being consulted, and with a thousand peculiarities and hereditary evils which we are no more accountable for than for the face we wear. The design of God, therefore, in its highest aim, can be no other than the blessing and glory of every individual in some station of use and dignity in the heavens. Whatever, then, pertains to the security of that destiny, (for it is to be wrought out by our own co-operative freedom) we may rest assured is the chief regard of the Divine Providence. In other words, it may be said that the Divine Providence, in all that it does, regards the infinite and the eternal. Necessarily so, because of man's immortal nature, and his *connection* with the infinite and the eternal. It is our salvation; it is our immortal welfare; it is the filling, in eternity, of that office or occupation for which every man and woman is designed, for which we are specially guarded through all this dubious and changing scene of time. Thus, it is not for the outward, but for the inward; not for the material, but for the spiritual, in all cases, that the order of providence is steadily pursued. This is the reason why we do not more clearly *see* the great truth of providence, in many dark and apparently untoward cases. It is comparatively easy for the mere naturalist to demonstrate the necessity and goodness of physical disorders, — the convulsions of the globe, "the pestilence that walketh in darkness, and the destruction that wasteth at noonday;" though he would shed a flood of more marvellous light upon the subject by the adoption of the spiritual theory. But it is not so easy to show from results, and from actual experience, the like necessity and goodness in evils which afflict humanity in many other ways. The reason is, their results lay out of sight, hidden in eternity, and in man's spiritual nature. But the great point is, that inasmuch as there *is* such an eternity, and a God who rules through all, it is a necessary consequence — it is a truth demonstrable and clear as mathematics, that all that transpires in time and in nature must have a bearing and reference to that end; or in other words, as the System of Nature (so to call it) is not so superficial as the mere naturalist would make it, — as it has a great interior, even a *spiritual*-natural, which concerns men's souls for eternity, so God can have no other reference, in all the outward and temporary, but that which ultimately pertains to the inward and eternal. Just the same as a man builds a house, not for the outside, but for the internal conveniences. Were it not so, it would represent God as working for the merest moiety of his creation, and as absurdly as he who should construct a delicate and intricate machine, the chief value and effect of which depended upon its interior arrangements, and yet spend all his time and supervision in taking care of the case that enclosed it.

The application of this truth is of peculiar value in many dark and bewildering circumstances of life, and especially in states of depression and discouragement. There is no obscurity about the *principles* of the subject; all the difficulty lies in the individual cases, the connections of which we cannot see, and the particulars of which are many times hard to bear. Thus there are cases of individual experience sometimes, characterized by a *constant succession* of rebuffs and disappointments, of the most trying and afflicting nature; — a constant thwarting of all the plans, and the crossing of all the chief endeavors, for a series of years, and perhaps for a lifetime. What a flood of light does the principle in question throw upon such cases! And what consolation may the stricken soul here find! The truth is, we know not frequently our own good, nor do we conceive of our own mission, nor what we are now being trained for. And yet it is clear that every man and woman must have a mission — must be fitted to perform some uses in the universal Kingdom of God, which no other being can perform so well. If we fail of it in time, it is in reserve for us in eternity. How extensive and wonderful does the subject thus become! And how little do we reflect upon the places and offices to which we are destined in the heavens, after all this checkered and limited scene of time! For the angels have employments, more complicated and more varied than man, and it is the ultimate end of the Divine Providence to advance us to the rank and office of angels.

Now, therefore, we are watched over for that end. From the time we first draw our infant breath, yea, and before that, in the germ and embryo of our pre-existence, and through that to birth into this natural world, and to the last gasp of old mortality, and to eternity beyond it, there is a constant, unfailing providence by the Lord, and by angels and spirits from Him, to make this our calling and election sure. There is no subject, therefore, so all-embracing and interesting to the individual as this. It is not to overlook at all the affairs of the world, but to invest those affairs with a seven-fold importance. For the heavens and the earth are so connected, that what is best for earth is invariably best for heaven, though not frequently as we are apt to consider it. Good institutions, reformed practices, a redeemed, and purified, and happy world, are mainly valuable for the production of a better heaven. Heaven is suffering now, comparatively, and the intermediate world of spirits is immensely degraded, from the imperfections, impurities, and degradations of earth. The earth also partakes of the reflux, and is weighed down beneath its power. The connection between all is what is essential to be most highly preserved.

By a Heaven from the human race, we mean an orderly, organized, societary MAN; — the Grand, or Universal Man, which corresponds in all respects to the individual man or angel. Heaven is supremely Human. It must have its head, its feet, its various external and internal parts, and all the functions which correspond precisely to the orderly, regenerated, human being. As the whole is made up of all the parts, and as one man is the whole in miniature, so the whole heaven, being made up of individual men, must, in the perfection of its organization, present to the creator one Grand, Harmonic, Societary Man, — emblem and outbirth of his own infinite Manhood, and corresponding to the church or Body of which the apostle speaks, having the head and all the members, in mutual order, reciprocation, and blessing. And the happiness of heaven is increased in proportion to the numbers of heaven. "The more, the merrier," is a proverb which rises up and becomes invested with transcendent sublimity in application to this theme of the immortals. It is indeed a wonderful and mighty contemplation. Too vast, too pure, almost, for mortals to indulge in, but the reality of which is not beyond the Divine Creative Goodness to bestow.

And heaven, too, is of infinite variety. Its infinite harmony is only possible to exist by the greatest multiplicity of genius, occupation, pursuit, and interest. And, not as a "church" merely, but as a church and world united, will every hallowed and divine thing, every production of exalted art, every science of the now opened and forever opening universe, every beauty, every use, which it is possible to conceive of in that orderly and thronging population, enter into and compose the business of the City of God.

"Glorious things are spoken of thee, O city of God!" and though we may err in striving too closely to conceive of particulars, yet, more than the imagination can conceive, may we build in assurance upon these foundation principles, which are correct, and scientific, and true in every particular.*

We may thus comprehend the value and significance of earth. This world is but the birthplace — the necessary introduction to a state of immortal felicity in active uses. As before said, it was not possible to form an angelic heaven without an ultimate foundation or basis in the natural mind, secured by this life in the world of nature. And it is here that Divine Providence so leads and disciplines us, that in the preservation of our utmost freedom, we may have that plane in the mind so formed and established, that the heavenly and more spiritual life may be everlastingly grounded in it. This is the meaning of the inspired passage, "Where the tree falleth, there it shall lie." That is, as the external life in the world, or the plane of mind in which the experience and memory of that life is fixed, becomes formed and characterized, so will the interior life and experience in the future world become conformed to this first foundation existence. The one rests upon the other. Not arbitrarily, but by divine and necessary order. But of this more will be said in the next chapter.

Thus, then, we see the uses of the world. It is the whole object of this world — it is why the planets were first struck out of the eternal substance, to people the immortal spheres

* The reader who would see this subject pursued in full, may consult Swedenborg's "Heaven and Hell."

with undying beauty, intelligence, and happiness in use. To this end are all the labors and reforms of the world chiefly subservient. It is a low view of them to consider them chiefly with reference to earth. They are mainly valuable for the production of a better heaven.

To view the world from this point of view is to remove the causes of much complaint for the thick-crowding calamities and disappointments of life. The success of life is nothing without the success of eternity. And it can be *afforded* that many a splendid plan of apparent usefulness be thwarted — many an enterprise overthrown — many an *honest* and *virtuous* purpose frustrated, if it is seen by the overruling Intelligence, that this is not, on the whole, so well calculated to secure the eternal good.

We frequently complain of our lot when no very visible wrong, certainly no sinfulness, entered into our calculations, but where we were only providing for our own necessities, and the necessities of those depending on us, and where no imprudence, no miscalculation of means to ends, were at all to be discovered by the keenest eye. It may be that nothing of this kind existed. It may be that we had made right calculations — that wisdom and sagacity were conspicuous in all our plans; and if there were no other end in view by the Divine Providence, we could have been suffered to have gone on with that to a most sure and speedy success. But God saw differently. And think you He had no means to thwart that plan of ours? We may talk of the laws of nature and of human life as much and as long as we please; and I do not mean to deny, on the universal scale of infinite being, a certain law, a certain necessity, by which even the Divine Being is in some sense limited to his own order,— by which his Love is controlled by his own Wisdom; but with the most rigid views of necessity and fate, what an infinity of truth is there in his personal Will and particular agency! Be sure the Lord can put forth his arm of power — can come by mediate or immediate influx — can send forth a thousand angels to do his purposes, and crush all the thoughts of man in a moment. And we can make no doubt that whole armies, in the clash and noise of contending arms, are thus influenced and controlled, and the battle turned to victory, on the one side or the other, by this powerful influx from the spiritual world. "It all flows in, from heaven or from hell; from hell from permission, from heaven from Providence." It is often called the *fortune* of war, and the fortune of this thing, and that, and the other. Men greatly overlook the surrounding influences of the spiritual world; it is but a thin partition that divides us; in fact, man already, as to his spirit, is in the spiritual world, and in company with spiritual beings.

Here, then, is a ground for resignation to the Divine Will. Complaints, and heart-sickness, and a multitude of anxieties, enter into our mortal life with the very necessity of being. But if we could only see how many of those disappointments which cause such feelings, were expressly effected by the superior providence to favor the grand end of our eternal destiny—how our purposes were thwarted to make room for the Divine purpose, there would arise from this view a deeper resignation to the infinite Wisdom. It is not in the common cant of religion that we speak these things. We can make no doubt of a plan, and a purpose, and a vigilant action on the part of heaven, more deep and real than our utmost imaginations. Indeed, in the spirit of a saying of Christ with regard to little children — "Their angels do always behold the face of my Father which is in heaven"— may we not conceive how from very *infancy* a child is watched and guided to his future mission? and when youth and early manhood come, then the commission is renewedly and imperiously given to the guiding angels — "See, now, faithfully to this your charge. See here, in this peculiarly constituted being, what he is fitted for, and what only he can best do. This is a work that was planned from eternity. He must perform it, for without him it cannot be done. Watch him now, through all his devious ways on earth. He knows not himself, what is his work, or what is his mission. It is not yet best that he should know. It would interfere with his freedom. He is, therefore, seeking another end, and marking out another course for himself. But see faithfully that it shall not take effect. Note all his hereditary tendencies; let him pursue this or that for a time; but rather than fail of the eternal purpose, which is for the good of earth, and for the good of heaven, and for his own good through time and eternity, cut him off in every direction. Disappoint him, if necessary, times without number. Strip him of all his worldly possessions, for he is one who needs to be tried in the furnace of affliction. His will must be bent; his nature softened; and these are the means, which, in his case, are most effectual for the purpose. He will call it calamitous. He will think it a hard lot. He will sigh and weep in despondency. But see that it is a work of love. It must be done. Count not upon earthly moments, but upon eternal realities. Through him shall come blessings to a multitude connected with him; and when he has accomplished this work to which he is appointed on earth, you shall still be with him, in his last hours, and welcome him then to these heavenly mansions, where he himself shall see and adore the Divine Providence, and be full of thankfulness that all things were so accomplished."

Yes, there can be no doubt that a very similar commission is given to many an angel who is appointed to watch over our earthly existence. Instead, however, of one particular angel for the whole life, our heavenly society is changed according to our changing states.

"Such spirits are adjoined to man as he himself is as to affection, or as to love; but good spirits are adjoined to him by the Lord, whereas evil spririts are invited by the man himself: but the spirits with man are changed according to the changes of his affections; thence some spirits are with him in infancy, others in childhood, others in youth and manhood, and others in old age. In infancy spirits are present who are in innocence, thus who communicate with the heaven of innocence, which is the inmost or third heaven; in childhood are present spirits who are in the affection of knowing, thus who communicate with the ultimate or first heaven; in youth and manhood are present spirits who are in the affection of truth and good, and thence in intelligence, thus who communicate with the second or middle heaven; but in old age, spirits are present who are in wisdom and innocence, thus who communicate with the inmost or third heaven. But this adjunction is effected by the Lord with those who can be reformed and regenerated. The case is otherwise with those who cannot be reformed and regenerated; to these also good spirits are adjoined, that by them they may be withheld from evil as much as possible; but their immediate conjunction is with evil spirits, who communicate with hell, whence they have such spirits as the men themselves are. * * * The angels, indeed, guide man, but herein they only minister to the Lord, who alone governs him by angels and spirits." H. H. 295; A. C. 50.

Thus it is, we have every reason to believe, with our attendant spirits. But how many lack this faith! The belief even in *angelic* guidance has almost died out of the heart of Christendom, or became so faint as to be ineffectual, where but an indistinct impression of the Divine Providence is left to cheer and to animate us.

In conclusion, let it ever be remembered that it is our eternal use and happiness in heaven that Providence invariably consults; and though there be a million of occurrences that tend to throw doubt upon the plan and purpose of this life, yet if we could see the whole of it, we might find that every thread in the great web of human destiny was woven by a divine hand for infinite purposes. And thus it is, spiritually speaking, that *the very hairs of our heads are all numbered;* that is, every least state of our spiritual life is pre-arranged and provided for.

But when we once give up special and personal agencies, and see nothing but the iron working of mechanical law, then woe to our faith. It is no faith, sufficient for a man. Often, very often, does the great universe bear witness to God's marvellous hand, touching the laws, but not violating them, which yield to his miraculous agency; and often is the course of our life interrupted, or its current changed, by the unseen beings who hover over us with their benignant power. Oh, this *dead* faith in the *mechanics* of the universe — this mathematical, sensual reasoning about nature's laws and forces! What a world this would be, says some one significantly, if two and two always made four! — if it didn't sometimes make five! What a world it would be, if every thing was governed by dead weight, and algebraic equations, and fixed, mechanical principles; — if there did not occasionally break out influences from above the region of mere law, and *force* upon us the observation of the unaccountable, the impossible!

But all this, in our theology, is made rational and consistent. Two and two always make four, but the spiritual arithmetic is larger than the natural — takes in more things — has wider connections. Oh! there is nothing too wonderful, or too minute, or too vast, for the computation of the Infinite One, or to order in eternity, and effect in time. And He who inhabiteth all the convolutions of all the spheres, and toucheth the secret springs of the will of every angel, and every man, and comprehendeth every least state of every creature throughout eternity, will yet continue the doings of that Wisdom which is "wonderful in counsel and excellent in working." Soon shall the few fleeting years of our mortal life be over, and then, seeing the great end of a heavenly blessing above all the conflict and all the darkness, we shall have a more abundant reason to thank the Almighty "for his goodness, and for his wonderful works to the children of men."

CHAPTER II.

THE ETERNAL MEMORY OF THE SOUL.

"Hail, Memory, hail! in thy exhaustless mine,
From age to age unnumbered treasures shine;
Thought and her shadowy brood thy call obey,
And place and time are subject to thy sway.
* * *
But is her magic only felt below?
Say, through what brighter realms she bids it flow;
To what pure beings, in a nobler sphere,
She yields delight but faintly imaged here;
All that till now their apt researches knew,
Not called in slow succession to review,
But, as a landscape meets the eye of day,
At once presented to their glad survey!"—*Samuel Rogers.*

should fail to receive an adequate idea of the truth of ubject, or how the Divine Providence is secured and plished in every one's life, without an understanding of the wonderful faculty of Memory. Many scriptures assure us of an opening — a revealing to be made after we have entered upon the eternal world; — that the "books are to be opened," and the judgment proceed according to them; and that there is "nothing covered that shall not be revealed; nor hid, that shall not be known." We can never know the spiritual import of such language without an understanding of the true psychology. The words of Scripture are the words of the Divine Creator, most particularly given through chosen mediums, and systematically expressed and arranged according to the constitution of the human soul, and its experience in all worlds. The *true* spiritual sense of them is, therefore, primarily *in the soul;* or more truly, the Word of the Lord is Himself, or his own Truth, as it stands connected with the human soul in all worlds. In our world it is embodied in writing. It is, therefore, nothing arbitrary, but a simple transcript of the Divine Mind concerning human experience and regeneration, as it is seen to exist in visible form *in* the soul, in the spiritual world, and in all that pertains to it. So that, with a true enlightenment, such as may be obtained from the Word itself, from the study of Swedenborg, and from all other sources of illustration and wisdom, we may find the written Word, and human nature, and all true philosophies, to exist in harmony.

But let us refer to one great truth, upon which so many passages of the Word are undoubtedly built. We mean this vital truth of the soul's eternal Memory. It is plain to be perceived that there is *some* faculty or capability in the soul, by which the hidden things of the spirit are treasured up and made possible to be revealed. There is some subtle and mysterious connection between all the motions and doings of the mind, which makes it possible for the *whole experience of an individual* to be recognized and identified in the spirit, after the body has been surrendered to death. This is evident from the words of the Lord, not only in the language quoted, but in many other passages of the Scriptures. Our question is — What is that connection, that power, or capability?

Some philosophers have supposed that there is a special faculty of Memory. But it rather appears that *every* faculty is a faculty of memory ; — that while one remembers words, another remembers ideas, another places, another times, deeds, persons, etc. One remembers forms, and another colors; one the quality of a thing, another its more external connections. Even Phrenology would teach thus much. Every faculty is impressed with its own appropriate objects, and retains and dwells upon the ideas which those objects excite. We speak sometimes of a good memory when reference is had chiefly to what we read or hear; but it is well known that while one remembers the words of a discourse, and can repeat it almost verbatim, and perhaps without understanding it, another will remember its ideas, and be able to tell us all about it, but have no memory of the words. While one will remember the faces of persons, and forget the names, another will remember the names, and have no distinct recollection of the persons. How evident it is that *every* faculty is a faculty of memory; — that whatever we see, hear, read, or experience, whether it pertains to intellectual, moral, or religious matters; whether it be of business, pleasure, sorrow, scenes of virtue or scenes of vice; whether it be what we do to ourselves, or what we suffer others to do upon us; in fact, our whole experience — makes its impression upon some one or more of the various departments of the soul, and there *leaves* its impress; so that, by being placed again in certain circumstances, or affected with a similar experience, it can be recalled and vivified before us as a present reality.

But now, *how* are these things impressed? or, what do we mean by an impression? Do we talk of a mere nothing — of a mere abstraction, without substance or form? How useless are these abstract terms without a substantial groundwork for the understanding! What is an idea? a thought? a feeling? We need not plunge into any abstruse metaphysics, for these things are clear to us in their first principles, so that even a child may understand them. Is not the soul a substance, and an organism? If it is not, is it not a nothing? How much have the metaphysicians done, and theologians, too, in an affected spirituality, to reduce all spiritual nature to nothing! How vainly have they talked of a human spirit! Spirit, we are told, is an essence or substance, without form, parts, color, extension, or any of the properties of material nature. But in our anxiety to escape entirely from the material, is there any necessity for going into nothing? If the human soul is any thing, if it is a substance, it must have form; and both reason and revelation concur in pronouncing the human spirit to be in a *human* form.

Now, then, what is a mental impression, an idea, or feeling? Is it not *real* and *substantial* in the soul? Without entering into any useless or minute considerations which are not appreciable, can we not say that all the operations of the mind are attended with absolute motions of its substance? *Substance and motion* — the whole universe is made up of this — God, angels, and men. And never a man thinks or feels without the movement of some of that fine and susceptible substance of the soul, which truly and literally *receives* impressions — as truly as the wax takes an impression from the seal. There is some stir of the constituents of a man's spiritual being — some trembling, vibrating, absolute motion of the interior organism, just as there is of the nerves, and sinews, and more manifest flesh. In fact, it is the motion of the spirit which is all that makes the body move; for the body without its spirit is unanimated and dead.

We begin now to perceive how a man's experience in this life can be treasured up in the memory, or in other words, what the memory is. What can it be, but the capacity of the whole soul to receive the impressions made upon it by all the experience which it undergoes? — a sort of daguerreotype susceptibility, by which the substance of the human spirit is wrought upon, and, with an exceedingly fine touch, receives the impress of every thought and feeling which may be made, like rays of light, to pass over it or into it? This may be confirmed by the process of recollection. Memory and recollection differ. A thing may be in the memory, that is, impressed upon, or formed in the soul, but forgotten — not able, for the time, to be re-ccllected, or called out into consciousness. But after some effort, or by some circumstance which throws us again into a similar state, we all at once re-collect it, or call it out from the chambers of the soul where it slumbered, to manifest life, presence, and reality again. Now, what is this getting into similar states? What can it be but fixing again upon those very impressions, traces, or lines in the soul, which are as real there as though they were made with a stamp upon wood or paper; and by which the very same things — the same thoughts and feelings, occur again?

There is, in fact, a more substantial philosophy in the purely mental operations of the human soul, than has been generally imagined. It may be illustrated even by material instruments. A celebrated violinist once took great pains to procure some pieces of the wood of an old violin which had been long played on, with which to mend his own. He assigned as the reason, that the very vibrations of the harmony of many years playing, had altered the quality and susceptibility of the wood. It was better than any new, or any old, which had not been submitted to this influence. It had probably acquired, by a succession of harmonious sounds being made so long to vibrate through it, some musical arrangement of the interiors of its fibrous particles. This is a piece of very fine, but very valuable and rational philosophy.

Now, just so it is with the human spirit, which has been played on for so many years, either discordantly or harmoniously. The effect must be lasting and permanent. It is just like bending an elastic rod: keep bending it, and it will stay bent.

Swedenborg has well said, that "all the cogitations of the mind are attended with variations of the form; which variations, in the purer substances, are such as cannot be described. Thought can no more be given separate from a substantial form, than sight separate from its form, which is the eye; hearing from its, which is the ear; and taste from its, which is the tongue. Since, then, affections and thoughts are mere changes of the states of the forms of the mind, it follows that *memory* is nothing else than their *permanent* state, [or thoughts which are *awakened* by their permanent state,] for all changes and variations of state in organic substances are such, that, being once accustomed, they are permanent; thus the lungs are accustomed to produce various sounds in the trachea, and to vary them in the glottis, to articulate them with the tongue, and to modify them in the mouth; and when these organic things are once accustomed, they [that is, the *states* and *potencies* of sound] are *in* them, and can be reproduced."

Thus, then, we have the real philosophy of Memory. It is not that naked, metaphysical thing which it is supposed to be. Memory, in fact, is nothing but the permanent bent of the elastic rod, or the fixed arrangement of the particles of a musical instrument by constant playing. Memory, in other words, is that permanent state — that absolute form of the substance and motion of a man's mind, which has been acquired by constant habit, and by all the experience which he has undergone. It must be observed, however, that while *all* the motions of the mind, however faint and transient, leave their impression, it is only the more powerful, or long continued, which are *generally* made the subjects of memory.

And now, what is recollection? or how is this operation of the mind performed? It would seem that this *effort* that we make to recollect a thing, does really, by the power of the will, reach substantially, as by a current of fine spiritual fluid instantly excited, to those places in the soul where the impressions or forms are made, and thus awaken the same idea into life. And when, without effort, certain circumstances bring the matter afresh into the memory, it is by a similar process, by which a substantial connection is made between the present state and the former impressions. And frequently, other spirits who are with us, touch and excite for us those parts of the mind. Thus, either by voluntary or involuntary power, by ourselves or by other spiritual aid, the soul does really undergo a process of refinding, or refixing upon certain impressions or forms made within it, by which the past experience is made a present reality.

At all events, we know that the soul *has* this power, account for it as we may. And it is a fearful power — a tremendous power — a power that may be used indefinitely, either for good or evil, and by which the great eternal Providence proceeds with steady and unfaltering step, to fulfil its designs and execute its purposes. For it would appear that *every thing* that in any way ever gets *into* the mind, in some sense remains there, and nothing, by any possibility, can ever be entirely eradicated from it. At least, while man retains his present identity it cannot be. It may be forgotten for a time, but it can be recalled. And if one thing may, every thing may. Why is it that some things are remembered, and others forgotten? The facts or experiences of the mind are strung or connected together into an absolute and convoluted series, touching each other all the way, according as we have experienced, having made their marks or impressions on the soul. And it is only owing to this power of the mind, either by effort of the will, or by circumstances, or by excitation from another spirit, to run back in a more or less connected chain, and to fix again upon certain previous states and impressions, that some things are remembered and others forgotten. And if so, it only requires a sufficiency of the same power to run back in an *unbroken* chain, to recover *all* the experience which we have at any time been made the subject of. Thus, *every thing* that gets into the mind, remains there with a wonderful tenacity, and passes to eternity. Many things may be forgotten, but there is not, necessarily and philosophically, any such thing as absolute and eternal forgetfulness. It may not, in eternity, be found necessary, or it may not occur by any of the connections of spiritual laws and facts, that we should *ever* be re-awakened to the remembrance of every little thing we have done or said; the memory of natural things is indeed, for the most part, quiescent in the spiritual world; but every thing *can* be made to start into the conscious mind again. There is this power latent in the soul. And occasionally, we are told, the soul *is* let into its past states of life, sometimes even as to natural things, for purposes of conviction and discipline.

It would seem, indeed, that such a power as the memory here

described, is a *necessary* provision for our human individuality. It is necessary for the preservation of our identity. It is this that gives the *me* feeling which we all have, or which distinguishes between the *me* and the *not me*. How could we preserve our individuality unless we had this power of treasuring up our past experience? Suppose any large or considerable portion of our experience should be so entirely and absolutely forgotten, as to leave no trace or impress of it in the soul; how could we live, the conscious beings that we are? How could we transact business, or fulfil any of the purposes of life? Strike out of all memory the last ten years of my existence, and how could I fulfil the offices of life, or live in future as a whole, individual man? Sometimes such cases occur in disease, and we see the sad effects of them. The person is as a new-born child, having lost all his former experience, and is obliged to begin again with the very rudiments of knowledge. Now, if it is true in large portions of experience, it is true in small. The large experiences are made up of the small ones—the generals of the particulars. And if one solitary particular, ever so small, could be really annihilated from our being, the law would be broken which makes us what we are. And the same law which requires large portions of experience to be preserved in this way, requires every particular, and it will secure it by the power of an infallible existence. In fact, our whole responsibility, as moral and accountable beings, is involved in this power. If we could not *remember* our misdeeds or virtues, or if they were not so engraved upon our very spirits as to enable us to see them and *be* them, where would be the justice of our continuous punishment? But man in eternity *sees* himself, and *is* himself, by this wonderful power of shaping, impressing, moulding, and treasuring up in the soul; he will see, as we shall soon show, his whole past life; and there is "*nothing* covered, that shall not be revealed; nor hid, that shall not be known." He will know by inspection and experience, graved and colored all over and through his soul, whether he is good or evil, and *how* good or evil he is, though he may err in the value of the estimate, and he will go, by visible accompaniments, with the hosts of his own kindred, to his own place.

But we proceed to observe, in the next place, that the memory, like every other faculty and sense of man, is divided into two parts, internal and external; like the sight, or the eye. The outward eye pertains to the body, and is comparatively dull. It sees only material things. But the inward, spiritual eye, is finer and more piercing. It sees spiritual things, and takes cognizance of a thousand particulars concerning the ends and causes of things, which the eye of the body fails to recognize. It is sometimes developed in certain abnormal phenomena — in those instances where, from involuntary or artificial means, the senses of the body are laid aside or put to sleep, and the soul-powers spring, as it were, into new life and superhuman activity. Wonderful are these powers of the soul, and they help very much to illustrate the truths which pertain to the eternal world. No one will question, at this day, who has paid any sufficient attention to the subject, the sight of a spiritual eye, which is used independently of the outward organ, and can see to read the finest print through thick, black bandages, and pierce through solid walls of masonry, and at almost any distance, yea, into the secrets of a man's soul. If it be said that the outward organ is still necessary, though blindfolded, and that the whole phenomenon is only a preternatural quickening of the bodily sense, what shall be said of the thought-reading? and of a thousand other more marvellous phenomena pertaining to the spiritual world? But it is not our purpose to *prove* a spiritual sense here; we trust that we have passed that necessity; but only to illustrate, from certain well-known facts, the doubleness of man's whole nature. For, as there is an inner and an outer eye, so there is a double set of *all* the senses — a complete set of spiritual powers, which, in fact, are all that make the body any thing; for this outward eye would be worth nothing, were it not for the eye of the soul; and the outward ear, were it not for the ear of the spirit. It was these interior senses which the Saviour referred to, when he said to the Jews: "Seeing, they see not; and hearing, they hear not; neither do they understand." (*Matt.* 13: 13.) Because they saw and heard with the external senses alone. So also in reference to the appearance of Jesus after his resurrection, to those who went with him to Emmaus. It is said at first: "But their eyes were holden, that they should not know him;" and afterwards: "And their eyes were opened, and they knew him, and he vanished out of their sight." (Luke 24: 16, 31.) It must have been the spiritual eyes that were here referred to, for Jesus then appeared spiritually, and could be beheld with no other eye.

And now, inasmuch as there is an interior eye, and an interior and exterior to every thing, just the same as soul and body, so there is an interior and exterior memory. For the memory, as before said, pertains to the whole soul in all its internal and external departments. The exterior memory relates more specifically to the things of the natural world, and of mere external thought, as distinguished from those which are the product of the life's love. Here is a grand distinction which is recognized by no merely intellectual philosophy, and which is nowhere so thoroughly unfolded as in the writings of Swedenborg. It is the distinction between the *Esse* and the *Existere* of our spiritual constitution; or it is the complete recognition that all thought is a mere form of some affection — the affection itself taking spiritual shape in the mind, and producing either a form of truth or a form of falsity, according as the affection is good or evil. But there are many thoughts and ideas flitting in the outer courts of the mind, which do not proceed from the *ruling* love of the man, but are mere stragglers, having gained admission by some subordinate affection, or some transient love, or perhaps by mere error and false education, which, when they are seen in their true light, or when the dominant love assumes its entire mastery, are extruded from the man, as having no part nor lot in his life. This may be the case either with good or evil thoughts, according as it is good or evil which finally gains the mastery. All such thoughts form no part of the interior memory. They are simply inscribed on the exterior, and, though they do not become extinct, because they have made their mark there, yet for the most part they become dormant or quiescent in the other life; they are *capable* of being reproduced, and *are* so produced sometimes; but they are finally, perhaps universally, passed to the region of buried and forgotten things. Not so with the things of the interior memory. These pertain to the very love, and hence the life of the man. These can be blotted out only when the man himself is blotted out. They run into the unfathomable depths of eternity. They constitute the very *form* of the dominant affection of the man. They are all, therefore, inscribed with the utmost particularlity upon the interior memory; and these two memories, the internal and external, become thus as distinct as two tablets, upon one of which are the immortal records of the soul; upon the other, the perishing things of time and circumstance.

Here, however, it should be observed that the external memory is not destroyed; it is *in* the soul, and becomes the foundation of the internal. The things of the internal memory rest on that as a basis; so that, while the particular things thereof do not appear, the internal memory is qualified and characterized by the ground and basis of the outer life. This, however, only where the ruling love has settled into its permanent control.

"The interior memory," says Swedenborg, "vastly excels the exterior, and in comparison as many thousands to one, or as what is lucid to what is dark; for myriads of ideas of the interior memory flow into one of the exterior, and there form a sort of general obscure principle; hence all the faculties of spirits, and especially of angels, are in a more perfect state, as well their sensations as their thoughts and perceptions. The superior excellence of the interior memory to the exterior may appear from examples: suppose one man to call to remembrance another man, who may be friend or enemy, and whose quality is known from the conversation of many years. In such case, whatever he then thinks concerning him is presented as one obscure principle, and this because he thinks from his exterior memory; but when the same man becomes a spirit, and recollects him, then whatever he thinks concerning him is presented as to all the ideas which he ever conceived respecting him, and this because he thinks from the interior memory. The case is similar in regard to every thing; the thing itself, of which many things are known, presents itself to the exterior memory as one general something; but in the interior memory it is presented as to all the particulars, the idea whereof had ever been suggested to him concerning that thing, and this in a wonderful form.

"Whatever things a man sees and hears, and is affected with, these are insinuated, as to ideas and ends, into his interior memory, *without his being aware of it*, and in that they remain; so that not any thing perishes, although the same things are obliterated from the exterior memory. The interior memory, therefore, is such that there are inscribed in it all the particular things, yea the most particular, which man has at any time thought, spoken, and done, yea, which have appeared to him as a shadow, with the most minute circumstances, from his earliest infancy to extreme old age. Man has with him the memory of all these things when he comes into the other life, and is successively brought into all recollection of them. And they are made manifest before the angels, in a light as clear as day, whenever the Lord permits it." A. C. 2473, 2474.

The truth of this statement is confirmed by many facts elicited even in this life, from a wonderful psychology. It sometimes happens, in extraordinary occurrences, that the soul becomes gifted with a power, or rather with the use of a power, which was always latent in it, to take this retrospect of its whole past life. It frequently occurs to persons who have been drowning, but who have recovered to relate their experience. It has happened to them, in what *would* have been their *last hours*, had no means been taken to resuscitate them, that they have had a strange vision of the past, in which their whole life seemed to float before them in a single view. There is a case recorded of an English captain, who fell overboard, and came very near drowning. After struggling for some time with the winds and waves that threatened to overwhelm him, and endeavoring to approach a small boat which he saw in the distance, he was observed to give out, and to manifest convulsive efforts, when suddenly his interior memory was opened, and all the chief events, history, and experience of his whole life, were exhibited before him, with a particularity and minuteness of detail which both astonished and admonished him. Also another case of a man who fell from his horse, and who received such a stunning blow as, in some sense, to start out this memory in him; when he saw at a glance, his past life, with the same vividness and accuracy. One of the Beechers has lately reported the case of a man who fell from the third story window of a house; and before he reached the pavement, he saw his whole past life. De Quincy makes mention, in some of his writings, how the *guilty* actions of a man's life have sometimes been reproduced in a like wonderful manner. I was once preaching in a neighboring town, on the subject of the Memory, and adducing instances such as the above, and after the meeting was dismissed, a man, a stranger to me, came out from the congregation, and confessed to me privately that he himself had been made the subject of a similar experience, which was so wonderful to him that he had never before told it to any one.

But there is a reason for these very striking phenomena; and that reason is to be found in the profoundest facts of our spiritual constitution. It is undoubtedly true, that at such times, the link which connects the soul with the body, or the internal with the external being, is somewhat loosened, which lets the man at once into his interior life. There he sees, as in a flashing panorama, the wonderful work of his past experience! But how could he see it unless it were graved, and cut, and colored into his soul? Cases have also occurred in severe sickness, where this partial separation has probably taken place, or where at least, the intellect has retired, as in sleep, from the outer to the inner chambers of the soul, and there merged and conjoined itself with the more interior and essential principles of life.

What a momentous truth is this that we are illustrating! How fearfully do such facts indicate to us the revelation of unseen things, and the uncovering of what is hidden! Even in *natural* life, the preternatural power of the memory is full of instruction, full of warning. How impossible it is to eradicate any thing that has once entered into it, may be instanced in some cases of diseases and injuries of the brain, where, after many years, the things utterly forgotten, have, by a restoration to the same state again, in which the injury was received, or the disease contracted, become suddenly and mysteriously reproduced in the mind.

"Dr. Abercrombie relates the case of a child four years of age, who underwent the operation of trepanning, while in a state of profound stupor, from a fracture of the skull. After his recovery, he retained no recollection, either of the operation or the accident; yet at the age of fifteen, (after the space of eleven years,) during the delirum of a fever, he gave his mother an exact description of the operation, of the persons present, their dress, and many other minute particulars.

"Dr. Pritchard, in a work on the Soul and Body, mentions a man who had been employed with beetle and wedges, splitting wood. At night, he put these implements in the hollow of an old tree, and directed his sons to accompany him the next morning in making a fence. In the night, however, he became mad. After several years, his reason suddenly returned, and the first question he asked was, whether his sons had brought home the beetle and wedges. They, being afraid to enter into an explanation, said they could not find them; on which he arose, went to the field where he had been to work so many years before, and found, in the place where he had left them, the wedges and the iron rings of the beetle, the wooden part having mouldered away." *

* Power of the Soul over the Body, by George Moore, M. D. pp. 153, 154.

In view of all these facts, and many more that could be given, pertaining both to our internal and external life, well may we ask, in the spirit of a profound Christian philosophy — *Where were* these ideas and images in the mind all this time? Surely they were there, and only waiting the recurrence of similar states, to bring them vividly into consciousness again. Thus, whether we understand it fully or not, in all the connections, there is an interior and an exterior memory; and it is upon this inmost tablet of the soul, that our whole life-experience is recorded with an exactness and particularity which admit of no power of escape. And even if we had no revelation so much fuller and more perfect, these facts would point to a fair and definite conclusion concerning our life beyond death. As it is, they mutually confirm each other. In that spiritual world, how surely shall we be the self-same creatures which we have made ourselves in this! For the spiritual world is but this world uncovered. And how fearful is the thought on the one hand, and consoling on the other, that, during our whole life here on earth, we are really treasuring up in the interiors of the soul, by every thought, feeling, and action; by all our sorrows, pleasures, temptations, successes, disappointments; by all our knowledge and wisdom; by all our folly and wickedness; by every association with persons and things, and by all our employments; — treasuring up a substantial form of life in the soul, which we must take with us into the spiritual world, and make the groundwork of our existence there! Nay, that we must *see* this panorama of our past life, and realize how fully and exactly it has become interwoven into the soul! And from this, too, we are to go on gathering a *new* experience, but infallibly connected with and likened to the past, through eternal ages and ever-increasing variety of life! "Memory, indeed, seems intended to qualify us to treasure impressions in all worlds, and to carry on the record and history of our feelings from time to time to eternity. The everlasting future grows upon the past; remembrance is the basis of eternal knowledge." And as no particle of matter can be annihilated, but is only passed through a succession of changes, so no part of spirit, and no part of the experience of any spirit; but what has been done *exists* — somewhere in the vast universe of souls — of which every individual is a part and parcel. And it can be reproduced with infinite exactness. But as before observed, it will not always or in all respects be necessary; we shall not have our past life *continually* before us; but the power to do this resides with God in the soul. And, at times, the soul *is* let into its previous states, that it may see itself as it was and is, for humiliation and correction. Even with the natural memory, such is sometimes the case.

"Although the external or natural memory is in man after death, still the merely natural things which are therein are not reproduced in the other life, [except occasionally, *H. H.* 461,] but the spiritual things which are adjoined to the natural things by correspondences; which things, nevertheless, when they are presented to the sight, appear in a form altogether similar, as in the natural world." *H. H.* 464.

In fact, to have any part of our experience annihilated would be to destroy the individuality of the spirit, and to imagine a providence without a purpose.

There is another idea connected with this subject. We frequently find ourselves in possession of stores of ideas, without previously being aware of it, or knowing how they got there. How often is this felt in writing and in speaking. The reason of this is, that in addition to a continual influx from the spiritual world, the experience of the past has been faithful to us. And it has not been in vain that we have been carried through this or that particular experience — directed to read this or that book — listened to this or that sermon — and passed so strangely through a multitude of occurrences. They all have done their part in helping to form and impress the soul, and have faithfully recorded their impressions in the "book and volume of the brain." Perhaps, now, in the future world, we may be privileged to see the *connection* of these experiences, and how every idea and feeling has had its orderly occurrence, so far as it could have, in reference to our various states, and the final end of all; so that we may be able to read the providence of God in the minutest circumstances of our life — to trace the connection between little things and great things — between what we are, and what we have been called to suffer and enjoy — to see how a train of mental associations was instrumental in exciting us to this or that course of conduct — and how necessary certain things were that we deemed trivial or disgusting — and how our whole life has been subject to the guidance of a wise and beautiful providence. In short, we may there learn the force of circumstances in developing character; and by the memory and experience of the past, be able to converse on this subject with higher orders of intelligences; and with a clear, unclouded reason, "see that our living spirits have been exposed in this world of trial and darkness, to nothing trivial, nothing accidental; but that other spirits, invisible to us, have been permitted to be busy with our sensations and thoughts, for specific purposes suited to our case; either for temptation, or for withdrawment from temptation, to turn us from our own devices, for spiritual exaltation, or, may we not say, for the more mysterious abandonment of the soul to evil; thereby the better to exhibit the awful sublimity of the Divine Government, which shall finally educe good from every evil, and render darkness itself the medium of glory." * The revelations of Swedenborg on this head assure us of the most thrilling interest and the completest satisfaction, in thus contemplating in the spiritual world, our past career and our varied fortunes in this life.

Finally, it is to be observed that this Memory of the soul is the *Book of our Life*, spoken of in the Scriptures. How often

* See "Power of the Soul over the Body," for this extract, and a few altered lines previous.

is it said that we are to be judged out of a book — that "a book of *remembrance* was written for them that feared the Lord and thought upon his name." (*Mal.* 3: 16.) It is sometimes called the "book of God's remembrance," but it is man's remembrance, given to him of God. It is the style of the Scriptures to speak of God's doing what man, by the divine providence, does in his own soul. Again, that "the dead, both small and great, stood before God, and the books were opened, and another book was opened, which is the book of life; and the dead were judged out of those things that were written in the books, according to their works." (*Rev.* 20: 12.) The books that were here opened were the *interiors of the minds*, or the memory of the wicked; and the other book, which was the book of life, is the interior memory of the good. What other books can be referred to? A book, in spiritual language, corresponds to the mind, because it contains the writer's thoughts and intentions. Book of life, sure enough! Book of our *own* life! — which we have written ourselves, and within whose ominous folds are recorded with infinite precision, every thought and act, upon immortal tablets! It is this volume, upon which we have been so busily at work for so many years, which is to be opened and read by us, from the beginning to the end of it. And how shall every villany, every secret sin, there stand forth in letters of living light! and every virtue, every holy aspiration, all that has been done in secret silence of the mind, also shine in characters of heaven upon the page of our existence! It is in this way that "God shall bring every work into judgment, with every secret thing, whether it be good, or whether it be evil." (*Eccl.* 12: 14.) Also, "that every idle word that men shall speak, they shall give an account thereof in the day [or state] of judgment." (*Matt.* 12: 36.) Idle words are expressions of thoughts; and thoughts, of some love or affection. We understand the philosophy of the statement, and we need be no longer in doubt of the fact.

Such is the Memory. It is the basis and instrument of the

eternal providence of God, and in vain should we attempt a clear and full idea of the great theme we are treating, without an understanding of its nature. It is by this that all providences are connected, and that nothing can happen to man's spiritual life without being carefully treasured up in the Divine substantial archives, and made to tell through infinity and eternity. Oh, wonderful and mighty contemplation! How applicable to mortal man!

"We take no note of time
But from its loss; to give it then a tongue
Is wise in man. As if an angel spoke,
I feel the solemn sound.
* * *
"My hopes and fears
Start up alarmed, and o'er life's narrow verge
Look down—on what? A fathomless abyss!
A vast eternity! how surely mine!"

CHAPTER III.

DIVINE PROVIDENCE IN THE REGENERATE LIFE.

"'Tis a new life: thoughts move not as they did,
With slow, uncertain steps across my mind;
In thronging haste, fast pressing on, they bid
The portals open to the viewless Wind,
Which comes not save when in the dust is laid
The crown of pride that gilds each mortal brow,
And from before our vision melting fade
The heavens and earth, — their walls are falling now!"
— *Jones Very.*

UNDER this head, which comprises, in fact, the whole aim and working of the Divinity with man in his present state, in order to an angelic heaven more and more perfect to eternity, we have to treat, first, of the Necessity of Regeneration; and second, of the Nature and Operation of it. And by thence following it through its various stages of Conflict, Temptation, Fluctuation, and final Rest, we shall thereby derive a more full and satisfactory view of the Divine Providence, and appreciate the varied means, trials, and experience, which the great Operator employs for our discipline.

First, then, of the *Necessity* for the Regenerate Life. We should not make this a question, were it not that we are writing for many who have yet either failed to see it, or see it only in part, and who do not appreciate the one great work of our earthly life. The bald naturalism of this age has at last laid its hands upon the very horns of the altar, and sought to quench its fires in a cold intellectual light. It affects to be philosophical when it is only sceptical — only superficial. "It says, Culture; it says, Nature;" and if it fails not to add, "There also is the Divine," yet it penetrates not to the core of our great Misery, and of course brings not the panacea for our ills. The Christianity of to-day is painful from two extremes. On the one hand it degenerates, thinking that it soars, into regions of mere Pantheism and transcendental mysticism; on the other, it revels in a morbid religionism, the very dregs of the spiritual nature. In the one class we have young ladies and misses, fine gentlemen and scholars, of truly amiable accomplishments and loving hearts, who think it an impertinence to speak seriously of the New Birth in any other light than natural progression; in the other we have a grovelling fanaticism, or a sepulchral and unnatural religion, irksome and constrained, the bane of all true cheerfulness and all hearty and healthful life. Let us seek the happy medium. Let us presume to be philosophical as well as theological, and to marry all things at the sacred altar of Truth.

There are but two theories of the origin and condition of man, which it becomes us to notice. One is, that he came gradually into being, by successive gradations from the lower animals, and his course from the commencement has been one steady, onward path of progression. Thus, that from a rude and undeveloped creature, very closely allied to the animals next beneath him, he first became Savage, then Barbarian, then Civilized, and then Christian; Christ himself being, according to many advocates of this theory, but the apex and head of our common Humanity, at the completion of one great cycle of the human race. And in still further consequence, that man will continue to go on as he has, without any backward movements, from one degree of perfection to another, perhaps forever; or at least till he reaches the highest possible state of manhood and excellence. This is the *natural* theory. It is the theory advanced in the "Vestiges of Creation," and other works of a kindred character; and with some variations as to the precise mode of the *origin* of man, it is the theory adopted by those

Christians who do not subscribe to what are called the more "evangelical" views of man and his necessities.

The second theory is, that man was created a pure and sinless being, and has *fallen* from that state into sin and degradation; and that, by his fall, he has so contaminated and perverted his original constitution, that a new spiritual birth is necessary in order to restore him to his pristine glory.

There are, to be sure, various modifications of this latter theory, and many errors connected with its evolution, but the theory in general is unquestionably correct.

It is manifestly true, that if the path of man has been steadily progressive, — if the mere powers of his nature, in connection with the ordinary operations of the Deity, have kept him in this onward march, without any backward movement whatever, and if they are sufficient to keep him so in all time to come, then the idea of a New Birth loses a large share of its significancy. It may indeed apply, in a moderated sense, to the first re-creation of man from a purely natural to a spiritual state, before the Fall — before his natural mind became defiled with evil; but nothing is plainer than that the Scriptures speak of man as we now find him, in a very different manner. In the Bible, Christianity is set forth as a *restorative* system. It is a reconstructive work — a building up of former ruins. If it were all mere natural progression, then we might as well shut up our Bibles at once; for Christianity teaches from beginning to end, the restoration of something that is lost. And has the account of the temptation and fall of Adam no meaning? Take also the following few passages from Isaiah, Jeremiah, and Romans. Speaking of the sins of many ages, the prophet says — " And they that shall be of thee [that is, of the true church] shall build the old waste places; thou shalt raise up the foundations of many generations; and thou shalt be called *The Repairer of the breach, the Restorer of paths to dwell in.*" (*Isa.* 58: 12.) Again — "Thus saith the Lord, Stand ye in the ways, and see, and *ask for the old paths,* where is the good way, and walk therein, and ye shall find rest for your souls." (*Jer.* 6: 16.) Again, speaking of the restored state of the church — "Whereas thou hast been forsaken and hated, so that no man went through thee, I will make thee an eternal excellency, a joy of many generations. * * * And thou shalt know that I the Lord am thy Saviour and thy Redeemer, the Mighty One of Jacob. For brass I will bring gold, and for iron I will bring silver, and for wood brass, and for stone iron." (*Isa.* 60: 15–17.) Showing the very perceptible advances from one state to another, after having been "forsaken and hated." And why is the Lord called a Redeemer and Saviour, if there is nothing to be redeemed, or nothing lost to be saved? The idea of redemption is very different from the idea of natural progression. But why multiply passages? What meaneth the whole story of deliverance by a Saviour — the death of all in Adam, and life and righteousness in Christ? What meaneth "the restitution of all things, spoken by the mouth of all God's holy prophets, since the world began?" (*Acts*, 3: 21.)

If there is any one truth in the Bible, plain to be read of all men, it is that our salvation, which is a misnomer in the naturalist's theory, is not trusted to natural progression, but is a supernatural restoration, by wonderful divine means, of something forfeited by the whole human race. It is this which renders a New Birth neccessary, in a sense very different from the first spiritual re-creation of man; and "if any man be in Christ, he is a new creature," not merely progressed upon the old plane. And what is the significancy of the word "regeneration," but re-creation, or to generate anew,— and as it is now always represented, amid conflicts and difficulties? As there are two worlds, a natural and a spiritual, so there are two births; one is of the body, the other of the spirit. The one is open, manifest, and introduces the human being into the natural world; the other is hidden, invisible, and prepares him for life eternal in the heavens.

But in regard to regeneration from the *fallen* state of man, the question is frequently asked — What light does *history* shed upon any backward movement of the human race? And we answer, so far as the light of *ordinary* history shines upon the fact, it is indeed comparatively obscure; for such history, in its most accredited portions, reaches back only about twenty-six hundred years, whereas the human race is probably ten times as old, at least. But what if ordinary history did differ from the testimony of the Scriptures? The Scriptures, which reach further back than any other history, and speak with a much higher authority, assert everywhere the fall and restoration of man. And does not the tradition of the whole ancient world point back to a Golden Age, then to a Silver, Copper, Brass, Iron? What is the meaning of all this?

But it is not our purpose to rest this discussion upon any doubtful authority. The external history of the matter is a question which we shrink from. There is one evidence, however, to which we would point in proof of the fall of man, which should seem enough to impress us sensibly with the truth. We allude to the prominent aspect of humanity now, lying as it does all about us, over the face of a corrupt world. What is the general impression, and the lesson that seems most deeply and spiritually taught, as by a sorrowful conviction in the soul? Is it that all has gone on orderly and well, thus far, from good to better, by a steady law of constant progression? or are we rather impressed with the signs of ruin — with noble natures fallen into decay — with virtues crushed out, and intellects depraved, and spiritual faculties quenched in sense and materiality, by some mighty and overwhelming calamity which has passed upon all mankind? What is the actual condition of the race? "Taken in the mass," it has been truly said, "it lies in spiritual darkness; each generation receiving from the past its gloomy superstitions and horrid idolatries. A race in its true condition, not less than a family or state, would form a certain organic whole. It would be a family of nations, society in its grandest form, and that a form of beneficence, taking up every people and every tribe into one circulatory system of benefits and blessings, that poured life and happiness from all to each and from each to all. Diplomacy, trade, commerce, would form a grand system that kept girdling the earth with charities: or perhaps, rather, the arteries and veins that kept sending life into all the members, and bringing it back. Instead of this, the nations and peoples are fallen asunder; we debate whether they belong to the same species; each is parted off to its solitary darkness and its bloody customs, and they present the spectacle of the fragments of a mighty ruin. If you choose to except the Christian nations, which are no exceptions at all, yet remember that three-fourths of the world lie under the night of barbarism, and need, not merely improvement, but re-creation out of chaos." *

And what, now, of the story of the street, and of the masses of humanity every day to be met with? We see, in forms that once were infants in some mother's arms, and even these shockingly disfigured and deformed at birth, the marks of every evil that could degrade and brutalize a human creature. What bodies! what faces! what expressions! Whither, ah, whither has fled the *beauty* of the human race? Our philosophy tells us that true beauty is but the outward form of goodness. Although the outward form differs frequently very much from the inward, and the face of the spirit is not as the face of the body, yet if sin had not at first deformed the human spirit, we should not have had such hereditary transmissions upon the faces of all human kind. The angels of heaven are all beautiful. Men and women would be, if sin had not deformed them. With the good, the beauty of mankind has also departed from the earth, and the form of devils has too frequently succeeded to the forms of angels. Bating the few exceptions, what a spectacle of hard, selfish, care-worn, unlovely, unspiritual humanity! — to say nothing of the haggard, the demoniacal, the brutal of all

* *Sears, on Regeneration*, pp. 19, 20.

sorts. And is this man?—the creature so noble, so godlike, so erect and like an angel? But if we look even to the higher classes, so called, it needs no great effort of the intuitive faculty, to read even there, the lessons of selfishness, sensuality, spiritual vacancy, pride, pomposity, and pitiable vanity.

And after all, we do not see into the lowest pits of this hell upon earth. How few there are who know the reality—who have any full perception of the kind of life in the dens of our great cities! So little of the angel—such a depth of manifest declension from all that is divine and human, verging to extinction even in a beast! We turn from it with loathing and sickness at heart.

Well—but only on the principle that "all 's well that ends well"—what is the inference from this whole aspect of humanity? Does it look as though this was an *unfallen* state? Is this the *beginning* of the human race?—this the way *God created* man? But alas! as though in tremendous mockery, we are told that this is a very much *progressed* state—that for ten, twenty, or thirty thousand years, man has been coming *up* to it, from the low stages of his original condition! Oh then, what could he have been at first? And at this rate of progression, how long will it take to reach a respectable manhood?

Folly, folly of deceived men! It is better to believe the simple story of the Bible;—that "God saw every thing that *He* had made, and behold, it was *very good;*"—that there was a time when "sin *entered* the world, and death by sin, and so death passed upon all men." It cannot be possible that God created his noblest work so—that, after He had finished all the previous creations, He then produced man in a stew of vice and misery—in brothels and pest-houses—rotting and scarred all over with diseases, both of soul and body, and then left him to work his way up, by mere ordinary means, to a pure and holy state. No, man has fallen from his first estate—plunged himself into these evils; and from the time that Adam walked in innocence in the Garden of Eden, and erred there, (explain the account how we will,) to the time of the advent of the second Adam—Jesus Christ upon earth, man, it appears, *continued* to fall, growing worse and worse, morally speaking, although he made some advances in civilized and merely intellectual life. We cannot estimate this matter by three or four thousand years; we must take the thousands of years that lie back in a distant antiquity into the account. The Golden age was real, and we have not seen its equal — nothing to compare with it, since. We have had more natural science, never so much spiritual life.

Look again, at another aspect of the matter. Sometimes we are pointed to the *lower races* as evidences of the first states of men; the North American Indians, for example. These, it is said, are a sample of men that have progressed no higher. But the true way to look upon them would seem to be, as to men *run down* — noble races, who once had the fire of a different genius in their eye, and the mystery of whose history is not yet opened to the superficial gaze of men. They do not look like men just raised up to this pitch of aboriginal humanity; they carry about them the marks of a fallen nobility, a departed glory. Their history is full of relics that are wonderful and sacred.

But we have no more time to spend upon this branch of the subject. The truth is, from all that appears, and from the testimony of Scripture, and also the testimony of Swedenborg who speaks in such fulness, having had his spiritual sight opened to *see* the condition of the ancient world, there has been a gradual fall of the human race, from the time of Adam to the time of Christ. Since then, we would fain believe the world has been progressing. But the Fall was not sudden, as in the story of the prevalent theology, but gradual, as before explained; and consisted in turning away from the Divine Life and turning to the human self-hood. It should be remembered that the most Ancient church, signified by Adam, or Man, stood the highest, in point of love, purity, and spirituality, of any church or race of men that has since lived upon the earth. It was, in fact, a church and world united. The separation had not yet taken place. It was a divinely conditioned order of society, but as yet infantile and inexperienced. They were opened to a more liberal influx of the Divinity into the interiors of their nature than any people who have lived since, and the angels of heaven were their visible and familiar guests. The very term *Golden*, which has become applied to the first age, is correspondential of the goodness of their natures, which had not yet degenerated into silver, or mere truth, and still worse, into copper, brass, and iron. The image of Nebuchadnezzar, seen in his dream, (*Dan.* 2: 31–45) whose "head was of fine gold, his breast and his arms of silver, his belly and his thighs of brass, his legs iron, his feet part of iron and part of clay," showed also the successive states of the church, or of mankind in their connection with God and heaven; and the terms here used were spoken in accordance with this wisdom of the ancients. But, although the most ancient men were in a high state of goodness and simplicity, yet they had not that peculiar intellectual culture that we have; in matters pertaining to heaven, and to a true religious and spiritual life, they were wiser than we; but in what pertained to the arts and conveniences of mere outward life, they were not so skilled.

In fact, the first ages were the infant ages. And precisely as an individual infant is in a state of comparative innocence and purity, and more like the kingdom of heaven, so the infancy of the human race: they were in a more truly heavenly state; they had not soiled and imbruted their natures with the lusts and evils of this life; and *by* their purity, tenderness, and love, and certain interior capabilities in consequence thereof, which we have not, they were receptive of a more generous influx from the heavens, and had open and conscious intercourse with the angels. "They had the most delightful visions of divine things, and a perception of all things relative to faith, almost like the angels with whom they had communication." — "Their voluntary and intellectual made one, thus one mind; wherefore they had a perception of truth from good, for the Lord flowed in through an internal way, into the good of their will, and through this into the good of the understanding, or truth: [which is different from the present state of men, who have to be led to truth first, and thence to good.] Thence it was that that church, in preference to the others, was called *Adam*, or Man, and also a likeness of God." (A. C. 1121, 1122, 4454.) They were pre-eminently in love to the Lord and in charity to the neighbor, and lived in peace and amity among themselves. It was the primitive Eden of the world.

But, as an individual infant is inexperienced in all that pertains to adult age and the outward accomplishments of worldly life, so the infancy of the human race: they were, therefore, not civilized, as we use the term; although, in respect to the true wisdom of life, they were better than civilized; civilization would be a poor term to apply to their state of simplicity and purity; they were, in short, an innocent, unsophisticated, good, spiritual, but otherwise ignorant people. But what they lacked in material science, they more than made up in spiritual science, and in the knowledge of Divine Truth.

"The man of the Most Ancient church," says Swedenborg, "had revelations, by which he was initiated from infancy into the perception of goods and truths, and as these were inseminated into his will, he had a perception of innumerable others without fresh instruction; so that from one general truth or principle, he became acquainted with particular and individual truths from the Lord, which in the present day must be first learned to be known. It is scarcely possible, however, now, to acquire a thousandth part of the knowledge which they possessed." A. C. 895.

From the state of spiritual vision which they were in, "the objects of the outward senses, such as terrestrial and worldly things, were to them as nothing, nor did they perceive any thing of delight in them, but only in the things which they signified and represented; when they saw such objects, they thought not of them, but only of their significatives and representatives; which to them were most delightful, being such things as exist in heaven, by virtue of which they saw the Lord Himself"— that is, his Divine Form as He appeared to their spiritual vision. (A. C. 1122.)

Such was the state of the Most Ancient Church. But they fell from this state. Just as an individual infant passes out of his infant innocence, and pure, artless beauty, and begins to show the buddings of passion, and the puttings forth of self-will, pride, and malice, till finally he passes into a selfish, proud, sinful, and unamiable manhood; so the first races of spiritual men passed gradually into a similar state. There was a gradual closing up of the internal mind and senses,—a gradual sensualizing and materializing of the better nature, and a diminishing of love to the Lord and the neighbor, through thousands of ages, each generation growing worse and worse by the accumulations of hereditary evil, till the heavens were closed to their eyes, and till finally men had filled out the measure of their iniquity, and made it necessary for the Lord to come himself upon the earth, to beat back the flood of gathered evil, and institute new measures for the salvation of men.

In all this, it will be observed that we preserve in full force the scientific conclusion, that when man was *first created*, he was but one remove from the highest animals: although that remove was distinguished by the communication of a human soul, an internal, spiritual nature, which the animals have not. We cannot tell how long a period elapsed from his original creation to his finished spiritual state. It is sufficient to say that he was at first natural, afterwards spiritual. This is referred to in Genesis on this wise:—"The earth was without form, and void, and darkness was upon the face of the deep." By which is signified, in the spiritual sense, not the material earth, but the *mind of man*, in its merely natural state. The Spirit of God then moved upon the waters; that is, upon such things as were treasured up in the human soul by the Divine Creator, which rendered it susceptible to regeneration. It was by a particular Divine Providence — by a holy angelic ministry, that man was brought up out of his original condition, to a high state of spiritual and celestial manhood. Then was the Golden Age, in all its early splendor and glory. Hence it is said of the first branch of the river that went out of Eden, that "it compasseth the whole land of Havilah, where there is *gold;* and the gold of that land is *good.*" (*Gen.* 2: 11.) Genuine celestial good, from love.

The human race, then, first ascended, then descended; first rose, then fell. And as before observed, the fall of man through thousands of years is not inconsistent with a *general* law of progression. Like a sinless infant passing into corrupt manhood, the very fall, in this sense, involves a progression. But it cannot be called an *orderly* part of it. It was not orderly for man to sin, and so to lose his pristine glory, any more than it is now orderly for him to do so; but *having* lost it, in this effort to exert and cultivate his sensuous, external nature, when he regains it, it will come with seven-fold power, with a more enlarged expansion of all the faculties of the natural mind, and be in reality a Golden Age of the future surpassing all the glory of the past. Thus, I say, although this kind of progression is not orderly, and *ought* not to have been so, yet like every other evil, the fall of man is overruled for good, even a greater good than could be obtained without it. A greater good could have been attained without the fall, if man *would,* but as he would not, the heavenly blessing is now made to come to him through clouds and darkness and difficulties. Such is the common lot.

But, having lost his infant purity in the process, it is first necessary to have that restored. And for this purpose, he needs to be "born again." We thus see the propriety of such phraseology. He must be restored to the infant state of simplicity and innocence, and grow up into a new manhood.

And here Christianity comes in to the rescue. Here, too, the significancy of the Apostolic statement — "As in Adam all die, even so in Christ shall all be made alive." (1 *Cor.* 15: 22.) And again — "As by one man sin entered into the world, and death by sin; and so death passed upon all men, for that all have sinned; even so by the righteousness of one, the free gift came upon all men unto justification of life." (*Rom.* 5: 12–18.)

But it is to be observed here, how different is the simple truth from what theologians have made it. "In Adam's fall we sinned all," says the Primer. Now the truth is, the Adam here spoken of is not merely an historical person — a veritable man who lived six thousand years ago, but the Adam of consciousness; and represents the whole past life of the sinning generations of men. The same as the Christ here spoken of, in which we are to be made alive, is not the mere historical person of Christ, but represents the Christ of consciousness, or that ever-present, divine influence from Him, in all who receive his life.

It has been well observed by the author before quoted — "It is obvious, on a careful analysis of the Pauline philosophy, how much more than his proper share of the evil brought upon the world, our common ancestor has been made to bear. Was ever the memory of man so wronged and abused by his children? So far from laying off upon him the whole business of man's fall, Paul does no more than designate how the work began, and how sin was first introduced. His successors kept adding to the work which he only commenced, and death passed upon all men, not because Adam sinned for them vicariously, but in that ALL HAVE SINNED. He sinned, and there, alas! *began* the work of the degradation of his species; the balance between good and evil began to dip the wrong way, his successors kept adding to the weight, sin became more facile with every generation, till the scale came heavily down. And this is THE FALL OF MAN.

So then, the Adam of St. Paul in this connection is a corrupt past which has become immanent in the present. It is an inherited, disordered nature, impersonated in each individual. With primitive man began the descending series, and it kept on till the time of Christ. Then the ascending series began, and it will keep on till it comes up to the level of that height where began the march of humanity. Or to seek an image which perhaps will give us at once the Apostle's unclouded meaning: He regards the race in its totality, as an organic whole, as making one orb of being. With the first man's sin, it began to dip in darkness, and the line of shade encroached upon it till it hung in disastrous eclipse. With Christ its emergence began; and it will continue till it rolls in complete glory along the latest ages." *

Here, then, we begin to see the necessity of Christ. It is He who accomplishes the new birth, as it was Adam who in his children consummated the "old man." Man himself had not power to break the spell that bound him. It was his outermost nature — what is generally known as the "natural mind," that needed to be wrought upon by the power of an indwelling life. All sin — all evils, both hereditary and acquired, dwell in comparative externals, or in the natural mind as distinguished from the spiritual. These external parts, (and some of these reach very deeply inward,) have become so encrusted with evil, and their fine spiritual vesicles so twisted and turned in every wrong direction, just as we see the human body and face deformed and ugly with sin, that the internal life could not pierce through into the ultimates of natural man, and he became an absolute *slave* to sin. In addition to this, and as a consequence of it, evil spirits from hell came flowing in and pressing upon him at all sides, making the bondage all the more hopeless. He had no power to liberate himself. "Who shall deliver me from this body of death? I thank God, through Jesus Christ our Lord." (*Rom.* 7: 24, 25.)

* *Sears, on Regeneration*, pp. 56–58.

Such, then, is the *necessity* for the Regenerate Life. "Marvel not that I said unto thee, Ye must be born again." Man has fallen, and he must be raised. He is made for the world, and he is made for heaven. Therefore he must be born into the one, and born into the other. If he had not sinned, he would have passed to the second birth and to heaven, without pain or difficulty, by a process of interior development beautiful to contemplate. Regeneration would then have been, as it was before the fall, "a strict progression, following in unbroken lines of continuity, from the dawn of self-consciousness to the noontide of a nature affluent with Deity." But now it is attended with the labor-pains of a difficult and dangerous parturition. The natural birth has become symbolic of the spiritual birth. The one is the correspondent of the other. It is in order for both to be accomplished without obstruction and with pleasure. Sin only has made it otherwise. But the process must go on; the necessity exists; and "Verily, verily, I say unto thee, Except a man be born again, he cannot see the Kingdom of God." (*John*, 3: 3.)

CHAPTER IV.

NATURE AND OPERATION OF THE NEW BIRTH.

"Nothing is better attested than the fact that men of our race, whether under Christianity, or without any knowledge of its truths, do undergo changes of character and life, that can no way be accounted for without some reference to a supernatural power such as Christianity affirms in the doctrine of the Spirit." — *Horace Bushnell.*

THE Divine Providence is nowhere seen more beautifully and systematically, than in reference to those processes which are instituted, and those means which are pursued, for man's recovery from spiritual degradation. How little of the human, how much of the sovereign Divine Agency, in the great work of our reconstruction into spiritual and celestial men! Truly is it compared to the "wind that bloweth." It bloweth "where it listeth," or where it inclineth, "and thou hearest the sound thereof; but canst not tell whence it cometh, nor whither it goeth: so is every one that is born of the spirit." The Holy Spirit is of course the great agency of the second birth; but we would observe here, that there are, and have been, two distinct dispensations of the Holy Spirit,—a general and a special one. In one sense, every operation of the Divinity in the mind of man, whether before or since the Christian dispensation, may be characterized as the action of the Holy Spirit; for it was the motion of the Divine Spirit in the human heart. But that a special dispensation of the Spirit was given by Jesus Christ, is familiar truth to every Christian. It is expressly said by Jesus — "And I will pray the Father, and He shall give you another Comforter, that he may abide with you forever." (*John*, 14: 16.) And "the Comforter, which is the

Holy Ghost, whom the Father will send in my name, he shall teach you all things." (26.) But this Comforter, or Holy Spirit, is said in another place to be dependent upon the departure of Jesus from this world. "I tell you the truth, it is expedient for you that I go away; for if I go not away, the Comforter will not come unto you, but if I depart, I will send him unto you." (16: 7.) Again it is said — "The Holy Spirit was not yet, because Jesus was not yet glorified:" but after his resurrection it is said — "He breathed on them, and said, Receive ye the Holy Spirit." (20: 22.) This outward breathing was a symbolical act, representative of the inward reception of the living spirit. And we all know, how, about ten days after his ascension, on the day of Pentecost, while the disciples were assembled with one accord in one place, suddenly the breathing influence came, "as of a rushing, mighty wind, and filled all the house where they were sitting." (*Acts*, 2: 1–18.) It elevated all their powers of utterance, filled them with new thoughts, "and they began to speak with tongues as the spirit gave them utterance." This was among the *first* effects of the new Spirit. Hence it is clear that the Holy Spirit thus referred to, is an express and particular impartation of the Christian dispensation.

But now how is it, and wherefore? And we reply, it was a consequence of the Lord's Glorification. This is an item of the true Christianity which is little understood, and little dwelt on, by the mass of confused Christendom. And yet nothing is plainer in the evangelists' records, than that our Lord underwent a continuous process of laying down his life for the world, that is, his derived, inherited life of corrupt humanity, from the very commencement of his labors. He took on the *whole* of humanity, in its worst estate, and by purifying it all in Himself, was thereby enabled to do the same or similar for mankind. Let any one follow the history of the Saviour from his first efforts, through all his temptations and humiliations, to his great triumph; let him observe with what greater clearness

He continually speaks of his unity with the Father, till He finally declares it "finished," and that "all power is given unto him, in heaven and in earth;" and let him divest himself of the thought that by the glorification of the Son of Man is meant any external honors or splendors which He is to receive in heaven for the work He has done on earth; and he will then gain some definite idea of a subject so unutterably grand. It was only at the Ascension that this work seems fully to have been accomplished, although the last temptation was experienced upon the cross. The truth is, when humanity had run to its very lowest ebb, and had reached a point of sensuality and corruption which it could not have remained in and survived upon the earth, then the Divine Essence itself, by a law and process which the understanding of angels is only adequate to fully comprehend, descended into the ultimates of human nature, and by investing itself in a body of flesh, and a corrupt human soul, was enabled to experience every possible temptation, to be assaulted with all the hosts of hell, and with every evil which could possibly enter into the experience of man. And by meeting and overcoming these evils by the divine ability which dwelt within him, He thereby removed them all from his natural humanity. He made that *humanity* Divine. He took upon his own nature, in amount and quality, the sins of the whole world, and resisted them all. And this was the accumulation of a long train of hereditary evils — the effect of the thousands of years' fall and corruption of humanity. And as they were resisted and triumphed over, the human organism which was assumed for this purpose, was successively cleansed and glorified. Every particle of the corrupt nature derived from the Virgin was thoroughly expelled from him, and replaced by a divine substance, so that he became a DIVINE HUMANITY. This is referred to in the following language of John. — "And now, O Father, glorify thou me with thine own self, with the glory which I had with thee before the world was." (*John*, 17: 5.) Also in the 12th chapter: —

"Now is my soul troubled; and what shall I say? Father, save me from this hour: but for this cause came I unto this hour. Father, glorify thy name. Then came there a voice from heaven, saying, I have both glorified it, and will glorify it again." That is, the process of glorification had been continual, all through the Lord's experience,—a continual putting off the human, with its corruptions and lusts, and a putting on of the Divine. And when this process was accomplished, then it was, and not till then, that the Holy Spirit could be imparted to men. "It was not yet, because that Jesus was not yet glorified;" (*John*, 7: 39,) but after He had ascended triumphant over the grave, a fully transformed and DIVINE MAN, in every vesicle and tissue of his immortal organism, then He could give forth from out that wonderful experience, the sanctifying influences of the new and renovating Spirit. (20: 22.) It was the same eternal and Divine Spirit, but given now through a new and adaptive medium. And it went forth freely, both by mediate and immediate influx, to all the sons of Adam.

Here was a new and living way open for salvation,—"a fountain opened to the house of David, for sin and for uncleanness." We may talk of being saved by precept and example, and the force of merely natural virtues, till we die the death; so did not Christ talk, but in part, and this is not the story of the old evangel. Precepts and virtue are good things, but they only have life through the Lord of glory, who has first glorified his own nature, and is now thoroughly able to regenerate ours.

It should be observed, too, that all who experience the New Birth are said to follow the Lord in a similar process. Speaking to his disciples on the subject of self-denial, he says—"Ye which have *followed me in the regeneration*." (*Matt.* 19: 28.) From which it is evident that Jesus himself experienced something analogous to the new birth in man. And what was that? Precisely, this glorification of the assumed humanity. The only difference is, the Lord, by virtue of the Divinity that dwelt within Him from the first, made his humanity absolutely

Divine, which is expressed by the word "glorification;" whereas He only *regenerates* ours, for man still remains human. And further, He cast out the evils of his human nature by his own proper and divine ability; whereas we put away ours by power derived from Him. And still further, if Swedenborg is to be credited, He utterly *expelled* his evils — ejected them entirely from his whole body of Humanity; man is only enabled to remove his from the centre to the circumference — to throw them out there, to the extremest verge of his external spiritual organism, where they remain forever, but become quiescent and inoperative. But upon this latter point there may be yet more light.

We can now understand what it is to "follow the Lord in the regeneration." He has truly "set us an example," more sublimely significant than any thing which is usually conceived by these words. If it be said that it is not a fair example, because we have not that divine power to expel evils which He is thus represented to have had, we reply, it is a good example and something more. The example remains in all its force and dignity, and with it, a truly divine power of salvation from it. But it is a mistake to think thus humanly of the gospel's influence,— to think that it consists so much of the mere power of a once acted example: it is only a truly *Divine* Saviour who can deliver us from the great bondage we are in, and this by a constant flowing of the divine life from Him. "A just God and a Saviour, there is none beside Me." (*Isa.* 45 : 21.)

The work for us to do, then, is simply the imitation of the great Exemplar — the removing of evils in the external man. It is the regeneration of the natural mind, — the seat of all evils and falsities. We are to become regenerated, as our Lord was glorified. The one is a perfect image of the other. It was necessary for Christ to pass through all this — to come from the heavens and to be incarnated and glorified, that he might reach man both inwardly and outwardly. Outwardly, he needed to see the image and glory of the Divine *Person* —

the God manifest to the *senses,* and to the mental eye ever afterwards in the heavens. This truth had become completely obscured, as the heavens became shut, by the fall and degradation of man. Inwardly, he needed to receive the spirit of the Divine Humanity, by which he might reach through to the outward, which had become so encrusted and hardened with sin, that the ray of internal Divinity was all too feeble to penetrate to the seat of the disease. Christ, then, does this work for us. He is still a *living, potential* Saviour; and having taken up within his consciousness the whole of man's tempted and sorrowful experience, and in the thirty brief years of his earthly sojourn, lived through all, and suffered all, in quality and principle, that can ever be gathered into the sinning generations of men, He is now able to come, and does come, both immediately and by his ministering angels, with an influx and influence adapted to every individual case. He becomes a divinely human *sympathetic* Saviour. "We have not a High Priest who cannot be touched with the feeling of our infirmities, for, in that he himself hath suffered, being tempted, he is able to succor them that are tempted." (*Heb.* 4: 15; 2: 18.) There is something divinely beautiful in this. He passed through all states, that He might save all. He clothed himself in infancy, that He might save infancy; (from the hereditary with which it is afflicted;) He clothed himself in youth, in manhood, and in all that old age could experience, (since "we live not by years, and figures on a dial,") that He might impart to all, his Divine-human properties, and save to the uttermost all who come unto Him. He was to help, not men only, but angels; to extend his divine strength to the highest up in glory and brightness around the Father's throne, and to the lowest down in the depths of earth's pollution. He was also to minister to the spirits of the under-world. The Holy Spirit which was so made to emanate from the Divine Humanity, is thus seen to be no third person in the Deity, but simply an afflux through a new and accommodated Medium, of the one, eternal God;—the outraying sphere of the Father through the Son. The truth is, humanity had descended so low in sin and defilement, that it could not be approached *directly* with a power sufficient to save it, without perishing in the consuming splendors of the Divinity.

Let us now observe more particularly the process and operation of it as indicated by the analogies of nature, and a true psychology. It is a *birth;* note that. Now, a birth, that is, a natural birth, is not a birth from death, but from something analogous to it. It is a birth from previous non-existence, except in germ and potentiality. And it is manifest that a second-birth cannot take place, when it is to proceed through difficulties and obstructions, without the death of what constituted the first. The "old man" must die, preparatory to, and continuous with, the creation and formation of the "new." And as before observed, all sin is in externals. It is in the natural mind. There is a spiritual principle which has been kept pure and uncontaminated through all the sinful experience of man. It has not come forth into action; indeed, it has been completely covered up by the foul incrustations which have been suffered to accumulate upon it, till only total corruption — total selfishness, has characterized the degenerate soul. Such is the state of all, before regeneration. The natural man is wholly evil because wholly selfish. It may show many an outward virtue, but the germ within will be corruption. But it must not hence be concluded that there are no glimmerings of the better nature to be found among common men and women as we see them, who make no pretensions, and have scarcely any acquaintance with the Christian life. The truth is, by what the divine Saviour has done for mankind, there are many gleamings of the better life, all over the world, by those even who have rejected Him and his gospel. They have rejected the *form* of the truth, as it has been presented in its perversions by the errorists of all times, but they have not been able to extinguish every vestige of the new life of Christendom.

Still, we ought not to hesitate to say, that our poor humanity did descend to that pitch where it could be said of the entire natural man, "the whole head is sick, and the whole heart is faint." "Every imagination of the thoughts of his heart was only evil continually." (*Gen.* 6: 5.)

Still the spiritual principle dwelt within. But it was inoperative, dead, buried. Man's outer nature enwrapped him like a shroud — enclosed him as a coffin. But it was a living death — the very breathing, active "body of death" which the apostle so wretchedly lamented.

If, then, man dies spiritually, he must die on the outside. His whole external natural man must be put to the crucifixion, that the internal spiritual principle may ascend into new life, and permeate the whole natural with its pure and blessed effects. There is a profound philosophy here which deserves to be better understood. Considering the human soul a substantial organism, or more properly speaking, the man himself, which gives to the physical form all its proportions, it is then easy to conceive the terrible and destructive work of sin. It has deformed the external of that spiritual body. If we could see it, as a purely spiritual being can, we should see that it was unbeautiful, sin-smitten, and marred. All its little vesicles, which are receptacles of the divine influx, are turned and twisted in every wrong direction. This is the significancy of the word depravity. *Depravus*, to twist from, or become crooked. Phrenology and Physiognomy show us this even in the body. It is just so in the spirit. It is the inner that has shaped the outer. And it is here, in these outer coatings and encasements of the spirit — rather, in the natural mind which surrounds the spiritual, that old Adam has done his dreadful work. The natural mind *in itself* considered, when unperverted, is not evil. It pertains merely to the things of outward nature — to the world and its objects, and it is admirably fitted for our existence in this life of the body.

But being so near the earth, it is liable, before spiritual

things get fully established in it, to become seduced by its vanities, and to make its tangible things of pre-eminent value. It also delights to reason from the senses alone, and is thereby involved in downfall and ruin. Here, then, is the whole cause and region of sin, — in the natural mind. And it being in itself a substantial organism — a part, in fact, of the whole man, the organic effect of sin is to twist and turn away the tissues and vessels of the spirit from their true upward spiral form, which is the form of heavenly receptacles, so that heavenly influxes can no longer descend into them; and then the man becomes, in all the convolutions of his active spiritual organism, turned *downwards and outwards*, and thus open to sensual and external impressions, and influxes from the hells. The natural mind thus becomes, also, hardened and coarse, unyielding and mutilated. The depravity here is thorough. But let us thank God, there was one receptacle into which the horrid monster could not enter. That was the DIVINE INMOST, or that sacred and inmost tabernacle of the soul, in which Jehovah Himself proximately dwells, where the divine influx is first received, and from which it disposes the other interior things, which succeed according to the degrees of order with every man. The celestial and spiritual minds also, or the two inner degrees which relate more properly to man, are there in potency, though not opened and active till regeneration. Here, then, is a region of purity in the midst of corruption. It has been forever sacred and undefiled in the sight of heaven; the fall of man has had no power utterly to extinguish it; and were it *not* for this, God himself would have no power over him to save him. As for all the rest of man, that is, as to his natural man before any regeneration, we speak but the psychological fact, and proclaim the Scriptural truth — " The whole head is sick, and the whole heart is faint. From the sole of the foot, even unto the head, there is no soundness in it; but wounds, and bruises, and putrefying sores." (*Isa.* 1 : 6.) This is proclaimed of the spirit of man as it appears in the light of heaven to the angels who so look upon him.

The Lord then came to *regenerate the natural man*, or to cause that to live the life of heaven, which before was dead in trespasses and sins. When the natural is made truly alive, then the spiritual acts through it, and by it, and the external is reduced to correspondence with the internal. How much of truth, the philosophy of which has never been fully comprehended, is there yet to be found in these old verbal petrifactions of the church:—"the crucifixion of the old man"—"the death of the natural man"—"the putting on of the new man." The truth is, as we attain to a true and comprehensive psychology, we shall systematize our ideas of divine things accordingly. The natural mind is regenerated by influx into it through the spiritual, and through heaven, from the Lord. And the natural being the outermost plane, it is the plane where the influx terminates. If then, that natural be full of evil and false things, each of them formed into substantial accretions, when the influx reaches there it is not freely received; for heavenly good and truth cannot enter into such perverted receptacles, and it is thereby dissipated or turned into evil. But when the old natural has become as nothing—has been made to die the death, then the spiritual can flow out into it and be received. And it does so gradually, as each evil is crucified and slain. The whole old man is thus rejuvenated with a new life; the health and sweetness of heaven come coursing joyously through all his veins; new tempers, new dispositions, sacred and beautiful affections, now take the place of unclean and hateful things, and God is glorified and man is saved.

We have said that this subject of the New Birth may be illustrated from the analogies of nature. By the *seed*, which is dropped into the ground, and which does not begin to germinate or have life, till the external is dissolved and changed. It first undergoes an apparent death. It is real, so far as the external is concerned. All that surrounds the germ of life within rots and crumbles away. It is the inmost only which springs into new life, and makes to itself a body from the purer substances of nature. So precisely with man in his sins. He is to put away that corrupt external — die on the outside, that the internal divine life may be ultimated in his outermost nature.

We are accustomed, I know, to speak of sin as something inward, and of inward purification; and it *is* inward so far as the body is concerned, and so far as the interiors of the natural mind are concerned; and it penetrates very deeply: but it is not in the inmost, and it is not in what are called the celestial and spiritual minds. These minds are indeed *obstructed* by the gathering folds of evil, and as already observed, lie shrouded and coffined. But the great Regenerator Himself dwells waiting there; and there, in those regions of celestial and spiritual things, from infancy to latest age, are stored up the remains of innocence and virtue not injured by the Fall, and kept pure through all generations, as the only hold the Lord of life and glory has upon our sin-encrusted natures. Is it not a divine and beautiful truth to contemplate? And should not the heart of man leap at it as precious joy, when he sees that the angel is within, or rather, that the germ of it is within, only waiting to be developed and liberated? But it is a long, hard, trying work, to which the whole of the divine providence is continually bent, and many fail in its first beginnings, and go discouraged, or worse yet, listless and indifferent, even to the grave.

But we proceed to observe, in the next place, that this new birth of the spirit is for the most part a *hidden, invisible* work. Necessarily so, from the divine means employed in it. "The wind bloweth where it listeth, and thou hearest the sound thereof, but canst not tell whence it cometh, and whither it goeth: so is every one that is born of the spirit." The meaning is, it is effected by the Lord alone, while man is ignorant of it. By the wind is represented spiritual influx; and as the natural atmosphere flows into the lungs, giving life and motion to them, and thence to the whole system, so the winds of the spiritual world sweep gently through the avenues of the soul, and in an imperceptible manner, do the work of the great Regenerator there. Man knows not, frequently, the influence he is under, except that he heareth the "sound thereof," the meaning of which is, that his affections are influenced by the spirit that controls him. For sound *corresponds* to affection. Hence it is that a man's feelings are frequently best known by the sound of his voice. The eye may more successfully practise deception, for it corresponds to the intellect. But the sound of the voice is the greatest revealer of character. Hence the significance of all the varying sounds of nature. And hence also their ability, as in the varying tones of the human voice, the articulation of beasts and birds, and particularly the sound of music, to awaken almost any sentiment of which the heart is susceptible. Now therefore, all that man does is to hear and obey. The wind bloweth where it listeth; the Spirit of the Lord goeth whithersoever it will, to the places of retirement, or to the scenes of active life; to some poor man or woman in a cottage, or to the halls of the great and affluent; and man himself, acted on invisibly by these gentle influences, and beset behind and before by the unseen angel ministries, is only to submit himself to the work of the Divine Operator. The processes of regeneration are hidden from him, lest, by his knowing it, or knowing precisely how and when he is taken, he might interfere by his self-hood with the work to be done.

I do not speak here the mere cant of the Church. We have a more sure word of testimony. We present the *science* of regeneration. We must understand these matters. The Church which will henceforth have power will be pre-eminently a *rational* one. And it carries its own evidences, its own strong, intuitive convictions of the truth, along with it. These are not mysteries in the sense of the old religionism. They are not miraculous, as being contrary to law. The new birth is indeed effected by the spirit of God, for nothing else can effect it. But the Divine Spirit observes its own laws. God is in closest unity and harmony with nature. It is only a mystery till it is understood.

We would remark, however, that many of the *providences* by which man is conducted to the great end of his regeneration are frequently *very* mysterious, yet only in the sense that they are not understood by us. It should ever be remembered that the great end — the one steady purpose which the Lord has in view with us here in this life, is to advance us to the highest possible station in the heavens. Now, so much depends upon a right improvement of this life, that it is in the highest degree rational to suppose that the Divine Providence is unceasing and universal, even to the smallest particulars, in order to carry us faithfully through these earthly scenes, and do the best possible that can be done, (for He sees what each individual is fit for, and what are the utmost capacities of his nature,) in reference to that eternity which is commenced, and very much to be determined here. He watches over us, and appoints his ministering angels over us, for this purpose. And well has it been said: — "It is not understood during the process of a man's regeneration; but as man becomes regenerate, he can look back and see how he has been led by the Lord through different states and circumstances, the origin and tendency of which at the time sorely puzzled him, or were involved in utter darkness; — why he should suffer this calamity, or be involved in that difficulty; — why, when he thought of making a short cut to the end, he was stopped, and taken round a circuitous course, reaching his ends only through a most tortuous and winding way; — these, and a thousand such like things, continually beset the path of every man. Truly it is said in the Word, that the Lord leadeth his people by a way that they know not; but which, though unknown at the time, becomes plain and clear as man advances towards the heavens. For all this hidden work comes out into broad day when man throws off this earthly tabernacle, and his spirit stands confessed, a devil or an angel." *

Another peculiarity of this work of regeneration, is its *gradual* process. There has been a doctrine current in the Church for many ages, and prevails now to a greater or less extent, that regeneration is or may be an instantaneous work. And no doubt, the proximate causes, and some sudden impressions which have been made upon the mind, have frequently, under providence, become the instrumentalities of a greatly and rapidly improved life. Paul's conversion is frequently referred to. His case, however, is not full to the point; for we find him, long after that, still in a grievous warfare, the flesh lusting against the spirit and the spirit against the flesh, and longing for deliverance from this body of death. But the truth is, conversion is by no means regeneration. It may be a part of it, and so far, so good. We do not deny that a man may begin, instantly, to live a good life. He may be more or less converted, that is, turned from a bad life to a good one, somewhat suddenly. *Repentance* may come suddenly. Many things may so be brought to bear upon the mind — many occurrences of a timely and well-ordered providence, with the express purpose of turning the man from the error of his ways; and he may so be arrested in his evil career, as to stop short at once, and resolve to be henceforth free. But surely, no *entire* freedom is gained thus suddenly. It may be the *beginning* of a glorious and heavenly career. And in so much the man may be said to be converted. But neither repentance nor conversion, to any great depth or thoroughness, can be said to take place by any such process. And even when these striking cases of sudden change and improvement do apparently occur, it is *but* an appearance to our partial view of it; the truth is, when such changes are at all vital and penetrating, there has been a long

* Crisis, Vol. II., No. 12.

train of previous preparation; the providence of God may have been dealing with such a soul for years; and when at length we see the open and apparent change flowering beautifully upon the character, it is as the plant that springs from beneath the surface of the ground. God has been working there with his heat and moisture for a long time; and it is the *appearance* only that is sudden to us, while the gradual process has been concealed from our eyes.

So it is with all the operations of the Lord in the soul. But when we come to Regeneration, of which repentance and conversion are the mere beginnings, it is then that we see the truth and labor of the toilsome work. The people of Israel did not flee on wings of haste and joy to Canaan. They did not conquer even one enemy without a struggle. "By little and little," saith the Lord, "I will drive them out from before thee; not in one year, lest the land become desolate, and the beast of the field multiply against thee." (*Exod.* 23: 29, 30.) That is, lest by a too *sudden* and *hasty* rejection of evils, the whole work should not only be ineffectual, and the proper life of man be jeapordized, but evils come rushing back again with a more grievous power. How often is it the case!

We need to look a little into the structure of the human mind to comprehend this. When a man's *body* is diseased,— when, by a long continuance in certain morbid and unhealthy states, he has contracted a disease which renders certain organs or parts of the body unfit for vital activity,—when obstructions exist, and impure matter has accumulated, and even, in some cases, that part of the body grown into chronic misplacement and deformity, it is frequently dangerous to remove the obstruction all at once, for fear of a greater injury to the patient's life. Nor is it any less so, but more so, inasmuch as spiritual things are superior to natural, in the life of the spiritual patient. He is under treatment by the Divine Physician. And when it is realized that every evil of his life has really *formed* itself in substantial accretions in the organism of the soul; that impure substances from filthy regions of the spiritual world have been allowed to collect, and to insinuate themselves by a vicious influx, and to grow by the indulgence of many years into a complication of spiritual disease, more rooted and more functional than any disease of the body can possibly be; that ossifications, enlargements, contractions, local and general disorders, afflict and permeate the whole spiritual structure, and make the man, like Isaiah's description of him, from the sole of the foot even unto the head, of no soundness at all, but wounds, and bruises, and putrefying sores; — when all this is realized, then we may comprehend the necessity of a different curative process than any merely metaphysical speculation has ever yet suggested. And further, the disease is strictly internal. Internal even in regard to the spirit. For it is the *life*, the very vital principle of the soul, that is afflicted. Its *cause* was there. Not by any external injury that has been suffered to mar and waste the spiritual body, and not even by any collocation of external *circumstances* which have so wrought upon the man, as to entice him into evil; these undoubtedly have had their effect; but it was his own free and inner choice, — the life of his will, — the love that ruled him, and was with him in quiet, and prompted all his thoughts, and by the most deliberate purposes has so woven this web-work and tissue of corruption around and through his soul, that he is *fast* there; he is fixed and formed in evil; his very and supreme life has organized itself in this body of sin and death, so that he needs all the strength so agonized and prayed for by the apostle, to be fully delivered from it. "Can the Ethiopian change his skin, or the leopard his spots? then may ye also do good, that are accustomed to do evil." (*Jer.* 13: 23.) Yes, we see but too plainly why it is and how it is. And now, to break up such a life all at once would destroy the man. Therefore it must be done "little by little."

The truth is also, that regeneration cannot be a quick or instantaneous work, because it is in part, the work of undoing what thousands of generations have been doing. The human race descended from a high, infant state of purity and goodness, down to the time when Christ made his appearance. Since then, we have no doubt it has been ascending. Everybody knows that the highest form of civilization is connected with Christianity,—that it received its quickening from its life-giving energies, and its crowning glory is the Christian faith. Now, the upward process, speaking of the race in its totality, must, as to time, correspond somewhat with its downward march. We do not undertake to say *as* long, but only to indicate the very patient steps of its toiling, upward progress. As to the individual, he *knows*, if he know any thing at all by worthy experience of the work to be done, that it is for the most part a laborious and protracted one. For the most part, too, it is quiet. It is often a still, quiet agony. Man indeed "hears the sound thereof;" his affections then are disposed to obedience; but he cannot tell whence frequently is the *occasion* of the strife; alas! *he* knows not how the winds of heaven, by the direction of a superior power, are made to sweep through all the channels of his disordered soul. And as he is frequently *unaware* of the work, so, instead of quietly submitting to it, as in the more advanced stages of regeneration, it is "too often only as the wind that bloweth, in fitful gusts and fearful apprehensions."

We revert again to the analogies of nature. The Lord compares the kingdom of heaven to a man casting seed into the ground, and he "should sleep, and rise night and day, and the seed should spring and grow up, *he knoweth not how*. For the earth bringeth forth fruit of herself; first the blade, then the ear, after that the full corn in the ear." (*Mark*, 4: 26–28.) This correspondence shows the part that *man* has in the great work of the regenerate life. It is not his to create himself anew, any more than it is the part of the husbandman to cause the seed to germinate and spring forth from the ground. All that the husbandman can do, is to prepare the ground, cast in the seed, and keep his fields from weeds and obstructions. The growth thereof, he knoweth not how it is. Paul may plant, and Apollos water, but God must give the increase. How perfectly plain it is, from all these analogies, that the chief work of man, in his spiritual re-creation, is simply a negative work! He cannot create any goodness nor any truth. He can only keep from sinning, (and he cannot do even this without the divine aid,) pluck out all the weeds of his spiritual nature, prepare the ground of his susceptible heart for the rains and dews of heaven, and for the Sun of Righteousness to warm and invigorate with life.

Sometimes Christians are seized with sudden resolutions. They are determined now to do some great thing. They say — "*I* am going to do this and this; *I* am going to accomplish so much." Alas! they know not the great secret of the whole of our mortal labors. It is only to abstain from evil, root out all obstructions to the heavenly influence, and let God do the rest. By removing obstructions the Divine life flows in all the more freely, and this it is which does the work. It is so in physical matters. No physician ever cures the body. He can only *remove obstructions*, and so aid nature herself, by a freer circulation of the vital fluids, to effect her own cure. Man, to be sure, has a practical free-will to do even the *positive* acts of a good life, but his will is solely stimulated by the divine influx consequent upon his removing of evils. A man *cannot* be thus engaged in removing evils without being at the same time engaged in doing good. For, every evil that he removes, as of hatred, adultery, theft, false-witness, covetousness, etc., prepares the way for the flowing in of the opposite virtues; and they do flow in from the Divine Humanity of the Lord.

The science of this matter, then, is perfectly plain. Do the negative part, and let God do the positive part. Or, do the positive part, feeling that it is of God. *Stop sinning*, and give the Lord a chance to act. *Cease to do evil;* and the learning to do well follows in necessary course, for man must be doing something. But while man is positive in an adverse direction, the Lord cannot be positive with him so successfully. Be not inactive, but *passively active* in the hands of the Lord. In short, realize our own feebleness, and our utter dependence on God, and look to him only for help, and our powers will be increased seven-fold. Man only fritters away his powers in any other attempt. He is never so feeble, never so inefficient, as when he says, in a spirit of self-trust and self-consciousness—"Now *I* will, or *I* am going to do this or that." To be sure, sometimes great things are accomplished by what we call the power of a resolute will; but when it is so, there is almost always a strong belief and reliance on some fate, or destiny, or providence, in man's behalf. *Bonaparte* was a man of indomitable will; but he believed in destiny. He believed that God had raised him up for just such a work. He believed that all the powers of heaven, or of fate, were on his side, so that he could *not* fail. And it is wonderful how such a faith in destiny stimulates the human will, — far more perhaps, than the extreme of the doctrine of absolute free-will. A man that really believes in it, does not sit down, and idly fold his hands, trusting to his faith, or to this Fate, or Predestination, to work it out for him. No, but he goes to work himself all the more vigilantly and vigorously, resolving that because it must, it *shall* be accomplished!

This is the true way. Combine both. This is the way in which providence is carried on. I say that a man who does *not* believe in this, but sets out with an air of importance, declaring what great things *he* will do, will only fret and fume his little self away, and in the end, chance if all he does be not to go headlong into folly's destruction. We have seen such people, and they are the most inconsequential little creatures in the world.

But the soul of great, calm, majestic resolutions, looking to the Lord, and relying on Him, quietly and noiselessly goes forth, accomplishing the mightiest results with the utmost facility and ease.

And so in this great work of the regenerate life. Even the sound of the wind may not be sensibly heard, it blows so gently and mildly, and through so accordant a nature; but the affections are all tranquil, and the thoughts serene; yet if the wind does rise, and sweep somewhat boisterously through the clogged and perverted channels of the soul, (and the wind always makes the most noise where there is the most obstruction,) then the man knows that he is wrought upon, but he cannot tell whence cometh the mighty spirit, nor whither it goeth. Fortunate for him, if he submit himself to this manifest effort of Providence to train him for the skies, and that he drive not off the angel guardians of his peace.

Finally, the essence of this New Birth is Love. If there was any one thing that distinguished the people of the primitive ages — the infancy of the human race, it was a spirit of love grounded in innocence. This is evident from several considerations; and it is plain to be perceived, that as the essence of all evil is selfishness, so the essence of all good is unselfishness, or love for one another. The mind of man, in fact, is made up in general of two parts, the Will and the Understanding, or the affectional and the intellectual natures. Now, the *fall* of man, or his gradual declension, consisted in the *separation* of the will from the understanding, or the good affections from the mere intellect, so that, in process of time, the intellectual principle came altogether to predominate; and such is the state of the world at this day. Faith pertains to the intellect, or to the understanding, rather than to the will; and it is conspicuous, that love or charity holds but a subordinate place in the faith of the church and in the practice of mankind.

Now, the New Birth is the *uniting* again of what has been so grievously sundered. And as the soul of all truth is goodness, or the soul of all wisdom is love, without which it is nothing but a cold, dead body, so this new birth of the Christian is so much *like* a birth as to be *the creation of a new soul in a new body;* viz., a new will principle in a new understanding. For the understanding itself, or man's rational powers, are as much vitiated as his love, by the Fall, and have become filled with abominable falsities. Hence it it so hard, frequently, to understand theological and spiritual truths. The popular mind has often an utter aversion to them. It is not because the truths themselves are so hard and unfitted to the mind, but because our own minds are pre-occupied with so much rubbish. Now, therefore, a *new spiritual infant is born,* — created of God in the substances of the human soul, and as it grows, and comes to maturity, the whole "old man" is made to die the death, and human nature is permeated by a new spirit, has a new life — a new will and a new understanding. And the beauty of it all is, these two parts of our nature are thenceforth perfectly and harmoniously united. There is a restoration of lost powers to the human soul, — a pure, divine marriage of Goodness and Truth, and God is glorified and man is saved.

CHAPTER V.

SPIRITUAL WARFARE.

"The more the interior man is searched and laid open by the Word of God, the clearer are the demonstrations of this divided consciousness; and it seems to the individual that two classes of powers are ranged in opposition, and seeking for the dominion of his nature. This conflict perhaps did not appear except under the light of Christian truth bursting on the soul in clearer splendor, — like the sun arising on a field where hosts are gathered and arranged for battle, but which lay in stillness on their arms until the morning light should appear."—*Rev. E. H. Sears.*

THE work of the regenerating life is everywhere represented as a work of strife and combat. The natural mind is full of evils, and the work of routing and removing them is sometimes very painful. In nothing, perhaps, does man feel his duality of being, that is, his natural and spiritual minds, so powerfully. For, unless he had two minds, as distinct in their desires and cravings almost as two persons, could it be that there would exist this warfare and division in him? The natural or external mind is, in all its characteristics, an image of the natural world, and finds its delight in the things of the natural world; the spiritual or interior mind is an image of the spiritual world, and loves the things of that world, or heaven. The spiritual, indeed, loves also the things of the natural world, but only as a master loves a servant, by whose means he performs uses; the natural world, by such an one, is held in subordination; it is not suffered to become uppermost, or chief. And when the natural is so regarded, then the natural mind *itself* becomes spiritual, or *spiritual-natural;* it suffers the spiritual to act through it and by it; it is thus at one and in harmony with the spiritual. But this is the effect of regeneration. Before this, it is not so.

And indeed, all through this life in the world, both with the regenerate and the unregenerate, these two minds are so distinct, that man does not know what is performing with himself in his superior mind; for with that mind he is in the spiritual world with angels, and with the other, in the natural world with men; and even when he becomes a spirit, which is immediately after death, he does not, according to Swedenborg, know what is performing in his inferior mind.

It was these two minds, so distinct and separate, that furnished the ground of the Apostle's warfare, and also the ground of every warfare experienced in the heart of the Christian. And it may be safely concluded, that until a person has begun to experience this warfare, that is, an unrest, a dissatisfaction with himself, and a conflict more or less painful with the predominant desires of the heart, he has not even *begun* the regenerate life.

This matter is so interesting, — it covers so large a field of human life and of the Divine Providence, — that we are moved to look at it still more analytically. And here may be contemplated a certain description of character which is common enough to be met with, and which frequently, perhaps, excites almost our envy, or at least our desire, that we could be of such a disposition. We refer to certain persons of a mild and even temperament, who never appear to be troubled much with any thing. Or at least, if troubles come they are soon over; they are met with a momentary shock and passed by lightly; and there is such a natural buoyancy and equanimity of spirit prevailing with them, and so much easiness, that it seems quite out of the power of this world's fortunes to produce any great or deep disturbance in them. And they frequently have, too, a certain amiability about them, — a quiet, contented, good-natured disposition, that seems to mark them out as made and fitted for enjoyment. In short, they seem to be what many truly religious people are, all but the religion. For it is not their religion which confers this enjoyment, for they have none.

It is a contentedness which springs not from any resignation to the Divine Will; it is a cheerfulness not at all referable to faith or reconciliation, except a reconcilement with the frivolities of every-day life; it is what many would call an easy, constitutional happiness. And it frequently manifests itself in all the attracting amiabilities of good companionship and unburdensome life.

Now, there are two ways in which to account for this, before we come to the real and deepest secret of such a phenomenon.

First, it may be partially accounted for by mere shallowness. There is not depth enough for much disturbance. It is not proper, perhaps, to speak thus of that deficiency which is a mere withholding of the gifts of God; but of that shallowness which is the result of indifference, it *is* proper to speak. And perhaps we may say it is a general truth, that never a truly noble and susceptible mind existed, without a larger proportion of trials than is permitted to inferior and thoughtless persons. We frequently at least see such persons, who pass their time quietly and tranquilly, with scarcely a ripple on their shallow lake; having no thought for the past, and no care for the future, living and enjoying the present, not as religionists do, but as animals do, from mere thoughtlessness. It is the great and deep ocean that is lashed into tremendous waves and surging billows. It is only a noble and sensitive mind that can be similarly disturbed. When the ocean *is* calm, and such a mind too, then what a splendid calm it is! And yet there are those who frequently give way to folly, and deem it almost a refreshment to meet with a person of the above description, who is not particularly interested about any thing, there is such a happiness! How little they know of the true elements of a happy life!

But again, the life in question may be partially accounted for from a nobler view of it; namely, from certain hereditary qualities which are really good in themselves, and which confer upon the person a truly equitable and harmonious character.

By nature he may not be disposed to much mental disturbance. He may have the gift of peace ingrafted in him from birth. And if it is *real* peace, that is, such as comes from an ancestry of virtue, and has been handed down to an offspring of fair and even proportions, and thus freed from a multitude of carking cares that otherwise would have disturbed and embittered the whole life, then indeed it can be said that there is so much hereditary *virtue* in the person. But it may be *only* hereditary; the person may not yet have made it his own by spiritually and deeply willing it; and if so, it is the merest natural, and may not abide the spiritual life. It may play within him beautifully, and pass from him felicitously, when in circumstances of ease and convenience, but a strong temptation may sweep it all away. For hereditary good, as well as hereditary evil, is not *truly* good until acted out from a more interior love of it, — from such a spiritual affection as cleaves to it in the midst of difficulties, and against strong self-interests. And in the spiritual world, where nothing abides but what is real, it may leave the man entirely destitute.

But there is still another and a truer way of accounting for that peculiar life which we have here set forth. And that is, to refer it all, or mainly, to the entire predominance of the natural man. The spiritual in such natures is not frequently waked up. It is asleep under all this covering of nature. The natural man is now enjoying, therefore, an undisturbed possession of its own proper domain. There is nothing to oppose it, nothing to trouble it. Hardly a twinge, perhaps, of genuine conscience, yet fully aroused in it. Being an image of the natural world, it enjoys the natural world. The things of heaven do not at all intrude themselves. The warfare has not yet commenced in such minds. Bating the other causes, this is the secret of all or most of their happiness. It is a happiness, a contentedness, such as the animals enjoy, only human instead of beastly. And it is capable of very much pleasure. There may be many a charm, and many a fascination, and even a ravishment with the things of this world;—why not, if the birds can sing so sweetly, and the animals hold such fetterless sport, and the whole brute creation ring with joy and resound with melody? Does not the lamb delight to skip and play, and the cow and the ox graze in luxurious comfort, and the shining snake, and every insect, enjoy to the full the measure of life which is allowed them? So does man, without one particle of the spiritual having as yet any exercise over him. And his natural has the advantage of being a *human* natural, with something of the *natural-rational* in it, upon a much higher plane than the beast's; why, then, should he not, in all the fulness of his unregenerate nature, find delight in the externals of his mind? This, indeed, is something of that poor enjoyment which is finally permitted to lost spirits who have signified their preference for the very lowest life;—with much occasional restraint, indeed, and the terrible liabilities and discomfitures attendant upon such a nature. What *must* it be, when the highest is put for the lowest, and the lowest elevated to the supreme rule? So, also, it is in the world. And there may be very much apparent amiability and satisfaction with such a life; no thought for the past, no care nor anxiety for the future; an enjoyment, such as it is, and a life altogether in the present; passing their time as listlessly, so far as any real anxiety for their spiritual condition is concerned, as though this world were all, and the joys of sense the only reality. All their affections, except the hereditary good already named, are "of the earth, earthy." They know not what it is to be troubled with any other. These are they who are spoken of in the Scripture: "I was envious at the foolish, when I saw the prosperity of the wicked; they are not in trouble as other men, neither are they plagued like other men." (*Psalm*, 73: 3, 5.) In short, the secret of such persons' happiness is, that there is as yet no warfare and division felt in their minds; the natural, perverted as it is, is not only in the ascendant, but has the field entirely to itself; the Devil reigns in undisputed and easy possession, and all the imps and emissaries of hell hold frequently high carnival in that man's mind. For a time, it may go comparatively well with him; especially if he avoids the grosser evils and more grievous crimes of the wicked. He knows no other life, he seeks no other. He is thoroughly alive to the life of nature, and thoroughly dead to all spiritual life. He has, therefore, that easy, contented, sometimes gentlemanly cast of mind, which so many enjoy who pass with the reputation of amiable and graceful characters; and if sickness comes not, and their outward affairs are tolerably prosperous, they are envied and honored by those who, like themselves, have no spiritual discernment.

Now, it is the object of Christ's mission to *break up* such a life. "Think not that I am come to send peace on earth; I came not to send peace, but a sword. For I am come to set a man at variance against his father, and the daughter against her mother, and the daughter-in-law against her mother-in-law, and a man's foes shall be they of his own household." (*Matt.* 10: 34–36.) This remarkable passage finds its explanation only in reference to the structure and condition of the human mind. And without going into needless particulars, it is sufficient to say that by the terms father, mother, son, daughter, daughter-in-law, mother-in-law, etc., whenever they occur in the Word, are spiritually signified such things as pertain to the heavenly marriage and progeny of good and truth in the mind. These may occur in their true order, or in their opposites; and when any strife is occasioned, it is by some truth in conflict with some evil, or some falsity with some good, so that "a man's foes are they of his own household,"—that is, of his spiritual house or mind, which is frequently represented by a house with all its apartments. By a sword is signified truth combating. Hence it is said of the Lord, "Gird thy sword upon thy thigh, O most Mighty! and in thy majesty ride prosperously, because of truth and meekness and righteousness: and thy right hand shall teach thee terrible things." (*Psalm*,

45 : 3, 4.) Also in the Apocalypse, he that sat on the white horse, and was called the Word of God, "out of his mouth went a sharp sword." (*Rev.* 19 : 15.) Now, by the truth which the Lord reveals in his Word, and the more abundant expositions of that truth which are unfolded in the latter ages, is this sword sent upon the earth. It is the sword of truth to the earth of the mind. And when it enters the mind for the first time, which was before dead in trespasses and sins, then it is that a spiritual warfare has commenced, which puts to flight all the peace and tranquillity of the merely natural man. It is a warfare such as none know who have not commenced in good earnest the regenerate life. It is this which is set forth so graphically, in the correspondential style, by all the wars of the Israelites, and it is this which our Lord himself first engaged in for the glorification of his natural humanity. It is not possible, as a general thing, to attain to the heavenly state, without much affliction, and much tribulation and conflict of spirit. It is different, indeed, with different individuals; the hereditary evils are lesser and greater with some; but in all, before regeneration, they are thoroughly spread through the whole natural man, and if we feel them not, it is just because the sleep of death is still upon us, and we are pleasing ourselves with the flattering testimonies of the heart of nature, and with a thousand amiabilities which have no depth and no root in any thing but hereditary good, or worse yet, in a secret and disguised selfishness which calls forth a thousand virtues to the eye, but leaves not one in the heart. Such truth, I know, is exceedingly hard to receive, for there is nothing which the natural mind is so averse to as the very truths which are levelled against it. But it is truth, and it should be understood. It is needed especially in this age of rationalizing, naturalizing, miscalled Christianity. The truth is, we have broken away in alienation from God. We have not known God, nor the Lord Jesus Christ. And in the pride of our fallen nature, we have dared to set up our own feeble and conceited intellects,

and to trust to our own natural and hereditary goodness, mixed with selfishness as it all is, and which can no more abide the day of the Lord's appearing, than the stubble that the wind bloweth and the fire consumeth. The truth is, also, we cannot *know* our evils till we feel them in this internal strife and combat. Even the *literal* sense of the Lord's words suggests something of the nature of it. To think of a *family*, bound together by the cords of consanguinity and the ties of love, where affection, and sympathy, and the dear delights of kith and kin, should enter into all and spread through all, making the interests of such a household a unity and a peace such as we might transfer in imagination to the very heavens, — to think of it as torn and rent with intestine commotion, — to see it in opposition and contention, — to hear the fierce wrangle of bitter words and contemptuous speeches, — to see the father against the mother, and the mother against the father; and the son, and the daughter, and the daughter-in-law, and the little child, in a tumult of wild and angry passion, or so thoroughly divided as to settle away into the scorn and hatred of a sullen and mutual silence which has more of hell in it than heaven, nay, which is the very picture of hell, in some of its outbreaks and unquelled disorders! — if there is a sight on earth to make an angel weep, it is such a scene of family disturbance. For the very *marriage* principle — the highest and holiest of heaven's best — is thus outraged, and with it, all the dear connections and tender relationships which follow from it.

But it is the *spiritual* of that scene, and that, too, which dwells in each individual heart, which is referred to in the remarkable words before quoted. It is a warfare between good and evil, truth and falsity. And in a more tremendous sense than was ever seen by human eye in such a family, do the angels look in upon a man so situated, and behold the foes which are of his own household! But if nobly resisted, it is a warfare that they can witness with joy. Nay, they can take part in it. They do take part in it.

These are *temptations* which the regenerating mind undergoes when it is thus subjected to this inward strife. So soon as a man *begins* to receive the truth, and apply it to the eradication of his own evils, so soon is there let in upon him such evil spirits as feel disturbed by the work he has engaged in, and who take up arms against him. And the angels, on the other hand, defend him. This is permitted in order that he may be more speedily and thoroughly convinced of the evils which are lurking within him, and also that those evils may be *stirred up* by the evil spirits who are attendant on the man, and thus that he may be aware of them and resist them. "Regeneration cannot possibly take place without such combat, for the life of the old man resists; nor can the life of the new man be at all implanted until that which resists is taken away." And not by one temptation, but by many, and of various kinds, according to the evils which are in the man. For these evils are inlaid in the very substances of the soul, and inhere pertinaciously, being rooted in the parentage of many generations, and confirmed by actual evils of the man himself. Thus, then, the combat must necessarily be firm, and if at all thorough, many times grievous to be borne. And if a man has not felt it, let him beware of the peace which he so much prizeth. For he is in the very worst security, crying Peace! Peace! when there is no peace, but such as may lead him along in a winsome way to the very deeps of perdition. He should rejoice at the very first sign of disturbance. If it be on account of sin or evil, he should pray for the warfare to commence; and no matter if his soul sink almost within him, he must have these feelings; ah! did not our Lord have them in all their bitterness? — and what a cross was that which he bore through a long life of toil, temptation, and conflict! But because He triumphed, we may triumph. Yet never, till we have passed through this ordeal of dread and fiery trial.

We are not sufficiently aware of the nature of the conflict we are engaged in. We are not aware of the invisible hosts constantly surrounding us. Jesus knew, and could see, the vast hell he fought against. He was "with the wild beasts" in the thickest of the battle;—in "the wilderness, and tempted of the Devil." (*Matt.* 4: 1–11; *Mark*, 1: 13.) The meaning of which is, that He encountered the very worst of those evil affections signified by beasts, and the whole organized iniquity of the spiritual world. Nothing is plainer, indeed, from the Scriptures and from other sources, than that the great battle of our earthly life is no mere matter of earth alone, but a more serious struggle between the spirits of light and truth who would raise us up to goodness and heaven, and the spirits of evil who would drag us down to hell. Along the whole play-ground of humanity they stretch their lengthening files, and with this distracted globe hung, as it were, in the midst, they extend on the one hand to the glowing heights of heaven, and on the other, to the dismal abysses of the nether hell. Man is kept in this equilibrium. His destinies are wrought out in the midst of such an encounter. If it were all of earth, Christianity would be a fiction and a mockery. The Apostle very plainly recognizes this warfare, in the following passage from his letter to the Ephesians: "For we wrestle not against flesh and blood, [that is, against mere men in the body,] but against principalities, against powers, against the rulers of the darkness of this world, against spiritual wickedness [or wicked spirits] in high places." (6: 12.) The principalities here spoken of are not of this world, but the same which are spoken of in Colossians, as those which Jesus triumphed over by his work of redemption: "And having spoiled principalities and powers [broken up all their confederacies in the world of spirits], he made a show of them openly, triumphing over them in it." (2: 15.) And throughout the whole course of our Saviour's life, how evident it is that he was engaged in a struggle with the powers of darkness! He cast out evil spirits, and gave the same power to the Apostles.

Concerning this warfare of the Lord while on earth, and in

the infirm humanity, it is well remarked by Swedenborg, that "All temptation is made against the love in which a man is, and the degree of the temptation is according to the degree of the love. The life of the Lord was love towards the whole human race, which was so great, and of such a nature, as to be nothing but pure love. Against this, his life, were admitted continual temptations, from his earliest childhood to his last hour in the world. During all this time the Lord was assaulted by all the hells, which were continually overcome, subjugated, and conquered by him; and this solely out of love to the whole human race. And because this love was not human, but divine, and all temptation is great in proportion as the love is great, it may be seen how grievous were his combats, and how great the ferocity with which the hells assailed him." (A. C. 1690.) "These temptations are not described in the Word, except in a few words; nevertheless these few involve all."

And thus also it is with man. The great conflict of our life is more insidious and dangerous than it can ever appear to us, being connected and carried on with powers invisible and personal. And in nothing do the angelic guardians of which we have spoken in a previous chapter minister more effectually to our peace, than in resisting all the attacks of such an adversary, in delivering us from their wiles, and in leading us on through the difficult and upward path to heaven, while temptations and enmities flow in upon us like a flood. It is thus that they ministered to the infirm humanity of Jesus. After all his temptations, which were firmly resisted, "Then the Devil leaveth him," it is said; "and behold, angels came and ministered unto him." (*Matt.* 4: 11.) Thus it always is. If, by our faithfulness and resistance, we drive away these evil spirits, then, after the trial, angels come and minister unto us. They cannot come effectually till we do resist. This is the law of our spiritual life. It is then their delightful work to insinuate the good graces of heaven into those parts of the soul where obstructions have been removed, and where the fortresses of evil have been weakened by resistance.

In regard to the conflict which is thus experienced in the soul, and its intimate connection with the spiritual world, it is remarked by Swedenborg, that it is perceived by man very obscurely; indeed, "so obscurely, that he scarcely knows otherwise than that it is merely an anxiety; for man, especially he who believes nothing concerning influx, scarcely perceives a thousandth part of those things concerning which evil spirits and angels combat; nevertheless, man and his eternal salvation are then at stake, and the determination of the stake is from man; for the combat is carried on from those things which are with man, and concerning them. That this is the case, has been given me to know with the utmost certainty; I have heard the combat, I have perceived the influx, I have seen the spirits and angels, and at the time and afterwards I have conversed with them also upon the subject." (A. C. 5036.)

This, then, we take to be the truth of the matter. This is the warfare in which every man who comes into heaven must be engaged in some degree, in some part of his life. "I came not to send peace on earth, but a sword." It is not of course implied that the ultimate end of all this is not a greater peace than can possibly be described. For the Lord is the very "Prince of peace," his Gospel is the "Gospel of peace," and peace, "unfluctuating peace," is the end of every battle carried on with the weapons of heaven. Yet the great battle must be fought first. Those deeply intrenched hereditary evils, which stand to us as the authority and affection of a father, which we love so well, and obey so well; those equally settled and compacted falsities, the pride of self-derived intelligence, and errors of the natural mind, which stand to us as the influence and affection of a mother, which it is so hard to part with, and which have nourished us so long; and those other dear and affectionate relatives, the legitimate offspring of so honored a parentage, whether they be wife, children, brethren, sisters, or more distant connections; — this whole family of most affectionate relationship and strong union is altogether to be broken up! If a man forsake not the *whole* of it, and hate not father, mother, wife, children, brethren, sisters, yea, and his own life also [own natural life], he cannot be my disciple. (*Luke*, 14: 26.) The warfare is to be carried into the very heart of the family. A man's very greatest foes are to be they of his own household. The truth of all this now stands conspicuous. It is no mere figure of speech, but a correspondential representation of the evil loves and false affections which are a man's hereditary heirship, and constitute his spiritual family and house. And "when my father and mother forsake me, then the Lord will take me up" (*Ps.* 27: 10): not till then, for the Lord cannot enter to dwell where such perverted natural affections make their abode and enjoy their life.

Let us, now, at the risk of being more practical and hortative than the naked disquisition demands, bring somewhat of this test to ourselves. Do these truths disturb us? Do they make us feel, in a degree, unhappy? Do they humble us under a sense of our own evils, and make us despise ourselves? Has this sword of truth entered into *our* minds, and do we feel it combating against some dear and cherished evil, or many of them? Then is the Divine Providence doing its legitimate work. For the good work is not begun in us till these effects are realized. There is no power at all in a merely natural Christianity, which does not recognize the thorough depravity of the natural mind, the root and element of which is selfishness in all its thousand forms, — no power at all, — especially where the Lord is not acknowledged in his true and essential Divinity, and the eternal distinctions between good and evil, — *no* power to purge thoroughly the diseased nature which so afflicts us, to probe to the quick, and to make a new man of us. It is a folly, a waste of time, and a delusion. It is not meant by this that the perverted Christianity around us is doing no good, for its broken and adulterated truths do serve with some power — many times with great force — against the corruptions of the natural mind. But they can do no *thorough* work. We must, eventually, either in this world or the next, be saved by the truth, before we can enter heaven. There is no entire salvation without it. When the light of eternity breaks in upon the sinful soul, if there are any remains of good in him that can be made effectual, if he has not experienced the conflict here, he will have to experience it there, — there in the world of spirits, where the processes of vastation he will have to go through with before he can enter heaven, are sometimes painful beyond expression. He had better do this work here. For as sure as the opening scenes of eternity, if he be only one of those easy, complacent, natural men, who enjoy, as it was said, but a constitutional quiet, and a buoyancy of spirit which may be the very fatal mischief of his life, he will find in that world, unrolled to him successively such inner deeps in his soul as he had never dreamt of, — and there, in those inner deeps, every vessel of his spiritual organism perverted and defiled with sin. Better, I say, make that exploration and discovery now. Be thoroughly convinced that there is nothing else worth living for, that the world and all it can offer is too small for the ambition of immortal spirits, but that there is an inheritance pure, undefiled, and that fadeth not away, reserved for all who covet purity of life, and make that the one grand object of all their struggles and all their enterprise. Oh, it is worth a world of painstaking ; and the victory once achieved, the battle never to be fought again, — never, never ! Eternal peace, angelic peace, will have settled forever in the mind, and increasing beatitudes forever and ever.

CHAPTER VI.

TEMPTATIONS OF THE REGENERATING LIFE.

"Temptations appertaining to man are spiritual combats between good and evil spirits, which combats are from those things and concerning those things which man had done and thought, which are in his memory. They are generally carried on to a state of desperation, which is their period and conclusion. In temptations man is in equilibrium between two opposite powers; one from the Lord in his inner man, and the other from hell in his outer man." — *Swedenborg.*

We shall ever find it our highest wisdom to recur to the *Divine Word* for instructions and illustrations concerning our spiritual experience. It is here that the whole plan of Providence and the map of human existence are unrolled before us. The Word being written with a much more specific fulness than it is commonly supposed to be,—it being, in fact, systematic and continuous, and having an internal sense originated from a standpoint in the spiritual world from which it was written, and where was seen, in divine light, all the states and experiences of the soul as in panoramic vision, it becomes our chart and guide across the ocean of life. Some general marks of the spiritual sense have always been discovered in the Bible; and nowhere perhaps more so, than in the account of the people of Israel in their bondage to the Egyptians, their deliverance thence, and their journeyings to the promised land: for Egypt has always been recognized as a representative of the natural mind untaught in spiritual things; the bondage endured there, as a figure of the like spiritual bondage; their deliverance from it, the commencement of a new life; their wanderings in the wilderness and the encountering of so many enemies by the way, the long and toilsome work of regeneration and the spiritual enemies that oppose and fight against this work; and their final routing of these enemies and entrance into Canaan, the triumph over every evil and the attainment of heavenly rest and peace. These and many other things in the history of the Israelites have always caused it to be read in the church as more or less of a spiritual history, full of significance to the life of man.

With this general view of the Scripture history, let us here introduce one passage which is full and pertinent to the point under review. *Deut.* 8: 15, 16.—"The Lord thy God, who led thee through that great and terrible wilderness, wherein were fiery serpents, and scorpions, and drought; where there was no water; who brought thee forth water out of the rock of flint; who fed thee in the wilderness with manna, which thy fathers knew not, that he might humble thee, and that he might prove thee, to do thee good at thy latter end." Here is a plain reference to the grievous *temptations* which they experience who from natural are becoming spiritual. The warfare before treated of relates more fully to the *commencement*, or to the *first states* of the new life. True, it is frequently more grievous as that life progresses to the interiors, and as deeper evils are brought to light than we had ever thought existed, even as the last temptation of our Lord was the most grievous of all, when it appeared that God had forsaken him. But in the first states we are frequently more apt to feel and speak of it as a warfare, from the fact that we have just began to *realize* the conflict. But all through it is a warfare, from which there is no discharge so long as a particle of sin or impurity remains. We must devote, then, another chapter to this subject, without which our treatment of it would by no means be complete.

The "great and terrible wilderness" referred to, which was true literally in the experience of the Isaelites, in the spiritual and universal sense is the barren and uncultivated state of the unregenerate mind. The prominent reason for this correspondence is found in the spiritual world: for there, they who are thus destitute of truth and goodness appear to inhabit wilderness tracts of land; barren and arid deserts; where there is no verdure in the plains, and no harvest in the fields, and no fruit-trees in the gardens; for all these things in the spiritual world are correspondences and outbirths of the states of the inhabitants. It would be tedious to enumerate passages where the wilderness is spoken of and set in contrast with the Garden of Eden, and the Garden of the Lord, and many fruitful places. Speaking of the natural man before regeneration, which is represented by Jacob, it is said — "The Lord found him in a desert land, and in the waste, howling wilderness; he led him about, he instructed him, he kept him as the apple of his eye." (*Deut.* 32: 10.) And what else shall we understand by "making the wilderness rejoice and blossom as the rose"?

Now, inasmuch as this wilderness is seen correctly in the mind of one man, when inspected by the light of heaven, — seen in miniature, — so a multitude of such men together would make a still greater wilderness: and in the spiritual world where the evil congregate, particularly in the hells, and from thence into the world of spirits, there is the "great and terrible wilderness" from whence proceed all our temptations. It is called great and formidable, because of the grievous nature of the temptations encountered thence. "Wherein were fiery serpents, and scorpions," and all manner of evil beasts. These refer not to natural creatures, but to spiritual evils which take these forms. Thus also it is said of Babylon, the perverted church, that it has become "the habitation of devils, and the hold of every foul spirit, and a cage of every unclean and hateful bird." (*Rev.* 18: 2) So also in Isaiah, speaking of the same or similar things, under figure of the land of Idumea and Zion, "The cormorant and the bittern shall possess it; the owl also and the raven shall dwell in it; it shall be a habitation for dragons and a court for owls. The wild beasts of the desert shall also meet with the wild beasts of the island, and the satyr shall cry to his fellow; the screech owl also shall rest there, and find for herself a place of rest. There shall the great owl make her nest, and lay, and hatch, and gather under her shadow; there shall the vultures also be gathered, every one with her mate." (*Isa.* 34 : 11–15.)

All this would be entirely unworthy of the Word of God, if the literal sense only were adhered to, for why such a particular enumeration and description of mere birds and animals? But when it is reflected that they every one signifiy some falsity or evil in the human mind, and how they mate, and beget their like, and that they are really seen, flitting about in the regions of darkness in the spiritual world, and in this world also, by the angels who can see what correspondences are around every man, then we may have a rational and spiritual idea of the great and terrible wilderness through which every man is led in passing from Egypt to Canaan.

The "fiery serpents" signify the lusts of the sensual man; and "scorpions" such deadly persuasions thence, of error and falsity, as quite deprive a man of his own proper life. For a scorpion, when he stings a man, induces a stupor upon the limbs, which if not cured is followed by death. This persuasion also of certain deadly falsities produces a corresponding effect upon the understanding. "In the spiritual world," says Swedenborg, "there exists a power of persuasion which takes away the understanding of truth, and induces stupor, and thus distress, upon the mind; but this power of persuasion is unknown in the natural world." (A. R. 428.) Yet perhaps we may now be opening to something of this kind, as we see the terrible fantasies and delusions which are being practised upon men in their near approach to the spiritual world.

The meaning of these words is rendered still more obvious by what follows. "Fiery serpents, and scorpions, and *drought*, where there was *no water*." That is, by a familiar correspondence, no truth.

And again — "Who brought thee forth water out of the rock of flint." Allusion is here made to the Rock in Horeb, which was smitten by Moses, from whence issued water for the people; that is, truths from the Lord.

"Who fed thee in the wilderness with manna, which thy fathers knew not, that he might humble thee, and that he might prove thee, to do thee good at thy latter end." The meaning is, that while in temptations, the Lord sustains man with spiritual meat and spiritual drink, which are the goods and truths from heaven: for by manna is understood the good of celestial love; and by the fathers of these Israelites *not knowing* of this manna is signified that the natural man is utterly averse to it: thus that the whole temptation is intended to separate the evils from the natural man, to make him spiritual, and to do him good in his final state; that is, in heaven to eternity.

Such is the graphic teaching of this passage of the divine Word. It introduces us to one of the most important and interesting considerations of the regenerating life.

But here we encounter a difficulty in the outset. There are many who are still so fast bound in Egypt, or who have made so little progress out of it, that they know scarcely any thing about these temptations. They live, for the most part, a purely natural life. As before observed — "They are not in trouble as other men, neither are they plagued like other men." (*Ps.* 73: 5.) Still, they have their troubles. They are, for the most part, griefs about worldly things, for the loss of property, sickness, and an unsuccessful ambition; and frequently, petty cares and irritabilities for things which in themselves are nothing, and amount to nothing; in short, for the mere hurt of the natural life, which is self-love and love of the world. But they have no *spiritual temptations.* These are such as belong to the interior man, and are assaults upon his spiritual life. But before a man has begun to experience this life, although he is in association with evil spirits, and lives and acts so much from them, yet he knows not what it is to have his faith and love assaulted — to be bowed down in despair on account of his own salvation: talk to such a man about a loss of truth, a separation from the Divine presence, and a great grief for that, and he does not comprehend you; this is not what he is concerned about; a heavenly life is not at all a matter of anxiety with him; therefore the devils have no power over him in this respect; he is on their side, and is at one, and in comparative peace with them; and he is only cast down by earthly misfortunes, such as a loss of property, honor or health.

In the systematic language of Swedenborg, "there are several kinds of temptations, which in general may be divided into the celestial, spiritual, and natural. Celestial temptations can have no place except with those who are principled in love towards the Lord; and spiritual temptations with those only who are in charity towards their neighbor. Natural temptations are altogether distinct from these, and are not indeed truly temptations, but merely anxieties from the assault of natural loves," as aforesaid. Hence it may be seen that "temptation is anguish and anxiety occasioned by whatever opposes or resists any particular kind of love. Thus in the case of those who are principled in love to the Lord, whatever assaults this love produces an inmost torture, which is celestial temptation; also with such as are principled in love towards the neighbor, or charity, whatever assaults this love occasions torment of conscience, and this is spiritual temptation. But with those who are merely natural, what they frequently call temptations and the pangs of conscience are not truly so; still their troubles are wont to be productive of some good, and are frequently the procuring causes of *spiritual* temptations; for when man is in disease, grief, the loss of wealth or honor, and the like, if then a thought occurs concerning the Lord's aid, concerning his providence, concerning the state of the evil, that they glory and exult when the good suffer, and undergo various griefs and losses, in such case spiritual temptation is conjoined to natural temptation." (A. C. 847, 8164.)

From this general view of the subject of temptations, we may now proceed to some further considerations concerning their source, their grievous nature, their use and end.

First, as to their source. We have all heard of the temptations of the Devil, and it has always been the belief of mankind that these temptations were in some sort from the spiritual world; although but one Devil or Satan, *in propria persona*, whose wiles are almost infinite, instead of many organized into one, has had to bear the chief blame of all the evils thus inflicted upon man. It is surely a relief to be delivered from so monstrous and shocking a conception; still, a dark and dread reality remains. Hell yawns, and its multitudinous emissaries issue forth from many an organized band of malicious and deceitful spirits, to flood the world with wickedness and crime. Each man, each woman, is plied daily and hourly with pestiferous streams of influx from those dark retreats, to say nothing of the more direct and personal assaults experienced by every one. This is certainly the doctrine of the Scriptures, was the experience of our Lord, and has been attested by many instances of open and partial vision into the spiritual world. We may even see the analogy of all this, and a certain necessity for it, in the condition and constitution of the spiritual universe. It is not always for the mere purpose of *tormenting* man that the spirits of evil ply him with their seductions, but to gain strength and power with him — to enlist him in the cause of their own life. It is chiefly a matter of affinity, and the love of rule with them. They seek to attract their like, and to make others like them. And the truth is, were there not some evil in ourselves, we could not be tempted *at all* from the infernal world; and man was not, originally; *he himself* turned away from the Lord to think too much of himself, and thus "brought death into the world, and all our woe." But after the hells had been created, by evil men passing out of this world into the spiritual world, then they existed, and do still exist, as the cause of many a combat, many a fierce and bitter trial, the source of which we are all too apt to attribute to what is in ourselves only. Yet it is this evil in ourselves which is excited by the evil spirits; and they are permitted to do this in order that we may be more sensible of the nature and extent of our own corruptions, and thus engage more manfully in the extermination of them.

And through all this process, there is a most distinct, particular, and beautiful Divine Providence. The Lord our God it is who leads us through this "great and terrible wilderness," wherein are fiery serpents, and scorpions, and drought; where there is no water; who brings forth water for us out of the rock, and feeds us with heavenly manna which the natural man knows nothing of, that He might humble us, and prove us, and do us good in the end. If He suffers us to be tempted, it is never above our ability to bear it, and with the temptation He makes a way of escape. And precisely as He himself was tempted, in his infirm and unglorified humanity, and as the account says, was "led by the Devil into the wilderness" for that purpose, so he permits us, and leads us by his own right hand through scenes as dark as night, and trials which sometimes make us sink in despair, with a view to exaltation and glory. But these temptations are wisely proportioned to our different states. If we have not the love of the Lord predominantly, we know nothing about the fierce tortures which the devils of the lowest hell are capable of inflicting upon that tender and celestial principle. If we are in some degree spiritual, and are really trying to live the life of charity which prevails in the spiritual heaven, then it may be that we need the trial in different ways. We know not our own weakness, and in those points wherein we frequently think we are the strongest, there we are the weakest. A man may *pride* himself, or feel elated, with some particular virtue that is in him. And if so, it may be a sure sign that it is a false or fictitious virtue, or mere hereditary good which he indulges in when ease and opportunity favor it, and which runs from him with a pleasure like the natural flowing of his animal spirits. But if it abides not with him in moments of trial, — if, when brought into straitened circumstances, and the temptation is on him to go counter to it for the sake of some earthly gain or honor, he then gives admission to an opposite principle of his evil natural mind, then does such good really belong to the man? — that is, to his *spiritual* man — the only man that can enter heaven? Most assuredly not, for his spiritual, more interior nature does not at these times will it; the natural only wills it when there is no gain and no honor at stake; or it may be when both gain and honor are seen to be promoted by it; how is it, then, that he is so elated with these natural virtues? The very fact that he is so shows that this virtue is not spiritual with him; and here is a point, therefore, wherein he needs perhaps the strongest temptations. He needs them to *save* that splendid endowment of hereditary goodness. He is a man of merely natural, ancestral virtue. These graces are not his, but his fathers'. He knows it, frequently, as well as anybody can tell him. He is peculiarly sensitive and complacent upon that point. It may be that *honesty* is the darling thing he doats upon, or benevolence; no matter what it is, there is evidently much reliance and strength placed upon it; and now it is that he is brought into circumstances to try and test it. He is brought, perhaps, into poverty and distress on account of it. Or if not real poverty, then an *imaginary* want is permitted to cast up its gloomy shadows in the mind's perspective, and the man is plagued and anxious about his future lot. He is made to suffer a thousand privations in the anticipation of a possible one. And under these circumstances, one satan or devil is permitted to suggest how, by a sacrifice of a little of that inborn good which sits so uncomfortably upon him, some large advantage may be gained in the line of wealth or honor; another suggests that the world is generally out of order, and that strict honesty nowhere exists, and cannot possibly thrive; another, that a surrender or two upon a golden occasion like this may be more than compensated by the good that will follow, — that a man once secured from absolute sinking in the slough of the world's penury, may do a great deal of good by the very abundance of his means; and in a variety of ways the Scripture is fulfilled — "Behold, Satan hath desired to have you, that he may sift you as wheat." And where a man's honesty may be seen to be invulnerable, still there are other and weaker points. And it may almost always be assumed as truth, that if a man *has* a weak point, more vulnerable than the rest, there will the Devil be permitted to enter, and try him to the uttermost. But it is never permitted to take away freedom. The spiritual man can resist if he will. We are not speaking, now, of many extreme cases of obsessed and deranged humanity, where rational freedom is manifestly overborne; yet even of those it may be said, perhaps in every instance, it was not so at first, and the power that has thus been lost might still have been retained.

But again, God also sends various *worldly afflictions* in reference to that weakest point in a man's whole nature. And hence it is, that in the midst of all our troubles, the exclamation is frequently heard — "Oh, I could have endured any thing but that. If only this trial, or that, or the other, had been sent upon me, I could have submitted, and bowed my head to the chastisement. But it seems as though the very thing which of all others I could have prayed to be spared from, has at last come upon me." Ah yes, and for the very reason that here was the tender point, and the seat of the most vital disease. Here, therefore, the most effectual medicines are to be applied. God loves his children too well to leave them unattended in their greatest needs. And whether it be a fancied strength with a real weakness, or a very manifest and conscious infirmity, or something, perhaps, which we least of all expected, which was lurking within us and keeping us from the paths of heaven, — there He comes with his providences and his secret ministrations, to drag out the evil from its hiding-place, to show us our weakness, and to lead us faithfully through this terrible wilderness.

Oh, if we could only look into it and see! — if we could only see unveiled before us and around us, the dark and desolating places through which we are travelling! — if the spiritual eye could be opened to behold only for *once*, the deep and dreadful forests, where no sun of heaven casts its light into its dens and caverns; where the wild beasts of the desert have their habitation; where serpents hiss, and scorpions sting, and every unclean and hateful thing is besetting us at every step; — a wilderness more terrible and more real than any which the material world has in it; and thus to see the places we have frequented so much, and how near we have lived to the brink of fearful and horrible destruction, and what human company in the shape of spirits we have allowed to be with us; how would the sight awaken in us the prayer of the Psalmist — "Lead me in a plain path because of mine enemies; lead me to the Rock that is higher than I."

And if the spirit of this prayer really dwells in us, the Lord *will* be with us, as with his people of old, "to guide our feet into the way of peace," to feed us with manna, and comfort us by the way. And then also will be fulfilled these words of the Lord, spoken to his disciples while on earth. "Behold, I give unto you power to tread on serpents and scorpions, and over all the power of the enemy; and nothing shall by any means hurt you." (*Luke*, 10 : 19.) Here is an allusion to the same serpents and scorpions, viz., those spiritual enemies which attack us in the wilderness of life.

Such, however, is the ignorance, and in fact, the total want of faith, concerning the temptations which man experiences from the spiritual world, that we are moved to transcribe a passage from the great Seer of the church, touching the particulars of this subject.

"Evil spirits never make assault against any thing but what a man loves, and their assault is violent in proportion to the intensity of the love. Evil genii are those who assault what has relation to the affection of good, and evil spirits are those who assault what has relation to the affection of truth. As soon as ever they observe the smallest thing which a man loves, or perceive, as it were, by the smell, what is delightful and dear to him, they assault and endeavor to destroy it; consequently they assault and endeavor to destroy the whole man, since his life consists in his loves. Nothing is more pleasant to them than thus to destroy man; nor do they ever desist from their attempts even to eternity, unless they are repelled by the Lord. Such of them as are more particularly principled in malignity and cunning, insinuate themselves into man's very loves, by soothing and flattering them; thus they introduce themselves to man, and presently after such introduction they endeavor to destroy his loves, and by so doing to kill the man; and this in a thousand ways and methods altogether incomprehensible. Nor do they carry on their assaults only by reasoning against principles of goodness and truth, such assaults being of small account, (for if they be baffled a thousand times, still they persist in their attempts, since reasonings against principles of goodness and truth can never be wanting); but they pervert the principles of goodness and truth, and enkindle a sort of fire of lust and persuasion, so that the man does not know but that he is immersed in such lust and persuasion; and these they inflame at the same time with a delight which they fraudulently steal from man's delights derived from other sources: thus with the utmost cunning they infect and infest the man, and this so artfully, by leading from one thing to another, that unless the Lord were ready to administer help, the man would never know but that he is really such as their suggestions represent him. In like manner they assault the affections of truth which form man's conscience. As soon as they perceive any principle of conscience whatever, they frame to themselves an affection out of the falsities and infirmities appertaining to man, and by this affection they overshadow the light of truth, and thereby pervert it, or cause anxiety, and thus occasion pain and torment. They have, moreover, the art of keeping the thought fixed intently on one object, by which they fill it with phantasies, and then at the same time they clandestinely infuse lusts into those phantasies. Not to mention innumerable other artifices, which it is impossible to describe so as to give any just conception of them." A. C. 1820.

So writes the Seer of the New Jerusalem. Is it possible to

invent such an account? Is it the language of imagination, or guesswork? No, it is undoubtedly the sober reality of the dangers amid which we are living. "Watch and pray, lest ye enter into temptation."

There are still a few particulars suggested by the subject here opened to us, which are profitable to attend to. One is, that notwithstanding the manna which was miraculously provided for the Israelites was constantly given, and was "sweet like honey to the taste," and was even called "angel's food," significant of the blessed properties of this principle of celestial love, yet they frequently turned from it with loathing, and lusted after the food of Egypt. "We remember the fish," say they, "which we did eat in Egypt freely; the cucumbers, and the melons, and the leeks, and the onions, and the garlick; but now our soul is dried away; there is nothing at all besides this manna before our eyes." (*Num.* 11: 5, 6.) That is, in the spiritual sense, concerning those represented by them, they looked back with pleasure upon the lowest things of the natural mind, and the "flesh pots of Egypt" began to be coveted as luxuries. But the heavenly manna was held in repulsion.

Is it not just so with many a regenerating mind? Oh! the terrible delusions of mere sense and nature! It is the Devil's business, thus to insinuate a distaste for heavenly things, and before a man has got half way — nay, before he has fairly entered upon the great life before him, to tempt him in a thousand ways, — to try him with all possible hindrances, — to spread out before him the enticements of the world, and the false glories of a perverted nature, and thus to send him back again in the way of death. How often is it experienced! That old sphere, — that old company of devils and satans which we are beginning to leave, but which is not so ready to leave us! It is, in fact, a dismemberment of spiritual societies. It is a strife and a struggle between opposing principalities. In the individual it is felt frequently as pain and anguish of spirit. The natural man dies hard. If we have not felt it, we know nothing about it, and have no right to attempt to describe it. But the moments are most sweet in the intervals of the conflict; — sweeter than honey itself is the heavenly manna to the pure soul who has acquired a taste for it. It is truly "angel's food." It is the good of that truth which can alone lead us safely through the wilderness; it falls every day if we will but gather it, and is the bread of heaven whereby only we can truly live.

Another particular suggested by this subject is, that of all who came out of Egypt, scarcely any entered the land of Canaan, but died in the wilderness through which they travelled. This is not to be viewed as a mere natural consequence of the forty years' travel, for that time was not too long to conduct many to Canaan, who even started from Egypt. But the truth here involved is of an exceedingly interesting spiritual nature. *None* that desired to return to Egypt were finally conducted to the promised land. But the *children* of the Israelites, those born by the way, with Caleb and Joshua, these entered into the land of Canaan. The truth here taught is, the destructive nature of yielding to temptations, and also, that the death of the natural man must be complete. All Egypt must be thrown off before entering Canaan. This desire to return back, and this murmuring by the way, are all significant of the evils and falsities with which the natural man is filled. These must all die in the wilderness. Only the spiritual, or the natural when it is made spiritual, can enter into heavenly rest; and this is signified by the children newly born to the Israelites by the way. These find the way to Canaan, and so does every man who is newly born of the spirit. Caleb and Joshua found the way there, for they "wholly followed the Lord." (*Num.* 32: 11, 12.) In like manner, all whom they represent.

Thus particular is the Divine Word! What treasures it contains, far beneath the letter, for our instruction and guidance! And in all our temptations, let us ever remember that there is ONE who hath endured them all as our great Leader and Deliverer, — who has passed through the same "wilderness," and is thus "able to succor all who are tempted." He knows the terror and darkness of the way, for he has been there before us. And He it is who gives *us* power "to tread on serpents and scorpions, and over all the power of the enemy." It is only by repeated and long-continued temptations, that we finally achieve a permanent victory. For by every successful resistance, something is weakened in the evil organism of the natural man; the spiritual vessels are then set up in their due order and consistency; good and truth flow in from the Lord; and the whole human constitution is thus by degrees permeated by a new spirit, and built up, fair and beauteous, in the form and order of heaven.

CHAPTER VII.

FLUCTUATIONS.

"O ever-swaying, conscious soul,
  What tidal mysteries are these
That through my very being roll,
  As borne upon the heaving seas?

"From wave to wave, from land to land,
  Of this vast inner world I'm tossed,
And now on heavenly heights I stand,
  And now in dreadful deeps am lost." — *Landerf.*

It is the experience of almost every one who has really begun the new life that leads to heaven, not only to be in warfare and temptation, but to be subject more or less to certain vacillations; — to be, at times, elated and depressed; — sometimes to endure the extremes of heavenly joy and assurance, and at others, to be cast into the depths of despair. Even in natural life, such fluctuations continually occur, but in spiritual life they are of a different character. They do not come of natural things, but of spiritual things. Who hath not felt them? We need not cite the experience of the "old saints," for it is the experience of the humblest Christian. And it seems almost invariably the lot of those who reach the highest summits of holiness and joy, who catch the clearest glimpses of the heavenly beatitudes, to be most familiar with the deeps that range beneath them. At least it is so until perfect rest is obtained. These fluctuations are frequently alluded to in the Psalms, and in other portions of the Word: — in the Psalms more particularly, because throughout this wonderful composition, the temptations of the Lord, his combats with the hells, and his victories over them, are continually referred to, and by connection and analogy, the like states in man who is regenerating. Thus, in the 69th Psalm — "Save me, O God, for the waters are come in unto my soul. I sink in deep mire, where there is no standing: I am come into deep waters, where the floods overflow me. * * * Reproach hath broken my heart, and I am full of heaviness; and I looked for some to take pity, but there was none; and for comforters, but I found none:" (1, 2, 20.) referring to the terrible inundation of falsities and evils which came flowing in upon Him from the hells, and the almost despair which enters the heart on such occasions. Again, but shortly after, being delivered from this state and mounting up to another, — "My lips shall greatly rejoice when I sing unto thee; and my soul, which thou hast redeemed. My tongue also shall talk of thy righteousness all the day long; for they are confounded, for they are brought unto shame, that seek my hurt." (71: 23, 24.) Again, from the gloomy depths goes up the cry — "Hear my prayer, O Lord, and let my cry come unto thee. Hide not thy face from me in the day when I am in trouble, for my days are consumed like smoke, and my bones are burned as a hearth. My heart is smitten, and withered like grass; so that I forget to eat my bread. By reason of the voice of my groaning, my bones cleave to my skin. I am like a pelican of the wilderness; I am like an owl of the desert." (102: 1–6.) And again, in the very next Psalm — "Bless the Lord, O my soul; and all that is within me, bless his holy name. Who forgiveth all thine iniquities, who healeth all thy diseases; who redeemeth thy life from destruction, who crowneth thee with loving kindness and tender mercies; who satisfieth thy mouth with good things, so that thy youth is renewed like the eagle's." (103: 1–5.) And so we might go on through many of the Psalms, from high to low, and from low to high, in a succession so rapid and consecutive, that, read with this point particularly in view, they present to us quite a new and interesting feature. The Psalms, indeed, without this view of them, are an unsolved problem. With all their beauties and manifest proprieties, there is no sufficient reason why a soul should thus pass so often from one state to another, and from the extremes of depression to the extremes of elation, without the admission of temptations and trials from the unseen world. It is strikingly manifest in the 107th Psalm. Six times is it there said that the people cried unto the Lord from the depths of humiliation and trouble, and as many times, that He "led them forth by the right way" — that He "brought them out of darkness and the shadow of death," and "out of all their distresses." And in a beautiful correspondence taken from a life upon the sea — "They mount up to the heaven, they go down again to the depths; their soul is melted because of trouble." Then "He maketh the storm a calm, so that the waves thereof are still," and with gladness and quietness bringeth them to the desired haven.

These things, in their spiritual import, all relate to the fluctuations experienced in the regenerating life. Human life is often compared to a voyage at sea, but the comparison becomes all the more interesting when seen in the light of genuine correspondence in application to our *spiritual* progress.

These fluctuations are also what is referred to in the account of the Flood in the time of Noah. The flood here spoken of was an inundation of spiritual waters — falsities and evils from the unseen world. And we read, according to the truest translation, that "the waters returned from off the earth [that is, from the earth of the natural mind] *in going and returning*." (*Gen.* 8 : 3.) That is, by a continual fluctuation between truth and falsity. The nature of the fluctuation, however, can only be understood by the nature of the temptation. If the temptation is celestial, the fluctuation is chiefly between good and evil; if it is spiritual, it is between truth and falsity. But inasmuch as the states of all, in the present condition of the world, are more or less mixed, that is to say, not celestial nor spiritual entirely, but a mixed mass of good and evil, truth and falsity, pertaining to the world as we now find it, so these fluctuations partake of a like varied and indeterminate character. And who hath not experienced them? What Christian — what humble and earnest-seeking disciple of the Lord, hath not, more than once, been made the subject of the like vacilla tions? A man, for example, starts out upon the course of a new life, is convicted of his evils, repents of them, and truly commences the regenerate work. For a time he does well. He may be always doing well, but it is not always so apparent to him. He acquires new truth, realizes more deeply the divine Word of the Lord; eternity, with all its hopes, and fears, and infinite realities, becomes to him a matter of more than mere speculation; he is alive to spiritual conviction, is thoroughly aroused, the old scales have fallen from his eyes, and he sees, oh, what wonders, and glories, and prospects before him! Shame and humiliation seize upon him for his past life; his understanding is stimulated by the new spirit, his affections touched, and he resolves henceforth to pursue the path which leads to heaven. But how little he yet knows of the "great and terrible wilderness" through which he is to travel! Yet still he is elated, and it is of the mercy of God that he should be. He has made some successful resistance, and has received some delights of the new life he has commenced. But they are mostly, perhaps, delights of the understanding; for the understanding can be elevated into the very light of heaven, and partake somewhat of its joys, while the will is yet in the gall of bitterness and the bond of iniquity. But now it is that he is greatly refreshed and inspirited. He is mortified that he never saw so much before. He *feels* himself a new man, in a dear and beautiful sense of the word. He says, perhaps, with David — "O God, my heart is fixed; I will sing and give praise, even with my glory." But this very light into which he is now elevated, by and by reveals new evils in him; he sees for the first time what he never could have believed before, that there are depths in his soul which he had never dreamt of; that his spiritual nature is a thing not to be trifled with; that it is more heavenly, and more devilish, than any human moralities or earthly philosophies had ever presented to him; that the very light of eternity which has broken into his poor soul, and the holiness of angel visions, and of Him who is himself the very Soul and Centre of Perfection, in all his majesty and glory,—that all this reveals to him such a contrast in his own sin-deformed and polluted character, that he turns from the contemplation with a sense somewhat of discouragement. He is oppressed and humiliated. There occurs to him, perhaps, the language of the patriarch:—"I have heard of thee by the hearing of the ear, but now mine eye seeth thee; wherefore I abhor myself, and repent in dust and ashes." (*Job*, 42: 5, 6.) Then it is that the spirits of evil are let in upon him to *stir up* his evil. He is now in a condition to profit by their aid. They can show him what he could not see himself. But, "not a hair of his head" will the great Father suffer them to injure; the angels of mercy stand ever by him to minister to him in this most necessary trial. But he falls—and oh, how low!—from his high ecstatic state—sinks away into discouragement and misery, and is overwhelmed with evil! Perhaps goes venting his ill humor upon his companions around him; perhaps is somewhat ashamed that he ever made so fully the *profession* of religion; perhaps, in fine, is throroughly miserable,—a scorn in his own eyes, and a reproach with his acquaintance. "I looked for comforters, and found none."

It is a true picture; it is this which is presented all through the Psalms, and in many other portions of the Word. These are the fiery trials that purge men's souls. We pine in secret over a hidden grief that we dare not reveal to any fellow mortal, and we go, perhaps, more penitently than ever, to Him who hath bidden us confess to Him, and lay our burden at his feet. Thus it is that we gain strength and encouragement for renewed efforts. We rise by the light of the same Sun with which we fell, and by the same reverse steps, till gradually again the glory-smitten summits appear to our eyes, we are uplifted into heavenly ethers, and feel the play of warmer and more joyful affections. "Out of the *depths*" we cried unto the Lord, for it was there alone that we could be *made* to cry. Such is the Divine Providence in all such cases. It is only through such vicissitudes that we gain at last the heavenly rest. At each wave of the advancing process we gain somewhat upon the previous state; "we sink to rise to higher heights," are humiliated to be exalted.

One truth in this experience it is of the utmost importance to know. Always, in temptations, when the moments of *despair* come, then it is that the Lord is nearest. For it is this very sense and realization of our own evils that *causes* the despair. And this is caused by an influx of the Divine Goodness and Truth. We fall, at such times, into the extreme of conviction. By the light of truth and the operations of the Holy Spirit, our sins have become intolerable. The work has penetrated more to the interiors. Then it is that we feel most miserable of all. But then it is that the Lord is nearest. Even so it was with Christ. It was the *last* temptation, on the cross, that caused Him to cry out — "My God, my God, why hast thou forsaken me?" The reason was, it was the *inmost* and the severest of all, as touching the very vitals of the humanity itself. But so far from being forsaken of God at that time, the unition of the Divine with the Human was then about being completed. So also it was in Gethsemane; but the face of a strengthening angel then became present at the scene; and so it is with every man. It is in these most trying and crushing scenes that the power of sin is most effectually broken with us. The old life is expiring amid groans and pains. But we must not deceive ourselves in this matter; we must not think that because we suffer so much, that this is always an evidence of the death of self. The truth is, it is the life of self that suffers. Were there not so much of the old life remaining, we should not so feel the dying. It is the throbbing heart-strings and nervous susceptibility of the "old man" that now shrinks from the separating process. When perfect death is effected, there is no more pain, nor sorrow, nor anguish.

But I am aware that I am describing an experience that will not be appreciated by many a nominal Christian; they will say that *they* have never experienced any thing so hard; and it may be that they will never need to. But O God, how many do! It is not for all to pass through these heaviest trials. The trials are great in proportion to the evils in the hereditary to be exterminated, and the height of angelic accomplishment to be attained. Some that do not go so high, do not suffer so much. But here another truth should be known. There are some even of those who finally come into heaven and enjoy exalted stations there, who are yet permitted to pass through all this life, not much disturbed or troubled by its fluctuating fortunes. They are comparatively exempted from the common lot of necessary trial. The reason is, many times, that they are so stated and circumstanced in this world that they cannot, in temptations, be sufficiently protected by angels. They would sink under them. Therefore they are spared till their entrance into another life. There they can be properly defended, and there they must drink their cup of the common suffering. (A. C. 270.) There is no heavenly perfectness without it, and whether here or there, there is only one thing to do when it comes; welcome it and drink it, saying — "Not my will, but thine, O God, be done!"

CHAPTER VIII.

THE WINDING WAY.

"We see the end, the house of God,
But not the path to that abode;
For God, in ways they have not known,
Will lead his own."

We not only have fluctuations of state — ups and downs of spiritual experience, but irregularity in the course of natural life. There is probably no one characteristic of human life more marked and observed, than its frequent *labyrinthic* course through every possible variety of experience, from change to change, in the shifting fortunes of the world. What a picture or map of one life might be drawn, if it could only be seen in all its bearings, as it has reference to the states of the soul! For let us not think that this mere surface experience — this seeming maze without a plan, has no complete and systematic connection with our inner life, for it must have; it is, either individually or collectively, or both, an outbirth from it and a ministration to it. It is necessarily so, from the sure operation of the law of correspondence between all things inward and all things outward. The whole material world is the result and ultimate of the Divine creative Essence through the spiritual world. Spiritual causes and material effects, — this is the law of the universe. And so in human society. Should we have all this external, in the way and fashion which we do have it, were it not for the internal? Has not confusion proceeded from interiors to exteriors, and not *vice versa?* And order also? and beauty? What were the surface without the soul? Here, then, we find ourselves fixed in a system of divine and inevitable, but not arbitrary, appointment. Do we ask the reason for the crooked way? Behold it in the deviations from the straight and narrow path of the soul. We are told, and not without reason, that ways actually appear in the spiritual world, according to the thoughts and intentions of the mind; for the spiritual projections of a multitude of minds there take shape and way before them; and a spirit is known as to his quality by the path he there walks in, or those which he most loves to frequent. Hence it is that to travel in the way, and to keep in the right way, are so frequently spoken of in the Word. Hence also the "broad way" and the "narrow way," which derive a more tremendous significance from the throngs of travellers seen in the precincts of the world beyond. It is the same in this world, when observed by the invisible witnesses. And it may therefore rationally be said, that all the ways and paths in which the multitude of the men of this world are travelling, are as distinctly seen, in the light of heaven which shines around every man, as though they were mapped out on the great chart of the world; and they are actually journeying, some in one way and some in another, to that eternal home of the soul which is every man's free choice and destiny.

But it is because of the *wilderness of sin* through which we travel, that the paths of our life are so crooked, both in a spiritual and in a natural sense. Thus it was with the forty years' journey of the Israelites. It is most significantly said of them — "And it came to pass when Pharaoh had let the people go, that God led them not through the way of the land of the Philistines, although that was near; for God said, Lest peradventure the people repent when they see war, and they return to Egypt: but God led the people about through the way of the wilderness of the Red Sea. (*Exod.* 13: 17, 18.) Reference is here made to those spiritual combats which all who make this journey are called to experience, and which, if they are led too hastily, by mere truth in the understanding, without sufficient experience in the will, they will neither be prepared nor able to endure the conflicts which will come upon them, and will manifest a disposition to repent and turn back to Egypt; that is, to the delights of the natural man. Therefore, God leads them about a more circuitous way through the wilderness of the Red Sea; — spiritually typical of those long-abiding evils and falsities which lie in the region of the road to heaven. And what a route it was which these ever-memorable people travelled! It has sometimes appeared to me, that a true and impressive idea of our spiritual pilgrimage cannot in any way be obtained without this external, natural correspondence of it. For so long as we have senses, and the things of the spirit *will* take form, how can it be otherwise than that some correct ultimate or imagery shall be found absolutely necessary to present the great reality in all its fulness and power? Herein is one great value of the correspondential style. Herein is the philosophy of all picturing and symbolism. We are forever children. We need the picture-books of the soul — the images of eternity. In God's Word we have them.

There is nothing so significant in all history as this most wonderful, miraculous, and imposing chart of the Israelitish journey. And let it ever be remembered by those who are inclined to doubt it, that the spiritual sense which is discoverable in this history is not the same in character which may be found in any other history. In *all* history there is indeed an interior meaning — a spiritual cause for its natural existence; for it is but the outbirth of spiritual transactions. But in the case of the Israelites, it is somewhat different. Their affairs were not left to the ordinary flow of natural occurrence, but were expressly ordered, many times, by a supernatural power, and varied from the course which they otherwise would have taken, for the *sake* of the interior sense. Had they not been, the Scripture of their history would not be capable of that systematic and particular internal meaning which is now evolved from them. This is just the difference between their history and common history. We make this remark once for all, for a better understanding of our repeated allusions. The history of the Israelites is thus, in a wonderful manner, the history of the human heart. We shall ever find in it, the more we study it, something new and instructive of our own soul-experience, and may forever take warning of their troubles. How much is contained, for instance, even in the *length* and *time* of their journey! It was but about three hundred miles, straight across, from Egypt to the Promised Land. And it might have been travelled in a few weeks at most, on foot; but they made of it some thousand or fifteen hundred miles; and by tarryings, difficulties, and rebellions by the way, consumed about forty years in the journey.

So it is in the regenerating life. But it should be remarked here, that there is no absolute necessity for all this trouble. There is an impression with many, that the regenerating life is of *necessity* a hard, long, up-hill work. It *is* more or less so, on account of the depth and extent of hereditary evil. But it need not be so much so. It is only our wilful sins and rebellions that make it the hard, intractable thing that it is. The work of regeneration might be more felicitous and easy. How many, through their unfaithfulness, have been many years in gaining that for which, in a more orderly procedure, and by submission and obedience, a much shorter time would have been sufficient! How much ground may a man lose in the divine life by *one* act of unfaithfulness or transgression!

And as to the *variety* of the life thus experienced, this also is foreshadowed in the journey of the Israelites. How often, for example, does it occur to us, that we find ourselves in places or states, precisely such as they were wont to pass through and encamp in, and how often is the course of our life interrupted by some new trial or trouble analogous to the experience of this mystical journey! Thus, sometimes they came into *straits* and *troublesome* ways, as at Pihahiroth (*Exod.* 14: 2, 3, 10); sometimes into *large and ample room*, as at the plains of Moab; sometimes to places of *hunger and thirst*, as at Rephidim and

Kadesh (*Exod.* 17 ; *Num.* 20 : 1, 2, 11); sometimes to places of *refreshing*, as at Elim and Béer (*Exod.* 15 : 27 ; *Num.* 21 : 16); sometimes where they had *wars*, as at Rephidim and Edrei (*Exod.* 17 ; *Num.* 21 : 33); sometimes where they had *rest*, as at Mount Sinai ; sometimes they went *right forward*, as from Sinai to Kadesh ; sometimes they *turned backward*, as from Kadesh to the Red Sea ; sometimes they came to *mountains*, sometimes to *valleys*, sometimes to places of *bitterness*, as Marah (*Exod.* 15 : 23); sometimes of *sweetness*, as Mithka.* And thus it is in the regenerating life. We pass through every variety of experience, and at the end of each state, something is completed in the character of the soul which *could not have been done* on the straight road to that which was near ; that is, in a hasty or less thorough manner. There are no short cuts — no avoiding of any of the ground to be gone over ; we must travel the whole distance which our evils and imperfections have made necessary ; and thus it is that we are to "remember all the way which the Lord our God leads us these forty years in the wilderness, to humble us, and to prove us, and to know what is in the heart, to prove us, and do us good in the end." (*Deut.* 8 : 2, 16.)

But the most singular turn in all this wonderful journey is that which the Israelites took from Kadesh-Barnea, near the South-western border of Canaan, out towards Eziongaber, on the shore of the Red Sea. After travelling perhaps five hundred or a thousand miles, in many irregularities, and arriving within about one hundred from Canaan, near the very borders of the promised land, they then take a turn directly out and down from their main course, coming again into the wilderness, by the way of the Red Sea. And then, after much wandering and crossing, they have to travel all that distance back again, coming to the same, or nearly the same, place from which they turned out. There are several different maps of this journey, none of which are probably correct in all points, but they all,

* See a note in A. Clarke's Commentary, at end of *Num.* 33.

as made out from the Scripture history, represent this turning as among the most conspicuous and wonderful of the whole travel. What, now, does it mean? Whence this sudden and retrograde movement for so long and wearisome a distance, after nearing the very precincts of the promised land, and the necessity of going over so much of the same, or nearly the same, ground again? We may be sure that the Divine Providence is most instructive here, and that it is not without a deep significance in the course of the regenerate life.

Be it observed, then, that the place of this turn-out, called Kadesh, and sometimes Kadesh-Barnea, the latter term signifying the *wandering son*, was distinguished for *contentions about truths*. It is thus spoken of in Ezekiel, where the borders of the Holy Land are described. — "And the South side, Southward, from Tamar even to the waters of strife in Kadesh." (47 : 19.) It was at Kadesh also where Moses struck the Rock, as before in Horeb, from which came forth waters which were called *Meribah*, by reason of the contention and strife there. (*Num.* 20 : 1–11.) In like manner it was at Kadesh that the spies were sent forth to the land of Canaan, and to which they returned, and where they murmured and made a strife, not being willing to enter the land. Their story was that it was a land flowing with milk and honey, nevertheless the people were strong who dwelt there, that the cities were walled and very great, and what frightened them more than any thing else was, they saw the children of Anak there. (*Num.* 13 : 27–29.) So gigantic and formidable did all this appear, that they were discouraged from entering into it; and for all their murmurings they were commanded by the Lord to turn back into the wilderness by the way of the Red Sea. (*Num.* 14 : 25.) By this is represented the exceeding greatness of the evils and falsities of the natural mind, which, at certain stages of the regenerate life, appear so great and formidable, that the spiritual principle is discouraged and falls backward, not having fortitude to go on any further. And this, frequently, is because *truths* have the predominance,— because truths are not sufficiently united to their kindred goods. By the aid of such truth, however, we are frequently enabled to *see* our evils more fully and clearly, and they frequently rise up before us in all the gigantic proportions of the Anakims of old. "A people great and tall — who can stand before the children of Anak?" (*Deut.* 9: 2.)

Now, it was at this place — at Kadesh-Barnea, that the children of Israel turned out from their track so strangely, and took almost a direct downward course, for a long distance, coming again into the wilderness by the way of the Red Sea. What does it signify, but that, in our onward spiritual course, next to absolute sinning and profanation, there is no danger so great as the danger of going too fast? — not too fast if it is really a progress in goodness, but too fast in one direction — in the direction of mere truth. This, in fact, is that way of the Philistines which is *near*, or which is first and most easily arrived at; Kadesh-Barnea was *situated* near the land of the Philistines; the Divine Providence had assigned them this locality for the sake of the interior sense; and the Philistines, we may all know, signify faith separate from charity, or mere truth in the understanding without good in the will. That such is the signification is evident from the character given to the Philistines wherever they are spoken of in the Word. Thus in Jeremiah, the Prophet is directed to speak against the Philistines, of the waters that rise up out of the North, an overflowing flood, which should destroy the land, the city, and all that dwell therein. (47: 1, 2.) That is, a flood of falsity which should destroy all truth and good. It is also apparent from the *wars* which the sons of Israel had so frequently with the Philistines, and the subjugation of the former by the latter. They are also called the "uncircumcised" and unclean.

But now, this is not only true of the people originally spoken of thus historically, but of every man, when he comes into the commencement of the regenerate life. There is a spiritual Philistea which is always nearest. It is comparatively a short cut from the Egypt of the natural mind to mere truth in the understanding. And many, on looking out upon the journey before them, would be strongly tempted to go that way. Who would think of going the other way — the long, fatiguing, circuitous route which the Israelites took? But it becomes a necessary route to nearly all who would reach the heavenly state. The nearest is always attended with most danger. It is comparatively easy to furnish the understanding with truth. There is a certain sublimity connected with spiritual truths, a feeling of elation and superiority, which is refreshing to indulge in, and which makes even controversy a matter of chief delight. The good of charity is very likely to be overlooked in a warfare and division about truths. These are our spiritual Philistines, in the Kadesh-Barnea of the soul. Hence it was that when the Israelites arrived here, they were brought into grievous temptations, fell into strife and contention among themselves, and had to turn directly out and down from their course to a far-off region by the Red Sea!

Thus it is ever with man. It is especially so with those who are most enlightened in spiritual things, and who will compose that more glorious church of the future, which will be known as the "New Jerusalem." I speak not here of any sectarian or ecclesiastical establishments, but of all those, wherever they may be, who will see the light which is soon to dawn more fully upon the world, and who will come into distinct spiritual associations. The people of this church will be more exposed to spiritual temptations, from the very plane of life and thought they will be in. And by the aid of so much truth, and so many fine discriminations, they will be able to *see* the promised land, as it was seen by the spies, and almost entered upon by the Israelites at Kadesh. The spiritual understanding can do a great deal in this matter. But oh! how much harder it is to practise! — to be fully true to our own ideal! And what a danger there is of mistaking our own ideal for our own state!

And now let us note another remarkable fact in this experience of the Israelites. It is singularly true in reference to their journey, that nearly the whole of the forty years was consumed after they had arrived at Kadesh-Barnea, on the very borders of the promised land. Thus it is written — "And the space in which we came from Kadesh-Barnea, until we were come over the brook Zered, was *thirty and eight* years; until all the generations of the men of war were wasted out from among the host, as the Lord sware unto them." (*Deut.* 2 : 14.) This, then, is certainly a most important period in the regenerating life. From the time the spies were sent forth, that is, from the time when we begin to see evils in our unrenewed nature with a truly spiritual eye, and to be concerned about them, to the time when we are ready to go bravely on and enter into Canaan, is within two or three years of the whole time of the journey! During all this time, or through all this state, which may be longer or shorter with different individuals, we are really beating about in the wilderness, making little or no progress in a direct line; on the contrary, experiencing temporary and apparent retrogressions, going back and forth, from which we only recover by a multitude of temptations, difficulties, and trials! "How oft did they provoke Him in the wilderness, and grieve Him in the desert! Yea, they *turned back* and tempted God, and limited the Holy One of Israel." (*Psalm*, 78: 40, 41.) And yet the truth is, these seasons when we *appear to ourselves* to retrograde are frequently seasons of progression — disorderly progression; they are necessary to the strengthening of the good we have acquired, to the confirming and enlivening of truths. The *danger* is in going too fast; we get puffed up with certain attainments which lie truly more in the understanding than in the will; we begin to think we are growing better, and it may be that we are; but then it is that we suddenly find ourselves turned back — humiliated, even from Kadesh to the border of the Red Sea; — and from thence into many irregularities of temper, disposition, and conduct, in the vast, untrodden wilderness of the yet uncultivated soul.

CHAPTER IX.

THE UNKNOWN PATHS.

"For God unfolds by slow degrees
The purport of his deep decrees,
Sheds every hour a clearer light
In aid of our defective sight,
And spreads at length before the soul,
A beautiful and perfect whole,
Which busy man's inventive brain
Toils to anticipate in vain." — *Cowper.*

THE paths of our life are not only *winding* and *labyrinthic*, both in the natural and the spiritual sense, but they are most *unexpected*, and *furthest from our thoughts*. We find ourselves in situations, frequently, which we never could have dreamed of previously, and which we shrink from with a sense of dread and of utter unfitness. This also is of the Divine Providence, which is the best acquainted with the state of every one. It should ever be remembered that the *whole* of Providence with us has reference to eternity;— to that state of life which we can attain to in this world, which is the ground or basis of our immortal life; — and to that *use* also which we can be best fitted to perform; — in short, to that highest possible station of life, usefulness, and happiness, which we can be brought to in the eternal world.

It is for this purpose that the spiritually blind are led about and instructed, and brought into ways and paths which they knew not, and that the whole of this life is frequently a wonder and a mystery to us. Who hath not reflected on it? To a contemplative mind it is perhaps the great subject of the most interior thought. And even with the frivolous and thoughtless, there are times when the thick coverings of sense and nature seem broken through, — when thoughts arise and feelings exist as to all the solemnity and significance of life. What is it — they say to themselves — that has brought me here? — that has made me who I am, and what I am? And even as Isaac, who went out into the field towards evening to meditate, evening signifying an obscure state of the mind, so these souls who for the most part are so thoroughly immersed in the world, have their evening hours of calmer and deeper meditation. "Oh! what is life? and what is human destiny? and what is all this toil and trouble for?" And "who will show us any good?" These are questions which are not easily put off, nor are they easily answered except from a standpoint of divine, interior truth. Only eternity can answer these questions. In the light only of that great and incomprehensible life which we must all live, and which cannot in one of its least issues be trusted to us, but to Him only who is infinite and eternal himself, can this problem be fully solved, and this mystery enlightened. Here the blindness is struck from our eyes. We do not, indeed, see the ways *in* which we are led, nor, specifically, the end *to* which we are led; but we know that it is a good end, nay, the best end; and that every path in which we are so providentially conducted, is a path either direct or circuitous, to the nearest attainment of that divine good.

Let us remember that we are journeying through a wilderness. There are many things that make it so, but primarily, only one. That is, Sin. We should not be so blinded were it not for our evils. The way would be plain before us, and the paths pleasant. But by the Fall of man from his innocent state, he has closed up those spiritual perceptions which most properly belong to him, and which, in a true state, would be his distinguishing characteristic; so that he cannot know so well what is his destiny, nor can he be so easily led into it. Hence we are often anxious about many things, which, if we could truly see, form no direct part of the doings of God with us here, and are only permitted us as a means of gratifying our perverse inclinations for awhile, and which we cannot be turned from without violence offered to our freedom. The Lord is kind to us even in our waywardness. He can do *nothing* for us in a state of non-freedom; for what we might be forced to in such a state, would not abide when the unnatural force was withdrawn. And He must keep us *forever* free, nor will it do to enlighten our blindness too suddenly. For, in a state of evil, if by a supernatural light which might easily enough be given, we could be made to see the end to which the Lord was conducting us, we should many times quarrel with it, and turn from it with loathing and horror. Our own evils would not appreciate the good held out to us, and we should strive all the more hardly against the Divine Providence. This would be particularly the case with such merely natural men as doated on riches and honors, and from whom it might be necessary, for their spiritual good, to strip them away. Therefore we are led blindly. And gently — oh, how tenderly, we are conducted over the rough places, and through the winding ways of this maze of human life, till by and by, if we are capable of being brought so far on in this life, He makes darkness light before us, and crooked things straight.

It should be observed here, that it is a distinct *law* of the Divine Providence, that we should not see it beforehand, but that we should look back and see it. If we could see it before, as already remarked, we should be constantly interfering with our own wills against it. But still, that we may know there is a Providence, we are permitted to look back and see it, and oh, how wonderfully! Perhaps there is not a religious, contemplative person living, who cannot look back upon his past life, and see some one or many instances where the guiding hand of the Lord is very apparent to his spiritual mind, and in cases perhaps where at the time it looked dark and adverse to him. He would have grasped the seeming good if he could have grasped it. He planned for it wisely, and worked diligently. But another hand unknown to him was in the work, and he was not permitted to seize the prize. By and by he begins himself to see that it would not have been good for him; he is thankful to heaven that it did not so occur; but how much higher than any mere earthly good, and how much further extending, is the Divine Providence in all such leadings!

It cannot be too deeply impressed upon the mind, that there is not even any *earthly* good granted for its own sake alone, but that the whole dispensation, whether of riches, or honor, or health, or sickness, or poverty, or disgrace, has an inevitable connection with, and reference to, the spiritual and final state of the subject of it. It must be so, differently as the men of the world may calculate. It is so from the very intimate connection of all spiritual and all natural things in the constitution and course of the universe. It is not an arbitrary, but a philosophical connection; although there are many personal and invisible agencies employed in effecting these dispensations of the Infinite, and our own freedom is largely concerned in the whole of it.

The contemplation of this one truth will solve a thousand problems concerning our earthly life; for it is not the truth alone, and the good which we receive, but the earthly circumstances which are the means of leading us to that truth and good, which form an interesting and highly important part of the Divine dealings towards us. The spiritual destitution into which the world is brought has created a great deal of bodily destitution, and our natural evils are the outbirths and consequences of our spiritual evils. Hence the wilderness of life is so dense and dark, not only as it regards spiritual truth and good, but in reference to those material conditions and seemingly untoward circumstances in which we are immersed in our struggles after a temporary subsistence. But the truth is, in every one of those conditions there is a providence no less direct and manifest in reference to eternal ends, than in the more immediate spiritual appliances of good and truth to the heart. It is in fact frequently *more* manifest, how we are led to divine and spiritual things from what we call worldly circumstances, than it is frequently with the more direct applications of truth to the mind. For in the one case the *means* are visible, in the other, invisible. Worldly conditions are indeed many times a hindrance to *direct* spiritual culture, because we are not yet capable of such direct leading; because there are many things yet to be adjusted in order to it; but who can doubt that they have *invariably* a good tendency, and the most intimate connection with spiritual states? Frequently this truth is very apparent. In cases of adversity and calamity, for instance.

"It sometimes happens," says a good observer of these changes, "that in the course of Divine Providence, when the mind of man, in the commencement of his regeneration, begins to be open to eternal views, his worldly supports are taken from him, sometimes gradually, sometimes suddenly, and with apparent violence, that he may learn to look upwards, and to find his support in the Lord alone; to disentangle his affections from the world, and to break all their bonds and affinities. This, at first, proves a severe trial to the new convert, who will often shrink during his passage through the wilderness, and will look back with regret to the sensual delights of Egyptian bondage. During this state, were the days of his worldly prosperity to return, his worldly affections, which are to be subdued, would return with them; he is therefore kept in straitness of various kinds. Still, worldly means are allowed for necessities, in various unexpected forms; a stranger hand will sometimes, like the raven, bring him food; he will at times discover the Divine Providence that brings him manna from heaven for his mental support, which he will loathe at times, and sigh for quails. When he falls into company with worldly minds, he is sometimes shocked and disappointed, and sometimes won over to his former delights; but in proportion as his spiritual mind is strengthened by privations, outward trials, and inward temptations, he blends with the world with less danger, can treat its levities and amusements which are not criminal, as children's play, reserving to himself his hidden satisfactions, which he feeds on, and ventures to impart only at prudent intervals. A ray of worldly prosperity which would before have dimmed the light of his spiritual mind, and darkened its views, may now serve to make them more luminous, by removing the shade of worldly cares and anxieties, from which the freed spirit, disencumbered, takes a wider range; the elevated affections are at length instinctively taught, as is fabled of the bird of paradise, to live on the wing; there is now no danger of their settling on earth. The divine favors, in the spiritual or natural form, are like grapes and figs from the promised land, and the triumphs of the humble regenerate mind are those of gratitude and tears." *

Such are some of the mystic paths through which we are led, and their nature and tendency. But there is only one thing, perhaps, which could *thoroughly* and *fully* convince us of this amazing and particular providence of the Lord. That is a *sight* of our past life, — the ways that we really *have* been in, — the paths we *have* travelled, — and the thousand places where was made necessary the interference of the Divine hand, to keep us from that course and that danger, which, if left to ourselves, would long ago have whelmed us in destruction. Could that map of our past life be spread out before us, so that we could see just how we have been guided, how blind we were in ourselves, and what stops, and what passes, what precipices, and what fearful heights and depths we have been upon and dwelt in through all that wilderness, then we should confess, with an overwhelming power, to the truth of the Divine Providence.

And now, it is according to all our best reason, and to the best revelations on this subject, that we *shall*, after death, be favored with that sight. We shall see and own the Divine

---

* *Arbouin's* "Dissertations on the Regenerate Life."

guidance. There is a case described by Swedenborg in the following language.

"There was a certain one who had confirmed himself in this, that nothing was of the Divine Providence, but that all things were of human prudence, and also from fortune and chance. When he came into the other life, he continued there his former life as all are wont to do; he inquired out and also imbibed all things, even magical artifices, which he supposed might be serviceable to him, and by which he might provide for himself, that of himself he might find satisfaction. He was amongst the evil, subtle spirits. Afterwards the same spirit was reduced to the state of his infancy; and it was shown by the Lord to the angels, what his quality was at that time, and also then what was the quality of his future life, which was foreseen, and that each of the things of his life had been under the Lord's guidance, and that otherwise he would have plunged himself into the most grievous hell, if there had been even the least cessation of the continual providence of the Lord. He was also asked whether he ever thought about eternal life; he said that he did not believe it, and that he had rejected every thing of that sort, by reason that he saw so much confusion, that the righteous suffered, and the wicked gloried, with other things of a similar kind. And he was in the utmost amazement when he perceived that he lived after death." (A. C. 6484.)

Such, undoubtedly, will be the surprise of many a one. We have not that faith in the future life that we might have, and we little reflect upon the leadings of Providence in reference to it. But our eternity is at stake. It depends upon us how we will form and fashion that eternity. And there is one thing to be done, if we would be led through this wilderness world aright. Give up our own will! Make that sacrifice, at any cost, for the Lord cannot lead a self-willed soul beside the still waters and in the paths of righteousness to heaven. But He leadeth those who will be led by Him. This is not only religious truth, but it is truth such as all may see. There is a great deal of cant expended upon this subject, but we need take no views but those which are sanctioned by the most practical and thorough philosophy. We may rest assured that it is the simplest and sublimest of all wisdom to surrender *every thing* at His discretion ;— to feel ourselves that we have *no* will but that which is given us from Him, and which is discoverable in all our circumstances, and in every condition in which we may be brought — to do the present thing well, and trust to Him for the results. O, eternity ! eternity ! How little are all the fleeting things of time, put in such a comparison as this ! Be willing to *die* — to be *flayed alive* — or to drag out the most miserable existence that can be inflicted upon man, if so be the Divine Will — if it be necessary to exalt us in the heavenly state. And let us remember that some of the best souls are tried in this way, to make them still more perfect. And many escape, because it is foreseen that such trial would be useless. There are many who are so thoroughly natural, so in love with self and the world, that such sufferings, instead of humbling and softening them, would only make them more irritable and rebellious. The same fire that softens the wax, hardens the brick. Therefore they are treated in another way, — are permitted to have wealth, and honors, and aggrandizement, here in the world, to keep them in that best state, which may only be the lowest natural, which they are capable of attaining. Like fretful and uneasy children, they are allowed these playthings to keep them still. But there are others who can not only endure, but will be highly exalted and spiritualized by sufferings. Our Lord himself was only perfected in his natural humanity by means of suffering ; and if there *is* a capacity in any one which cannot be improved and brought out but by these severer methods, then the Divine Mercy will not shrink from the work, and the Divine Wisdom has all means at command, to carry it forward to its utmost completion. And the sooner we surrender the better. We delay the work, and protract the suffering, many times, by this resistance on our part. It is the *will* that the Lord is after. Give him that. Place your right hand in his, for Him to lead you as a little child, and the suffering will be diminished a thousand-fold, nay, perhaps brought to a speedy termination; for it is the whole object of it to subdue and break down this evil life of nature, and make that spiritual which before was only natural; or rather, to make it spiritual-natural, — to bring the whole man in conformity to divine order, and thus to confer upon us an eternal blessing. When this is accomplished, there is no further need of any suffering or conflict. The way is dark, and long too, frequently, because our wills are evil. *We can shorten it immensely by immediate surrender.* The paths are devious and perplexing because we are yet in the wilderness. But as we perfect and regenerate, and attain more to the state of the angels, the paths will not appear so dubious and uncertain, but become manifestly the plain way of the Father's will. This is clearly taught in these words of the Lord. "I will make darkness light before thee, and crooked things straight." Our whole mind will be illuminated by the Divine Truth, and the crooked, zigzag road of the evil of ignorance will give place to that which leads straightway to the heavenly city. Thus it is written of the journey of the Israelites. "They wandered in the wilderness in a solitary way; they found no city to dwell in. Hungry and thirsty, their soul fainted in them. Then they cried unto the Lord in their trouble, and He delivered them out of their distresses. And He led them forth by the right way, that they might go to a city of habitation. Oh! that men would praise the Lord for his goodness, and for his wonderful works to the children of men." (*Psalm*, 107: 4–8.)

Such, then, is the issue of the journey. It is a mystical, spiritual journey, which every pilgrim to the heavenly Canaan is taking, and countless foes and hindrances exist by the way. The prayer should ever be with the Psalmist; — "Lead me in a plain path, because of mine enemies," — invisible, spiritual enemies, direst foes to the soul's peace.

How great will be the surprise, when we stand upon the hills and plains of the immortal country, to look back with our fellow travellers, and see how variously we have been led! One has come up through a world of tribulation, amid temptations and anguish enough to have almost sunk him in despair; another, through scenes of turmoil and difficulty, and bodily discomforts all his life long; another, through spiritual trials which have almost broken his nature, nay, quite broken the perverted nature of his own unregenerate heart; another, through more prosperous circumstances, so far as the earth-life is concerned, but has not, perhaps, attained so high a place in the celestial kingdom; another, by the very means of his wealth, by the *good* he has done with it, has come to inherit those riches which are imperishable and ever-increasing; and all — all conducted through paths of mystery and ways unknown to them, till the blindness has clearly gone from their eyes, and the light of eternity shines over all the past, and covers them with glory, and assures them for eternal ages to come. Well — pray God that it may be so. And what, now, are all the sufferings of time? What are all our repinings and murmurings by the way? The Lord has numbered all our sorrows, and counted every tear, and precious, far more precious than the heaps of gold which others have been suffered to accumulate, He has enriched our spiritual nature with every necessary good, and there, in the land of eternity, spread a heaven of glory and magnificence around us. We shall there look back upon this whole track of time, and see that there was no other path through which we could have been so safely led. And through that — winding and circuitous, and dark and uncertain and painful as it was, the poor blind man was led, and saved from a thousand pitfalls by Him only who could see. At last the prayer — "Lord, that I may receive my sight:" — and lo! He makes darkness light before us, and crooked things straight. Now we may progress forever and ever, with an assured and enlightened footstep. For we have but begun the journey here. We have passed through the wilderness. We have entered the heavenly Canaan; and there still, but not in conflict, not in darkness, the Lord is ever with us to conduct us through the heavenly mansions, and abroad through the vast stretching fields and glories of eternity, forever perfecting, forever increasing in love, and purity, and happiness, — pursuing still those paths of immortality which lead forever upward, to holier visions and diviner joys.

CHAPTER X.

VIEW FROM MOUNT PISGAH.

"On Pisgah's height the aged prophet stood,
And viewed the extended scene. Fair Canaan's land,
Judah and Gilead, to the utmost sea,
Outstretching unto Zoar, in richness and
In beauty filled the eye, but not to him
Was promise of the blessing. He should see,
But not inherit. So to man, proud man,
Perched high upon an eminence of faith,
Gleaming afar in visioned intellect,
Ray out the unspoken glories; rapt he stands,
Admires, exults, and spies the heaven beyond,
Then sinks into himself, and weaves his shroud
For blindness and for death." —*Landerf.*

THERE is one elevation of so peculiar a character in our regenerate experience, as to demand particular attention. It is an elevation of a purely mental nature, and so entrancing and glorious, and withal so deceptive, that we must not fail to comprehend it thoroughly. And this too is graphically described in the Divine Word. It is found in the experience of Moses. It is familiar knowledge with every student of the Bible, that this distinguished lawgiver and leader of Israel, who was at the head of all their hosts, who led them forth from Egypt amid many wonders and miracles, and was with them in the wilderness, leading, guiding, instructing, was not himself permitted to enter into Canaan. But the *interior, spiritual* lesson intended to be conveyed by this, has not yet fully dawned upon the understandings of many. So particular, indeed, is the Divine Providence in the lesson conveyed by this great piece of history, that it was specially ordered that none but Caleb and Joshua, of all the men of war that came out of Egypt, should find their way to the promised land. But yet unto Moses, and to him alone, was granted the privilege of *seeing* the land, in its whole broad extent, from the top of Mount Nebo, the highest summit of Pisgah. Others saw it as they approached its borders, — the spies, for instance, who were sent forth to explore it; but no one but Moses was permitted to have this broad and entire view of it. And for this he was expressly brought to this high elevation, being commanded to go there for the purpose. The meaning is to be found in the *representative character* of Moses, and in that stage of the regenerate life which is here signified. Moses was the inspired *Lawgiver* of the Israelites; and as such, represents the Divine Truth instructing and guiding, but not in action or in combat; and before truths can be of any effect in securing heaven for us, there must be this combat against evils. There was indeed some warfare against evils, in the journeyings through the wilderness, but it related chiefly to a more external state, — to a state of reformation rather than regeneration; or to regeneration of the understanding rather than the will: regeneration more fully and properly commences after the passage over Jordan: hence it was that Moses, the Jewish lawgiver, was full of instruction for the understanding, gave all laws and regulations for the people, instituted all the particulars in the multitudinous ceremonial service, but could not himself lead them into Canaan. For this purpose a *Joshua* was necessary, who represents Truth combating, and routing the enemies of the land. Hence, as soon as he arrived within the country, there appeared an angel unto him with a *drawn sword* in his hand. (*Josh.* 5: 13.) His mission was to expel the Canaanites. After all outward enemies are conquered, and reformation has done its work in the wilderness, then there are *internal* foes to combat, signified by "the inhabitants of the land." Mere truth in the intellect cannot do this; but it is of wondrous service in sharpening the vision, and preparing the way, and leading right up to the very work to be engaged in: thence it was that Moses, so pre-eminent in wisdom, was elevated to a very high mountain — went up even from the plains of Moab, which represents a low state of mere natural good, to the top of Pisgah which was over against Jericho, — a city on the borders of the promised land. All this signified the near approach to the heavenly Canaan. But he did not abide there. He merely went up to see the country, as it lay outstretched before him in all its grandeur, and to die there. Alas! how strikingly it prefigures the power of truth to elevate the understanding and quicken the intellect, and to see, on many and many a time, the glories which burst upon the spiritual vision, when the will, not being in the love of that truth, cannot abide there, and too frequently dies there! It is expressly stated in the Divine Word, that neither Moses nor Aaron should enter the promised land, because of a strife at the waters of Kadesh, and because they sanctified not the Lord in the midst of the children of Israel. That is, because of a contention about truths, and because of an omission to make that truth holy by an indwelling principle of good. This cannot be done by any mere temporal elevations, ever so high and exciting, of the powers of the spiritual man; and hence it was that of all the men of war that came out of Egypt, none save Caleb and Joshua finally found admission into Canaan. They represent the truly spiritual principles that remain, after the whole of the evil natural has been thrown off in the wilderness.

But Moses *saw* the land — saw it in all its extent and glory, for one at that distance from it. It is said that "the Lord showed it to him." The principal of Divine Good *can* so quicken the understanding as to cause some temporary elevations; it is in fact only this that ever enables us to see the truth and to acknowledge it as such; but until it is acted, and made enduringly spiritual, it does not abide by us, although the vision may be full, and the prospect most extensive. Thus the

Lord showed to Moses "all the land of Gilead, unto Dan, and all Naphtali, and the land of Ephraim, and Manasseh, and all the land of Judah, unto the utmost sea, and the south, and the plain of the valley of Jericho, the city of palm-trees, unto Zoar." (*Deut.* 34 : 1–3.) And as all the possessions of the tribes of Israel were thus pointed out, so all the goods and truths of the church are thus frequently depicted to the eye of the believer, and in this state of elevation of the understanding above the will, the prospect is refreshing indeed. How much does it include! "This," says the Lord, "is the land which I sware unto Abraham, unto Isaac, and unto Jacob, saying, I will give it to thy seed." (*v.* 4.) Every possible good and truth which can enrich the celestial, spiritual, and natural departments of the human mind, — this is the prospect which appears from the mountain top; — "I have caused thee to see it with thine eyes, but thou shalt not go over thither."

How often is it verified in the mind of the believer! There is many a Pisgah — many a Nebo, visited by the enthusiastic admirer of spiritual truths, especially such truths as are now revealed for the New Jerusalem : and it is a part of the dispensations of Mercy, that we should thus be capable of interior elevation even above what we find it possible to practice. It is a peculiarity of life introduced into human capacity after the Fall. Before that, the men of the first church, according to Swedenborg, received divine truths by an internal way, into the good of their will, and through that into the truth of the understanding; and whatever was thus received was immediately reduced to life and practice. Hence they received no more truth than what was united with the good that was in them. Such continued to be the state of man till the period of his fall, when the will, in process of time, became so corrupted with evil, that if divine truth had any longer been inseminated in this way, it also would have become utterly corrupted, and his salvation made impossible. He would have perished from the earth. To prevent this catastrophe, a new church or state of humanity was instituted with the posterity of Noah; and it was providentially ordained that the will principle should thenceforth be separate from the intellectual, and that man should no longer be reformed and regenerated by the reception of good immediately into the will, and thence truth also, but should receive truth first into the understanding, by which the will might be rectified, and regeneration effected. This is the state of the world now; we are led to good by truth, and not *vice versa;* hence the remarkable power of seeing so much more truth than is generally reduced to life and practice. It is a provision of the Divine Mercy. If we could not, by some effort of the intellect, lift ourselves above all that pertains to the will, we should not, in our present corrupt state, see enough of the truth to enlighten the dark and deep recesses of the depraved soul, and to save ourselves from imminent destruction. Therefore it is that the spectacle is so frequently presented, of a man well stored and furnished with all the principles of a correct life; with an intellect of shining and brilliant qualities; who can even understand the most divine truths, and take delight in their promulgation and defence; and yet whose life is a sad comment on the influence of those truths to bend the will, or soften the asperities of the natural man. He is indeed like a traveller over mountain heights. And if he be a man of taste and imagination, how well does the experience which he then undergoes illustrate the phenomena of such spiritual quickenings! He may not only see, but feel strongly, and be entirely overcome by the excitement and power of the occasion. There is not, perhaps, a better illustration of the subject in hand. He may give way, for the time being, even to religious feelings, and realize within him all the glow of a most rapturous adorer. Powerful feeling is *frequently* produced by the survey of some vast field of natural scenery. Suppose, for instance, the man really stands upon some conspicuous mountain of the earth; and as he views outstretched before him the prospect of an almost boundless vision; — as he stands in the centre of a horizon embracing earth, and sea, and sky, and all the picturesque and surpassing beauties of Nature in her grandest attire;—here, for miles around him, a connection of cultivated fields and waving harvests ready for the reaper's hand; — there the towering hills and loftier mountains of a more distant scene;— and the thousand-fold area of diversified land, and flowing streams, and scattered towns and villages, with the spires of still more distant cities enriching and giving interest to the whole prospect; — when all this enters the mind, and impresses itself upon the still more imaginative faculties, how common it is to feel one's self elated, and carried away with a rapture of profound and religious contemplation. The man finds awakened in him susceptibilities which make him almost feel that he is equal to the prospect before him. He feels truly religious. He *cannot* look upon such a scene, and feel no rising emotions to Nature's God. And he makes use of the occasion, perhaps, for new and more profitable reflections. He carries it all to the more sacred retreat of his own soul, and secretly resolves to *live*, henceforth, in accordance with a nature more sublimely grand than all the materialism which is thus lighted up in glory around him.

But he descends from the mountain, and meets with his fellows who live in the plain. Alas! how often is it that the descent is made spiritually as well as naturally, and, the *sight* out of mind, out of mind also all the high feelings and lofty thoughts which have been inspired by the scene. He descends to the plain level of the natural man. He mixes with all the frivolities of a world lying in wickedness, and instead of a survey from the top of a mountain, his understanding has fallen, and his will has fallen, into the dark and narrow boundaries of sensual indulgence, and the dwellings of the unclean.

So it is with many a beholder of the spiritual truths of the New Jerusalem. A vast field of vision is opened to us here. Indeed, there is nothing equal to it. By this capacity in some men of fine parts, of the elevation of the understanding above the will, one may stand upon an eminence of all-commanding survey. Oh, how great it is!—and as he looks with mental eye upon the spiritual prospect spread out before him,—the vast realities of the eternal world,—the glories of heaven far above him, and the deeps of hell beneath him,—the far-off mansions of the eternal city,—the green pastures, the still waters, the fields and paradises more real and more substantial than all the solid materialism of the world,—the fruits of every month which hang upon the trees of life of every heavenly inhabitant; —and as the songs and rejoicings of that world come even now to his spiritual ear, and he realizes that all this is or may be for him, and such as him, truly it would be difficult *not* to feel strong emotions rising within the breast, which might convince a man that he was far, very far, from that thorough depravity which preys through all the natural mind. And besides all this, there is the whole system of doctrinal truths presented for a refreshment to the understanding. And if he be a man capable of appreciating consistency, or revelling in the midst of mental beauty, then I know not of a richer banquet that can be spread to the intellect, than the treasure-house of such truth affords. For there never was so sublime a philosophy, and never such thorough satisfaction to all the hitherto divided faculties of the human mind. What, indeed, are all the philosophies, from Plato down to the last improvements of unaided human science, compared with the clear, analytical and synthetical presentations of the illuminated Swedenborg? Now, all this is augmented a thousand-fold by being pressed into the service of religion,—by being sustained and systematized by the Word of God,—by being supported by so many consentaneous and minute particulars,—and by being in every way such as to enlist the whole man—affection, imagination, thought and all, in the most stupendous and consistent system ever presented to the human mind. Is it any marvel that many are captivated? Were it not for the greatness of the theme, and the life that it requires, would there not be ten thousand more? These indeed are the Pisgah heights of the New Jerusalem. Whether or not we have adopted *all* the truths of this spiritual church, these are the heights over which the intellect must frequently travel. It is here that we are led by the Divine Providence, that from such an elevation we may view the country that stretches far into the promised land,—a land flowing with milk and honey, but which none but the faithful, like Caleb and Joshua, are ever permitted to enter. We cannot be too thankful even for the *sight* of such a land. How stimulating it is, or may be, to all good endeavor! What a prize for the ambition of immortal spirits! And in our *sins* and *defilements* too, to be able thus, not only to form a mere ideal, a sentiment, but to catch an intellectual view of so divinely authorized a prospect, and hold it steadily to the mind, —how should it affect us in all our trials, in all our disappointments, and our labors of love for one another! Oh, it were a pity that we should be transported to the mountain tops only to die there;—to see the glorious country beyond, and not to go over thither. And yet if it be all that we can attain to in this part of our pilgrimage, well were it still that we should die at one hundred and twenty years, like the patriarch before us, with the "eye not dim, nor the natural force abated." (*Deut.* 34: 7.) For in this is contained a spiritual promise and prophecy, that if we do not *abuse* the knowledge we possess, even if we do not fully *use* it, the life that remains in us will be quickened and animated beyond the grave, and lead to the Canaan of heavenly rest. Yet often, even in this life, we have to descend from this Pisgah of faith and intellect, to fight with the enemies that dwell in the plain. We deceive ourselves with the mountain view, and are only brought to our senses again by the sad reality of so much to do before we can "go over thither."

CHAPTER XI.

FINAL REST.

"One of the peculiarities of the Quietists, and which undoubtedly has some connection with the origin of the name, is what their writers have denominated the *permanent* or *continuous state.* They sometimes denominate it the *fixed state.* They do not mean by this a state which is absolutely immutable; although, when it is once reached, it is not very likely to change; but a state which is *established and at rest in itself by a continuity of nature."*— *Madame Guyon.*

WE should fail entirely to appreciate the end to which all the operations of Providence were leading us, did we not bestow one chapter upon the great and final attainment. "Rest for the weary soul!" — It is the aspiration of universal humanity. And if there were no other evidence, it would be quite sufficient to prove that the present condition of man is a lost and wandering one — this universal restlessness! Nowhere is repose. Everywhere is inquietude. And whither hath contentment fled? What would we not give to realize in divine presence before us, not occasionally only, but as a constant, ever-present guest, that perfect image of Repose which artists dream of, but fail so frequently to produce! A form and countenance of expressive peace! A divine serenity! Only beauty can dwell with this; and where true beauty is, there also is repose. It is the product of a complete life. Or rather, it is life itself, in that perfect harmony which is the rest of all its faculties even when in highest activity. Far is it from inaction. It is the repose of life, not of death. But how hath it forsaken man! He is not at rest; life is but a "fitful fever" with him; and scarcely ever can it be said of him, when it is over, "he sleeps well." Even in his most prosperous circumstances, there is, almost without an exception, a vein of discontent running through all his experience; the moments of gladness give way to the seasons of sadness; the tincture of melancholy insinuates itself more or less into the cup of human life as drank by almost every one; and how large a portion of our time is afflicted with that restless oppression and *ennui* which weighs upon the spirits day by day. Where was there ever a contented man? — one who had *no* desire to change his condition, except to progress in the Christian life and in the order of Providence? No doubt, there have been such; but in the present unregenerated state of the world, and the consequent fluctuating condition of human fortunes, there come times — alas, how frequent in the life of almost every one — when the soul, tired and burdened with its earthly cares and painful uncongenialities, would escape with loathing from all present scenes, to something far off and unrealized. "Oh, that I had wings like a dove! for then would I fly away and be at rest." (*Psalm*, 55 : 6.)

But the boon is not far off. The truth is, this *rest* that the soul covets so longingly is nothing more nor less than harmony of action. It is at once apparent that there can be no rest nor ease in *discordant* movements, — nothing but chafing and discomfort: and surely none in inaction or idleness. The whole secret and element of happiness may be expressed in two words — harmonious activity. There must not only be harmony in the soul itself — in its whole structure and organism — in the play of all its parts, and the interior with the exterior, but between the soul and its outer relations, — the body and its surroundings, — and the occupations in which the soul engages. Also in its connection with other souls. Then there is rest and happiness; perfect rest, and the perfect soul's joy. Such rest is never fully attained in the world. It may, however, be approximated to, by progress in the regenerate life. The great aim of Providence is to complete this whole circle of harmonious movement, in the soul and out of the soul. It is only completed in eternity. There it will be found that the true rest takes its rise from the centre and spreads to the circumference. Perfect individual regeneration, a consequent harmonious outward world, congenial minds in association, and a multitude of agreeable pursuits and pastimes, varying incessantly with the ever-varying wants of the soul. Such is the heavenly rest. Such is the soul's Sabbath. In the natural world, of course it can be only partially realized. Much as we may perfect and harmonize our spirits, we cannot throw off this load of materiality. We cannot rise fully above the discomforts of the outward world. The very best of souls may sink into occasional depressions, and give way to consuming anxieties. But with only ordinary spiritual attainments, the burden is far more discouraging. Ah! truly, external things do have almost a superhuman power to throw the whole nature out of balance, and heap up discomfiture like a flood. But the question we have to put is — *Would* they have this power, if the soul itself was in the high attitude of life it should be in, or is capable of attaining? It is a secret yet but little known and appreciated, how much a purely spiritual power can overcome the annoyances of the outward world. I will not say that it is miraculous, but that it approaches to the miraculous. Else why is it that the very flames of martyrdom, — the fierce destruction which, in ordinary circumstances, racks the whole body with keenest torture, is deprived of all its power to torment, and is only attended with unspeakable pleasure in the soul? Unless there was a power in the heavens, of spiritual life and joy, to interfuse into such a soul at such a time, and thence into the very body, could the stake and the faggot be spoiled of all their power to hurt? But the testimony is better than this, for the very faces of the angels themselves have been seen at such times, and their gladness and triumph added to the triumph of the victim. And who does not know what moments of intense excitement can do, even in ordinary life, towards banishing all consciousness of pain? "But these are exceptions," says one, "to the common, every-day experience." Yes, but they reveal the *law;* they show that the spirit can triumph over the worst physical circumstances, — that there is a fountain of power that can be and is made efficient, to infuse gladness, and trust, and victory, into the upright soul, over all the power of the enemy. Now, therefore, it is but a fair inference that this fountain may be made to flow into human life in its *ordinary* circumstances, with the most marked and successful experience. And it does so. Christian experience is enough to assure us; the history of the faithful is enough to put it beyond doubt, that, aside from these extraordinary examples, the Spirit that supports us — that enlivens us through all, is a "spirit of power and of might," — a "Comforter" indeed, which can put far away the evil and feeble life of the merely natural man, and impart to the soul something of its own heavenly supremacy.

And besides all this, so evident it is that it is the *mind* that does all, or nearly all, and that this alone is capable of rising superior to all its circumstances and to be happy in spite of them, that it is only necessary to refer to certain *natural* or *hereditary* phenomena, where, in certain well-built and happily attempered men, who have no particular religious supports, there is a cheerfulness and buoyancy preserved through the most embarrassing experience. Contrast them, for instance, with certain others of an opposite make. And in their common, worldly circumstances, while the one would go downcast and discouraged, plunged in trouble, and letting his pecuniary misfortunes extract from him all the sweet peace and comfort of his mind, the other would live through continual embarrassment — debt upon debt, with no ability to pay, overwhelming him all the time, and yet, by this gift of a buoyant and cheerful nature, or, call it if you please a careless nature, he passes merrily through the whole of it — it is almost impossible to cast him down — and he manages to maintain himself as freely and blithely as a bird of song through the air. Now, what nature does for some men, it is the province of religion to do upon a more exalted scale. Such facts show that it is all in the *mind*, or at least very greatly, and may be altogether so, whether a man will be miserable or happy. Say, if you please, that it is very much in the body, and in the circulating fluids; in health and a good digestion: it is granted most cheerfully: and with all due credit to the bile, the spleen, and the stomach, we can readily appreciate how the mutterings of such a rising host as too often appears in some haggard son of dyspepsia, are enough, like the touch of Ithuriel's spear, to put to flight a world of comforters, charm they ever so wisely, and in the name of religion. But, aside from the reflection that such an array of bodily invaders is too often induced by *mental* foes and diseases, there is still the truth that mere animal happiness is but a small part of human enjoyment, and that all bodily delights and outward things are nothing for conscious, rational satisfaction, only so far as they affect the mind. A man may have ever so healthy and harmonic a body, yet if he has a mind disposed to melancholy and the dark side of things, he will turn every pleasure into insipidity, see a lion in every prosperous way, and infringe even upon his bodily health and comfort by this cheerless tendency to the lower regions of the soul.

And, truth to say, it is such, that is, the spiritually diseased, and not those who are surrounded with external, worldly annoyances, who are most disposed to the literal sense and aspiration of the Psalmist — "Oh that I had wings like a dove! for then would I fly away and be at rest." They think they can find rest by escape from external inconveniences. They do not mistrust that the chief trouble is in their own souls, and that if these souls were right, external things would have scarcely any power to harm them.

Let us not be stoical here. We realize too painfully that man has a body, has senses to be gratified, lives in an external world, and has frequently several dependent on him and his means and labors for support. A man must be a block, a stone, not to feel this. And the cases are frequently severe and hard to be borne. It is not in the power of any religion to administer perfect peace for any great length of time, under such extreme circumstances, for a man cannot live as a pure spirit in this natural world. But then, there are two considerations which come in here: one is, that this very deficiency and discord in the external world has had its origin in the *spirits* of men; if not in the individual, in the ancestry; and the world in general cannot flee from this without fleeing from those spiritual states which are the *cause* of all the poverty and discord of the external conditions. Another is, that with the *individual* frequently, there is more of a correspondence between his internal state and external condition, than he is apt to imagine. And when, as is often the case, the correspondence is not such as exists in the heavens and hells, that is, a perfect representation in exteriors, of the internal state of the soul, yet it is *invariably* the truth that the external conditions here are such as the internal state requires, for the regeneration, and for all the connections of the individual. It may be difficult for us to believe this truth, but a moment's reflection may convince us. It is true from the very *necessities* of the Divine Love and Wisdom. God, being infinite in his perfections, can do nothing else, and permit nothing else, but what has a relation to the highest good of every one; and that good is the life eternal of the soul. It is an optimism which connects all things into one grand system, material and spiritual, timal and eternal. Not a single particular can be left out, not a hair of the head can perish.

Now therefore, while under the power of these external afflictions, a true spiritual philosophy will, in proportion to a true discernment and a regenerate ability, turn them all into discoverable means for the soul's best possible welfare. This alone would lighten their weight in a great measure, and lessen the disposition to flee from them. The soul would rest *in* them, or make itself much more contented than it does, while they were all working out their providential mission.

But the truth is, with those who are regenerating, it is not outward circumstances, not worldly things, but *spiritual temptations and combats* which are felt to be most annoying, although the source of the annoyance may be oftentimes unsuspected. And in a more interior sense than is commonly dreamed of, it is not literally to fly away from one's present position—from present surroundings; alas! the evil is in himself; and he may exclaim with the utmost truthfulness—

> "Me miserable! which way shall I fly?
> Which way I fly is hell; myself am hell!"

The object is to escape from the hell within. By taking wings like a dove, we may do it. That is, by an elevation into the superior regions of spiritual light, we may at first look down into the dark and guilty caverns of the soul, and the all-revealing truth will point out the way of escape. To fly away and be at rest is thus to be delivered from those temptations and infestations of evil spirits which cause all the unrest and torment. But that those spoken of in this connection of the Psalmist had as yet no hope of deliverance, is signified by the words that immediately follow:—"Oh, that I had wings like a dove! for then would I fly away and be at rest. *Lo! then would I wander far off, and remain in the wilderness.* I would hasten my escape from the windy storm and tempest." To remain in the wilderness is yet to linger in the state of evil which *causes* the unrest. And this is the inevitable condition of every soul who aspires to that high and heavenly blessing consequent upon the New Birth, and the final completion of its life in the soul. We would "hasten" from the unrest—be quickly delivered from the "windy storm and tempest"—and many are the impulses which stir and agitate the mind, and move it at times to noble resolutions. We are *impatient* for the promised deliverance. But we still linger in the "wilderness." This is the lot of all human advancement. It can never be sudden, but gradual. Our evils are too many and too heavy, and they drag upon the wings which would bear us away to the regions of bliss. So it was with the Lord himself. "The child grew, and waxed strong in spirit, and was in the *deserts* [or wilderness] till the day of his showing unto Israel." (*Luke*, 1 : 80.) That is, his humanity was yet in a state of little comparative life, from the abounding evils of the hereditary nature. It is also said of the New Jerusalem, that, on its first descent from heaven to earth, "the woman fled into the *wilderness;*" signifying its small and feeble state, and its dwelling with those who are not in truth, because not in good. So also of the forty years' journey of the Israelites.

But there is a rest. The wings of the heavenly dove are abundantly sufficient to bear us away above all earthly obstructions, so that we no more flag, no more falter, but reach in triumph the mountains of peace. This is signified by the dove that went out from the ark of Noah. She at first "found no rest for the sole of her foot, and she returned unto him into the ark." The reason was, the yet abounding falsities and evils of the natural man, and the tumultuous state thereby induced. Nothing of good and truth could as yet take root in the mind. Although much instruction may be imparted in such a state, and much truth received into the understanding, yet if falsities abound, and evils still prevail, the truth can only gain a superficial entrance, having no good to support it, and there is thence produced a necessary turbulence, unrest, and dissatisfaction with one's self. The very evils of the heart, being brought in contact with so much truth, are quickened into a mutinous and rebellious state, spreading gloom and discontent through all the regions of the soul. Then it is that the true *spiritual* aspiration begins to escape from us. Then it is that one would fly from one's self. Then it is that self-condemnation, spiritual *ennui*, and a thousand hypochondriac emotions, exist to plague the soul; and in the mistake sometimes of the real causes, the person would mainly seek a change of his circumstances. He knows not what to do with himself. But now it is that the Lord's spirit is doing its work with him. It is spiritual conviction which is causing all this disturbance. And he must not expect a too hasty deliverance from the windy storm and tempest, but be content to remain in the wilderness for a while, if he is only travelling with all possible speed through it.

But there is, we say, a rest;—a holy Sabbath of the soul;—and this is indicated by the seven days which the dove remained in the ark, after the waters abated, when she was again sent forth, and "returned not again any more." By this is represented a state of *liberty* from all the lusts and fallacies of the natural man; when the true rest is found, and the true peace secured.

It is also indicated by the rest of the seventh day, after the six days of creation. That these days or periods are spiritually to be understood of states of the soul, in that spiritual creation which is called regeneration, we cannot stop here to explain. We would only remark upon the insufficiency and unsatisfactoriness of every other interpretation of this much tortured portion of the Word. Only in the spirit will these absurdities of the letter disappear; and the geology of the soul—its strata of experience, and its fossil remains, and high antiquity, will yet be found in scientific harmony with the utmost particularity of Genesis.

The truth in question is also indicated by the rest of the seventh day, after the six days' labor of man. "Six days shalt thou labor, and do all thy work, but the seventh day is the Sabbath of the Lord thy God; in it thou shalt not do any work." Thus it ever is with the regenerate life. There is first a labor to be performed, then a rest. It is during the labor states — the states of combat and strife with one's own evils, that the aspiration so frequently escapes from the soul, to fly away from its burdens. But the rest is only partial that is obtained at such times; the soul may wander far off *towards* the rest, but it will remain in the wilderness. The *perfect* rest —perfect Sabbath of the soul, is only at the seventh day. And this is the origin and correspondence of our Sunday. How beautiful it becomes when seen in its true light! What a divine significance in all this cessation from bodily labor, every seventh day,—the wheels of industry all still,—the strife and noise of the world all hushed,—when seen as emblematic of this hallowed rest of the soul!

In that day, it is said, "Thou shalt not do any work." Here also is a sense of the spirit. It is not alone taught that the *body* shall not labor, that worldly business shall cease, but that on the attainment of the seventh state of regeneration, all combat ceases in the soul. Evils become extirpated, and there is henceforth nothing of *proprium* — nothing of the evil that properly belongs to one's self, suffered to work and labor against the Lord's own operation. All is submissive stillness. Not inaction, but passive activity. No murmuring, no rebellion. The Great Spirit circulates at ease and in harmony through the perfected soul, and there is the repose of action. At the completion of the sixth day evil spirits also retire, for there is now no more to attract them, and good spirits and angels succeed to their place.

There is indeed a difference between the rest of the celestial man, and the rest of the spiritual man, or him who is in love predominantly, and him who is in truth; but both have their seventh period; and so particular is the Divine Word, that this distinction is especially referred to. The rest of the celestial man is expressed in the original by a word which means the *Sabbath*, while that of the spiritual man is expressed by another word, from which the name *Noah*, which means rest, is derived. But both, after enduring temptations and combats, have a rest of the Lord, and also become a seventh: the celestial man the seventh day, and the spiritual man the seventh month. Hence it is said — "The ark rested on the seventh month, on the seventeenth day of the month, upon the mountains of Ararat;"— signifying the holy light from the elevated divine good in the soul.

There are many who will read this for the first time, and doubt the particularity of any such sense in the Divine Word. But we can only say to all such, we know whereof we affirm; we know that the Word *is* thus particular, and that, from beginning to end, it contains beneath its letter a systematic reference to the regeneration of man. Would that we could more fully expatiate upon it. But let the present suffice, if for nothing more, as a kindly hint, a providential introduction, which may be the means of further inquiry at the proper sources.* And be assured, in the language of John Robinson to the pilgrim fathers, "the Lord has more truth yet to break out from his Holy Word."

By such unmistakable teachings of the inspired Records, we are enabled to see in a more conspicuous light, and by the aid of a divine science, the sublime capacities of the human soul. We can hence appreciate that genuine *repose* which has been the dream of artists and the theme of genius in all ages of the world, but which the Spirit of God can only effect in the regeneration. How greatly has the world mistaken it! And in its discontents, its despondencies, its ten thousand troubles and annoyances, how has it wandered from the true sources, to external bewilderments and internal misery! How little has it exerted itself in the true direction, to rise above the fogs and damps, the darkness and terror, of its own evil and false nature, to the heavenly mountains of sunshine and joy! It is not mere poetry that is here used. There *is* a sunshine of the *soul.* The sublime orb that hangs in glory and effulgence in the spiritual heavens, sending its light and heat through all the regions, may shine into our hearts, and impart to us of its warming beams. It may elevate the whole man to the holy moun-

---

* See, for a good exposition of the interior sense of the first eleven chapters of Genesis, Rendell's "Antediluvian History:" or, the first volume of Swedenborg's Arcana.

tains of Ararat. There a man may stand above his circumstances. There, upon that holy height, may he feel the refreshing breezes of heaven playing through his restored and healthy mind, and with all the world beneath his feet, may realize his victory over it and his superiority to it. In silent thankfulness may he raise his eyes to the blue deep above, in calm and humble emotion for its divine beauty, reflected only from his sun-bright soul. It is the Repose of heaven. It is Peace and Rest such as "the world cannot give, neither can it take away." It will fit us for all earth's trials that remain, which will now be only of the body and of worldly necessities, which we shall meet with welcome, and adopt as friendly to the consummating Perfection.

The fruits of such a life are more than can be enumerated. Then a thousand delights, of which the previous states know nothing, take up their abode in the mind; the internal and external parts of it being now harmonized, conduce to that true action in which the very essence of happiness consisteth; instead of tiresomeness and discontent, a serene and joyful sense of life flowing continually from the Lord, and a constant recognition of his providence in all things; instead of melancholy, cheerfulness of spirit; instead of the restless aims of ambition, gratitude and thanks for the smallest favors, which are all that can be most safely bestowed; and the lapse of time continually filling us with new delights, as it bears us perceptibly onward to an immortal existence.

CHAPTER XII.

RETROSPECT AND PROSPECT.

"When Providence intends to accomplish any thing, it does not do it by halves, but entirely." — *Stilling.*

It is of the utmost importance, in travelling to a new country, not only to have a general acquaintance with the way, but to be furnished, if possible, with such guides and directions as shall lead somewhat into the particulars of the journey. We not only want to know the end and object of it, but the chief points of use and attraction, and the things most necessary to be provided with. It is so in the great spiritual journey. If I know not what the Great Leader aims to do with me, and the chief means which He will seek to use in my furtherance to everlasting possessions, in vain do I try to obtain a correct idea of the course and experience of the work. To appreciate what Divine Providence is, we must know something of the extent and nature of its aims. Before we can submit ourselves most readily to the discipline, we must understand what is to be done. It is for this purpose that we have gone over the ground of the few preceding chapters. If the great object is a heaven from the human race; if the ground of it is in so substantial a nature as the eternal forms and memories of the soul; if the necessity of regeneration is so urgent, and its nature and operation so radical and thorough; if the warfare is so formidable, and the temptations so great, and the fluctuations so mighty, and the way so winding and labyrinthic, and the view from some of its highest points so untrustful and deceptive; and after all, the final rest so glorious; — if *this* is the work and leading of Providence, what a theme it is for angels and for men! We need not wonder at the prompting curiosity of higher and holier beings, when the mystery of the incarnation was presented to them, and it became a subject which they "desired to look into." And now, inasmuch as our fallen humanity may still partake of the nature of angels, in that proportion may we hope to be attracted more earnestly to the remainder of our chosen theme. We know of nothing so comprehensive, nothing so interesting and glorious. We pray for the unction of a holier spirit, for deliverance from all doubt and trifling in spiritual things, and for truth and freedom even to the end. The region to be explored is alike fruitful of all high trust, and of the weightiest responsibility.

> "No more we slumber on the brink of fate;
> Roused at the sound, the exulting soul ascends,
> And breathes her native air; — an air that feeds
> Ambitions high, and fans immortal fires,
> Quick kindles all that is divine within us,
> Nor leaves one loitering thought beneath the stars."

CHAPTER XIII.

DIVINE PROVIDENCE IN THE MODERATION OF THE HUMAN WILL.

"O all-preparing Providence Divine!
In thy large book what secrets are unrolled,
What sundry helps doth Thy great power assign,
To prop the cause which Thou intend'st to hold!"
— *Michael Drayton.*

THE rational freedom of the human will is the one thing, in all our experience, that the Lord guards as the apple of the eye. It is man's pre-eminent gift. And we can have no distinct views of the divine government, without a clear conception of the causes which are made to influence our freest determinations, and which operate to perfection in the spiritual world.

"That it may be known [says Swedenborg] what free-agency is, and of what quality, it is necessary that it should be known whence it is; its origin is from the spiritual world, where the mind of man is held by the Lord. The spiritual world consists of heaven and hell, and between heaven and hell there is a great interstice which appears to those who are there like an entire orb. Into this interstice evil from hell is exhaled in all abundance; and on the other hand, good from heaven flows in thither also in all abundance. It is this interstice, of which Abraham said to the rich man in hell, 'Between us and you there is a great gulf fixed, so that those who would pass over from hence to you cannot; neither can those who are there pass over to us.' (*Luke*, 16: 26.) Every man, as to his spirit, is in the middle of this interstice, solely in order that he may be in free-agency." T. C. R. 475.

"There is a sphere exhaling from the hells, which may be called a sphere of endeavors, which is a sphere of doing evil;

this sphere it has also been given occasionally to perceive; the endeavor is perpetual, and soon as any opportunity is given, an effect thence bursts forth; but that sphere is checked by the sphere of the endeavors of heaven which is from the Lord, and which is a sphere of doing good, wherein is all power, because it is from the Divine. Nevertheless, between those endeavors diametrically opposite to each other, an equilibrium is kept, to the intent that man may be in freedom, and thus in election." A. C. 8209.

It should be remarked here, that this middle state of which Swedenborg speaks, is strikingly confirmed by the theology of the church in its first ages, and by the very evident scriptural teaching in regard to *Hades*. Indeed, the idea of immediate entrance into heaven or hell, at death, is comparatively of recent date. It seems to be an off-shoot of the Lutheran Reformation, and introduced into Protestantism by a too fierce assault upon the Catholic Purgatory. In destroying Purgatory, it destroyed the true doctrine of the Middle State with it. It has been well remarked, that since the time when the Christian Churches first came clearly into the light of history, which was the last quarter of the second century, "we find them universally in possession of the idea of a mediate place of souls, — one which was neither heaven nor hell, but preliminary to either. It was not an idea broached by heretics here and there. It was the belief of the Church Universal, which nobody called in question. Out of this belief the papacy shaped its purgatory, and practised on human credulity and fear." *

From the position of man's spirit in this middle state, and his consequent freedom, we may appreciate something more of that constant and providential moderation of his will by the angels of the Lord, as he works out the problem of his life. For by being thus situated, and acted on equally by heaven and by hell, that is, fairly and impartially, according as he

* See Sears' "Foregleams of Immortality," pp. 258–324.

himself chooses good or evil, he is at liberty to turn himself to either. But he is assisted and regulated in this process by the most careful ministry of angels. Through years and years of the most trying and varied experience, the man must be watched by the angels who are thus placed over him; and those angels must be changed according to the man's changing states; he must be withheld from this thing, and encouraged to that; he must be supported in temptations, while those temptations are continually moderated to the extent which he can bear; he must be apparently left to himself, and still most closely attended; and through the whole experience of so vast a life, involving every moment eternal consequences, it must all be done with such perfect wisdom and precision as to keep the will in its utmost freedom and equilibrium between the powers of heaven on the one side and the powers of hell on the other.

"The angels, by whom the Lord leads and also protects man are near the head; it is their office to inspire charity and faith, and to observe the man's delights, in what direction they turn themselves, and to moderate and bend them to good, so far as the man's free will enables them; it is forbidden them to act violently, and thereby to break man's lusts and principles, but the injunction is to act with gentleness. Their office also is to rule the evil spirits who are from hell, which is effected by methods innumerable, of which it is allowed to mention only the following: when the evil spirits infuse evils and falses, the angels insinuate truths and goods, which, if they are not received, are yet the means of temperament; the infernal spirits are continually making assault, and the angels affording protection; such is the order. The angels principally moderate the affections, for these constitute the life of man, and also his freedom. The angels also observe whether any hells are opened, which were not open before, from which there is influx with man, which takes place when man brings himself into any new evil; those hells the angels close so far as man suffers it, and if any spirits attempt to emerge thence, they are likewise removed by the angels. The angels also dissipate foreign and new influxes, from which are evil effects; especially do the angels call forth the goods and truths which are with man, and oppose them to the evils and falses which the evil spirits excite.

By such things the angels of the Lord lead and protect man, and this every moment, and every moment of a moment; for if the angels should only intermit a single instant, man would be plunged into evil, from which afterward it would be impossible he should be extricated." A. C. 5992.

Thus it is with this most delicate instrument — the human will. If we fail sometimes to comprehend the mystery, — if we find ourselves balked, and discouraged, and our most cherished plans defeated by some new emergency or old continued difficulty, let us not forget the many connections which run out far beyond this world, nor the myriads of wills, connected with the One Great Will, which are all invisibly acting in concert with ours, for eternal ends of salvation and use.

CHAPTER XIV.

DIVINE PROVIDENCE AND HUMAN PRUDENCE.

> "There is a destiny that shapes our ends,
> Rough-hew them how we will."—*Shakspeare.*

It is a frequent remark of those who have had much experience in the world, and especially those who have met with many disappointments, that "there is no use in planning." Indeed, how often do we hear it said — "Nothing that I ever undertook to do yet, came out as I intended. I never did any thing that I wanted to do, in my whole life. I have been balked in every thing. I seem to myself like drift-wood, floating down the great stream of life, not knowing what I was made for, or whither I am tending." Ah, yes,

> "A greater Power than thou couldst contradict
> Hath thwarted thy intents."

But it is one straight and continuous story; God hath an *infinite* use for thee — an eternal ocupation. Thou must fill that place in the universe which from eternity was foreseen and provided. Thou art a particle from the Infinite Deity. And as sure as God exists, thou must do that work which was wrapped up in the germ of thy destiny from the very first.

Truly, there is but little use in planning. Many of us have lived long enough to see our most cherished plans utterly frustrated, and ourselves in such uses and stations as no human sagacity could foresee or imagine. "Man appoints, God disappoints." Look out into the world, and see the currents of its mighty forces, and the strongly interlinked connections of all its business, activity, and enterprise. And when we think of how it all came into being, — how much the past generations have had to do with the present scene, — how a child is born, and endowed, and circumstanced from the very first; then may we ask ourselves how much of destiny, and how much of free-will, compose this complicated web and mystery of life.

But there is one thing connected with this subject, that we do not sufficiently reflect upon. It relates to the *inmost affections* of man, which form and determine his active thoughts. Whenever man acts or does any thing from what seems to him his own prudence, it is always from some love or affection from which the thought is. Now, it is the *thought* alone which comes into his sight, and not by any means the affection alone. Love in itself has no form, and only comes into manifest perception from the form which it takes in its own thought. As truth or falsity, it can be seen and taken cognizance of by man, but not as good or evil alone. Every truth is the form of some good, and every falsity of some evil. There are indeed certain gross and external affections which manifest themselves in the sensations of the body, but seldom ever in the thought of the mind. "But the *internal* affections of thought, from which the external exist, *never* manifest themselves before man; concerning these one knows no more than one sleeping in a carriage concerning the road, and no more than he feels the circumrotation of the earth." D. P. 199. Now, it is these internal, hidden affections, which are the more immediate subjects of the divine operation. And how innumerable, how infinite they are! And when we reflect that the externals, which alone come into our sight, are *from* these internals, and it is these only which form the thought and reflection of man, and constitute all his prudence, how little does that prudence become, and how manifestly under the divine control!

Providence with God is prudence with man; and with those who are in the love of self and the world, all their thoughts and actions, plans and schemes, are from the low and base affections which favor these two loves. The Lord sees these affections, and the angels also who are set over man, and they understand them much better than the man himself does. Hence the plans which grow from them are so frequently thwarted by unforeseen occurrences, and are either turned to favor man's salvation, or to lighten the evil of condemnation which he would otherwise bring upon himself. They are permitted to succeed for a time, — they go on bravely and well, as though in truth the man had power in his own hands to become "the architect of his own fortune." But by and by he is circumvented in a way he least suspected. Some change of societies in the spiritual world, or power applied there, starts up an obstruction here in the ultimates of nature; all his boasted power is humbled into nothing; the mighty fabric of his pride topples down before him as he looks on in astonishment; and he is obliged to confess to that mysterious destiny which the natural man knows nothing of, only to dignify with the name of Fortune.

And in like manner also, if the man is principled in the love of the Lord and the neighbor. He may need a lighter or even a heavier treatment; more or less disappointment or success; but inasmuch as his aim is now heavenly, he is more fully within the sphere of the Divine Providence, and less implicated in the mistakes of mere humanity. He is therefore carried to his goal in a more orderly manner.

It is one's own prudence that lies hid in every evil from its origin, and in which also is concealed the acknowledgment of nature alone. Hence also it is that those in the future world who have most relied upon their own prudence against the Divine Providence, become, according to Swedenborg, mere worshippers of nature, and more than others, magicians also, and skilled in wicked arts. For it is by these means that they hope to affect more fully their own purposes, to circumvent the laws of nature, and to provide for themselves.

It will not of course be inferred, or felt in the least, from any thing which has been said of the perfection and fulness of the Divine Providence, that any relaxation of effort is encouraged on the part of man: for inasmuch as the whole of nature is in effort, or *connatus*, to effect its own results, so man, as a part of it, though acted upon continually by the Divine Will and by influx from the unseen world, must still continue with all energy to exert himself, and to contribute his part to the mighty movement. Because there is so resistless and continual a Providence, that is no reason why man should not act with all diligence as of himself; for it is the very order of Providence to cause man to act, and thus, by means of his free powers, receive and appropriate those blessings which he can thus only enjoy. He could not enjoy them unless he appeared to acquire them himself. How great is the satisfaction of accomplishing any thing of one's self! What a divine pleasure in the very work itself! In fact, Providence can only come, most fully and successfully, where the free-will of man is most active to admit it. It thus opens the doors, and throws open the windows of the mind, for influx. Hence the proverb — "Providence helps those who help themselves." But if we deny it, or do not look to it, our own power dwindles into imbecility. We may succeed for a while, but the great currents of influx and of destiny will sooner or later assert their mastery, and man be humbled and carried away with them.

"I have discoursed with good spirits," says Swedenborg, "concerning the Divine Providence, and concerning man's own proper prudence, and they showed me about this by a representative familiar amongst them, namely by a mote scattered and rare in the atmosphere, saying that man's own proper prudence is to the Divine Providence as that mote is to the universal atmosphere, which mote is respectively nothing, and also falls down. They added, that they who attribute all things to their own proper prudence, are like those who wander in thick forests, and do not know the way out, and if they find it, they attribute it either to their own prudence, or to fortune." A. C. 6485.

"But I know that human prudence brings over the rational

more to its side, than the Divine Providence does to its; for the reason that the latter is not apparent, but the former is apparent: it can be more easily received that there is one only life, which is God, and that all men are recipients of life from Him; and yet this is the same thing, because prudence is of life. Who in reasoning does not speak in favor of one's own prudence, and in favor of nature, when he reasons from the natural or external man? but who in reasoning does not speak in favor of the Divine Providence, and in favor of God, when he reasons from the spiritual or internal man? But I say to the natural man, pray write books, and fill them with arguments, plausible, probable, and likely, and in your judgment solid; one in favor of one's own prudence, the other in favor of nature, and afterwards give them into the hand of any angel, and I know that he will write below these few words: 'They are all appearances and fallacies.'" D. P. 213

CHAPTER XV.

DIVINE PROVIDENCE WITH DIVINE FORESIGHT.

"Thou only knowest,
Thou, whose broad eye the future and the past
Joins to the present, making one of three
To mortal thought: of two eternities
Amazing Lord!" — *Young.*

It is doubtless very difficult for our finite faculties to realize how such a truth as the infinite Divine foresight can possibly exist. It seems almost too much for even Deity himself. That some *generals* of the universe should be previsioned to the Deity — that the planetary systems, for instance, and the nature of man, and his fall and restoration, with other things of a like general character, should be known and seen by the great Creator from all past eternity, is a truth we can very readily admit. We can seem to comprehend how such a thing could be. But that all the minutiæ — the infinite and everlasting complication of events in all worlds — the smallest particulars, with all the thoughts, motives, and actions of man, spirit, and angel, should be thus seen and scrutinized — what an overwhelming contemplation! And yet if we will stop upon the very threshold, and consider what the generals are *without* the particulars — that they can in fact only be made up of each several particular, we may infer that one can be foreseen, on the same principle as the other. How is a general seen? How does God see *any thing* before it comes to pass? This question answered, the whole is answered; for the difference between one such thing and many is only that which is involved in the infinity of the contemplation. The *infinity* of the subject may perplex us, but the principle not at all.

Let us then proceed to narrow down the contemplation to the nature and proportions of a man. We know that man is the image of God, created from Him, and spiritual like Him. And now the astounding fact presents itself that *man* foresees, with wonderful accuracy, an event before its existence in the world of nature. How often is it the case! It is proved by prophecy, by dream, by presentiment, by actual spiritual sight, either in sleep or wakefulness, in numberless instances. And it is a truth of the most wonderful and interesting nature. *How is it* — we have asked ourselves many a time — that the future can be foreseen? We can understand how the *past* can be seen, and this even by the spiritual vision of one who has never known the history of it — never heard of the events which are now for the first time discovered, and which are viewed and read distinctly by a clairvoyant power, on the records of the bygone. There is a very appreciable philosophy for this. The past has existed. It has therefore *made its impress on the substances of the world*, either material or spiritual, or both; either in human souls, or in the general sphere of spiritual existence from them; and it is so indelibly engraven that it can be read there by the eye of the soul as from the page of a book. Let none think that the actions of the past are not preserved, and stratified, as it were, in the earth of human experience. Witness the truths in the previous chapter on Memory. Most astonishing is the reality — most thorough and substantial the philosophy which so interprets it.

But how can the *future* be seen? — that which has not yet existed — which no human soul has felt or sensed in any way — which depends upon the concurrence of a thousand wills, and purposes formed and annulled, and re-formed and re-annulled, and ten thousand contingencies. How can such a thing be seen even for a day, much less a year, or many years in advance? And yet we know that it *is* seen, and with the most amazing particularity, even in the recognition of accidental circumstances. How is it?

Let us observe, then, in the first place, that it is *not true* that these things never have existed. They *have* existed in some sense, as before observed, in the general substances of the spiritual world, and in the Deity Himself. The Infinite embraces from eternity all the finite, which are only so many variations and complications of possible existence comprehended in the Divine Essence, but not yet ultimated into nature. [See pages 70, 71.] There is, therefore, a general pre-existence to all things. And in the spiritual world, which is all *from* the Deity — more especially that part of it which is nearest to earth, there is a more definite, formal, and active theatre of effects, which are the causes of much that we see here in natural existence. In one sense it may be said *all* that we see here; for every thing exists in spirit before it takes on natural ultimates. Now it is by seeing the *causes* of things — which exist in substantial essences in the pre-existent world, that things in this world are sometimes foreseen with such fatal precision. These causes form an infinite network of most infallible connection, and of course, by the Deity, can be *all* comprehended in his Infinite Mind. But *some portion* of that prescience can be imparted to created beings. An angel, standing above the human plane, can see much more than we can, and predict to a much greater extent the forecoming history. He may do this by taking into his view a greater number of causes. And in proportion to the really spiritual capacity of a human being, whether by natural refinement, by culture, or by states induced by normal or abnormal processes, is he so much nearer the spiritual world, and can see so much more of the forthcoming natural. Hence it so frequently happens that the most surprising things are pre-visioned and pre-intimated to mortals here below, which are fulfilled with the greatest accuracy. There is no chance, no accident. All is absolute, connected, and causative existence; and to the Omniscient who can take in all, it is not so much foresight as insight; not so much foreknowledge as eternal verity. And yet not by arbitrary predestination on His part, but by certain knowledge of the movements of created freedom.

Thus it is that we are frequently *forewarned* of dangers, which warnings are intended for our safety, if we would heed them; and that they are most accurately foreseen is proved sometimes from the apparently *accidental* nature of the occurrences so previsioned. Take for instance the following case reported by Mrs. Crowe, in her "Night Side of Nature." It is related from the best authority, as communicated to herself, and is given as an instance of the "inexorable fatality which brought about the fulfilment of the dream."

"Mrs. K——, a lady of family and fortune in Yorkshire, said to her son one morning on descending to breakfast: 'Henry, what are you going to do to-day?'

"'I am going to hunt,' replied the young man.

"'I am very glad of it,' she answered. 'I should not like you to go shooting, for I dreamed last night that you did so, and were shot.' The son answered, gaily, that he would take care not to be shot, and the hunting party rode away; but in the middle of the day, they returned, not having found any sport. Mr. B——, a visitor in the house, then proposed that they should go out with their guns, and try to find some woodcocks. 'I will go with you,' returned the young man, 'but I must not shoot, to-day, myself; for my mother dreamed last night I was shot; and although it is but a dream, she would be uneasy.'

"They went: Mr. B—— with his gun, and Mr. K—— without. But shortly afterward the beloved son was brought home dead: a charge from the gun of his companion had struck him in the eye, entered his brain, and killed him on the spot."

How purely accidental seems the occurrence here related, and how many were the chances, humanly speaking, that it should not so have happened! Going back into all the connections of the generations past, or even only for a few days, how many separate wills, and motives, and contingencies, had to concur for the production of this incident! The day might not have been fair, which would have prevented the excursion altogether. Or that particular visitor who carried the fatal gun might not have made his appearance. How many causes might have detained him! Or, having been present, he might have been more careful. Ten thousand things may be imagined in defeat of such an occurrence, but *it was to be!*—and it is a truth overwhelming to think of. Not, I say, predestinated, in the common understanding of that term, but made certain by the working of human agencies, and hence foreseen.

But on the other hand, when such warnings are obeyed and the casualty prevented, it alike proves the fore-knowledge, not of the event, but of the impending danger or nearness of it, which is equally out of ordinary human sight, and in the pre-existent future. Many instances might be related, but our limits forbid. The life of the great Harvey, the discoverer of the circulation of the blood, "was saved by the governor of Dover refusing to allow him to embark for the continent with his friends. The vessel was lost, with all on board; and the governor confessed to him, that he had detained him in consequence of an injunction he had received in a dream to do so.*"

"Seeing in dreams," says Ennemoser, "is a self-illumining of things, places, and times;" "for relations of time and space form no obstructions to the dreamer; things near and far are alike seen in the mirror of the soul, according to the connection in which they stand to each other; and as the future is but an unfolding of the present, as the present is of the past, one being necessarily involved in the other, it is no more difficult for the untrammelled spirit to see what *is* to happen, than what has already happened.†"

"Sir Humphrey Davy dreamed one night that he was in

* Night Side of Nature, p. 79. † P. 49.

Italy, where he had fallen ill. The room in which he seemed to lie struck him in a very peculiar manner, and he particularly noticed all the details of the furniture, etc., remarking in his dream how unlike any thing English they were. In his dream he appeared to be carefully nursed by a young girl, whose fair and delicate features were imprinted upon his memory. After some years Davy travelled in Italy, and being taken ill there, actually found himself in the very room of which he had dreamed, attended by the very same young woman whose features had made such a deep impression upon his mind."

A most remarkable instance of this foreseeing power was related to me by a personal friend but a short time since. An acquaintance of his, a few years ago, dreamed one night of being in a very difficult position, in a street in New York, with a coach, and in the rain, when he came to a certain locality, and found himself, in the midst of other troubles, in great *pecuniary* need. He was relieved by the presentation of some silver money, among which was noticed a number of pieces of very singular coin, the like of which he had never seen before, supposed to be foreign, and the value of which he could not tell. But what should be his surprise to find himself, several years after, in the very same difficulty, in the same locality, and actually relieved by money containing a number of the *new three-cent pieces*, which had just made their appearance, and which were an exact *fac simile* of the coin he saw in his dream! Then, too, for the first time since its occurrence, flashed the whole dream into his mind. The dream occurred before any such coin had been struck or ordered in the country, and before any one, so far as he knew, had conceived of the device.

Such facts seem almost to show that our whole experience in this world, and indeed, upon the same principle, forever, is woven into a fatal pre-existence. It *is*, so far as certainty is concerned, but in perfect consistency with the utmost practical freedom.

But the most singular instance, I think, that I have ever heard of, of such pre-vision, or pre-intimation of the future, is related in the Memoir of the celebrated Lavater, prefixed to his work on Physiognomy. Professor Sulzer, a young man of his aquaintance, had one day fallen into unusual gloom and depression, which he could in nowise account for, and which was continued for several hours with the most dismal apprehensions. All his affairs, so far as he knew, were going on as well as usual, and what the cause of the forebodings was, could not possibly be divined. Yet the *distinct impression* was, that his *future wife* was in danger of some terrible accident. The doctor was but twenty-two years old, and had as yet formed no alliance with any one who most distantly promised to come into that relationship. He had not even seen the lady whom he had been encouraged to *think* of in that connection. And it was *ten years* from that time before he entered into the marriage relation. The circumstance had almost become obliterated from his mind. Yet one day it came to his recollection, and was made the subject of conversation between him and his wife. And by referring to dates, it was found that precisely the day which had overshadowed the doctor with such fearful apprehensions, his beloved companion, then a little girl but ten years of age, experienced a violent fall which came very near causing her death.

Wonderful — wonderful such truth is! Innumerable such facts might be adduced. The connection in the latter case was undoubtedly from a very near spiritual relationship, and perhaps effected or aided by the angels who were the mutual guardians of both the parties.

And now is it any more wonderful that God the Infinite should see *all* occurrences, or have in some way a knowledge of them, before they transpire in the natural or spiritual world? Whence all the *rills* of foresight but from the infinite Fountain? And if one thread of the infinite warp and woof of destiny can be foreseen by men, surely He who filleth im-

24

mensity with His presence can comprehend all breadth, all length, and the whole infinite connection.

And be it observed, the infinite *eye* of God, the same as his infinite power, or love, involves a spiritual faculty in its own ineffable organism. God is infinite Man. "He that planted the ear, shall he not hear? He that formed the eye shall he not see?" (*Psalm*, 94: 9.) And these infinite things in the Deity do not act without their proper mediums, any more than man sees without the aid of light. The whole spiritual world is full of light from its own Sun, and it is by this light that God sees into the minds of angels, and also of wicked spirits. If, therefore, we cannot comprehend the infinity of the subject, we can the *rationale;* and inasmuch as man the creature foresees, we have only to transfer the mediumistic connections of his creatureship, in an infinite amplitude to the Creator, to conceive how He can see, not only by Himself, but by angels and spirits from Him, which is the same thing, and from eternity to eternity inspect the myriads of thoughts, feelings, and actions of all his creatures, and every position and circumstance into which they may come! It all results from the germal and infolded Essence of all things from the very first, and from the fact that God is all in all in a most necessary connection.

Mighty and overwhelming as the truth is to all finite faculties, yet it is from such a truth that the very best of consolation is derived for poor and helpless humanity. If God did not foresee and foreknow, how could he *provide* for every thing? If it were possible that any thing, ever so small, could start up in his dominions without his previous knowledge of it, then a greater thing may, and still a greater. And where shall limits be set? And in such a contingency, what certainty is there of absolute and abundant provision? Things, therefore, are not only *pro*vided but *pre*vided; and though all eternity, which with the Infinite is an ever present Now, they are arranged in the most perfect order, because *of* order and *from* order: that is to say, not arbitrarily or artificially, but essentially and necessarily, as flowing from the Divine Nature Itself. What man perverts to disorder is provided with its proper limits, checks, and regulations.

Such is the truth as it pertains to man's whole existence. It is only thus that the Divine Providence is rendered perfect. But it is seen to be of the most essential importance to the *regeneration* of man. There are many progressions and periods in the regenerate life, from old states to new ones, both in the understanding and the will. It must be, therefore, by a continual moderation of man's free-will throughout the whole process. "Such progressions and derivations," says Swedenborg, "are perpetual with the man who is regenerated, from his infancy even to the last of his life in the world, and also afterwards, even to eternity; and yet he can never be so regenerated, as that in any measure he may be said to be perfect; for there are things innumerable, yea, indefinite in number, which are to be regenerated, as well in the rational as in the natural, and every one of them has shoots infinite in number, that is, progressions and derivations towards interiors and towards exteriors. Man is altogether ignorant of this, but the Lord is acquainted with all and single things, and provides every moment; if he were to intermit his providence for the smallest instant of time, all the progressions would be disturbed; for what is prior respects what follows in continual series, and produces serieses of consequences to eternity; hence it is evident that the divine foresight and providence is in every thing, even the most singular; and unless this were the case, or if it were only universal, the human race would perish.—(A. C. 5122.)

"How precious are thy thoughts unto me, O God! how great is the sum of them! If I should count them they are more in number than the sand; when I awake I am still with Thee."—(*Psalm*, 139 : 17, 18.)

CHAPTER XVI.

DIVINE PROVIDENCE IN THE PERMISSION OF PARTICULAR EVILS.

> "From seeming evil, still educing good,
> And better still, and better thence again,
> In infinite progression."

HUMAN nature is frequently appalled and its reason confounded, by the prevalence and outbreak of such gigantic evils as carry terror to all hearts. Most bloody cruelties, most hellish and heaven-daring crimes. The butchery of thousands to gratify the caprice of one petty and contemptible tyrant; and the violation of all innocence, all honor, and every sentiment of respect and humanity. The most detestable brutality, the most heartless shame. Women and children treated as dogs, and in fact worse than any animals, and such scenes enacted in the face of heaven as even the sun might refuse to light, and angels weep over in bitter tears. We forbear to paint the picture; there are no colors black and bright enough, and no art adequate to the awful drawing. The facts are such as to prompt the hearts of natural men, frequently, to exclamations like the following: — "Why does not God strike dead such miscreants at once? — If there is a God of infinite power, why does He not hurl destruction on them in an instant?"

But what says cool and sober reason? In the first place, the *amount* of crime is of but little consequence so long as there is any; why is there any? why does God permit any evils at all? We do not propose to enter here again into the question of the *origin* of evil; but evil having gained admittance, what is the providence in such outbreak — such terrible ultimation? And it might be a sufficient reply to this, to ask another question. Why are the diseases of the human body permitted to break out upon the surface? Wherefore the hideous eruptions upon the skin and exteriors, so afflicting and offensive to man? Manifestly, there is a correspondence. The human race as at present existing is an organized body of corrupt humanity; and if the evils wherewith society is impregnated did not thus appear, no one would know of their existence, and hence know of the application and the remedy. The external, criminal manifestations of a sin-smitten humanity are symptomatic. It is by observing the symptoms that we get at the disease. Or, to speak individually, if our evils did not appear to us; if we were not, time after time, notified of their existence by the *external* malady; if they never broke out into acts of disorder, into ungoverned passion, unbridled lust, and strifes and tumults of various kinds; to say nothing of the little acts of impatience, hatred, and folly, every day appearing; we should never know what a gangrenous mass of corruption the internal man was affected with, and hence should not be so well aware of the stringent necessity for cure. It is of the Lord's divine mercy that sins are thus manifest in outward act.

And besides, if they did not break out, the spiritual internals would be still more affected, and like a cancerous gangrene, would spread through the whole soul, and consume all human vitality. There is as much use and advantage, therefore, in the eruption of spiritual, as of physical diseases. And when we hear of some violent outbreak of crime or villany, — some murder, or wholesale butchery of humanity, or demonstration of an infuriate mob, we can look upon it frequently with the same cool philosophy as we look upon the sore which discharges its virulent matter upon the human body. Not by any means that the sore *ought* to be, either physically or socially, but that the outbreak is, under the circumstances, the best thing that *can* be. It were better to put off the corruption peaceably and quietly, without injury to others, as a common sinner does his evils; but if this cannot be, as is manifestly the case in certain stages of the body politic, then it is better to have the storm and fury, and the thunderbolts of God's vengeance along with it. We are not arguing for crime, but discovering the providence in crime. It is one God who rules in heaven and in hell. It is one Almighty Disposer who governs in the natural and the spiritual worlds. Whence earthquakes and volcanoes? The earth must have vent; its pent up gases must find escape; and better at an earlier stage than a later. Best at the *right* time.

> " If plagues and earthquakes break not Heaven's design,
> Why then a Borgia or a Catiline ? "

The penalties of crime are none the less sure for its usefulness, nor the wrong any the less flagrant. It is the " order of disorder," and the Divine Providence is equally concerned in it.

The whole process, too, is *corrective* in its nature, and tends to greater and greater harmony. The same as the storms and convulsions of the earth. It could not *at all* be permitted without this tendency, and the true and manifest principle is that no evil is permitted which is not the most direct means of preventing a greater. We cannot see, in each individual case, the justice of their sufferings who fall *victims* to the desperadoes of earth; they are frequently innocent and harmless. Whole populations of unoffending inhabitants may be swept off by one unholy war, and countless human beings fall a prey to unconscionable villanies. But yet we should remember that sin has defiled more or less the whole human race, and though we cannot see the cause in many individual cases, yet the cause undoubtedly exists, in some plague spot or other, of many a sacrifice to mysterious death. We shall not presume, as no man can, to scrutinize and comment upon all such providences, in all their bearings; we have frequently to bow our head in most humiliating ignorance, and in silent, painful wonder. But through all the darkness there is at the same time a general truth that streams in light upon the whole contemplation. That truth is, that the involvements of evil in those who are called innocent are frequently much greater than we imagine, and oftentimes so great, and so peculiar, that the cause of their sacrifice may be clearly found in them. Indeed, we may lay it down as a *principle*, which in some degree covers all these cases, that no one can be made to suffer from the wrongs and violence of another, who is not to some extent, directly or indirectly, nearly or remotely, so implicated in the whole wrong as to find the cause of it in that connection. But when we speak so, we do not mean specific sins of the character of those which create the immediate outbreak, but still *some* evil, more or less distant, either hereditary or actual, which enters into and forms a part of the general disorder. Were there no disorder at all, *none* would suffer: and were any one individual so perfect, and disconnected from the common confusion, as to be altogether guiltless and exceptionable, it is probable that that individual would either be removed from the scene of the present disaster, or translated to the spiritual world. Christ himself would not have suffered but from the evil hereditary that was in him; and when that was all purged away in the glorification, He arose by pure and necessary attraction to the heavenly world. In his great experience may be found the experience of every man; and in the light of pure and absolute truth, may be read the teachings of a providence most particular and impartial, and beautiful to behold.

But let us leave these generalities and come to some specifications. How much more, then, is a *principle* once gained in the world — an established principle of liberty or justice, than the sacrifice of whole armies in war to secure it! What were all the cost of the American Revolution, in blood and treasure, compared with liberty and free institutions? The blessings thus secured will descend to uncounted generations through all time; while the men that perished in the struggle were few comparatively, and even these lost no life but the bodily life, and passed by that conflict, by divine appointment, to their proper places in the spiritual world. And so when God lets loose some tyrant to scourge the human race, and destroy property and men by the hundred thousand, we may rest assured that it is not without some cause in the evils of that very humanity, and to procure blessings which by no other means could follow. It is disorderly, but it is the "order of disorder." Evil has created the crisis, and by evil, under a good providence, it must be met. So of all pestilences, famine, and corruption in church or state.

But speaking of wars, we cannot do so well as to introduce an extract from the great Seer and Enlightener.

"The causes that the greater wars, because they are united with homicides, plunder, violence, and cruelties, are not repressed by the Lord with kings and generals, neither in the beginning, nor in progress, but in the end, when the power of the one or the other has become so weak that danger of destruction threatens him, are very many, which are stored up in the treasury of divine wisdom; of which some have been revealed to me; among which is this; that all wars, how political soever they are, are representative of the states of the church in heaven; and that they are correspondences: such were all the wars described in the Word, and such also are all wars at this day: the wars described in the Word are those which the children of Israel carried on with various nations, as the Amorites, the Ammonites, the Moabites, the Philistines, the Syrians, the Egyptians, the Chaldeans, the Assyrians; and when the children of Israel, who represented the church, receded from the commandments and statutes, and fell into the evils which were signified by those nations, (for every nation with which the children of Israel carried on war signified some evil,) then they were punished by that nation: as, when they profaned the holy things of the church by foul idolatries, they were punished by the Assyrians and Chaldeans, since by Assyria and Chaldea is signified the profanation of what is holy. Like things are represented by wars at this day, wherever they are; for all things which are done in the natural world correspond to spiritual things in the spiritual world, and all spiritual things concern the church. It is not known in this world what kingdoms in the Christian world resemble the Moabites and Ammonites, what ones the Syrians and Philistines, and what the Chaldeans and Assyrians, and the rest with whom the children of Israel carried on wars; but still there are those who resemble them. But what the church is in the countries, and what the evils are into which it is falling, and on account of which it is punished by wars, cannot be at all seen in the natural world, since in this world the externals are only manifest, which do not make the church; but it is seen in the spiritual world, where the internals, in which the church itself is, appear; and there all are conjoined according to their various states: the conflicts of these in the spiritual world correspond to wars, which are governed on both sides by the Lord by correspondences according to his Divine Providence. * * * Successes also, and the affairs of war managed fortunately, are called, by the common phrase, the fortune of war; and this is the Divine Providence, especially in the plans and deliberations of the general; although he should then and afterwards ascribe all things of it to his prudence. He may do this if he will, for he is in the full liberty of thinking in favor of the Divine Providence, and against it; yea, in favor of God and against Him; but let hi know that no jot of the plan and deliberation is from himself it all flows in either from heaven or from hell; from hell from permission, from heaven from Providence." D. P. 251.

Thus we have reason to believe it is with all the various evils which afflict humanity. The Divine Providence is as much in the evil, or over the evil, as in the good. And how much cause of gratitude we have, and what consolation should we take, situated as we are in this evil and calamitous world, to know that the plan is so vast, so complicated and grand, embracing with the most wonderful particularity both worlds and all eternity in its reach, and that our little affairs which so perplex us are conducted with the same steady and everlasting order as the movements of the planets, or the quenching of a sun in the mighty constellations!

CHAPTER XVII.

DIVINE PROVIDENCE EQUALLY TO THE GOOD AND TO THE EVIL.

For He maketh his sun to rise on the evil and on the good; and sendeth rain on the just and on the unjust."—*Matt.* 5 : 46.

By the sun, in the spiritual sense of the above passage, is signified the Divine Love, and by the rain, the Divine Wisdom, or truth. And inasmuch, as before explained, it is not any absolute and essential malignity, but only the Divine Essence received into perverted and inverted human forms, which causes all the evil, so it may be comprehended how all only live from one Divine Life, even when sunk in the lowest depths of sin and defilement. But the providence towards the evil, though of equal goodness on the part of the Divinity, is still different in its character and operations. It is the eternal state which is contemplated in both cases. But in the case of the good, or those predominantly in the aim and endeavor of good, while all things succeed according to order and in order for the soul's regeneration; with the evil, who themselves have inverted that order, they proceed according to that inversion. In both cases, calamities, afflictions, successes, disappointments, worldly prosperity and adversity, come to the individuals, and in every instance for good: the difference being, that in the one case, these dispensations succeed in order to our regeneration to eternity; in the other, in inverted order to the next best thing that can be done for us; which is an abode in some selfish sphere in the spiritual world, where obedience may at length be secured from the love of happiness, but the soul is still left in a form of inversion. But as to the *finality*, in the great eternity, we advance nothing over-confidently, nor dogmatically. There are no limits to the Divine Mercy, and none to our hope and faith. We believe in the ultimate destruction of all evil, though at the cost, if it may be, of the sinner's identity. This is a consequence, however, not *necessarily*, perhaps, included in the process; that which is saved—that inmost germ of life which *cannot* be destroyed, may perhaps realize some conscious and eternal good from the terrible destiny through which it has passed. It may *know*—not as a human being in full ultimates of life, but by some interior process unappreciable by us, and for an humbling experience to the whole soul ever after, of the dreadful passage of the "second death." Or in the new creation, if not alive to that experience by its own conscious identity, as an angel, such knowledge may be then newly communicated. But of all this we cannot here speak.*

It is here to be noted, that deliverance from evil in this world, and also in the next, as it takes place in the Middle State, or World of Spirits, is deliverance from infernal societies. In those societies man lives continually while in evil, nor does he think, will, or do any thing, which has not connection with some combination of iniquity there organized.

* He who would see an able dissertation on the end of evil and the final destruction of the wicked, from an old church point of view, may consult a recent work on the "Doctrine of a Future Life," by C. F. Hudson. For a mere exposition of the *literal* sense of the Word, in those passages which speak of the punishment of the wicked, as to time and eternity, we know of nothing equal to it. We have here the whole literature of the question. And the reader will be well repaid by a masterly accumulation of testimony, as to the meaning and usage of terms, and the faith of eminent Christians, through the whole history of the church. Also by many worthy and truthful reflections. Of course, a true *spiritual* philosophy will reveal a ground of hope and faith quite superior to absolute and thorough annihilation; and though the real truth of this subject may have been hitherto, in a great measure, providentially concealed from the world, yet who may not hope, that in those depths of the Word not yet fully opened, the heart of man may rejoice to the full, in the most complete and celestial satisfactions?

Fearful indeed is the thought, and we little mistrust, in our moments of indifference, how the spots of corruption that exist within us, as to every kind and character of evil, send out their threads of quickest communication—stretch abroad their spiritual wires—and lay the roads of most facile intercourse, from land to land, and station to station, in the great spiritual country! What a reflection it is, that by every species of wickedness in which we may engage, and by every remaining spot of evil, we really have connection and communication, now with a society of knaves and deceivers, now with liars, now with adulterers, now with haters of God and the church, and now with profaners; not to mention unnumbered other evils which organize themselves into societies in the spiritual world, and which lay their plots so deeply and cunningly, to entrap the unwary travellers of earth! What a motive it is to search the heart and know the thoughts, and see if there is any wicked way in us, and be led in the way everlasting! For these ways are *really there*, spreading as a net-work through many avenues, over the whole tract of eternity.

It is in the deliverance from these wicked societies in the spiritual world, that the whole of the Divine Providence with us is concerned. But differently with the evil and with the good. "If the affection of a man be evil, he is, [while yet remaining in the world,] carried about through infernal societies, and if he does not look to the Lord, he is brought into those societies more entirely and deeply, yet still the Lord leads him as by the hand by permitting, and withdrawing so far as the man is willing to follow from freedom; but if he looks to the Lord, he is brought forth from those societies successively, according to the order and connection in which they are; which order and connection are known to no one but to the Lord alone; and thus he is conveyed by continual steps out of hell upwards towards heaven and into heaven. This is affected by the Lord whilst man is ignorant of it, since if man knew it, he would disturb the continuation of that process by leading himself. A. E. 1174.

From this it may be understood how the Lord follows the wicked, and how with the determinedly wicked there is a continual permission of evil *to the end that there may be a continual withdrawment.* Nothing can be more merciful, or beautiful to contemplate, except the more orderly leading of the good, and of the angels themselves. So perfect indeed is the divine government as thus represented, that there is *no place in the universe* where the divine laws can be violated with impunity, or where the chastisements consequent upon such violation do not tend more and more to obedience and peace. And so complicated, and yet so systematic are these movements, that the withdrawment from evil is done in a thousand ways, even the most secret, with man, comparatively as the food which is received into the stomach, which first undergoes a separating or digesting process, by juices prepared for that purpose, and is then converted into chyme, and next into chyle, from which the blood is made, and for this purpose is passed through various organs of the body, by innumerable little ducts, and vessels therewith connected, — the intestines, the heart, the lungs, the kidneys, in each of which a separation is made, and a purification from the grosser and more unsuitable substances, till what remains is thoroughly prepared to enter into the composition of a healthy human body. It will sound strangely, without doubt, to a merely material science, to say that all this is the effect of the secret operations of the soul. But when men learn more familiarly what the soul is, and come to view it as an organized human form, having in itself all the organic apparatus which the body possesses, only of a spiritual nature, then they will be prepared to admit a philosophy into their theology which is now little dreamed of. It is a familiar expression enough, that the soul lives upon Divine Goodness and Truth, — that this is its spiritual food, as bread is the natural food of the physical organism. But when all this is seen in reference to the very *substance* of the Divine Spirit, and to the human soul as the interior organic body, of which the material frame is the outer symbol and expression, what have hitherto been used as mere figures of speech will assume a reality surpassing our utmost imagination. It will then be understood *how* the soul lives upon the divine Good and Truth, and how it spiritually appropriates, by its own receptive and digestive apparatus, the divine and living substances which enter into it.

It is thus true — true in its utmost extent, that these involuntary operations of the bodily organism in regard to its food and sustenance, are effected by the operations of the soul. They are correspondences. One is the cause, the other is the effect. Hence it is that a healthy, cheerful, pure, and vigorous state of the mind, is so conducive to good digestion, and to unobstructed physical health. But of these secret spiritual operations, the man himself knows nothing. He does not attend to them, and he cannot, any more than he can to the involuntary movements of the heart in sleep. Who does attend to them? The Lord only, in his Divine Providence. And so it is with regard to all man's evils and sins, both hereditary and acquired. The whole spiritual world is at His command, and every variety of angelic and spiritual ministration. And by innumerable hidden methods, he accompanies man into evils, and leads him out of them; works upon his affections, and controls his motives; arranges all his circumstances; opens and closes each day for him in the best possible manner; and as far as *can* be done, consistently with his freedom, is continually operating to withdraw him from evils, to separate them from things not agreeing and discharge them by unknown ways, and to lead him from one society to another in that eternal world which closes in upon all sides around him! "Many, O Lord my God, are thy wonderful works which thou hast done, *and thy thoughts which are to us-ward;* they cannot be reckoned up in order unto thee; if I would declare and speak of them, they are more than can be numbered." (*Psalm*, 40 : 5.)

One chief method of governing the wicked is by external restraint and fears. They cannot, for the time being, be led to good from the love of good, but they can frequently from the love of happiness. That is, to external good, but not internal. But God will not forsake them even upon that plane of the mind; and though they may never thus attain to the enjoyments of the angels, yet they may be made receptive of many uses and delights of such a life, which, to them, are all the heaven they can imagine or enjoy. We will not pretend to say how high such a life may ultimately ascend, or how low and devoid of life it may frequently find them, or precisely what deliverances, as to mode and operation, in the long ages of eternity, may in God's great mercy await them: we have no desire, nor is it at all profitable, to speculate much upon such a subject; enough that the Great Father loves *all* his children with an undying, inexhaustible affection, which many waters cannot quench, nor floods drown, and which sin itself has no power to diminish. Enough that all his providences tend invariably to some kind and degree of good, forever and ever. Our soul is made glad within us, and shouts with an interior joy, for what *unknown* mercies must eternally be measured out, and what more than puny human thoughts are in the GREAT EVERLASTING LOVE. We can trust it for any thing. It is no less alive and active in the lowest hell, than in the highest heaven. It must prove efficient just so far as the creature will consent, and *whenever* it will consent.

It is thus that the very selfishness of man is made an instrument and a means for his security, to prevent him from sinking into deeper and deeper wretchedness. What a powerful principle is the love of honor, of gain, of reputation, and the fear of the law! How much may it do for God's eternal universe! And beyond all this, what other principles of the everlasting

Jehovah may operate, to complete the reign of moral evil, and glorify all human souls! Thus, with the poet Gambold:—

> "I'm apt to think the man
> That could surmount the sum of things, and spy
> The heart of God, and secrets of his empire,
> Would speak but love. With him, *the bright result*
> Would change the hue of intermediate scenes,
> And make one thing of all theology."

CHAPTER XVIII.

DIVINE PROVIDENCE IN EARTHLY AND HEAVENLY RICHES.

"Ye vainly wise! ye blind presumptuous! now
Confounded in the dust, adore that power
And wisdom oft arraigned: see now the cause
Why unassuming worth in secret lived,
And died neglected; why the good man's share
In life was gall and bitterness of soul:
Why the lone widow and her orphans pined
In starving solitude, while luxury
In palaces lay straining her low thoughts
To form unreal wants." —*Thompson.*

PERHAPS there is no one feature of our earthly life which appeals with greater force to the reflecting observer, and especially to those who are in any way tried with want, than the *vast inequalities* which are visible in human society:—the dire *extremes* of immense wealth on the one hand, and squalid poverty and misery on the other. What a spectacle does our civilization present! What occasion, even in a single city, for sad and sorrowful reflection! But there is no occasion for discouragement; for if the providence of God is seen anywhere, and can be most triumphantly vindicated, it is in this spectacle of confused outward relations, and in true and false riches. Let us be most devoutly thankful, that here on this dark problem, the light shines so abundantly, and that more than common cheer may be administered herewith to man. It is because the riches of the world, when truly held, are so necessary to the *very life of the soul*, that we feel their deprivation so painfully. We do not now have reference to what is commonly called *religious* life,—that word in its common acceptation is so narrow and fractional. But if true religious life may be defined to include our *whole spiritual culture and support* — the full and harmonious activity and enjoyment of what is sometimes called the *æsthetic nature*, — all the devotional, moral, intellectual, and spiritual faculties, in their utmost extent of varied and multiform uses in the world of nature, art, and all human industry, — then indeed may we say that the riches of the outward world are indispensably necessary to the true life of the soul. This *is* religion, and nothing else is, in the full, broad extent. The *whole man*, and not one corner of the mind devoted to the faculties of veneration, faith, benevolence, and justice, is to be attuned to harmony with the great Divinity. When a man is truly God-like, he is not a mere religionist in the praying, conscientious sense, but is an artist, a philosopher, a mechanic, an author, an agriculturalist, an exchanger, a producer of all sorts of useful and beautiful things, with an abundance of means for the pursuit of his occupation. Then his soul truly lives. Not till then. O detestable and infernal poverty! thou art not of heaven; from hell thou art, and to hell shalt thou return. In those dark and damnable regions thy rags become thee; they are the fashion of the place; but not in heaven, where bloom and beauty, in the most flowing and ample abundance, and all rich and adaptive outward things, make every man the lord of his own house and manor, with the most unstinted privileges.

Now, it is because this is so thoroughly and necessarily true, that every soul, in proportion to its genuine refinement and aspiration, feels painfully the deprivation. Poverty is not, in a single instance, the orderly condition of the world. The poor, in the literal sense, we shall *not* always have with us, any more than we shall have vice and imbecility. Poverty is the curse of evil and the child of sin. The riches of the soul require the most ample material riches; and it only truly and *fully* lives when these riches are provided.

But what has the Divine Providence to say for such a

subject? How shall these ways of the Lord be made to appear equal?

In answer to this questioning, let us first consider the law operative in *this* world in regard to the acquisition of worldly riches. And the Lord himself hath given the law: — "Seek ye first the kingdom of God and his righteousness, and all these things shall be added unto you." (*Matt.* 6: 33.) But how so? Must not this be received with palpable restrictions? Is it indeed true, that those who make these heavenly matters the first and primary objects of life, are most prospered in their temporal concerns? Indeed, is it not often the reverse of this? And is not the case so conspicuous as to attract the attention of every observer, and fill the minds of many with the most bewildering contemplations? The privations of the good, the prosperity of the wicked: this is the old complaint — the old stumbling-block. And yet it has not escaped the notice even of the superficial observer, that each state has its corresponding compensations; that those who have made this world their portion, with its rewards get also its deprivations, its desolations, its cares, its emptiness, and its "many sorrows;" while those who have made heaven their portion in this life, not only enjoy it hereafter, but enter now into that peace which the world knoweth not of, — into comfort and assurance forever. And hence, with all the confusion, it would be impossible to find a truly spiritually minded and virtuous person, in the greatest of earthly poverty, who would, to the sacrifice of his virtue, exchange circumstances with the richest and most affluent. He knows, if he knows any thing at all, that he is the richest of the two; and that God has not a government, even in this world, so at odds with equity and righteousness.

But yet the great law is explicit and unmistakable. It speaks plainly of earthly goods, and it is the letter of the Word that we are now concerned with. There are many confirmatory passages. Nothing is plainer, throughout the whole Scriptures, than that, with certain exceptions, the blessing of an ample abundance of all material good is promised us, as an aid to our complete existence. In the Old Testament it is "basket and store, field and house, the precious things of the earth, and the fulness thereof;" in the New Testament, though with a more obvious reference to our spiritual welfare, it is still the emphatic words of the Lord—"Your heavenly Father knoweth that ye have need of these things; and if ye seek first the kingdom of God and his righeousness, "they shall be added unto you."

Now, that there is a *law* here—a law as inevitable and regular as that by which the planets roll and the grass grows, is manifest from several considerations. It may be seen first, from the very intimate *connection* between all spiritual and all material nature. Take, for example, the human body, which is a miniature representation of the entire universe. It is well known that certain spiritual states cause certain bodily states; that a sound mind is indispensable to a sound body, and *vice versa*; that particular affections, whether of fear, hope, joy, grief, elation, or depression, operate so seriously upon the physical organism as frequently to occasion severe sickness; and nothing, as before alluded to, is so favorable to a cure of bodily distempers, as a cheerful, hopeful, vigorous *spirit*, which can act directly upon the material structure, and even banish its disorders. It is not without science, therefore, that many skilful physicians frequently prescribe nothing but sham medicines, with the most confident assurance of success, knowing well the power of faith or imagination to do what no drugs have power to do. It is *called imagination*, but it is in fact the inducing of a new spiritual action in the organism of the soul, which of itself creates a new influx into the body, causing a different movement there, and thus effecting a manifest cure. And how many diseases and disorders of the body are *first caused* by sins committed in the spirit! Whereas, if the kingdom of heaven had been preserved there, health and harmony would have been maintained in the body. "Thy kingdom come on *earth*, as it is in heaven."

We may see by this, how closely the laws which govern the spiritual world and the laws which govern the material world, are connected. What is true of the human soul and body, is true of the whole spiritual and material universe. For they are connected as soul and body. Man is the microcosm, or lesser universe, in which we may see by analogy, the macrocosm, or greater universe, in complete miniature.

But if it were necessary to illustrate any further, we might point to the well-recognized fact of how the whole spiritual and material worlds *are* connected, — how the laws of the one are interfused and blended with the laws of the other, — how the outer and material world is but a *development* from the inner and spiritual world, — and how we are frequently led by agencies operating in the heavens, by Divine Providence, to stations in this world where material conditions are largely concerned, but the end of which is invariably some spiritual advantage, either to the person himself, or to others.

Now, therefore, if there is a connection between the two worlds and their laws, then there must be a sense, and a very substantial sense, in which worldly prosperity is attendant on spiritual riches. There must be some way or degree, in which, by seeking first the kingdom of God and his righteousness, all these other things — these necessaries of bodily life and comfort — shall be added unto us. It is a prime part of wisdom to see this — to comprehend and appreciate the law; for we shall thereby have a better opinion of the world and its transactions, and be more contented with things as they are.

First, then, we may observe the fact. Do we not see, in the midst of all the confusion, that in general this *is* so? — that it is not, generally speaking, the worst and most abandoned of the earth who have the most of external riches? True enough, it may be said that it is not the most spiritual men, or even the most intellectual; they are generally too intent upon the higher matters to succeed best in material things. But it is, generally speaking, the men of at least an average standard of morality, *combined with other faculties which eminently fit them for business.* I think that any one of correct observation may discover that, even in material riches, God has not distributed it without some reference to the moral worthiness of its possessors. Let us make allowance for all the exceptions, which, for particular reasons, are allowed to exist; as wherein it may be seen sometimes that a determinedly good man, not yet fully delivered from his evils, would be hurt by a superfluity of wealth — that he would not, with this, attend so diligently to the perfecting of his spiritual nature; that a bad man would not be hurt by it, as it may be foreseen that, with ever so much trial and affliction, especially of the nature of poverty, he would only be hardened, and made more irritable and rebellious by it; therefore he is suffered to have wealth; again, that sometimes the morally unworthy are permitted to amass it for the good of others to whom it may come; *somebody* must roll up the material wealth of the world, and it is frequently permitted to those whom the Lord sees are as yet fit for nothing nobler; sometimes the worthy also are permitted to amass it, seeing that they will make a good use of it; — let us, I say, make allowance for all these exceptions, and then can we look abroad upon the world, and say that the distribution of material riches is not seen to observe some law connected with spiritual worth? There are other exceptions; as that some need more, and some less, for their respective enjoyments; that what would be an abundance for one, would not fill, even to comfort, the capacities of another; they are of a larger make every way — the Mastodons and Behemoths of humanity; — let us subtract from the contemplation all the exceptions, (and they are very many, Providence is very particular and fitting in its dispensations;) and then can we say that this material wealth, which the world so much doats upon, is distributed without any regard to moral law? Preposterous and impotent conclusion! We cannot live *spiritually* without living materially; it is the appropriate and necessary ultimate of a whole and perfect life. The soul of a good man, religiously be it spoken, has an imperative *claim* upon all the riches, and beauty, and convenience, of the outward world.

But we must remember that the world has fallen into disarrangement. By the fall of man from his primal innocence — from his Golden Age of spiritual plenty, when the earth brought forth abundantly, and suffering poverty was a thing unknown, he has lost not only his spiritual, but his worldly prosperity. With sin, unquestionably, material disorder has entered into the world. Impoverished outward conditions are the necessary effects of impoverished inward conditions. And if we wanted the fairest comment on the spiritual condition of this world, we might find it in the terrible physical condition — in the unequal distribution, the fearful extremes, the dreadful strife of the social and material relations. Surely, moral causes must be allowed to have entered in here; the Devil, in the shape of human selfishness, has done this outward, as he has this inward work. Now, therefore, the whole world being out of its proper order, it involves individuals who are not always themselves to blame for their stinted supply of earthly goods. Were it not for others, they havo frequently virtue enough, and power of mind enough, and tact enough, to amass a competency of this world's goods, and *would* do it. But they are involved in a general system of injustice. Therefore, they have to suffer as individuals for the sins of others. But no more than we do hereditarily for the evils of a *moral* and *intellectual* nature which we bring with us into the world. Every child who is born inherits a more or less discordant organism, and brings with him a load of hereditary evil which he individually is not responsible for. If the simple distinction had been made among theologians between hereditary sin and hereditary organization, everybody would have understood it. Yet this is a most wise law — this law of hereditary descent; for, as before observed, it is the same law which transmits all the good and all the evil. It is one law which makes both heaven and hell. Obeyed, it is the acquisition and perpetuity of all good; disobeyed, of all evil. Therefore it must remain, and therefore individuals must suffer for the sins of others. The hope is, however, nay, the faith and Divine assurance are, that this train of hereditary evil shall one day be broken — that the time shall come when children shall be born into this world *without* any hereditary evil — that the power of regeneration shall be so in the ascendant, that it shall no longer be said in any sense, " The fathers have eaten sour grapes, and the children's teeth are set on edge;" for there shall be nothing of evil in the child's hereditary for him to appropriate; " the whole earth shall be full of the knowledge of the Lord as the waters cover the sea," and the Lord shall "make an end of sin, and bring in everlasting righteousness."

But now, precisely as it is with moral and intellectual evils, it is with these evils of the social world in its impoverished material conditions. The world is out of order almost entirely. Whereas, were it in true and heavenly order — had we that divine form of society which we shall have, when the Church and the world shall become one — our point is, that the best of men would invariably fare the best, in material as in spiritual conditions. And if they did not always have the most of outward wealth, it would only be in those instances where Providence should see it would be better for them not to have it. Or, where their wants and uses and capacities did not require it. Or, in more general terms — for it is impossible to be exact here in all the particulars — there would be no suffering poverty. The plenty of a Golden Age would be more equally distributed. The evil of poverty is needed now frequently, for trial and discipline of our sinful natures; — to *impel* us to humility and spiritual attention; — to turn us from the world to Heaven; and to keep us from those abuses and indulgences, which, if we only had the means, we should rush into with all the pride and lust of our unregenerate natures. But surely, were the world entirely regenerate, and did purity, piety, and human perfectness everywhere reign, we should not need this hard discipline to turn us to more heavenly things, or to keep us from greater evils. Christ himself was only made perfect in his natural humanity through sufferings and want; and man must "follow Him in the regeneration." But when that perfection is attained, all strife ceases. The heavens are not in warfare; the internal is there in harmony with the external; the individual with the universal; and we may there enjoy the "Saint's Rest" from all our labors, the employments which we shall there have being only such as are congenial to every soul, and in which the very happiness of heaven consisteth.

So eventually it must be on earth. The kingdom of Heaven must come here as there. The good shall be rewarded, both internally and externally. Can any man tell why it should not be so? Nay, is it not an intuitive dictate of the rational mind, that virtue—true moral worthiness—should have its outward, as well as its inward, spiritual rewards? Else, why do we confer honors upon the truly good, and reward with prizes the meritorious aspirant? Are they not symbols—outward correspondents of internal states? And why is it that in heaven, all the most glorious mansions and the most magnificent surroundings, are the portion of the brightest angels; and "outer darkness," obscurity, mean and impoverished conditions, the portion of those who inhabit the spheres of evil? Trust me, these human conditions will be *reversed* in the next world, and the *truly* rich—the rich in spirit and in heart—will be the rich also in external possessions, by a law of correspondence which, invariably, in true order, and especially in the spiritual world, adapts the outward to the inward through all the Kingdom of God.

Here, indeed, we are introduced to a most stupendous philosophy. If it could only be realized by the men of the world, we should hear less, I apprehend, of the mysterious and unequal allotments of Providence in this life. This life is but a small portion of our existence, and we may rest assured that the great Creator has not overlooked those adaptations which are so necessary to the complete existence and comfort of man. He is to be ushered into the other life with all his faculties, and with the most abundant provision for their exercise and enjoyment in the whole outward creation. For there is an outward creation there as well as here, and quite as distinct from the internal, mental world. But the difference is, the substances of that world, being spiritual, are more plastic to the operations of the spirit within, and are formed and molded in perfect correspondence to the reigning quality of the place. Here, by the aid of material wealth, acquired without any regard to moral character, a man may gather around him an external which is not in correspondence. There he cannot do it. Here, be his character ever so sinful, he may surround himself with all the glory and beauty of the outward world. There, his surroundings will partake of the quality of his own spirit. It would be more so, even in this world, were this world in true order. But the *extent* to which it would be so, would exceed, perhaps, our imaginations to conceive. All things, even now, which exist in nature, exist by correspondence from the spiritual world; for they are created from the Divine Essence *through* that world. But our world, being in such disorder, those correspondences are frequently so inverted, and mixed with good and evil, and with the relations of time and space, that it is difficult to trace them. We can do it in general, but not in particulars.

In the spiritual world this correspondence reigns to perfection. It is the adjusting, equalizing, beautifying or deforming, principle of the place. We say place, because it must exist there as much as it does here; its spaces, however, being measured by states only, instead of feet and inches, and the inhabitants of that world appearing more or less distant, according to difference of spiritual character. And what a world must such a principle there create for us!—where we shall all appear, both personally and by surroundings, precisely according to the reigning spirit within! Such a principle is frequently recognized in the Scriptures; they speak oftentimes very definitely, of an objective, correspondential world. The scenery of the good spirit in heaven is invariably represented as beautiful; the scenery of the evil spirit in hell is invariably represented to be dark, forbidding, and ugly. So also the very forms and faces of those angels that appeared on various occasions are spoken of as beautiful. At the transfiguration of Christ, when the divine glory broke through to the senses of those who observed it, "his face did shine as the sun, and his garment was white as the light." The redeemed were seen as "clothed in white." On the contrary, we read of "outer darkness," "the bottomless pit," "the smoke of their torment, which ascendeth up forever and ever." These are not mere figures of speech; they are spiritual correspondences —actual appearances, which are the outbirths of the qualities of those who inhabit the different spheres. Just as a man's own thoughts and affections will sometimes take form and correspondence in his dreams, and his "night seasons" become quite as instructive as his meditations by day; or as a good clairvoyant will see, even now, the aroma and halo, colored and varied according to its character, which surrounds and emanates from the head of man. Were the visions of the prophets all unreal? Did they *see* nothing when heaven was opened to them? They saw into the interior world, where are the shapes and substances of all things spiritual, either good or evil. Thus saith the prophet:—"The spirit lifted me up between the earth and the heaven, and brought me in the visions of God to Jerusalem—[the spiritual Jerusalem.] And there stood before the idols seventy men of the ancients of the house of Israel—*every man in the chambers of his imagery.*" (*Ezek.* 8: 3–12.) Ah, mighty and all-revealing truth! Every man in the chambers of his imagery! So it will be through all eternity. So it is ever in *this* world, to the angels who can thus look in upon us. For, remember, when the angels look down upon this world, and exert the vision of which they are capable, they look not at the outward aspect, the fine person, the stately mansion, the exalted office, the glow and glitter of material wealth, but at the soul and its possessions. And to their eyes, how rich and shining may be the scene of some humble life, where the world is not attracted, nay, where it is positively forbidding to the superficial eye — where the dull routine of a scanty subsistence, and a life of jaded toil and drudgery, are the portion of all its participators. Yet the *interior* of that scene may appear like a celestial mansion of God. There are bright and beautiful spirits, beaming with love and affection for each other, aiding each other in the struggle of life, full of sympathy and concern for the best good of the soul, with a rational faith in the immortal life, and the practical connection of this life with that; and the very *spheres* of such a place — the spiritual aromas which emanate from the souls, and the works, and the general unanimity of agreeing affections, make it beautiful and hallowed to the sight of the angels. They do not see it as low and obscure, dingy with the lack of physical splendor, but as high and conspicuous; radiant with the light of an effulgent beauty; every affection sparkling with the good of love, every truth shining as precious stones, and the correspondences of their outward spiritual scenery, in connection with the interior from which it all emanates, constitute the true splendor and affluence of life. Such is the scene as it appears in the sight of heaven.

Again, the angels look down upon what the world calls rich and splendid — upon the prosperous and honored — upon those in stately mansions and "independent circumstances." And I say not that they do not see frequently the same prospect. Riches in themselves considered are no hindrance, neither is poverty in itself any aid, to the true wealth of the soul. But I say it may happen, and frequently does happen, that those places are, to the eyes of the angels, low down in the dingy obscurity of impoverished conditions. There are visible correspondences to the interior states. Dilapidated dwellings, streets of filth and impurity, an atmosphere of dark and uncongenial character, uncolored and unbeautified by the emanations of love and goodness, foul and pestiferous by the exhalations of hatred, envy, and every evil and impure passion; the bright scintillations of truth and rectitude all missing, the faces of the inhabitants deformed and forbidding, their voices unharmonious, their manners repulsive, their vestures in rags, their whole outward spiritual scenery gross and unbeautiful, the fitting and necessary correspondence of the interior life of the place.

These things are no fictions. They are the facts of a spiritual science well understood and appreciated. And if the church were spiritually enlightened, if it had any distinctive philosophy *worthy* of the great subject of the eternal world and its many mansions, this consideration alone would go very far towards the victory which overcometh the world, and all its vain and artificial distinctions.

We hear much of the fashion of this world which passeth away. And it is most true, the *material* forms, the riches of gold and silver, "the cloud-capped towers, the gorgeous palaces," yea, all the fashion of a world so out of divine order as this is, where the magnificence of the outward is so disproportioned frequently to the riches of the inward, and where the finest spiritual riches sit in obscure places, clothed in poverty, and destitute of the needed comforts of life — it is most true that all this will pass ingloriously away. But oh! if we mistake not God's Word, and the sure analogy of all things outward to all things inward in the world to come, there is a truth yet remaining — a mystery unrevealed to the mere worldling — a fashion of eternity, quite as substantial, and more thoroughly real, which passes not away any more than heaven itself passes away. Sometimes the man of the world is disposed to pronounce all these things of religion — these enjoyments of the mind so much spoken of — something which he never realized, mysteries.

As purely mental realities, no doubt they frequently *are* mysteries to *him.* He has a property which is altogether more palpable and real. There is something in a substantial farm, and a princely mansion, with so much solid stock in trade or stock in bank, which is palpable and real. "What do you mean by all these riches of the mind? Does it look as though the best of people fared the best?" We will tell you what we mean by it. And we will address ourselves to that very external, sensual nature, which may possibly comprehend it. What if these riches of the mind take to themselves outward forms? What if, while whole ranges of granite and brick — vast establishments of wealth and beauty, yea, and the exterior of all the equipage, and the train of honor and glory — what if, while the fashion of all this passes away like the fabric of a vision, at the all-devouring gate of death, *another fashion starts up!* — as real, and every way as formal and substantial, only more fitting, and entirely becoming the denizens of that not undiscovered country? What if the rich in mind and heart be there the rich in *exterior* comforts and possessions? What if the poor in spirit, as Christ called them, be there the rich in all outward as in all inward things? And what if the poor in purse — those who have gone clothed in rags, and inhabited hovels, should there take on the white, whole garments of redemption, or the purple glory of a celestial angel of love, and inhabit those higher mansions, of which Christ hath told us there are many; while those who have lived splendidly and fared sumptuously every day, if they have been selfish and wicked, should there appear in rags and poverty; — sitting in waste places and in darkness; — the glory departed, the exterior altogether conformed to the interior, and thus there should be realized all through that world of eternity, which is no mere shadow, what Christ hath told us — only with a fuller meaning than we have ever attributed to it — that the one party, in their lifetime, received their good things, and the other their evil things, but now the one is comforted and the other tormented?

Far be it from us to hold out any false fears, or to suppose there is any thing unnatural or arbitrary in the whole apportionment of the other life. We know there is not — that there cannot be. But I say, that a man who regards spiritual riches, or the man who prides himself upon the fashion of this world, will most surely find an outward world no less real and objective than this, when he casts off his mortal incumbrance; and therefore if that palpable, tangible realization of a property that is so appreciable, be of any special consideration to him, then *both* parties may be admonished, that along with all the *mysteries* and *mentalities* of the soul and of a religious life, there is all the *objective reality* of such a life; if not here, hereafter; and thus it is that this faculty of our nature which so clings to the visible and the formal, is undoubtedly to be gratified by the Author of our being; it was conferred to be gratified; and thus it is also, that the whole of the argument is taken away from the worldling, and from the sceptic, and from him who would taunt the poor man in his poverty, or envy the rich in his possessions; and there is positively an entire and thorough reconciliation to be made of all the nameless ills and inequalities of life. We cannot be satisfied with any less or half-way attempt to justify the ways of God to man.

Heaven and Hell are from internals to externals. It is not possible to escape the externals if we are in the internals. In this world we can, but not in the next. And hence it is that the idea of place, which is so commonly indulged in when thinking of the spiritual world, is founded in reality. To be sure,

> " The mind is its own place, and in itself
> Can make a heaven of hell, a hell of heaven : "

but these internal states create for themselves *apparent* places, of more reality than those which surround us in the material world: because they are more fitting and characteristic, being the very forms, and colors, and outbirths of the state itself. But instead of being fixed, as they are in matter, or changed by mere whim, or for convenience, by material means, they are varied as the states vary. Thus in heaven, with a continual succession of beauties and glories, the off-throw of the Divinity into correspondent creations through the minds of the angels; in hell, with a like succession of deformed and barren prospects. The natural inspiration of men in every age has conceived something of the truth here expressed. It breaks forth from the poetry of Milton thus: —

> " Though what if earth
> Be but the shadow of heaven, and things therein
> Each to the other like, more than on earth is thought?"

And from Wordsworth thus: —

> " Of all that is most beauteous, imaged there
> In happier beauty. More pellucid streams,
> An ampler ether, a diviner air,
> And fields invested with purpureal gleams;
> Climes which the sun, that sheds the brightest day
> Earth knows, is all unworthy to survey."

But it took Swedenborg to see the actual and substantial source of all this poetry, and to describe it in terms of sober reality. And thus it is that the true Seer is ever the greatest poet, and as Emerson has truly observed, "Melodious poets shall become as hoarse as street ballads, when once the key-note of nature and spirit is sounded." It is sounded now; but one cannot sing and find ears too.

What a momentous truth is this that we are here setting forth! Viewed practically, in reference to these inequalities of earthly fortunes, what a perfect annihilator it is of all visionary and vain pursuits, and all just cause of complaint for ill-success! When we consider what it is for which so many are engaged in this intense struggle of life — this stir, and bustle, and activity of all the world, — that it is that they may have outward wealth, outward magnificence, splendid and commanding mansions, rich and extended lands, and all the beauty, decorations, and conveniences of the external world, we are overwhelmed with the truth here presented. In the other life, this is precisely what the good will come to inherit, with all their internal joy. *They* only will have the most magnificent mansions — the most splendid surroundings — and the largest areas of beauty and delight, in which to expatiate forever and ever. While littleness of aspect, mean and inferior habitations, and all the appearances of external poverty, with deformity of person, will be the portion of the evil and the false. I know not of a more affecting consideration; I know not of a more tremendous rebuke — a more startling truth, could it only be seen and appreciated in the light of a true spiritual philosophy, that could possibly be administered to the mere lover of external riches. I wish that I could sound it far and wide throughout the land, to the solemn consideration of every votary of mammon.

"Why all this toil for triumphs of an hour?
What though we wade in wealth, or soar in fame?
Earth's highest station ends in '*here he lies,*'
And dust to dust concludes her noblest song."

Ah! but if it *did* all end here — if it were not still substantially existing, but lowered and brought into correspondence in the life beyond the grave, where the "true riches" take to themselves the corresponding outward appearances, and the only true poverty can never find that rich external which it frequently finds in this world! And this life is but a moment long — then comes all the true wealth of the soul!

We ask the reader's indulgence for more than usual prolixity in this chapter, for we feel that we are in direct contact with the world, and touching it in its sorest spot.

Let us now look a little more particularly into the fortunes of *this* world. I do it for a most practical purpose, and to call attention to the great law, operative even now, of the connection between internal and external riches. And after all the exceptions are made, and all considerations of a disorderly world, it is evidently true now, that, as a general thing, the best of men succeed best in the world. Sometimes, it is true, and perhaps frequently, the very wicked contrive to amass very large amounts; but it is not apt to *remain in their families* from generation to generation. And I believe it will be found, on looking deeply into the history of the world, that there is and must be some moral stamina or foundation upon which the riches of this world are mainly built, and by which they are continued in the same succession from generation to generation. So that there is *some* foundation in *truth* for that idea of aristocracy, or that superior respect which wealth has always commanded. Wealth truly belongs to the good. It is the *correspondent* of both good and truth. And even now, I say, if the wicked get it in large amounts, or by any unjust or fictitious means, as by speculation, deception, etc., it is not apt to remain in those families; it is soon dissipated; a few generations are commonly sufficient to run it all out; so that it has passed into a proverb, that "evil gains do not come to the third heir." By a righteous providence it mysteriously disappears, and by laws as truly fixed and operative as any in the natural world. "It has this day been confirmed to me by the angels," says Swedenborg in his private diary, "that this is the case, and that riches fraudulently acquired pass away, or are dissipated, so that the parties themselves know not by what means; whereas, others are enriched thereby." — (S. D. 1212.)

Now, to deny a Providence in all this, or to say that it all takes place according to natural laws, is to talk foolishly. God operates *by* his laws; and if He has so constructed the world as that *by laws* the good are generally favored and the wicked unrewarded, there is as much of a Providence in it as though it were done without law. *It is done,* and that is the main point. And if it were not that the present state of society is in such gross disorder from man's wickedness, it would *always* happen, that the most worthy in a moral point of view would have at least enough of this world's wealth to make them comfortable and easy, and, much more generally than now, the most of it. Such is the true philosophy with regard to the fortunes of this world. It is not fortune, but Providence.

But it is to be observed in reference to this grand law — "Seek ye first the kingdom of God," etc., — that it is not meant first in *time*, as though we were to give attention to religious matters before we attend to our worldly concerns, or to the neglect of them; but first in *importance*, or *primarily* and *centrally*; as much as to say — "Let this matter of your relations to God and heaven be the chief and predominant aim of your mortal life; seek this as highest and greatest, and all these other things — these necessaries and conveniences of bodily life, shall be added unto you — shall flow in appropriate order from the Great First Cause of all spiritual and all earthly good."

It cannot be otherwise than it should be so. This is the law. The movements of the planets are not more necessary. Although, from involutions and convolutions, and connections and adaptations touching man's spiritual needs, and reaching into eternity, we frequently lose sight of the law in individual cases. Still there are individual cases enough to assure us of the general principle; and the marvellous providences which we read of sometimes, whereby poor and destitute ones have been provided for in an unearthly manner, show well enough what God is able to do, would man but conform to his requirements.

By availing one's self of the power of this great law, a man is in league not only with God, but with all the angels of heaven; and he can be led by Divine Providence, and will be led, to those worldly stations, and that worldly good, which is best for his spiritual life. I know not indeed how much it would be possible for a man to realize, in a purely worldly way, would he only give himself up, once and entirely, and forever, to the determinaton of a spotless and religious life, — to a trust in the Lord with all his might, and the interests of his kingdom first. Let there be no half-way, no compromise about it, but let the man give himself entirely up to God and his Providence, doing only right in every particular, and helping others all he can, though death stare him in the face, and such a man would be taken care of in the most marked and supernatural manner. He would be in league with all high ministries on earth and in heaven. The God of Elijah would be able to have him all the more effectually in his hands. Angels and good spirits could come nearer to such a man, not being repelled by an evil or unbelieving sphere. And if he were not thus provided for to any great extent, it would be because he did not need that kind of prosperity which some more earthly natures require, and God was training him for the skies in a more eminent manner.

O sad and suffering world, how has man's wickedness hung thy faith in disastrous eclipse, and darkened all the heavens with its shadow! How little of love, of simple, childlike purity and truth! How easy to *write* on the Divine Providence, how different to practise! I tremble as I write, to think that I can practise no better, truths which must brighten the intellect of an angel, and fill all heaven with glory and rejoicing!

But I proceed to observe in conclusion, that there is a more spiritual meaning still, in the passage remarked upon, than has reference to mere earthly goods, and in which the Divine Providence may be still more fully seen. Earthly goods are in fact nothing, in themselves considered, only so far as they conduce to human uses, and are made subservient to the kingdom of God. Now, therefore, if a man is in true order of life, not seeking riches for themselves, but for the use they may be made to subserve, — for the real good of himself, his family, and the world, — even though it be only for the uses of the business world, in manufacture, exchange, and supply, (for the spirit of religion enters into all these; the immortal kingdom of heaven itself is nothing but a kingdom of varied uses;)

then he has a spiritual end in view. He is seeking to augment the general amount of good. And if he does it not in *highest* ways, he does it in some ways; and such a man may truly be said to have his riches *added unto him.* They are, in the use he makes of them, added to his spiritual nature. They really form, beautify, and build up the structure of the soul. And they prepare him for the kingdom of heaven on high. But if he only doats upon them as riches, and hoards them up, and sees them not in their connection with the good of mankind, then instead of being in any good sense added unto him, they are only a curse to him; and they will make him fall short of the kingdom of heaven.

Such is the true order of Providence in respect to earthly and heavenly riches. How much is there to be thankful for, and what an unusually clear light is thus shed upon one of the darkest and saddest problems of the world! Who has not reason to be grateful for his existence, and for the ability conferred upon him to enrich his interior nature with every possible perfection and delight, and to gather around him to all eternity, the beauties and glories of the angelic world?

CHAPTER XIX.

DIVINE PROVIDENCE IN ANSWER TO PRAYER.

"The Scriptural authors support the opinion that the Deity causes that to come to pass which is prayed for with firm faith. 'God heareth the prayer of the faithful.' The effects which they ascribe to prayer are not mere natural consequences of the act of prayer in the heart of the person who prays; they are positive, external effects, which have no visible connection with the prayer itself. This doctrine they teach by precepts, and confirm by circumstantial histories." — *John Casper Lavater.*

"More things are wrought by prayer
Than this world dreams of. Wherefore let thy voice
Rise like a fountain for me night and day.
For what are men better than sheep or goats
That nourish a blind life within the brain,
If, knowing God, they lift not hands of prayer
Both for themselves and those who call them friend?
For so the whole round earth is every way
Bound by gold chains about the feet of God." — *Tennyson.*

WE approach, now, a subject of the most interior and sacred nature, and one which we shall contemplate with the intensest satisfaction. We desire to put off the shoes from our feet, for the place is holy. And yet we must be consistent with the plan of this work, which is to present the *rationale* of every subject we are called to consider; more especially, perhaps, those subjects that are most interior, for it is here that reason so frequently fails, for the want of that solid support which is longed for in the externals of the mind, and a secret scepticism is engendered in the natural man while all faith is cherished in the spiritual. Thus there is a conflict and dissatisfaction, even where none is expressed. It is an age too, when the philoso phy of *all* things pertaining to religion is imperatively demanded.

What, then, is the real nature, philosophy, and effect of prayer? Many questions are continually asked concerning this subject, some of which are the following: How can God be affected by our prayers? Is not God unchangeable? And if prayer has any effect at all, is it not all with man, in changing his dispositions, and putting him in a right frame of mind? Can we expect any thing directly from God, by asking, which we should not obtain without asking? Does He not always know the things we are in need of, without our telling Him, and before we ask Him? These are questions which have disturbed many minds, and caused this subject of prayer to be enveloped in a great obscurity, and much diminished its importance and practice.

In approaching this subject, therefore, it were well to inquire first — What is meant by the unchangeableness of God? He is unchangeable in respect to always acting according to immutable and everlasting laws: but what if one of those laws is this very law of asking and receiving? What if He has made it a condition, in the constitution of the universe, that certain desires shall exist on the part of man, in order to the receipt of certain blessings? Now, nothing is more evident than that such is the case — such is the kind of a universe we live in.

The truth is, God wills to have his children realize that their highest happiness consists in their seeking Him, and the blessings that flow from Him. He desires that they shall acknowledge the Divine Source, — that they shall not be inflated with self-conceit, — well knowing that such a state of self-dependence and self-sufficiency is most inimical to the peace and welfare of humanity. And for this purpose, He has made the condition of our receiving certain blessings, this act or posture of the mind which we denominate prayer. But there is nothing arbitrary in it. It cannot be said that these blessings might have been bestowed without prayer, but that God has annexed this condition to their reception in order to draw and attach us to Him. They could *not* be bestowed without prayer. This desire on the part of man is the necessary cause of their reception. The *law* only operates by the desire. And both the state of dependence—the gratitude and religious effects, and the receipt of the blessings, are alike bound up in this divine system of necessary operation.

But again, we may now not only understand that this is the *law* of asking and receiving, but we may understand how it is that God exists in his own laws, and in fact only answers what He himself has caused to exist in the form of a desire. It should ever be remembered, for the clear understanding of this subject, that in all true and effectual prayer, it is God himself who *inspires* these desires in us towards Him. Do not all holy desires, all pure aspirations, all goodness and truth, come from God? God then has not only made it a law that we shall desire towards Him for certain blessings, but He himself comes into our hearts at such times to *create* those desires, and to give us a certain intuition of the things to be prayed for, and which He designs to bestow: or in other words, it is God himself who *prays in us;* according to the words of an apostle:—"Likewise the Spirit also helpeth our infirmities; for we know not what we should pray for as we ought; but the Spirit itself maketh intercession for us, with groanings which cannot be uttered." (*Rom.* 8: 26.) Now, this being the case, how easy it is to understand how God can answer prayer! He responds to his own desires. He inflows into the human heart, and touches its pure aspirations, excites its holy desires, all in accordance with his own will, and *of course* answers what He himself has caused to be asked. It is in this sense that it is written—"If ye abide in me, and my words abide in you, ye shall ask what ye will, and it shall be done unto you." (*John*, 15: 7.) The reason is, because in such a state of mind nothing is asked but what is in accordance with the Divine Will, and it is the Divine itself that inspires those desires. It is well observed by Swedenborg—"The Lord gives man to ask, and what to ask; but still the Lord wills that man should first ask, to the end that he may do it as from himself, and thus that it should be appropriated to him: otherwise, if the petition itself were not from the Lord, it would not be said in those places, that they should receive whatsoever they asked." A. R. 376.

The truth is, there is a continual circulation of the Divine Spirit, from heaven to earth, and from earth to heaven, and to the Throne and Centre of the universe. It is very much like the circulation of the element of water. It ascends in silent and invisible vapors from the earth and ocean, and is thence condensed, and dispersed in light and fleecy clouds through the atmosphere, and from thence descends in refreshing showers to the earth and ocean from whence it arose. So it is with the circulation of the Divine Spirit. God himself is the Author of all holy desires, and from thence they take their rise in the human heart, and ascend again to Him who gave them, and return with blessings to the thirsty soul. Now it would be manifestly improper to say that we will not pray, God knows what we stand in need of, and is unchangeable, and therefore nothing that we can do can alter his determinate purpose. The truth is, this round of circulation from God to man, and from man to God, and thence to man again, is a *part* of the unchangeableness; it is the system established; and the earth and ocean itself might as well say, supposing it endued with rationality,—"I will not send up my vapors; God knows I am in need of rain; therefore I will roll on here without a thought of any thing but myself." Now, the only difference is, man has free-will; and his aspirations and prayers go up with a willing heart; but still like ascending dews and vapors from the earth; and they descend to him again—yea, as saith the Psalmist—"He shall come down like rain upon the mown grass; as showers that water the earth;"—as the "dew of heaven," and the "small rain upon the tender herb."

The analogy is perfect and beautiful,—putting the system of nature and the system of divine grace at one. And as it all depends upon the free-will of man, or upon his free co-operation with the Divine Will, whether he will pray or not, so he might as well say of any virtue, or of any obedience,—"I will not exert myself; God is unchangeable; what can I do to command his blessing?" Prayer, in fact, is but the labor of the spirit for certain influences from God; and what more is any moral exertion which the spirit of man puts forth? All our virtues are derived from God, and every increase of goodness that we make is but a draft upon the unchangeable Deity.

The Lord indeed changes not, in his laws and nature; but man changes, and by that variation does really attract more of the Divine Spirit into his opened soul, and can thus be led more effectually into paths of the Divine Providence, and this even in answer to prayer.

Prayer in itself is nothing but desire; and this desire, when it exists on the part of man, has the effect to open up the vessels of his spiritual organism towards the Divine Being, thus causing a larger influx of his Spirit. The word — the external asking, is simply the outward expression of an internal psychological operation. It is stated by Swedenborg, and no doubt truly, — we can see the rationality of it, — that the higher portions of a man's spiritual brain, when in the act of devotion, are really raised into a convexity upwards, and that they fall again into a depression when he ceases from that state. Now, therefore, while God is immutable, it is still a divine and sacred truth that He can attract us to Him, and in turn He can be attracted to human states and conditions, by virtue of those affinities which exist between God and man, just as they operate between man and man. The influence is mutual and reciprocal. "Draw nigh to God," says an apostle, "and God will draw nigh to you." And by placing ourselves in proper positions towards God, by calling on Him with a pure mind, by seeking Him in the exercise of high spiritual qualities, we do, without any change in the essential principles and laws of action of the Divine Mind, inevitably *attract* those qualities in the Deity which are nearest akin to our own reigning spirit at the time of supplication. It is thus that the Lord "gives the Holy Spirit to them that ask Him." And the Spirit which is thus given, leads also to many other things, both of a temporal and spiritual nature, consequent upon this desire on our part.

But we proceed to observe again, that the Lord frequently sends his *angels* in answer to prayer. This perhaps is the general way of complying with human petitions. It is, however, by immediate, as well as mediate procedure. Here again may be seen the *reasonableness* and the *efficacy* of prayer. Take the following instance from the prayers of Daniel. "O my God," says the prophet, "incline thine ear and hear; open thine eyes and behold our desolations, and the city which is called by thy name; for we do not present our supplications before thee for our righteousness, but for thy great mercies. O Lord, hear; O Lord, forgive. Hearken and defer not, for thine own sake, for thy city and thy people are called by thy name. And whilst I was speaking and praying, even the man Gabriel, whom I had seen in the vision from the beginning, being caused to fly swiftly, touched me about the time of the evening oblation. And he informed me, and talked with me, and said, O Daniel, I am now come forth to give thee skill and understanding." (Chap. 9.)

Surely here was answer to prayer, in a visible and tangible manner, and an angel of God called out for the purpose. Would he have come *without* the prayer? Surely not, we may say, for the prayer was the very means, though it were inspired by the Lord himself into the free-will of the prophet, of putting him in a state to attract the divine attention or influx more interiorly, and to cause the angel to come at that moment. If we would accustom ourselves to think of this whole matter as *influx*, more or less interiorly, instead of a separate Divine Being coming and going, we should form more rational views, and believe more easily. But we may think of the angels, more distinctly, as coming and going. "*While I was praying*," says Daniel, "he was caused to fly swiftly, and touched me about the time of the evening oblation." How beautiful is this reality of prayer! How truly *any* man may thus draw the angels around him! As David says,—"This poor man cried, and the Lord heard him, and saved him out of all his troubles." (*Psalm*, 34: 6.) "The angel of his presence saved them." (*Isa.* 63: 9.)

Again it is written of Cornelius, "a devout man, who feared God and prayed to him alway," that on a certain occasion he saw in a vision an angel of God coming to him, calling him by name, and saying—"Thy prayers and thine alms are come up for a memorial before God." (*Acts*, 10: 1–4.) Then was given him direction how to proceed and what to do, with the whole announcement of Peter's vision concerning the gentile world.

Again, it is well known that while Jesus was praying on the Mount of Olives, "there appeared an angel unto him, strengthening him." (*Luke*, 22: 41–43.) Also it is said, in reference to an erring disciple who would have smote one of the enemies of Jesus,—"Put up thy sword; thinkest thou that I cannot now pray to my Father, and he shall presently give me more than twelve legions of angels." (*Matt.* 26: 52, 53.)

From all which it appears, that the sincere prayer of the heart is the *appointed medium of connection* between man, the Lord, and the heavens. And can there be any thing more touching and beautiful? To think of a *direct chain* of connection and communication, from God the Father, down through intermediate ranks of glorified beings, to the children of earth and mortality, by which their faintest aspiration, if it be true, touches some bright link in the chain of being, and wafts it successively to the throne of God! Indeed the universe is such a reality. We are not commanded to pray always, and not to faint, to no purpose, or for a half, or mutilated purpose. There is a wholeness in our devotions, and a reality surpassing our utmost imaginations to conceive. A praying spirit is a strong, a mighty spirit. The expression of the old pietists, "wrestling with God," means something; though it is not a scriptural expression, and is liable to perversion. The Deity is not that fixed, immovability of Nature, which never bends or is pliant to His creatures' wants. Why, even Nature itself is not such a fixity. Is not all Nature in incessant motion? Is not Matter itself in everlasting action? And do not all things have secret affinities, attractions, and tendencies? So also the mighty universe of spirit. So also the Spirit of the infinite God. And connected as He is with all created spirits through all dominions, there cannot one of them move without affecting, by successive steps, the whole host of created intelligences, and the Lord of all to whom they are united. Call this only *apparent* truth, if you will. Say that, more really, it is God who affects us, and moves all with his own will. Still, so far as *we* are concerned, it is a practical reality. It is our free-will that is concerned in the work. How truly are we told the philosophic fact, that we cannot lift a finger without moving, by some imperceptible degree, the distant spheres! — or sound a voice without undulating through the depths of space! Much less can we think a thought without moving the heavenly societies, or be stirred with deep feeling without pulsating through the immortal kingdoms. "There is joy in heaven over one sinner that repenteth." Can a man then pray, — can he bend himself in deep, strong humiliation, and pour out his desires to the Lord of mercy, especially if he is in any exercise of penitence, or distress of mind, and not pierce the ear of the Great Father of spirits, and move Him to compassion on a helpless mortal? The movement, I repeat, is chiefly the opening of our own souls to a larger influx of the Divine Spirit than could otherwise possibly be given. And God gives the prayer for that very purpose — that man may feel it as his own, and that the proper blessing may be given and appropriated.

Thus we understand the whole subject of prayer in general.

We see its profundity, its clear rationality. Our prayers indeed are not all answered; they frequently remain *un*answered, as to the specific things which we ask for. Hence it is so often inculcated that we must pray in submission to the Divine Will. "If ye abide in me, and my words abide in you, ye shall ask what ye will, and it shall be done unto you:" because in this state, all the desires are in harmony with the will of God. But yet it must be observed, that our prayers are *always* attended with a blessing; for the very *desire* towards God, even though we ask amiss for the particular things, cannot but prove effectual in procuring an influx of his Spirit, which unfailingly leads to many varieties of good. And, truth to say, it is only in these specifications for particular blessings, which for the most part ought not to be indulged in, that we are likely to err; for we know not, frequently, what things we are in need of; and hence it is that the *Lord's* prayer is so appropriate and compendious a form; and even the simple state of mind — "Thy will be done," if it be persevered in till it becomes a devout habit of the mind, is a very sufficient form of prayer. There are few, however, who attain to this simple state. What we nearly all need, in the present state of religion, is earnest, deep prayer, of a character sufficiently specific for each individual case. And until a man does come into this state, of greater or less simplicity and surrender, he is not in a condition where he *can* receive the highest divine blessings, his own will continually interfering with the divine efforts towards him.

The question has frequently been asked by those more spiritually minded, whether we should pray for *material* blessings; to which it is answered, that in this whole subject of prayer, much is to be deferred to the state of the individual. What is fit for one is not fit for another. Our Lord himself did not, from all that appears, use the form He prescribed for us, even so far as He might have used it consistently with his nature and office; but varied his petitions according to the circumstances, and the nature of the temptations of the infirm humanity. Nor is that one prescribed form the most proper for all persons, on all occasions. Nor is it literally and punctiliously enjoined. "After this *manner* pray ye."

As to praying for material blessings, is it not included in the literal sense — "Give us this day our daily bread?" Sometimes, however, it is said that it is no use to supplicate God for worldly prosperity, for temporal gifts, for however much our *spirits* may be changed and varied by communing with the Divine Spirit, it is plain to see that we can have no effect upon the laws of the material world. But is not this to cut off a large portion of our interests in this life? It is true, all our material things, and all the circumstances with which we are surrounded, are provided and arranged with reference to our spiritual and eternal good; but for that very reason it is, that many a man is directly benefited by a prayer of this nature. God *knows* of this connection, and He frequently puts the prayer into simple minds, gives them an intuition of what they ought to ask for, and the prayer is many times wonderfully answered. It is no use to become so very intellectual and spiritual about this, that we will not, on any occasion, bend the knee for the ultimate things of this life. Many a poor man needs and is blessed in this way. He gets what he prays for. And he would not get it without. The annals of devotion are *full* of wonderful and interesting occurrences. And the *rationale* of this method of procuring earthly blessings is perfectly appreciable. God can commission an angel to carry a loaf of bread or a barrel of flour to a poor man or woman who needs it, as easily as He can give the Holy Spirit to them that ask Him. He does it by means of human instrumentalities. It is a mistake, and a serious one, to deny this kind of prayer. It argues not superior spirituality, but ignorance and pride. Some may call it "old church" praying; I call it proper to any church, just according to the condition of the individual. A praise and a glory to God.

To be sure, this is not the *ordinary* means of the procurement of such blessings; God regards his natural laws, and the work and labor of this busy world; and the best of all prayer is continual and cheerful industry. But there are cases, and always have been, which, by a complication of human misfortune, lay out of the reach of the ordinary methods, and where the Divine Providence is especially manifest in the play of *spiritual* laws, by prayers and answers from the ever-present, all-merciful heavens. How many monuments of the Lord's marvellous and condescending love to poor, and forsaken, and suppliant ones! How have the heavens sent answers in the form of the most material aid!

We cannot let pass a subject of such vital importance as this, without offering some illustrations from actual life, in proof of the position here maintained. And we are happy in being able to present them so full, and well authenticated, and to the point.

A very remarkable illustration of the power of this kind of prayer, may be found in the life of Rev. William Huntington, of Providence Chapel, London. He appears to have been of the Methodist persuasion, and was a Minister who was raised from great obscurity to great popularity and influence among the poorer and more ignorant classes. He was the author of a small Treatise called "THE BANK OF FAITH: or, *God the Guardian of the Poor.*" He travelled much, and preached among many people, under circumstances the most trying, and at the same time the most comforting to the exercise of faith. The whole history is the history of a manifest and visible providence, by the instrumentality of prayer. The occurrences are so numerous and continuous that there is no room for doubt. There are indeed certain trivialities and particulars in relation to his material concerns, which some would be repelled from by pride, and some by ignorance. Doubtless the author has suffered himself to be betrayed into needless minutiæ. Nevertheless, it is a conspicuous monument of the Divine Mercy in token of God's care for poor, and suffering, and trusting ones. Says the author with great truth — "The only way to prove Christ's Divinity, is to go to Him when overwhelmed with guilt and horror, and pray to Him as the Eternal God." Again he says — "One reason for my writing this treatise is, because we are often tempted to believe that God takes no notice of our temporal concerns." We can quote but an instance or two from this remarkable book, while we fully sympathize with the author in regarding the providence of God a "great mystery," — he "could not unriddle it, even while daily exercised with it." How many more capacious intellects have felt the same mystery, with the same facts!

On one occasion he had been greatly exercised with debt and embarrassment, and his patience was severely tried, not only on account of himself, but his friend, who was in great distress, and stood much in need of a little relief. His never-failing resort was to the Great Father of bounties, in earnest and sincere prayer. And God who heareth the ravens when they cry, thus answered him. It was the evening previous, that he made the subject a matter of special supplication. The next morning a person knocked at his door, desiring to see him. When he came into the study, he says — "I looked at him, and perceived him to be a gentleman that I had never seen before. He told me that he had once heard me preach at Dr. Gifford's meeting-house, and once or twice in Margaret Street Chapel, and that he had heard me greatly to his satisfaction: and the reason of his coming to see me now was, that he had been exercised the last night with a dream — that he dreamed the Word of God came to him, saying, 'If thy brother be waxed poor, thou shalt open thy hand to thy poor brother,' etc. He asked me if there was such a portion of Scripture; I answered, the words were these:— 'If there be among you a poor man, one of thy brethren, within any of thy gates, in the land which the Lord thy God giveth thee, thou shalt not harden thy heart, nor shut thy hand from thy poor brother' — (*See Deut.* 15: 7–11.) He then told me that these words came to him in his sleep; and in the morning when he awoke, he felt the power of them. In wondering who this poor brother could be, he informed me it was impressed on his mind that I was the brother about whom he had dreamed; and asked me concerning my circumstances. I then told him of the trial I was in; and as he was fully satisfied it was of God, he wondered much at it. At his departure, he gave me money and goods sufficient to relieve my own circumstances, and also the condition of my friend. Thus, God, who commanded a widow to sustain Elijah, commanded this man to relieve me." (Pp. 98, 99.)

Such a circumstance will undoubtedly be viewed lightly by those who have scarcely any faith in such providences, and the more so because they do not understand the method of them, and have no idea of their frequency. But is it at all unreasonable that by means of the supplication the night before, some angel or spirit could be commissioned to the sleeping man, and thus a connection be established which was efficacious? How many such instances there are!

At another time, our author was in debt to the sum of twenty pounds. "This sum," says he, "hung long in hand, I looked different ways, and chalked out different roads for the Almighty to walk in; but his paths were in the deep waters, and his footsteps were not known. No raven came, neither in the morning nor in the evening. There was a gentlewoman at my house on a visit, and I asked her if she had got the sum of twenty pounds in her pocket, telling her at the same time how I wanted it. She told me she had not; if she had, I should have it. A few hours afterwards the same woman was coming into my study, but she found it locked, and knocked at the door. I let her in, and she said, 'I am sorry to disturb you.' I replied—'You do not disturb me; I have been begging a favor of God, and I had just done when you knocked. That favor I have now got in faith, and shall shortly have in hand, and you will see it!' The afternoon of the same day, two gentlemen out of the city came to see me; and after a few hours' conversation, they left me, and to my great surprise, each of them, at parting, put a letter into my hand, which, when they were gone, I opened, and found a ten pound note in each! I immediately sent for the woman up-stairs, and let her read the letters, and then sent the money to answer that demand." (P. 211.)

And now for the *rationale* of such demonstrations as these. We need to quote *many* of them to feel their full force. They are altogether too numerous and wonderful to be the effect of chance, or of a lucky coincidence. Indeed, there *is* no such thing. It is either by natural laws or spiritual laws, with divine and personal agencies, that every thing transpires. But in such manifest spiritual interpositions, was the will of God changed by the man's prayer? By no means. Would he then have obtained the gift without the prayer? Not at all. But God saw, and undoubtedly some angel from Him saw, that such a gift the man should have, and such a *prayer* the man should have. In *his* case they could be made to exist together. He was a devotional, spiritual man; and could be made, more consciously and sensibly than others, to look to God and ask Him for any thing. The prayer, therefore, took almost the form of a divine presentiment in his mind. God had determined to bless this man in precisely such a way; He meant to lead him, and did lead him, by his holy providence, and sustain him in a wonderful manner, because He saw that He could trust in Him. His trust was ministered to and cultivated in this manner. His whole life was a continued series of such experiences. This man had such a sense of the Divine Will, and such an intuition of what the Divinity meant to bestow upon him, that his prayers fell instinctively into the same current. God, therefore, was not changed by them; He himself it was who *gave* the prayer, seeing how it should be answered. But because of all this, should the man not pray? Should he expect the blessing *without* the prayer? It might as well be said that we will not try to be virtuous; we will not exert our free-will at all; seeing that it is all of God, and he is unchangeable. The truth is, with such as can be led in this trusting, prayerful way, these are the *necessary links* in the chain of the divine providence: but the *will* is as free as in the *lowest moralities;* the man cannot do without them, and God cannot do without them; and blessed is he who can be made to realize such effects.

Take another instance in the life of our own beloved countryman — Washington Allston.

"Soon after Allston's marriage with his first wife, the sister of the late Dr. Channing, he made his second visit to Europe. After a residence there of little more than a year, his pecuniary wants became very pressing and urgent—more so than at any other period of his life. On one of these occasions, as he himself used to narrate the event, he was in his studio, reflecting with a feeling of almost desperation upon his condition. His conscience seemed to tell him that he had deserved his afflictions and drawn them upon himself, by his want of due gratitude for past favors from heaven. His heart seemed filled all at once with the hope that God would listen to his prayers, if he would offer up his direct expressions of penitence, and ask for divine aid. He accordingly locked his door, withdrew to a corner of the room, threw himself upon his knees, and prayed for a loaf of bread for himself and his wife. While thus employed, a knock was heard at the door. A feeling of momentary shame at being detected in this position, and a feeling of fear lest he might have been observed, induced him to hasten and open the door. A stranger inquired for Mr. Allston. He was anxious to learn who was the fortunate purchaser of the painting 'Angel Uriel,' regarded by the artist as one of his master-pieces, which had won the prize at the exhibition of the Academy. He was told that it had not been sold.

"'Can it be possible? Not sold? Where is it to be had?' 'In this very room. Here it is,' producing the painting from the corner, and wiping off the dust. 'It is for sale, but its value has never yet, to my idea of its worth, been adequately appreciated, and I would not part with it.' 'What is its price?' 'I have done affixing any nominal sum. I have always, so far, exceeded my offers, I leave it for you to name the price.' 'Will four hundred pounds be an adequate recompense?' 'It is more than I have ever asked for it.' 'Then the painting is mine." The stranger introduced himself as the Marquis of Stafford, and became, from that moment, one of the warmest friends of Mr. Allston. By him Mr. A. was introduced to the society of the nobility and gentry; and he became one of the most favored among the many gifted minds that adorned the circle, in which he was never fond of appearing often. The instantaneous relief thus offered by the liberality of this noble visitor, was always regarded by Allston as a direct answer to his prayer, and it made a deep impression upon his mind. To this event he was ever after wont to attribute the increase of devotional feelings, which became a prominent trait in his character."

Suppose now it should be said that it was not Allston's prayer that procured this benefit, for the stranger was at the door while Allston was upon his knees. He must, therefore, have been influenced before Allston prayed. But what if God, willing to make his mercy felt all the more forcibly, was pleased to give Allston the prayer and send the man at the same time? It seems that he had about concluded that God would so attend to him, if he would acknowledge his ingratitude and ask for divine aid. Now to say that in his case the help would have come without the prayer, is to talk foolishly. In *this* case, it was a part of the necessary connection; and we might as well say that some other stranger could have been sent, or that the money could have been given without parting with the picture:—folly, folly of mere natural reasoning. *The Almighty Lord chose this way and no other.* That Allston did not understand the philosophy of it, is nothing to the purpose. That he might have ascribed *too much* effect to his prayer, is nothing to the purpose. That *he* could not precisely adjust the divine and human agencies, is all nothing. It had the desired effect upon his mind, made a deep impression, and increased his devotional feelings ever after.

At the risk now of being tedious, we shall present another account which comes to us well authenticated, and also from a Methodist source. It affords an instance of help in *extreme difficulty*, where the usual labor which should ever accompany our prayers cannot be performed, and where the spirit can do nothing *but* pray, and let God find the means.

"Dr. Joseph Stennet resided in Wales several years, and preached to a congregation in Abergavenny. There was a poor man, a regular attendant on his ministry, who was generally known by the name of Caleb. He was a collier, and lived among the hills between Abergavenny and Hereford; had a wife and several small children, and walked seven or eight miles every Sunday to hear the doctor. He was a very pious man; his knowledge and understanding were remarkable, considering his situation and circumstances. Bad weather seldom hindered Caleb's attendance at the house of God; but there was a severe frost one winter, which lasted many weeks, and blocked up his way so that he could not possibly pass without danger, neither could he work for the support of his family. The doctor and others were concerned lest they should perish for want; however, no sooner was the frost broken than Caleb appeared again. Dr. S. spied him, and as soon as the service was ended, went to him and said: —

"'O Caleb, how glad I am to see you! How have you done during the severity of the weather?'

"Caleb cheerfully answered — 'Never better in my life. I not only had necessaries, but lived upon dainties the whole of the time, and have some still remaining.'

"Caleb then told the doctor, that one night, soon after the commencement of the frost, they had eaten up all their stock, and not one morsel left for the morning, nor any human possibility of getting any, but he found his mind quite composed, relying on a provident God, who wanted neither power nor means to supply his wants. He went to prayer with his family, and then to rest, and slept soundly till morning. Before he was up, he heard a knock at his door; he went and saw a man standing with a horse loaded, who asked if his name was Caleb. He answered in the affirmative; the man desired him to help him take down the load. Caleb asked what it was. He said, provision. On his inquiring who sent it, the man said he believed God had sent it; no other answer could he obtain. When he came to examine the contents, he was struck with amazement at the quantity and variety of the articles; bread, flour, oatmeal, butter, cheese, salt meat and fresh, etc., which served them through the frost, and some remained to that present time.

"The doctor was affected with the account, and afterwards mentioned it in hope of finding out the benevolent donor; but in vain, till about two years afterward he went to visit Dr. Talbot, a noted physician in the city of Hereford. This Dr. T. was a man of good moral character, and generous disposition, but an infidel in principle. [Infidel to what? — to certain errors in theology?] His wife was a gracious woman, and a member of the church. Dr. Stennet used to go and visit her now and then; and Dr. Talbot, though a man of no religion himself, always received Dr. S. with great politeness. As they were conversing pleasantly one evening, Dr. S. thought it his duty to introduce something entertaining and profitable. He spoke of the great efficacy of prayer, and instanced the circumstance of poor Caleb. Dr. Talbot smiled and said: —

"'Caleb! I shall never forget him as long as I live.'

"'What! did you know him?' said Dr. S.

"'I had but a very little knowledge of him,' said Dr. T., 'but I know he must be the same man you mean.'

"Then Dr. Talbot related the following circumstances: He said — 'the Summer before the hard Winter above mentioned, he was riding on horseback, as was his usual custom, when he had a leisure hour, and generally chose to ride among the hills, it being more pleasant and rural. As he was riding along, he observed a number of people assembled in a barn; he rode up to the door to learn the cause, when he found to his surprise that there was a man preaching to a vast number of people. He stopped and observed that they were very attentive to what the preacher delivered. One poor man in particular attracted his notice, who had a little Bible in his hand, turning to every passage of Scripture the minister quoted. He wondered to see how ready a man of his appearance was in turning to the places. When the sermon was over, he walked his horse gently along, and the poor man whom he so particularly noticed happened to walk by his side.

"The doctor asked him many questions concerning the meeting and minister, and found him very intelligent. He inquired also about himself — his employment, his family, his name, which he said was Caleb. After the doctor had satisfied his curiosity, he rode off, and thought no more about him till the great frost came the following Winter. He was one night in bed — he could not tell for certain whether he was asleep or awake, but thought he heard a voice say, '*send provision to Caleb.*' He was a little startled at first, but concluding it to be a dream, he endeavored to compose himself to sleep. It was not long before he heard the same words repeated, but *louder* and *stronger.* Then he awoke his wife, and told her what he had heard; but she thought it could be no other than a dream, and she fell asleep again.

"But the doctor's mind was so impressed that he could not sleep; at last he heard the voice so powerfully saying, '*Get up and send provision to Caleb,*' that he could resist no longer. He got up, and called his man, bid him bring his horse, and went to his larder, and stuffed a pair of panniers as full as he could of whatever he could find, and having assisted the man to lade the horse, he bade him take the provision to Caleb.

"'Caleb, sir?' said the man; 'who is Caleb?'

"'I know very little of him,' said the doctor, 'but that his name is Caleb; he is a collier, and lives among the hills; let the horse go, and you will be sure to find him.'

"The man seemed to be under the same influence as his master, which accounts for his telling Caleb, 'God sent it, I believe.'"

We shall not, now, undertake to tell how all this was done,

nor strive to make ourselves too familiar with the ways of the Almighty. After what we have said, and with the principles unfolded and illustrated in this book, we shall leave it to the reader to decide for himself. Surely such a thing *can be done;* we understand sufficiently even the ways and means. "Trust in the Lord, and do good; so shalt thou dwell in the land, and verily thou shalt be fed. Commit thy way unto the Lord; trust also in him; and he shall bring it to pass." (*Psalm*, 37: 3, 5.) And greater wonders than these shall He do, if only we will be childlike and pure. I have not adduced the above instances because they are the most important; by no means; for the concerns of the soul are of far more consequence than the wants of these perishing bodies; but because, from their material nature, they are so *palpable* and *visible;* we cannot *see* so plainly what is done for the soul; it never *will* be seen till the book of life is all unrolled in eternity, and the Lord is manifest in his judgments. But that similar things *are* done, and that by prayer, is known very well. Perhaps, when we stand upon the eminences of the immortal country, and look back to see how wonderfully we have been led, we may recognize some of these very means. Indeed, if there is any truth in the Word, any efficacy at all in the divine instrumentalities so numerously employed, we may rationally expect that some of the *most* efficient will be those which have operated in the deepest secrecy;—the very sacredness of which, concealed in the inmost of the human soul, and in many unobserved experiences, have kept them from the common gaze of man.

To return to the generalities and principles of our subject, we have now an answer to that frivolous objection which is sometimes put, that prayer is nothing without work. Who does not perceive from the premises, that prayer *itself* is a work — a labor of the spirit, and that the body's working is nothing but an effect and correspondent of this working of the spirit? Thus, that the body is stimulated by influx flowing into it from the spirit, by which the hands are made to labor, and the whole man to be active in the cause of the soul. To be sure, prayer is comparatively nothing without work, but we have abundant evidence to prove that by this work of the *spirit alone*, the most surprising effects have resulted from prayer, by that strong influx flowing in from the heavens, by which many a man is not only refreshed and strengthened, his feet set agoing in the right direction, and his hands too, but by which also, without stirring a single step, *others* have been blessed by his prayers, and even at a distance, without the distant one knowing any thing about it. Cannot a swift angel go, and by as simple an operation as that by which we ask a man to go, to our friend or enemy at a distance, (for the heavens are all-communicative,) and implant his blessing on the desired head? Therefore there is a benefit in praying for one another, both near and at a distance. It was in a similar connection that Peter was influenced, while he was at Joppa, and Cornelius who prayed was at Cesarea, and the men who came with Peter had not yet come to the house. (*Acts*, 10.)

Let us never despise or disparage this privilege and necessity of labor, but let us ever remember that there are circumstances of such extreme difficulty and embarrassment, and perhaps many ordinary occasions in human experience, where the soul is so hedged in by the divine providence, that it can do *nothing* but *be still and pray*, and see the salvation of God! It is a most omnipotent instrument in the hand of every sincere believer.

Again, prayers for the *sick* and *afflicted* may also prove greatly instrumental. And it cannot be doubted that were men purer and more believing than they are, more surprising effects would follow. There is no doubt that some of the cases called miraculous, reported in the Catholic Church, were truly and worthily operated. And the gift was also with the early Christians. What is it, in fact, but a certain transfer of the divine magnetic properties, by which the currents of disease are arrested, and life sent flowing through its healthy channels?

Or more specifically, perhaps, by the expulsion of those evil spirits who infest the sick person, and who cannot endure the sphere of the Lord from the man who thus looks to Him in behalf of the afflicted? That diseases generally furnish points of attraction for evil spirits, even if not immediately caused by them, is thus evidenced in the case of some with whom Paul had to do. "And God wrought special miracles by the hands of Paul; so that from his body were brought unto the sick, handkerchiefs or aprons, and the diseases departed from them, *and the evil spirits went out of them.*" (*Acts*, 19: 11, 12.) When, therefore, it is written — "Is any sick among you, let him call for the elders of the church, and let them pray over him, and the prayer of faith shall save the sick, and the Lord shall raise him up," (*James*, 5: 14, 15,) there is no reason for disbelieving it. But the people of those days had a church that *was* a church, and such works of the spirit had not departed from it. It may come to us again. Yea, there is every reason to think so. These are not miracles, but the appropriate powers of a church, particularly of the New Church that is to be, when it shall become more spiritual, in the exercise of powers from the sphere of the Divine Humanity.

I know of a man who is accustomed to private, secret prayer, when he goes about to effect any object, and when he is conversing with others in regard to it, and who has assured himself that he has stood and watched the influence, and seen the countenance change upon the person he was in conference with, as by thoughts and feelings flowing in from above.

But in conclusion we would remark of this whole subject, that notwithstanding the prayer or desire is so essential, and so crowned with success, the primary essential of all prayer is a good life. The desires of the heart are indeed always according to the quality of the life. We can only truly pray for that which we most truly live, — for that which is the heart's secret, — its delight and love. And it is plain to be seen, that if we do not ultimate into actual life, or striving, what we pray for, we do not most sincerely and deeply pray. The life therefore *is* the prayer, most thoroughly of all; for when it is true, the man is continually in the desire and endeavor to receive of the Divine influx, and does receive it, and is directed most faithfully in the paths of providence, although unconscious of the means. His whole life, therefore, may be a continual prayer, and more full of true worship than the most unfeigned devotions of the closet or the temple.

Finally, we need not wonder at the effects which have been ascribed to prayer, in all ages of the church. If we have become more rational and intellectual, let us beware that we quench not the spirit in the cold waters of truth. We need it, humbly, patiently, perseveringly. Nothing is more dangerous than to become so philosophical as to be impractical. "If ye know these things, happy are ye if ye do them." And if we have succeeded in presenting this matter so as to encourage *any* one to a more prayerful spirit, our labor will have been not in vain. Confident we are, it is a great secret of success in many an adventure, many a danger, many a trial, many a complete life. God cannot do for us without it, any more than we can do for ourselves.

But the grand prayer of all is, next to a good life, "Thy will be done." If we are in this state, then, even though we may not have answered to us all the prayers of the heart, we may be more thoroughly assured of the answer of so much; and that is all that man really needs. And frequently, when we have long and earnestly sought, and ardently desired of God to bless us in this or that particular manner, it is not granted according to our requests, because it would not be good for us; but in another way, and when we are not thinking of it. Thus it is that we have power with God by our prayers. Nothing is plainer, nothing simpler. Here is philosophy, and here is faith; and it is high time they were put at one. And to say nothing here of mere forms, which may be left to every individual to settle for himself, a praying spirit is a mighty spirit — a spirit at one with the deep secrets of the universe, and at one with God: and man, so feeble and so sinful, yea, and even a little child, is gifted with a power in the heaven of heavens, to array Omnipotence on the side of its interests, and live like an angel defended from on high.

CHAPTER XX.

DIVINE PROVIDENCE CONCERNING FORTUNE, CHANCE, AND ACCIDENTS.

> "One adequate support
> For the calamities of mortal life
> Exists — one only: an assured belief
> That the procession of our fate, howe'er
> Sad or disturbed, is ordered by a Being
> Of infinite benevolence and power;
> Whose everlasting purposes embrace
> All accidents, converting them to good."- *Wordsworth.*

THERE is nothing, perhaps, which tends more to create an occasional shock of our faith in the Divine Providence, than the many things which are continually occurring that look so much like chance and accident. As observed in our opening chapter, it is the *confusion*, the *hap-hazardness*, with the apparent necessity that reigns through all human affairs, involving not only indifferent things, but many great and alarming evils, which sometimes bewilders all faith, and casts a momentary shadow over the brightest soul. But here let it be observed, that it is in *little* things, chiefly, where fortune and chance are most apt to be recognized; and in *evil* and *calamitous* things where accidents are most thought of. No rational and religious man ever thinks of attributing to fortune or chance the movements of great nations, the rise and fall of empires, the inauguration of particular persons as kings and governors, and the advent of men who exert vast influences for good or evil on the destinies of the human race. These are all acquiesced in as *providential* occurrences. So, also, in great and conspicuous *natural* events, such as earthquakes, floods and storms; even the natural laws are sufficient to account for these; they are as far from chance as heaven is from earth. But why, then, in little things do we reason or think any differently? Had we the ability to trace the origin of many a mighty nation, king, potentate, or movement of mankind, (that is, what *we* call the origin,) we should find it in things quite as little, and apparently the merest chances, as any thing of fortune that is daily occurring in the world around us. If Rome was "saved by the cackling of a goose," or if it was not, it is all the same: how many things are daily happening which are both unnoticed and unnoticeable by us, which must lead, inevitably, to the mightiest results! Thus, "a fit of passion in Mrs. Masham arrested the course of Marlborough's victory, and preserved the tottering kingdom of France; a charge of a few squadrons of horse, under Kellerman, at Marengo, fixed Napoleon on the consular throne; and another, with no greater force, against the flank of the old guard, at Waterloo, chained him to the rock of St. Helena."* In a true sense, there *are* no little things; all are but parts of a stupendous whole; and it is thus that we feel the importance of our least actions in the great and universal connection.

As to accidents, who, for instance, would think of denying a Providence in the results which have been attained by the art of printing, by the mariner's compass, and the telescope? And yet each of these great discoveries, to say nothing of many more, has been by what we call the merest accident. One man, sauntering in a wood, and idly cutting some letters in the rind of a beech-tree, and then fancifully impressing them upon paper; some other curious persons amusing themselves with a piece of loadstone attached to a cork, and causing it to swim in a basin of water; and still another, in the merest pastime, happening to hold two spectacle glasses between his finger and thumb, and varying their distance; and lo! the world is teem-

* Alison's History of Europe.

ing with books, the ocean is traversed and all lands discovered and enriched, and everlasting science looks down upon us from the stars, with hopes and aspirations infinite! Call you this accident? Then every thing is accident, or every thing is most particularly and wonderfully providential.

But the trouble is, we do not make the proper distinction between intimates and ultimates. The moment we admit a God, that moment we admit a Providence in every thing. Every thing *must* have rolled out from his Infinite Essence, which is Divine Love and Wisdom itself. Then it cannot be mere nature; much less chance. Every thing *must* be originated in infinite Wisdom, and be governed *by* that Wisdom — even the perversions which take place by man. These latter were not originated by the Divine Being; but they could not have existed without his permission, and they are governed on all sides by him. For this, the reader must be referred to the chapter on permissions. If, now, we could look into the *interiors* of this vast universe, and behold the wonders that are going on there; if we could see — reverently be it spoken — into the mind of God, and behold those thoughts, those infinite substantial connections which, in the intimates, embrace all future ultimates, then we should comprehend how these apparently fortuitous things are simply the Divine Providence in the ultimates of nature. And in these ultimates, where there are so many things hidden, which exist to perfection in the spiritual world and in the mind of God, and where the connections of such things even in this world are but very imperfectly seen, there is much of the *appearance* of fortune and chance. But we may know that it is not so, as sure as there is a God who is the First Cause of all things. We may know, as has been before said and illustrated, that there must be a *necessary* universal Providence.

But again, another distinction must be made between what may be called constant and inconstant things. By constant things is meant those laws of nature which are established and fixed, and the great processes of which are continually repeated without variation. But on this point the great philosopher himself shall illustrate.

"There are many constant things, which were created that inconstant things might exist: the constant things are the stated alternations of the rising and setting of the sun and moon, and also of the stars; the obscurations of them from interpositions, which are called eclipses; the heat and light from them; the seasons of the year—spring, summer, autumn, winter; the times of day—morning, noon, evening, night; also the atmospheres, waters, and earths, in themselves considered; the vegetative faculty in the vegetable kingdom, and the prolific faculty in the animal kingdom; also the things that take place constantly from these, when they are put into act according to the laws of order. These and very many other things are from creation, being provided that infinity of varying things may exist; for varying things cannot exist except in things constant, stated, and certain. But let these things be illustrated by examples: the varyings of vegetation would not be given, unless the rising and setting of the sun, and the heat and light thence, were constant: harmonies of sound also are of infinite variety; but they would not be given, unless the atmospheres in their laws, and the ears in their form, were constant: the varieties of sight, which are also infinite, would not be given, unless the ether in its laws, and the eye in its form, were constant; just so colors, unless light were constant. As regards the varieties themselves, which take place in things constant, fixed, and certain, they run into infinity, and have no end; and yet there is never one altogether the same with another in all and each of the things of the universe, nor can be given in successive things to eternity: *who disposes these varieties advancing to infinity and eternity, that they may be in order, except He who created constant things, to the end that they might exist in them?* These things are said, because some natural men, from things constant and fixed, which are necessities for the sake of the end that varying things may exist in them, catch at arguments of their delirium in favor of nature and in favor of one's own prudence." D. P. 190.

Now, in regard to the things which are called fortunate, and which break forth frequently as of mere chance or accident, it is to be observed that they are nothing but such inconstancies which result from things constant and established, and are therefore included in them. How much of light may be derived from this one principle, in reference to the great apparent confusion in the affairs of the world and in the actions of men! Does any one doubt the Divine Providence in such things? He might as well doubt the flying of the chips from the hand of some human workman standing at his bench and guiding the operations of the lathe: or the dust and waste of a large factory which is all set in motion by the main-wheel, and from which every random thing and particle results. The cases are parallel. There is much of our daily life, very much of our years, which seems as meaningless and insignificant, and as little under any law or guidance worthy to be called providence, as the scattered and confused things which play about the shop of the mechanic. And those who dwell in mere externals, who are disposed to take natural views of every thing, will laugh to scorn the belief in a particular providence, pointing to such trifles and such hap-hazardness. But these are no less included in the Divine plan, than the great ends of providence themselves. They are the flying chips from the turning-lathe, or the waste of a great factory. The great wheel of Providence continually moves on, turning out the most splendid fabrics, and the most beautiful and useful styles, which are wrought into garments and comforts for man; and is it strange, that in so great a workshop as the universe, the Almighty Architect and Artist should, to the eye of his finite creatures, appear in many things as merely fortuitous and lawless? But we may be assured that there is no waste, that every fragment will be carefully gathered up and wrought into the great fabric of eternity, and that all these things which men call fortune and chance, are simply the Divine Providence in the ultimates of nature, where all things are respectively inconstant. Such men are merely ant-eyed: they see the chips flying; they see not the hand at the wheel, nor the beautiful object which is there being wrought.

But again, we shall not attain to an adequate comprehension of this subject without connecting it more particularly with the action of the spiritual world. As in orderly and more important things, so in disorderly and accidental: the world of spirits is largely concerned. From principles before laid down and illustrated, it will be perceived very readily, that all the evil and false of the spiritual flows into and makes the evil and false of the natural, and even of the material. For, as the whole natural world has *first proceeded* from the spiritual, so eventually all the particulars. Not a piece of machinery that whirls in any mill or factory, not an engine or engineer, or little spring anywhere agoing, but derives its perfection and trueness from *spiritual* good and truth, and its imperfection and irregularity from spiritual evil and falsity. It is first substantial in the spiritual world and in the minds of men, and then in natural and material things. And thus it is, that from the vast sphere of evil and falsity now existing in the world of spirits, there inflows into this world a sphere of disorder, mischief, misfortune and accident, at which, could we see and realize it, we should be astonished. The connection is most intimate. When a good and safe sphere prevails on earth, then a good and safe sphere prevails in the world of spirits; and *vice versa*.

"When an accident befell me," says Swedenborg, "which appeared fortuitous, it was said by the angels, that it befell me because such spirits were present, and that when the accident is evil, the sphere of such spirits prevailed. Evil spirits also by their arts, had the skill to produce a sphere, from which were unfortunate circumstances, which circumstances appeared absolutely as of chance." A. C. 6493.

Again:—"The inmost and interior heaven, as mediums or mediations, arrange and administer the things which are foreseen and provided by the Lord as salutary to the human race; which things, when they come to men who trust in themselves, and indulge in the loves of self and the world, are immediately changed into evils, and also into accidents." S. D. 224.

When it is reflected that the things which are thus arranged in the heavens take the form of absolute substances, with a perceptible sphere flowing out and around them, and that when this sphere comes in contact with the evil earth-sphere, there is an absolute concussion or breakage in many points, not unlike the meeting of two opposite currents of electricity, the philosophy of such accidents will be more apparent to the natural mind. There are also *individual spirits* of a wicked and malicious character, whose delight it is to stand by man, and watch their opportunity for mischief. No doubt many a fall from the window, and death by such casualties, are the work of such spirits. Children and others, therefore, should be all the more careful not to expose themselves to the way of such spirits. Such things, indeed, can never take place unless divinely permitted for some good end; but so we may say of any other evil; *they do take place*, and they are ministered to form the infernal world. It is our part not to *tempt* the Divine Providence, but to observe all care, that such disorderly things may not happen. Virtue is virtue, in natural as in moral laws; and prudence is prudence. The addition of an invisible world only makes it more vast and important, but does not alter the principle at all.

But it is *goodness*, and *trust in the Lord*, that most effectually guards against such accidents. These afford a sphere of angelic protection. "I perceived," says Swedenborg, "that no disasters or fortuitous evils can happen to a man with whom the Lord is; for when by the agency of evil spirits who were present, a restive horse threatened injury to his rider, those spirits were suddenly cast down. They that were with me observed, that from such things it might be perceived what kind of spirits they are who bring misfortunes with them, which was afterwards confirmed." S. D. 4138.

How admirable all this is, and how well adapted to beget in man the principle of a nobler trust, a purer life, and a more expansive and rational religion, even in relation to all the little occurrences of his daily experience! I know not how these things will appear to many, but to me they are only expansions into particulars, by a noble Seer who was permitted to see them, of the wisdom and truth of the word of God.

"He that dwelleth in the secret place of the Most High, shall abide under the shadow of the Almighty. Surely He shall deliver thee from the snare of the fowler, and from the noisome pestilence. A thousand shall fall at thy side, and ten thousand at thy right hand; but it shall not come nigh thee. Because thou hast made the Lord, which is my refuge, even the Most High, thy habitation; there shall no evil befall thee, neither shall any plague come nigh thy dwelling. For he shall give his angels charge over thee, to keep thee in all thy ways." (*Psalm*, 91: 1–11.)

There is a deeper and fuller wisdom in all this than any of us can fathom. It is the spiritual sense of the words as it regards our salvation to eternity, which is most important, but it literally includes the most trivial and accidental things. So true is this subject, in the particulars which we have here endeavored to set forth, that it is really a matter of *practical wisdom*, as I heard a good lady once express herself, whenever an accident of an evil or calamitous character breaks forth in a family, to look diligently about the house, and examine one's self interiorly, to ascertain, if possible, the cause, and remove it from our own little spiritual society. The worldly wise may laugh, but there are more things yet in heaven and earth than are dreamt of in our philosophy.

That such providences as the *prevention* of disasters, even when danger exists, do frequently occur by these means, is confirmed by many particulars. We do not always see them as thus prevented, for indeed we cannot know, in many instances, what dangers we are exposed to. History, however, is abundant, and the cases are remarkable. How often was *Washington* fired at in the army, till an observant Indian made the remark from his own experience, that the fates were against him. He was often heard to swear that Washington was never born to be killed by a bullet, for said he, "I had seventeen fair fires at him with my rifle, and after all could not bring him to the ground." Could he have looked into the spiritual world he might have seen the reason. How easy it may have been, when the deadly aim was made at him, to turn the arm a little out of the way, and maintain the eternal purposes of God! But Washington, it must be remembered, was pre-eminently a *good* man, as well as the chosen leader of the liberties of this nation; hence a protecting sphere came *necessarily* around him, and a more than soldier-like defence from the unseen world. This is the more remarkable from the fact that several horses were shot under him, and his regimentals pierced in several places, and also from the fact that in the celebrated action that issued in Braddock's defeat, he was almost the only officer who was left, and the very one who, from his conspicuous position and activity, was particularly selected to be brought down. How powerless are the efforts of man; how sure and how resistless is the decree of God!

Again, how many *blunders* have been expressly arranged in war by the invisibles, for purposes of circumvention, safety, or defeat!

How thoughtless and unreflecting is man! Passing, for instance, under the great sheet of water at Niagara Falls, the projecting rock above looks threatening and fearful. I was told by my guide, that as often as *once in two or three weeks*, pieces of a size large enough to injure or kill a man, fell from the projecting cliff above. But no one was ever known to get hurt in this way. After escaping in safety, and looking up to the danger I had been in, — "It is the merest luck," said I. "*Providence*," said my simple African guide. And I could but discern Providence in his quick and apt reply. By how Providence? Could any thing be more natural than the trickling water slowly loosening the fragments of rock, and the influence of the seasons gradually wearing it away, as it fell in pieces from time to time? But then the spirit of a man might be impressed *not to go there* at a time of danger; and this would be Providence from the interior; or again, it is no extreme supposition, but what could be done very easily, did the man and all the connections admit of it, and were it absolutely necessary to be done, that a piece of loose and threatening rock might be *absolutely held*, by a strong angelic force, from falling at that time and in that direction! Or again, without any such supposition, it must be remembered that every law and circumstance of nature connected with the falling of every piece of that rock, had its origin in the Divine Mind or Essence; and the event, whatever it might be, (evil and its inversions excepted,) when so happening in nature, was only that which distinctly pre-existed from all past eternity, and was but a development or ultimate of that Providence which embraces all things. Nothing is more evident than that the great mistake of the natural mind, in any such contemplation, is to stop in "second causes," and to veiw only the *ultimates* and *instruments* of God's working; whereas it is plain that the chain *must* be continuous from all that is natural up to all that is Divine; and when we reflect upon what that Divine is — how much it embodies — how personal, exact, and infinite it all is, then we have the comforting assurance that all *is* of intelligence and wisdom — that Nature in her extremest outskirts is all full of God, all full of love, all full of pity, even in her roughest moods. There is an eye and a heart there, but concealed in the vast interior!

But our great lesson from all this is practical wisdom. It lies in our power greatly to abolish accidents, and restore the order of the world. When we reflect upon the frightful number of distressing casualties that are almost daily occurring among our railroads, steam-vessels, vast machinery and business everywhere agoing, it is our place not to ascribe it too readily to a *mysterious* Providence, though many mysteries must ever attend us, but to evils and falsities which connect us with hell and its disorders. Would that our practical men might think of this! What a large share of ruinous and fatal disaster is ever breaking in upon us from that sphere of mental and moral lawlessness which prevails among selfish and abandoned spirits, and which is here ultimated into similar disorder! Correct the evil here, and it would not flow in upon us from thence. But so long as selfishness, in the shape of hot-headed haste, avarice, vanity, and ambition, continues to reign in this world, so long will it be prompted and ministered to from the world of spirits: and so long will there be plot, contrivance, intentional and unintentional evil, flowing in upon us from invisible sources, to make more complicate the vast but permissive dispensations of God.

Take, for instance, the great calamity on the Amboy, N. J., Railroad, a few years since, whereby about fifty persons were sent prematurely into eternity, by the carelessness of man. The cause was the leaving of a drawbridge open. But now let us suppose that whole company of operatives — stockholders, officers, tenders, conductors, engineers, passengers, neighbors and all — to have been good and true men; then, in case any danger should have existed, some one — either the bridge-tender, the conductor, or some available person in the vicinity — might have been impressed with sufficient spiritual power to have removed the danger and prevented the accident; or, even, the danger might not have existed at all. But an evil sphere prevailed — a sphere of self-interest, carelessness, animal passion and headlong enterprise. A like sphere prevailed of necessity in the world of spirits; and the parties concerned, by a more stupendous connection than they were aware of, were run into destruction.

True, seen from the other side, it was not as it seems to us here. The destruction of physical life is regarded by God as a mere circumstance. We mourn over mangled bodies and sudden departures; but life, immortal life, only went coursing all the more rapidly through the eternal spaces; and the conclusion is just, that the time had come when it was best for every one of these persons to close his earthly career. He whose complicated thought includes infinity saw it all from eternity — the day, the hour, the number of persons, every minute particular. But it was disorderly, and as such it ought not to have been. One great object of Providence in permitting these things, is that we may *learn wisdom by experience*, for it is seen that we can learn it in no other way. And in every shock of terror that comes thus appallingly to human sympathies, — in every shipwreck, collision, explosion, fire, on sea or land, involving such havoc of human beings, it is intended to be taught us more respect for those calm, quiet, and harmonious laws, which make the music of the spheres, both spiritual and natural, and would, if obeyed, prove the harmony and safety of all human operations.

In concluding this chapter, and for the still more emphatic enforcement of a lesson so practical in little things, and so conducive to trust, we cannot omit an allusion, still more direct, to that changeful and fickle thing — the god Fortune. It is so wonderful and capricious, and yet so apparently knowing in many of its freaks, that it is no surprise at all that the ancients recognized the little deity, and even built a temple in honor of its power. To them it *was* something; and to many others it is. Even gamesters, and men of no religious principle at all, have been known to declare that, *according to the doctrine of chances*, such and such a thing could not have happened; for be it known, that the arithmetic of this doctrine is reduced by science to somewhat of remarkable precision.

Take, now, the following passages from Swedenborg:—

"During several years I have attentively observed whether fortune was any thing, and I have observed that it was, and that prudence in such case availed nothing: all, likewise, who have long reflected on the subject, know and confess this, but they do not know whence it is; scarcely any one knows that it is from the spiritual world, when yet it is thence.

* * * * *

"Take dice or playing cards, and play, or consult players; who of them denies fortune? for they play with it, and it with them, wonderfully: who can act against it, if it is steadfast? does it not then laugh at prudence and wisdom? is it not, while you shake the dice and shuffle the cards, as if it knew and despised the shakings and shufflings of the joints of the hand, to favor one more than the other, from some cause? Can the cause be given from anywhere else than from the Divine Providence in ultimates, where, by constancies and inconstancies, it acts wonderfully with human prudence, and at the same time hides itself?

* * * * *

"On a time, when I was playing at a common game of chance with dice, in company, the spirits who were with me discoursed with me concerning fortune in games, and said that what is fortunate is represented to them by a bright cloud, and what is unfortunate by a dusky cloud; and when a dusky cloud appeared with me, that it was impossible for me to win; and also from that mark they predicted to me the turns of fortune in that game: hence it was given to know, that what is attributed to fortune, even in games, is from the spiritual world; much more what befalls man as to vicissitudes in the course of his life; and that what is called fortune is from the influx of Providence in the ultimates of order, where it so exists: thus, that Providence is in the most singular things of all, according to the Lord's words, that not even a hair falls from the head without the will of God."—A. C. 6494; D. P. 212.

CHAPTER XXI.

DIVINE PROVIDENCE IN SORROW AND AFFLICTION.

"For till the bruising flail of God's corrections
Have crushed out of us all our vain affections,
Till those affections which do misbecome us,
Are, by thy sacred spirit, winnowed from us,
Until from us the straw of worldly treasures,
Till all the dusty chaff of empty pleasures —
Yea, till his flail upon us He doth lay,
To thresh the husk of this our flesh away,
And leave the soul uncovered, — nay, yet more,
Till God shall make our very spirit poor,
Through the transmuting process used by fire,
We shall not up to highest wealth aspire."

AND so it is that we are all, more or less, subjected to the terrible ordeal of suffering. But after so much which has been said of it already, in the chapters on the regenerate life, we shall not need a long matter here. There are a few things, however, which still remain to be said, and there is one thing which it is well to bear prominently in mind concerning this whole subject. It is that suffering is not the *orderly* way of perfecting any man. And nine-tenths of the wonder and mystery connected with our great afflictions would disappear at once, could we only make the distinction between what is from order, and what is from disorder. Every thing that God does is indeed of order on his part, but He himself is compelled to the "order of disorder" by the sins and follies of men. The great object to be attained by our whole discipline on earth, is the highest state of the soul's regeneration. And if sin had never entered the world, divine *Truth*, with an unsuffering earthly experience, would have been the sufficient and orderly means to that end of good. But, now, the sins and iniquities of men have made necessary an immense amount of human suffering. "Behold, I have refined thee, but not with silver; I have chosen thee in the furnace of affliction." (*Isa.* 48: 10.) That is, in the language of correspondence, not with truth alone, but with suffering. How much of it is necessary! Trials and afflictions which eat into the very soul and life, and destroy for the time being all peace of mind and body; which lay whole families prostrate under the awful blows of the divine displeasure; and which roll their surging billows, ages long, over desolate nations, and deluge the whole world with calamity; alas, there would be none of it, were man but a pure and sinless being! It would be no more needed on earth than it is in heaven. Nor is it by any means an arbitrary infliction as it is. It breaks forth by correspondence from disorderly human states. Not indeed that those who suffer most, sin most; this is far from being the case; but still, if there were not some disorderly conditions existing, either hereditarily or actually, all such suffering could and would be spared. It should be particularly observed that the law which here operates is not always of sin and punishment; many times it is so; and a great proportion, both of our physical and mental suffering, can be traced directly to laws violated on the part of the sufferers. But when it is not so, the causes must be looked for somewhere in the ancestry. We belong to a fallen world, — one of the most fallen, and most corrupt, if not *the* most, there is reason to believe, of all the universe. We are the ruins of many generations. Sin undoubtedly was the *first* cause of all the suffering in the world. The early, unfallen inhabitants of the earth were not sick, nor weighed down with a load of mental sorrow. We may, of course, reasonably suppose them to have had their little trials, their cares and anxieties growing out of their human and dependent conditions, the rearing of their children, and attention to all their worldly and heavenly concerns; but it is impossible that the iron of consuming grief, or the sting of misery, could have entered into their experience, before sin had entered with its wretched train of disorders. Upon this point we may acquiesce entirely with the great poet who is so well sustained by the Scriptures, in recognizing

> "—— The fruit
> Of that forbidden tree, whose mortal taste
> Brought death into the world, and all our woe."

So far as we have any spiritual revelations on the subject which are worthy, they accord with this view of it. There was no sickness in those times, neither in child-bearing nor death. But now, it is impossible to tell the amount of those hereditary conditions which cause both sorrow and pain to man, when he himself is not personally accountable. "The whole creation groaneth and travaileth in pain together until now."

Let it be understood, then, that while sin is the *first* cause of all suffering and affliction, (or nearly all—all that has any sting to it,) yet to many who have not sinned most grievously, —nay, to many of the very best and purest of humanity, the dispensations of sorrow come most heavily, and in various ways and kinds. It is of disorder, but not altogether of *their own actual* disorder. They are involved in a corrupt past. And their purification is to be effected by suffering, not altogether because *they* have sinned, but because their ancestors have sinned, and they are brought now into such an organic condition that nothing but a disorderly process will cure them.* They need this suffering to expel *hereditary* evils, or to prevent them from adopting them as their own, in the same way that others (and themselves partially) need it for their own *actual* evils. If it were not for this afflictive and painful dis-

* If any should be disposed to fault the justice of this hereditary law, they are referred to the chapter on the "Nature and Origin of Evil," pp. 38, 39.

cipline, these evils might break out in them more fiercely than in many actual transgressors. Who can tell, but the Lord who sees into all hearts, and knows the secrets of all constitutions, how much pride, how much lust, how much vanity and poor ambition, grosser and more evil than any could imagine, would spring up in many an humble heart which is now a subject of divine grace, and which is only prevented by these kindly chastisements? The seeds are all there, but in their case, it is seen to be better not to allow of their vigorous growth. They can be expelled without it. Therefore they are crushed within them before they are ultimated to that extent which some more hardened and daring natures require. In these latter, the weed must grow before it can be rooted out. It is also to be noted, that misfortunes and sufferings frequently happen to the faithful, in order that they may not attribute good and prosperity to themselves. If they were not of such a nature as to do this, and thereby become involved in sin and folly, they would not so frequently become the subjects of misfortune, which is only intended to rebuke their self-confidence, and lead them to look more fully to the Divine. There are, therefore, latent causes that operate, far more than appears. So of many other cases. Our kind and loving Lord knows how to discriminate, and it is all, therefore, of the Divine Mercy, whether we have sinned equally or not. The disorder is in us, and it is to be eradicated by these severe means. It is thus that the evil proprium is weakened, and such an experience does for us what truth alone could not do. "I have refined thee, but not with silver; I have chosen thee in the furnace of affliction." How many such there are, — children of sorrow, misfortune, and misery! They know not why it is, nor whence it is, that they are called to suffer, but the Lord hath seen in them from the beginning, a heavenly principle that could not otherwise be awakened. Indeed, without suffering, by which we are weaned from the world, divine truth would have frequently no attraction for us. The Lord should be set forth in all his loveliness, the unrenewed heart would have no affection for Him. Heaven should be set forth ever so brightly, the world would be brighter still, and nearer still. We cling pertinaciously to its outward shows. Its riches deceive, its glories cheat. But there is within, deeply imbedded under all this crust of worldliness, a principle of life which can be made available for the eternal heavens. The Lord seeks it as a jewel of his own. How shall He bring it forth? Only by suffering. It is the lot, more or less, of every human being, but of many in the highways and hedges of life, it is frequently a hard, compulsory lot, and they are made to feel in their very souls that there is no other path through which they can enter the kingdom of heaven.

> "The path of sorrow, and that path alone,
> Leads to the land where sorrow is unknown."

An eminent instance of this kind of discipline may be given in the case of that peculiar class of men known as authors and artists, and literary men in general. And to borrow the words of another—

"God's providence is in a most peculiar manner indicated in the life of authors and artists; for it is probable that there is no class of men whose desires are less satisfied, or who oftener languish in poverty. An eminent writer informs us, that 'next to the Newgate Calendar, the Biography of authors is the most sickening in the history of man.' This arises from the fact that they possess, above others, qualities which if allowed to predominate would cause their ultimate ruin. Thus a learned man has, as a general thing, though he may be ignorant of it, more vanity, more pride and arrogance than others. Now permit such a one to become wealthy, and, to use a common saying, there would be no living with him; for his superior attainments would cause him to look down with contempt upon those who were his inferiors, and which, joined with a superciliousness of manner, would render him unendurable except by those who were willing to become his parasites. Such a man ever in some manner desires to be flattered, and which flattery in reality is the same adoration, the same enjoyment on a miniature scale, which the Oriental despot tastes when his subjects prostrate themselves in his presence; and is that which in ancient times caused men to be worshipped as gods—and which, if permitted to go on, would take up arms against the Deity himself for universal empire: hence, rather than permit the man who prides himself on his own intelligence to rush into the very sin which above all others was the primary cause of man's fall, riches and prosperity are not given, and bitter medicine, even the very dregs of the cup of sorrow, are administered by the great Physician for his restoration, and to prepare him for the eternal scenes of the future. Yet in all this, not one law of the Divine Providence is violated, and success or failure, as a general rule, can be traced to natural causes, which ever are the substratum of the moral and spiritual."*

Notice, then, the law of these sufferings. It is not, personally, so much penalty for so much sin, but it is, (with respect to a state of general disorder from sin in the first place,) so much suffering, trial, and affliction in various ways, *for so much that can be done for our spiritual natures.* It will be manifest in the spiritual world. Beautifully and sweetly has it been said, "When the freed spirit shall ascend from its shackles of clay, in the clearer light of a better world, it will be seen how necessary was this compulsory training, to bring forth, and ripen to perfection, the willing fruits of obedience and love. Those who are called, in the economy of God's providence, to some important sphere of uses in this life, but more especially with reference to the life to come, are proven, even to the seventh time, if need be, in the purifying furnace of affliction."

How great a truth, and how comforting, have we here! We know not, any of us, for what offices in the spiritual world we are now being trained, nor how much our present trials and

* "The Nineteenth Century, or the New Dispensation, by a Layman." P. 284.

afflictions are necessarily connected with the nature of that office. What if we are to become ministering angels to those who will be left to suffer here? I often think, when I read the accounts of terrible and mysterious sufferings, how most befitting such persons may become to minister to those who may suffer in like manner, and how sweet and high will be the satisfaction of doing it. It was thus, be it observed, that *Christ* suffered. It was not in order for Him alone; He had not sinned; and had man not, it would not have been necessary for Him to have come thus into the world. But man had sinned and corrupted his nature beyond all possibility of redemption without His divine aid. Therefore, the Lord assumed an hereditary, and suffered for us in that — suffered for his hereditary only. And so it came to pass that the best and purest soul that ever lived endured the most awful afflictions. Why may not man consent, all cheerfully and willingly, to pass through a similar experience, even when sin has not set its seal most distinctly upon him? By the Lord's experience in this world, He is able now to minister to us from the heavens. His sufferings had eternity and all mankind in view. Can man's have any *less* than eternity? Oh, it is beautiful to think, amid the terrible and confused scenes of this world, how surely the whole experience connects with eternal things, and how our most severe and bitter trials may be preparing us for our sweetest offices of love and tenderness, from which we shall derive the most heartfelt pleasure! For who so fit for such angelic deeds of pitying love, not amid hospitals, and all the repulsive and loathsome circumstances of sick and lacerated bodies, but in heaven's pure and spiritual heights, where mortal infection never comes — who so fit for such ministrations, in a thousand ways, as those who have themselves suffered, and been wrung with anguish? And who, when all suffering is removed, both from the spiritual world and from a regenerated earth, so well fitted to enjoy the release and to appreciate the harmony, as those who have passed through the most terrible calamities? What can a mediocre person do or realize, who has passed through this life indifferent and insensate, not keenly alive to its joys or sorrows, and not greatly susceptible to either, compared with a soul who has most sensitively mingled in its great experience, and been mellowed and affected by its many changes? Here, again, is the *compensating* law, which will eventually reconcile all conditions, and equalize all fortunes, that to the very

> "Height of this great argument,
> We may assert eternal providence,
> And justify the ways of God to men."

But there is one consideration yet to be named — one great general view of the whole subject, which, perhaps, better than any other, affords the broadest and clearest light upon it. It is the argument from analogy between the spiritual and natural worlds. It is the same God that rules in the human and spiritual — that rules in the natural and material world. And no matter what may be the causes of the direful commotion which human spirits are made to feel — it may be sin, or it may be some more proximate natural causes, which have no direct connection with the creature's moral nature — the effects and operations of all this commotion are no doubt analogous to the disturbances of the material world. Nobody, for instance, doubts the utility of earthquakes, volcanoes, and storms; every one points to them as of admirable advantage to the physical world, and to the inhabitants who live upon it. The earth, as was said, must have vent; and if the accumulated gases created by the immense internal heat did not find this vent in the natural and comparatively harmless outlets made by earthquakes and volcanoes, the earth would be rent in twain — a catastrophe much more awful than a shaking and breaking here and there, as occasion demanded. Storms purify the atmosphere, and restore the equilibrium; and every such apparent disorder in material nature is made the subject of scientific computation and admiration by all who would speak of them rationally and wisely, and in connection with the Divine Goodness. There were times, in the early geological developments, of much greater devastation. These were very tempestuous periods. Gradually, the earth has subsided into calmer and more peaceful conditions, and it is not without scientific promise that it will continue to progress into a still more equal and harmonious state.

Now, humanity is evidently passing through the same analogous states as the physical world; and these unnumbered ills which flesh is heir to, even the most tremendous of them, are but a part of the universal disturbance, and the fitting correspondence of the spiritual state of the world. They, like the convulsions of the great globe itself, are necessary to the bringing in of higher harmony. It matters not, for this consideration, that sin is the cause of them, or of most of them; their tendency is the same. And precisely as the matter of the material world is crushed and bruised, and heaved to and fro in tremendous earthquakes, volcanoes, and storms, so the matter of the human world, human souls and affections and feelings, are ground and crushed and bruised in this terrible commotion of life. Suppose, now, that material nature could feel; what terrible agonies would there be in the bursting rocks, and the grinding abrasion of the convulsed earth! what awful groanings of the rock-ribbed hills! what pain of universal nature! But human nature can feel: that is all the difference.

"And oh, the difference to me!"

But from that very difference comes all our enjoyment. The more sensitive and susceptible the nature, the keener and more exquisite both the sorrow and the joy. How great will *be* that joy, when human nature is attuned to harmony!

We cannot refrain here from introducing a similar comparison by Mrs. H. B. Stowe: "The good of affliction is not often perceivable as the result of one paroxysm, but rather as the aggregate of several. The mechanic who would bring out the clouds and veins of a precious wood, seems to harass and torture it in various ways; and if the wood were a sentient creature, it might well complain as the saw, and plane, and the rude pumice-stone pass successively over it, and each varnish is scraped and rubbed; — nor till the last touch has been given, does one see the final result. So of afflictions. Some are like strokes of the axe and hammer, splitting and rending the heart of the soul; others are wearing and long continued, like the slow work of the file and the polishing-brush; and very seldom, under the process, does the soul recognize their use; but after long years, a softened melody of spirit is produced as the result of all.

Could a diamond speak when the lapidary is leisurely filing away its glittering particles, and vexing it with many frictions and polishings, it might say — 'I could bear a good hammer stroke, but oh, *this* is wearing my very soul away!' Nevertheless, the artisan knows that it is not the hammer, but the weary polish that the diamond must have, to make it glitter royally at last in a diadem. Such are some of the most common, least valued of our afflictions, — a slow, wearing, heart-eating process,— an affliction, oftentimes known and recognized as such only by God who orders it, and knows the precise moment when it is possible to let it cease.

Then let the soul deeply engrave in its belief this answer to its oft-recurring question — Why am I thus tried? *Because this affliction and no other could save thee.* The Great Father is an economist in all his lavish profusion of riches, but of nothing is He more saving than of the sorrows of his beloved; not one tear too much — not one sigh, not one uneasiness nor anxiety too many, is the lot of the meanest of his chosen."

But in the contemplation of this divine and beautiful truth, we are made powerfully aware of an objection which is continually recurring to the merely natural mind, that all these things take place by *law*, and therefore that they cannot rationally be considered in that very religious light which the pietists so affectionately rejoice in. And true indeed it is, that all our fortunes and changes befall us, or overtake us, by law, as determinate and fixed as that which rolls the planets in their orbits. But in spiritual nature, and in the vast spiritual world, how many agencies and personalities are forever operating, which do not appear in the laws of material nature! And even in the natural world, how different is the agency and ministration of men and women, from the operation of gravitation and chemical affinities! In the inmost heavens is it not more wonderful still? And in the Lord himself more wonderful still? The truth is, we loose ourselves in the abstract infinite, or in the "natural" infinite, when in fact there is no such thing. God only is infinite, and He is personal. And it is only when we come to see Him in the Lord Jesus Christ, his very and crowning manifestation, that we see Him at all as suited to our finite natures, and to our affections and sympathies. In Him may we understand the Being who appoints and permits our sufferings. In Him may we have a faith better than mere nature — than mere law, — a loving Divinity who is Himself the Law-originator and the Lawgiver. Then does religion come to us under all our circumstances with her sweetest and most affectionate embraces, and we learn to kiss the rod and submit to suffering, both as from law and from the Lord. The Lord governs *by* his laws; and from all eternity, as included in the everlasting Order, it was seen and permitted, what afflictions were best for our respective cases, and how and where they would find every one of us.

Let us, then, consecrate this chapter to a devout recognition of that great mystery of our life — human Sorrow. It comes to all, and is withheld from none. It comes to us in various forms, in disappointment, poverty, chilled and blighted affections, sickness, death, and "all the sad variety of pain;" and in every one of these forms, as a ministering angel disguised in sackcloth, to do the bidding of the Almighty Father. In each visitation, and at every blow, something is done to break up and dissipate the evil life of nature, to destroy our own selfish desires, and turn the thoughts to higher and holier and more substantial things. At least, this is its *heavenly* and *legitimate* use; sad is the visitation to the soul who will not profit by its crosses, but turns the cross itself into an instrument of fretfulness, unreconciliation, and rebellion. For we are thus resisting, through very selfishness, the most gracious and adapt ive means for our recovery, and virtually saying — Not Thy will, but mine, O God, be done!

CHAPTER XXII.

DIVINE PROVIDENCE IN REGARD TO LITTLE CHILDREN.

"Children are roses in the hand,
And stars that gem the nuptial band;
They are celestial flowers, dropped down
From inmost heaven's conjugial crown.
Soft smiling, with a tender grace,
Through their material forms we trace
The fair immortal's living charms; —
They wake — they breathe from God's own arms.
To inward vision they appear
Surrounded by an angel sphere;
Three heavens above the cradle bend;
Mercy and peace their steps attend." — *Rev. T. L. Harris.*

In approaching a subject so interior and holy as the Divine dealings with little children, we feel oppressed with a sense of our own insufficiency. And as we have already much exceeded the limits which we had proposed to ourself for this book, the most that we can pretend to do here is to bring forth some general principles concerning the nature and mission of children, the structure of their infant minds, and the provisions which the Lord has made for their salvation. For it is only by conforming to the *laws and principles* of the Divine Providence, that that Providence is most fully accomplished; and nowhere, perhaps, is this conformity more neglected on our part, or is this neglect attended with greater and more fatal consequences, than in reference to the *children* which the Lord our God hath given us.

How divinely sacred and holy is a new-born child! We know not if there be a greater mystery on earth: we doubt if death itself can be contemplated with half that sacredness and devout wonder, with which we justly look upon the birth into this world of a new immortal. For what is death but the continuation of life? And under what aspect does that life most deeply affect us, if not when it first opens upon us from its mysterious sources; — when it comes, all helpless and dependent, in the form of a human infant, with the faculties of an angel; — the genius, intellect, and affections of a mighty man or lovely woman, and the possibilities of a devil in hell, wrapped up in germ in its most tender brain, which a breath even, a rude touch, may cause to perish from our mortal sight forever? To think of the *eternity* of such a child! Surely, if the Divine Providence is to be exercised particularly any where, it must be in reference to such a being. The very *hereditary* of such a being, — that it should come into this world,

> "Not in entire forgetfulness,
> And not in utter nakedness,
> But trailing clouds of glory do we come
> From God our common home" ;—

"shades," too, "of the prison house upon the growing boy;"— and the truth also that the myriad inclinations to evil, and susceptibilities to good, which every such child brings with it into this rudimental sphere, must be in a measure the limits of action of the Divine Spirit for a whole eternity of varied and wonderful life; — when we consider all this, it would seem that there *could* not be a more suitable case for the Divine Providence to exert itself, than towards such a creature.

But first, in reference to the *source* of this wonderful creation. Be it understood, then, that every human spirit comes down in creation from Jehovah God through the heavens. There are, we are told, above the inmost heaven, or what is the same thing, within and beyond the inmost and celestial degree of the mind, the substances of what are called *human internals.* These human internals, however, are never conscious in man; they constitute a deep and sacred region in the mind, and are the veriest and most immediate entrance of the Lord himself. Swedenborg's language in regard to them is, that "what is done and transacted here, cannot be comprehended by man, because it is above his rational principle, from which he thinks." A. C. 1940. Again — "The heaven nearest to the Lord consists of these human internals; this, however, is *above the inmost angelic heaven;* wherefore, these internals are the habitation of the Lord himself." A. C. 1999. It is by these human internals, which are so near the Lord, that He has "the whole human race most intimately present," and "under his eye." The substances, then, of which these internals are composed, we can easily comprehend, are the exceedingly pure and almost divine substances which emanate in a very immediate sphere from the Divine Human of the Lord Himself. They are the first proceedings, next to the Spiritual Sun, (so far at least as we can conceive of it) of the Divine Love and Wisdom. And every particle of that substance may be conceived of as the proximate germ of a human soul.

"This germ, however, descends first to the celestial heavens, in whose sublimated auras it weaves for itself a body which is its celestial will-principle, and is the beginning of a finite individuality; thence it descends to the spiritual heavens, and there clothes itself in the initial form of a spiritual understanding, which is also in a perfect human form; then again it descends to the spiritual-natural heavens, and there takes the initiament, the first and inmost form of a spiritual-natural body." *

As yet there is no consciousness, for the human soul must descend still further into the world of *nature*, and through the father to the mother, ere that life begins which is so wondrous in its working and divine in its origin. And even when it commences, it is as yet unperceived, and is only per-

* *N. C. Repos.*, Jan. 1857, p. 24.

ceived obscurely, even in adult age, under cover of natural and worldly things.

Such being the origin of the human soul, it is easy to be perceived that in infancy, before that soul has become perverted and corrupted by any actual evils which it has made its own, it is necessarily the subject of many high and celestial influxes from the Lord, and is a peculiar charge of the celestial angels. Indeed, before birth, and before even conception, it may be conceived how the Divine Providence must operate to bring together such human pairs, so far as they *can* be thus influenced in this corrupt and sensual state of the world, as shall most conduce to the perfectness and purity of the new-born soul. Even while in the mother's womb, and through the whole process of gestation, those angels are appointed to watch over the germal infant, and the embryotic form, who dwell in provinces in heaven which correspond to Conjugial Love. By them the infant soul and body are protected from any harm or injury which might otherwise accrue to them. At birth, there are also angels who assist in the process, and who separate, as we believe, any impurities or external obstructions which may gather upon the spirit to prevent its more perfect refinement and expansion. They assist at birth into this world in like manner as they do at death, or birth into the spiritual world. Also, infant spirits who have passed into the other life, afterwards frequently attend them, and confer upon them peculiar influences. The hereditary evils of children, not having as yet become active, they continue for a long time to receive of the purest and best influxes, and these become the first inseminations, which serve as a foundation for the after life. "Their angels," said the Lord in reference to this subject, "*do always behold the face of my Father in heaven,*" (*Matt.* 18 : 10.) This is said in reference to the exceeding purity of the inmosts of children thus descended from the heavens, which, not being as yet contaminated with any actual evils, are so holy that their angels behold the Divine Humanity of the Lord continually with them. This perception is through the interiors of the child. By this direct influx from the Lord and his angels, and by the tender associations it brings them into with parents, nurses, and other children, which is of love most heavenly, they have prepared in their minds such receptacles of divine good and truth as constitute for them the ground of their future regeneration.

But here we are introduced to a subject which is one of the most remarkable and important in the whole arcana of spiritual things. And we are compelled to present it, not in our own language, but in the language of him—the distinguished Seer of the New Jerusalem. The truth here contemplated is denominated by Swedenborg the Doctrine of *Remains;* that is, the remains of innocence and goodness which have been preserved in man uninjured by the Fall, with the addition of those given in earliest childhood, and treasured up in his interiors from generation to generation. These, in after life, become the sole ground of regeneration.

"Remains are not only the goods and truths acquired by man from infancy, from the Word of the Lord, and thus impressed upon his memory, but likewise all the states thence derived; as states of innocence from infancy, of love towards parents, brethren, instructors, and friends; of charity towards our neighbor, and also of compassion towards the poor and needy; in a word, all the states of goodness and truth. These states, with their goods and truths impressed on the memory, are called remains; and they are preserved in man by the Lord, being stored up in his internal man, without his consciousness, and carefully separated from whatever is of his proprium, or from evils and falses. All these states are so carefully treasured up in man by the Lord, that not the least of them is lost, as was proved to me by the fact that every state of man, from infancy even to extreme old age, not only remains in another life, but also returns, and this exactly such as they were during his abode in this world. Thus not only the goods and truths stored up in the memory, remain and return, but likewise all the states of innocence and charity; and when states of evil and the false, or of wickedness and phantasy, recur, which do so both generally and particularly, as to every minute circumstance, then these latter are attempered by the Lord, by means of the former; from which it is evident, that unless man had some remains, he could not possibly avoid eternal condemnation." A. C. 561.

Here, then, we are introduced to a most momentous consideration. If there had been no other doctrine unfolded by Swedenborg, this one of Remains, systematically expounded as it is, from the unfallen, primal state of celestial manhood, through all the successive churches and ages which have distinguished the world into so many periods; and individually too, from the infant to the man; would be enough to signalize him as an eminent teacher. It is continually alluded to in the Scriptures, but by language which has hitherto been understood to signify only some remains of people and nations who have escaped certain destructions. But wherever, in the Divine Word, people and nations are spoken of, reference is always had to principles of truth and good which have distinguished those nations; as concerning Adam, Noah, the Jews in general, and all the distinctive tribes. There is, therefore, a more spiritual sense to such passages. And when the subject is applied to individuals and to children, it comes to us with great power. Long enough have we heard in common phraseology, that "the child is father of the man," and "just as the twig is bent, the tree's inclined;" but when we are once introduced to the scientific exposition of this doctrine of "Remains," all our former knowledge seems but the dim light of an intellect clouded and hemmed in by natural things, so that we not only could not see how the case was in eternity, but could not even see how the spirit was *here* introduced to its various and successive states of orderly development.

The nature of these remains may be further conceived of by the fact that they are from the Lord, and not from man. That is to say, they are such goods and truths, and states thence derived, as are not at all from the selfish proprium of the man himself, as what he does from gain, honor, and glory; but such as he acquires from purely unselfish actions, and such also as are insinuated into him before he has any consciousness as a moral agent at all. For these only are holy, and can be made efficient for salvation. It is these which are stored up in organic forms in the interiors of his mind, and carefully separated by the divine providence from any thing that can pollute them. Even a mother's prayer, breathed out for her infant babe while all unconscious of the celestial influences inspired by it; or the most infantile and innocent act, or emotion of love towards parents, nurses, brothers, and sisters; any thing and every thing that partakes of heaven and heavenly life, which is derived from first infancy to extreme old age, and from instructors, friends, books, experience, from preachings and readings of the Word;—all this is substance for the Lord's treasure-house: and the fact that these things can and do return—can be vivified and brought out into consciousness again, after having slept in forgetfulness for many years, and are thus made instrumental in regeneration; nay, the fact that they are all brought out in the other world, just as they were here, (for they lie imbedded in the spirit,) and are even there made use of for perfecting the spiritual life,—I do not *know* of a truth, except it be the Lord's existence and experience itself, more vitally and practically affecting.

But now, the *germ* of all this is received in *infancy* and *childhood*. It is received from the Lord alone, as may be seen from the *states* of infants and very young children. They are states of innocence, affection, and tender mercy. They are not yet the child's own, in any sense. He did not originate them, and does not even will them, only as an instinct. Heaven itself "lies about us in our infancy." And in proportion as man in adult age extinguishes these states, or covers them up, he becomes spiritually dead; and when about to be regenerated, these remains constitute the rudiments of that process. The man is then led back into them by the Spirit of the Lord.

For the more systematic understanding of this subject, it should be known that

"Goods of a three-fold kind are signified by remains—*viz.*, the goods of infancy, the goods of ignorance, and the goods of intelligence: the goods of infancy are those which are insinuated into man from his first nativity, even to the age when he begins to be instructed, and to know something; the goods of ignorance are those which are insinuated when he begins to be so instructed, and to know; the goods of intelligence are those which are insinuated when he is capable of reflecting on what is good and true. The good of infancy is inseminated from man's infancy to the tenth year of his age; the good of ignorance from the tenth to the twentieth year: from this year man begins to become rational, and to have the faculty of reflecting on good and truth, and to procure to himself the good of intelligence. It was on this account that all they who went forth out of Egypt were reckoned from a *son of twenty years* and upward." A. C. 2280.

Still more interestingly is it said, and educed, also, from a passage in the Divine Word, that

"Man, from first infancy until first childhood, is introduced by the Lord into heaven, and, indeed, among the celestial angels, by whom he is kept in a state of innocence; which state, it is known, infants are in until the first of childhood; when the age of childhood commences, he then, by degrees, puts off the state of innocence, but still he is kept in a state of charity by the affection of mutual charity towards his like, which state, with some, continues until youth; he is then among spiritual angels; then, because he begins to think from himself, and to act accordingly, he cannot any longer be kept in charity, as heretofore, for he then calls forth hereditary evils, by which he suffers himself to be led; when this state arrives, then the goods of charity and innocence, which he had before received, according to the degrees in which he thinks evils and confirms them by acts, are apparently exterminated; but yet they are not exterminated, but are withdrawn by the Lord towards the interiors, and are there stored up. But inasmuch as he has not yet known truths, therefore the goods of innocence and charity which he had received in those two states have not yet been qualified; for truths give quality to good, and good gives essence to truths; on which account he is from that age imbued with truths by instructions, and especially by his own proper thoughts and thence confirmations." A. C. 5342.

Such is a sufficient exposition of the scientifics and philosofics of this subject, though it is necessarily meagre and imperfect, for want of space. But from what has been said, something may be concluded of the nature and scope of that system of divine economy which is laid in the first germ of infant innocence, and which, by spheres and grades of angelic influence on each side and at every step of the ascending process, extends to infinity, and is conducting the young voyager through seas of unknown breadth and of immense peril, to the final haven of rest and peace! What power can compute the responsibility placed upon parents and teachers? There is so much commonplace upon this subject, that it is difficult to receive a suitable impression. We ought to consider ourselves more as spirits already; time and place should not so much affect us; and here we are, in God's eternity, building a temple which shall last forever! — doing it not only for ourselves, but for little ones who cannot do it for themselves — who know not how to do it — who are entrusted to us, and whom the Lord, in his merciful providence, has lent to us for a little while, and put under our tuition, that we may do this work, and do it for eternity. What if we are not faithful?

There is one thing not yet mentioned in this subject of Remains, which is of peculiar importance to know; that is, the peculiar sanctity of the *father's* instructions. The mother, indeed, has the chief charge through the first years, and generally molds the future life of the child; but the father represents more particularly the Lord. There is a different and more interior influx into his mind. Hence it is affirmed by Swedenborg that "what is once implanted from infancy as holy, particularly if it be implanted into children by their fathers, and thereby rooted in them this the Lord never breaks, but bends, unless it be contrary to order itself." A. C. 2180. Do we, as fathers, think enough of this privilege? Indeed, do fathers in general exert themselves as they might, by availing themselves of their greater authority, and standing more fully in the place and as the representative of the Lord, and thereby insinuating into their children the divine things of heaven and the church? Alas! we know that it is not so; and in too many cases it is mainly the mother's love, and the little nightly prayer, and the familiar verse, which is all the child receives from such sources, who is storing up remains for eternity.

To illustrate and set forth the truth of this part of our subject, we may here revert to a phenomenon which is frequently observed, and felt in the inmost soul. I allude to the fact, that when any guilty action is performed, or wickedness meditated in the heart of man, there is so often a running back in the memory to the scenes of childhood. Sometimes by a strange revision of the whole scene of the early home;—the house of nativity, and all its surroundings, starting up in complete picture in the mind, as if, by a sudden power of introversion, it were turned back to the days of childhood again. And all this in connection with some meditated wickedness about to be committed. Why should crime have such power to paint these early scenes? Ah! it does not paint them; it only brings out the old colors and impressions, by the holy power of *Remains* thus operating. These things start out in horror and resistance at the act! That mother's prayer—that father's warning and instruction—that sister's, brother's, playmate's innocence and goodness—those verses of the Holy Word daguerreotyped upon that tender organism,—these are all the Lord's implanting there; and they are treasured up within those sacred archives for reference and use for all time coming. True, they are not *generally* suffered to come out, except in seasons of goodness, humility, and the like, which pre-dispose to heavenly things. For the natural man is so full of evils, that there is great danger of pollution and perversion, or the mixing of these remains with things vile and evil, in which case they would be liable to perish. Therefore it is, frequently, not in health and prosperity, nor in states of wickedness, that they are felt to be most powerful, but in seasons of misfortune, sickness, or anxiety, which tend to the inducement of some holy state. Then remains are suffered to come forth and conjoin themselves to the natural man, that it may be regenerated. But they may be *felt*, and *are* felt frequently, when crime and wickedness stare us in the face, and we are meditating a surrender. Thus it is that the scenes of childhood are projected to the vision for guilt to look upon, and to blush in their holy presence.

If, then, we would do any thing effectually, to aid the Divine Providence in regard to children, we must do it by assisting them in the storing up of "remains." Here is a vast work as yet but little understood. It is only by seeing it systematically, that we become fully impressed by it. When it is reflected that the whole process of regeneration in adult life is grounded upon these remains of good and truth received in infancy and childhood, with what latent and concealed good is handed down from past generations, it will be confessed that we have here opened into a subject, the like of which does not often present itself. And yet it will be seen that *without* these early receptions, it would be all over with man, his evils having accumulated to such an extent that nothing otherwise could be done for him.

"Man at his birth has not the smallest portion of good of or from himself, being [in his natural mind] totally and entirely defiled with hereditary evil; *but all the good that he has enters by influx.* * * * Without these remains of things celestial, it would not be possible for man to become a man; for his states of lusts, or of evil, without temperature by states of the affection of good, would be fiercer and more savage than those of any other animal. [This is scarcely reflected on, because whatever is imbued in infancy appears born with it.] In the subsequent period of his life he is also gifted with new states; but these are not so much states of good, as of truth." A. C. 1906.

Thus it is seen what a work, under providence, we have to do for our children. Can it be possible, with such a system of divine economy, that the child is not cared for in the most particular manner,—that it is not led, from its earliest days, (so far as it can be, in a wicked world like this,) and brought into such situations and experiences as shall tend most effectively to the storing up of these heavenly remains? And is it not here, if anywhere, that the parent's chief work may be found, and prove most successful? O, eternity, eternity, how much depends!

And now, what we have to say most emphatically is—*Begin early.* We cannot begin *too* early. Much as we have heard of forming and impressing the mind, we do not yet realize the substantial philosophy of the subject. The mind itself being an active substance, the speaking of men as "clay in the hands of the potter," is no mere figure of speech. We can be literally *formed* into vessels of honor or dishonor. And in some of the representations of Swedenborg, we see how true it is that one mind is hard and bony, another soft and flexible, one in beauty and another in deformity. Thus, "with those who in the life of the body have studied only for the memory, and have not cultivated their rational, the brain in the other life appears with a hard callosity, and streaked as with tendons."—With those who have studied for self love and love of the world, it appears "conglutinated and ossified."—"With those who have been deceitful and hypocrites, it appears hard and bony, like ebony, which turns back the rays of spiritual light." H. H. 466.

What a comment is such a representation upon the interior sense of our common proverbs and phrases! "Hard characters, and cases."—"*Form*ation is better than *re*-formation."

Now, in an infant, or very young child, the substance of the mind is yet unformed except by hereditary evils. And these, we are assured, are distinguished both by forms and colors. (S. D. 1311.) Such minds are so tender and susceptible as to be "mere receptivities." But this is spoken of the infant mind. Soon, hereditary evils begin to appear and to be appropriated; but here, if anywhere, is the field for diligent culture. How much might be done, only by beginning early! "*Train* up a child," not let him *come* up, like a weed. *Re*-formation is comparatively a hard work. "Go out," said a noble and eloquent champion for early education — "into the *forests*, and attempt to turn the old and gnarled oaks, which have grown into deformity, and *curled as they have grown*, by the potent influence of a hundred summers' suns. Alas! if you had taken them as saplings, you could have shaped them into beauty, an acre in a day." *

By beginning early. I say, we cannot begin *too* early. And so far as good is concerned, rather than truth, the very first breathings of a child's life in this warm and pulsating world, may be made the signal for celestial influxes through the heart and prayer of the mother. A child a year old may, from feeling, signs, and intelligent discipline, be made to know very quickly what right and wrong are. Two years old may see a possessor, if not a professor, of the substantial rudiments of moral philosophy. Three years may bring forth fruits meet for repentance. Four years may see hereditary evil strangled in its first life. Five years — alas! if something radical and effectual has not been accomplished yet, power on the part of the parent is very perceptibly lost. Six, seven, ten, twelve,— if in mercy they are not already removed to the spiritual world, out of the reach of such parents, to the hands of better instructors, which by a well ordered Providence is frequently done, then what have we but a hard and wilful boy, or a pouty, unsubdued, and contrary girl, with whom all the power of divine grace is not perhaps adequate to bend the stubborn will, while we are continually assured that the Lord will not break

* Horace Mann.

it, and the Word of Truth is ever upon us — "Bring them up in the nurture and admonition of the Lord."

Many things must be omitted here concerning the state of infants and children after death, and why they are removed in so great numbers so early from the natural world, both because we have not space, and because, in another chapter, something of this will be alluded to. Infants in heaven perform for man in the world some of the most important uses of regeneration. By their tender and celestial quality, they can approach him in his more infantile states, and do for him what no other spirits can. It is not in divine order for infants to die, but since by a general state of sin and disorder they do depart thus early, they perform a very necessary work for man — indeed, an indispensable work. But it is for us, more practically, to recognize the wonderful Providence in the *creation and care* of these infant souls; and if we are at all impressed with such an amount of divine, interior truth, to let it have its proper influence in rebuking our indifference, and in leading us to coöperate more faithfully with the Lord of all souls, in bringing many children to heaven.

CHAPTER XXIII.

DIVINE PROVIDENCE IN MARRIAGES.

"They who enter into a state of marriage, cast a die of the greatest contingency, and of the greatest interest in the world, next to the last throw for eternity." — *Jeremy Taylor.*

"Those who are in love truly conjugial, in marriage regard what is eternal, because there is eternity in that love." — *Swedenborg.*

"Thou shalt not commit adultery." — *Exodus,* 20 : 14.

"What God hath joined together, let not man put asunder." — *Matt.* 19 : 6.

We have now approached a subject to which we have been looking from the commencement of this work. The Marriage of Human Souls! — and external relations in correspondence therewith. It is a theme most vitally practical, most fundamental, lying as it does at the very root of all good and evil, all happiness and misery. It regards not only the parties themselves, in their most sacred and intimate relations, but their offspring, and their eternity. Here, it must be confessed, is the germ of the soul first molded into its ultimate form, which, to a certain extent, it never recedes from. Say, if you will, that all deformities and evils may be eventually outgrown or eradicated; still, if there is any truth in eternal causation, what takes place here will *never* utterly cease, while life or being continues. The inexorable law which from the beginning eternally governs degrees, comes here into operation. Had nobler parties united in marriage, nobler beings would not only have been born into the world, but born into eternity. And hence, though it is not strictly true, as shown in the last chapter, that souls are *first* formed in the womb of the earthly mother, for they have come down through three heavens previously to that, yet it is true that they here receive their outer integuments and coverings, to which the interiors are in a degree limited and confined, and by which they are forever characterized, more or less, in the peculiarities of individual genius.

Certain hereditary evils too are thus permanently introduced into the human constitution. On this subject there is the profound psychology of Swedenborg, so foreign and even contrary to the prevailing science, which assures us that the soul is from the father, and the body from the mother. And it cannot, I think, be doubted, that the descent of the soul is *through* the father, as a graft or off-shoot of the divine spiritual principle in orderly succession, and that it is the office of the mother to clothe this germ with its suitable investment, from which the body is ultimately evolved. This is evinced from the fact that the disposition, affection, and peculiarity of the father, more than of the mother, is transmitted to the child, and appears conspicuously from generation to generation. Also that facial resemblances distinguish for so long a time whole families and even nations of men, from their first father. The body, which is from the mother, may resemble either parent, according as more external influences operate to mold it; but the soul, being more interior, is continually in the effort to break through; and if it does not so fully in the immediate offspring, it will reappear after a while, apparently overleaping three or four generations. On this account it is, that "there are two hereditary principles which are connate in man, one derived from his father, the other from his mother;" as it was with our Lord in the incarnation. "The infirm part or principle which man derives hereditarily from his mother, is somewhat corporeal, which is dispersed during regeneration; but what man derives from his father remains to eternity." A. C. 1414. By this it is to be understood, not that the evil necessarily remains *active* to eternity, but that still it remains, in a certain inherent form of character, as may be seen in the chapter on memory. Or, not to be dogmatical, it remains *far into* eternity.

In earthly marriage, then, in two distinct senses, is the beginning somewhat of eternal character. Souls that are to be married for eternity, are here, by this marriage, formed and characterized. Shall human beings at all *regard* so fundamental a truth? or shall they rush on, indifferent to eternal things, peopling the world with discords and miseries, and eternity itself with imperfections and abortions? We may be assured that *God* will regard it, and that in a system so vast and comprehensive as his universe, He will, despite all the sin and folly of man, conduct an ever-watchful providence, to right as far as possible the gigantic wrongs of the world. Man will co-operate as fast as he is regenerated. He will grow rational and considerate of eternal things, in proportion as he grows spiritual. What tremendous responsibilities are men and parents now incurring, and (illustrative of their own state) what inconsistencies are they guilty of! They will frequently send over a whole country, and to other continents, to procure good seed corn, fruit grafts, and other seed, to improve and replenish their granaries and orchards, and take special pains to cull out the finest and fairest of the seed, while they will encourage the most pitiful and indiscriminate marriages of themselves and their children, thus producing a harvest of discord, extending indefinitely beyond the bounds of time. What they will do for a potato patch, or a field of corn, they will not do for their own eternal sons and daughters!

We have alluded to this earthly *beginning* of human souls, that the subject may rise before us in its own true proportions, and rest upon the foundations which God has designed for it. Here we are, planted in the natural, and adjoined to the material. We are bound to respect it. If we do not, then our professions may be what they will; it is plain to perceive that we do not regard them, and that we are not what we would seem to be.

But we ascend to what with most persons will be deemed more easily practical. Men do not in general so much regard what offspring they may produce, as their own happiness and improvement, in this act of marriage. And here it is that the highest principles of the Divine Nature, as they are humanized in men and women, come into play. We are happy or miserable, exalted or degraded, according as we embody more or less of the Divine Nature in our own humanity, and in relations of principles such as they sustain in the Divinity. Now, a divine marriage is the first thing discoverable in the Deity. It is the ineffable and perfect union of the Divine Love and Wisdom. These are equally related parts (so to speak) in the Divinity. They form the infinite Oneness of his nature. It is the primal marriage, the first cause of male and female human souls, and the origin of the bond between them. Human souls being but offshoots from the Deity, the woman, predominantly, is an embodiment of Divine Love, and man of the Divine Wisdom. We say predominantly, for both the woman and the man have love and wisdom, each as an individual. But as finite beings, being made to share each other's happiness to the very utmost, they are so constituted as greatly to predominate, the one in the affections, the other in the intellect; and still, each to possess a degree of what the other is distinguished for. Were it not for this, they could not associate as they now do, but would be merged into a more monotonous life, at the same time separated by a greater interval; whereas now they can unite, and still be distinct; increasing the happiness by union in separation, and separation in union.

But it must be distinctly remembered that these particles of human essence have come down from God. They are distinct emanations from his own Divine Substance, mysteriously but beautifully formed and endowed. Must there not, then, have been a perfect marriage in first principles? How is it possible that male and female souls could proceed from the Divine

Essence, without being first and originally united in that Essence, not as conscious individualities, but as germal particles, and as male and female? — like the positive and negative particles of all matter. Must they not, from all eternity, have existed as germs of distinct humanity, each united to its own, in the great Fount of Being? Was not I distinct from you, and from every other being, in germal peculiarity from eternity? If not, then it would seem there was confusion in the Divine Nature. If we cannot go back to eternity with them, and in pairs, then we must say, that on a time, germs were created, or else that those germs which from eternity were united in other pairs, then became paired differently; either of which suppositions is absurd. We have no objections, however, to the idea that primal germs, as well as individual souls, were *developed* or *unfolded* from the Divine Essence, more and more distinctly; but that they were ever primarily and substantially *created* — that any substance was ever *added* to the One Infinite and Eternal Essence, we cannot admit. To our mind, it is as great an absurdity to create *more* matter or substance than eternally existed, as to create it at first out of nothing. It may be *developed* or *unfolded* into more, that is, into apparently more, as a rose bud opens and expands into the flower; but if there is a real addition of more in amount, then whatever this addition is, by so much must the principle be admitted of something being made out of nothing. We reject it therefore as an absurdity. These primal germs of human souls we take to be eternal in God. Or, if any choose to say they were on a time created, it makes no difference for our theory of marriage. If so created, it must have been either in equal pairs, or in unequal. We do not choose the absurdity of unequal, and are necessarily shut up to the conclusion of equal pairs — miniature representations of the Divine Love and Wisdom. Indeed, it was not so much *pairs* of germs, as individual particles in the most perfect dual unity, — like love and wisdom, or affection and thought, as they appear in an individual soul. These were the original archetypes of human beings. We become Platonic here, inevitably. True and deep thought strikes home to the reality at once. Such germs of souls were married from all past eternity in God.

> "Married in God, thus only sure
> To re-unite in heaven again."

The principles of the subject, then, being admitted, we proceed to say that there is a corresponding duality to be seen in all nature. Fortunately, this subject is not left to obscure, metaphysical abstractions. We see in nature what exists in God. "The invisible things of Him from the creation of the world are clearly seen, being understood by the things that are made," (*Rom.* 1. 20,) even this duality of the sexes. All things in nature are paired. The marriage principle is everywhere. The principles even of *material* nature unite in this dualism. There is the positive and negative force, action and re-action, giving and receiving, everywhere. There are not only two sexes to humanity and all animals, but a remarkable tendency to pairs in the parts of every individual. In man, there are two chief faculties of the mind — will and understanding, and two chief organs of the body — the heart and lungs. Each of these, again, is divided into two. There are two lobes to the brain, two to the lungs, two parts in general to each of the internal viscera; and even those which appear as one, are in two distinct divisions, united by a common covering. There are two eyes, two ears, two cheeks, two arms and legs; and although the nose is one organ, there are two nostrils; and so in the mouth; there are not only two lips, but each lip is divided by a perpendicular line, so that there are two halves to the lips; and the same may be said of the tongue. So in the lower natures, even in the shell-fish, which open with two shells; in the leaves of plants, which are beautifully halved; in the sexes and loves of the plants; in seeds also, which are similarly divided; and even in the mineral kingdom, how completely magical, how similar to affection and choice, is the action of chemical affinities! "Behold," saith the son of Sirach, "all things are double, one against another, and God hath made nothing imperfect!"

Now, there must be a reason for all this; and that reason, clear and conspicuous, is found in the two chief attributes of the Divine Mind — Love and Wisdom; for these include all the other attributes. Power is nothing but Love and Wisdom in actuation; and Justice, Mercy, Goodness, and Truth, are but modifications and outbirths of the one only Essence, whose nature is Love and whose form is Wisdom.

Here, then, is the foundation of all this duality which exists in nature. It is in the dual unity of the Divine Mind. Creation is an outbirth from Deity. It must, therefore, image the Deity, from its greater to its lesser parts. Everywhere and forever, it takes two to make one. Nothing stands alone, in a cold, solitary individuality; every perfect individual is a dual unity. The *proceeding sphere* of such a duality is the *third* element, or that which gives the *trinity*, also, which is observable in nature.

Now, therefore, man and woman are similarly married, from eternity to eternity. They are parts of the eternal substance. Not parts of God, now that they are separated and born *out* from Him; but they were originally, and are now, parts of the eternal substance. As germs, or monads, or married particles of that Substance, from eternity they existed in divine and secret unity. Male and female, they belonged to each other. They separated in coming out through nature into individual, conscious existence. Thus saith the devout Watts, with as much philosophy as poetry:—

"The mighty Power that formed the mind,
One mold for every two designed,
And blessed the new-born pair:
'This be a match for *this*,' He said;
Then down He sent the souls He made,
To seek their bodies here.

But, parting from their warm abode,
They lost their fellows on the road,
And never joined their hands:
Oh! cruel chance and crossing fates,
Our heaven-born souls have lost their mates
On earth's cold, barren sands."

Verily so. To *sinful nature* is chargeable this confusion of the married world. In the beginning, we are assured it was not so. The pairs have mis-mated. But the great fact that they *were* together from the beginning of things, coupled in the substance of the eternal Divinity, is the reason why, when harmony is restored, they again find each other, on earth or in heaven. At least, so we are obliged to conceive of it.

Or without this theory, can it be possible that God has permitted, or is it consistent with the Divine Nature to permit, the very *highest* creations — the ultimates of His own Divine Love and Wisdom — Man and Woman, to remain either imperfectly or temporarily united? Must not the union be both perfect and eternal? If marriage is really a union of souls, as we shall soon see more distinctly, can it be possible, where this union exists, that it can be broken at the threshold of death — at the very point where, by a long life of intertwining and regenerate affections, the parties are ripened for a still more heavenly and unobstructed union? From whence is the instinct so often felt in husbands and wives of an eminently religious experience, of a re-union beyond the grave? It were cruel not to gratify it; it is blindness not to perceive it. There may be much mistaking as to the parties who are to be thus united; there can be no mistake as to the principle. The Deity Himself is not more indissolubly and eternally united in the infinity of His own Divine Love and Wisdom, than are male and female human souls destined to a similar union. If either man or woman stood alone, or could even maintain their perfect existence alone, for a single moment, this conclusion would not follow. But requiring two to make one, perfect and entire, they can no more be separated in eternity than they can in time — nay, not so much. Nature is ever seeking higher and higher affinities, and what is not perfectly united in this world must conform to the law of divine association in the world to come. Souls formed to flow together, come so inevitably. Distance may sever, or circumstances prevent their connection in time, but they will gravitate together in the spiritual spheres, where the false ties formed in time have no power over them.

This is the way we are compelled to view the subject of marriage. It is inevitable as Fate. Of course, the free-will of the parties is consulted, and seen from eternity, bound up in the germ of destiny, and exercised in consistency *with* that destiny. It is the same with this as with all other subjects, where the Providence is necessary, and the freedom of the creature is a part of that system. There must be human endeavor, obedience, purity of heart, striving in the regeneration, all as essential to the *security* of this marriage, for it is not forced upon us, and is only given to regenerate souls. As we realize the marriage of good and truth in our own individual natures, so do we approach its counterpart in the joining of two souls in one. We may, therefore, postpone it, and that indefinitely, but it is the blessed purpose of God, founded in his own eternal nature, to unite all souls in such a heavenly marriage. And however rare such marriages may be in our day, owing to the sunken and corrupt state of the world, it is an important and comforting assurance which we have for the Church of the Future, that still such unions are provided by the Lord for those who from an early age have loved, have desired and have asked of Him, a legitimate and lovely connection with one of the sex, shunning and abominating wandering lust. How much should parents, therefore, try to instil this into the minds of their children! How greatly would the Divine Providence be facilitated by such means! Indeed, it is because of the immense and eternal consequences resulting from such a marriage, some of which have been already mentioned, that the Divine Providence is most particular in relation to this whole subject. There is a providential education and preparation for this end. And thus it often happens, that from very infancy, or youth, a boy and a girl are watched and trained for this purpose,—that a holy, angelic ministry is over them,—that, while each is ignorant of their coming destiny, they are prepared for their coming union,—and that finally they are brought, as by accident, or fate, sometimes from opposite quarters of the globe, and from the most opposite circumstances, to meet together, to know each other, and to enter into that unity which is from eternity and to eternity. It is no romancing that we have here. It is truth stranger that fiction. Indeed, all the truth there is in fiction is inspired from this source.

But let us now speak more particularly of the sex of the spirit. It is on account of the non-recognition of this truth, that all idea of marriage has degenerated into the most natural thought, and it is supposed to have no existence except in the natural world. And even in this world, it has become from the same reason, so grossly deteriorated, as to be entered into from the most external considerations, from bodily desire, domestic convenience, wealth, beauty, etc. There can be no greater error than such a view of the sacred institution of Marriage. It is the cause of more unhappiness than any other evil with which man is afflicted. For in losing the conjugial, he loses the inmost element of his nature. He invades the sanctuary of good and truth in the holiest recesses of the spirit. He divorces love from wisdom, and tears up the very foundations of heaven. For he should know that that which is recognized as impossible to be permanently embodied in the most outward spiritual forms, even in the relations between man and woman, is so recognized because of a defect in interiors; and that defect, unconscious as he may be of it, is no less than a total misconception of the very nature of the spirit in its masculine and feminine relations.

Let us consider this point in the light of the Divine Word. In Genesis 1: 27, it is written, "So God created man in his own image, in the image of God created He him; male and female created He them." (*Matt.* 19: 6.) The word man here, (*homo*) is applied to both male and female. He created *man* male and female. This is more evident from the literal sense, where it appears that the woman, as commonly understood, was not created till after the seventh day, as mentioned in the second chapter. From which it is plain that something more is meant by male and female than the mere sex of the body, and we may look therefore for the divine image, not only in each singly, but in both unitedly,—in the full *man* of the union thus symbolized. Considered as *individual human beings*, each is *singly* and *equally* an image of God; but considered as *male and female*, each is an image of God more particularly as to a distinct principle of the Divine Nature.

There are but two principles which constitute the Divine Nature, and these are the Divine Love and Wisdom. Both man and woman receive of both of these in an eminent degree, but not in an equal degree. It is the predominance of one over the other which constitutes the difference of sex; and also the remarkable fact that with man, his love is inmost, and with woman, her wisdom is inmost: or with man, it is love with a covering of wisdom, and with woman, wisdom with a covering of love. Any one may notice this from the fact that man in his social life is not at all unsusceptible of love; it glows in his breast with great vigor and strength, but it does not manifest itself so readily and easily; it flows not from him with such a constant and effortless exuberance; and it is more apt to be selfish and withdrawn: woman, on the other hand, outflows with her nature as though affection came first and uppermost; it is all on the outside; not in a superficial sense, but in a sense of "first have, first give;" she does not wait for it to well up through the great deeps of thought, of a calculating intellect, and many prior considerations; she is too frequently the dupe of her own quick affections for *not* so doing; but, being first placed, it first flows—ever ready, spontaneous, free and graceful. But to show that she has wisdom beneath all this, and very deeply, it is only sufficient to notice how admirably reflection comes, looking as it were *through* that love, to the subjects which love was first taken with. How fondly *contemplative* of such objects of affection! Her intellect seems to have love's eye, while man's love has intellect's eye. And in company with men, though she is not disposed to converse so much on the higher subjects that come within the range of his intelligence, yet her concealed wisdom shows itself in that appreciative listening which is sometimes so terrific!

The difference in consideration may be seen again from another point of view. Woman is more quickly roused than man, in any cause which appeals to the affections, because she is not reached so invariably through the intellect: but when man *is* roused, as he is capable of being, it is astonishing to see how his love will sometimes break forth with the most burning and terrible power. What feats of daring is he capable of! You cannot suppress it; he will not be reined in; he shows the might of all a woman's affection, and pushes on with it under the guidance of an intellect which is all-executive. But this love dwelling in him more interiorly than in woman, it takes time to arouse it: being surrounded and covered with his more sluggish intellect, it must first have *that* interested; it must break through that; when it does, then there is power.

And so with woman. In her common life, in the more gentle sphere of the every-day affections and domestic duties, she does not manifest the wisdom or intellect of man. But how common it is, when her outward supports begin to fail, when man forsakes her, or he is removed by death, and trials of her powers begin to set in; or when, in some emergency of business where she *must* act, and act too in very difficult and important cases; how common it is to see a wisdom and an intellect breaking forth, to which before she was a total stranger, and which is adequate to the most arduous undertakings! Here she frequently outshines man, in all his boasted strength and comprehensiveness. Thus in the experience of Madame Guyon, after her husband's death, who was called upon to settle an important part of his estate, involving a considerable amount of property, about which there had been dispute, and in which no less than twenty persons were concerned, which rendered the case one of great delicacy and perplexity. She accepted it, laid aside all other business, and shut herself up in her closet for about *thirty days*, not going out except for meals and for religious worship. She at length completed the examination, formed a final decision, and drew up the writing. The parties concerned were so much pleased with it that they not only commended it but published it abroad everywhere. But of this she says with her characteristic piety, "The hand of the Lord was in it. It was God who gave me wisdom. So ignorant was I then, and so ignorant am I now, of affairs of this nature, that when I hear persons conversing about them, it appears to me like Arabic." *

Here was an instance where the wisdom which is interiorly resident within the nature of woman, was permitted to come forth, and was probably ministered to by attendant spirits accustomed to such business. So in many more common occurrences. But such cases are always more or less abnormal; that is, where the inmost principle, whether in man or woman, is brought into a state of abnormal activity. In a true and normal state, intellect governs the one, and affection the other, the opposite principle lying more deeply within; and thus the sexes are each in their proper sphere, and each more fitted to unite with the other. Such cases, however, serve admirably to show the *precise nature* of both man and woman, and the exact difference between them.

Here, then, is the true spiritual distinction between the

---

* Life of Madame Guyon, by Prof. Upham. Vol. I., pp. 172-174.

sexes. It is not a distinction grounded primarily in the body, at all. On the contrary, the sex of the body is *from* the spirit. This is manifest from the whole texture, form, and constitution of the physical organism; in that in the woman it is soft, tender, and more beautiful; in man harder and rougher, with many differences of gesture, manners, voice, etc.

> "For contemplation he, and valor formed,
> For softness she, and sweet attractive grace."

It is the qualities of the *spirit* that have produced these differences, and not *vice versa*. Even the more prominent physical distinctions, such as are usually known as altogether sexual, are nothing but a *reversal* of form and organism.

Here, too, may be noticed the whole mooted question of the *equality* of man and woman, as it regards mental endowments. It has been greatly misconceived. It is not, to be sure, altogether without effect, that we are pointed to such minds as Hannah More, Maria Edgeworth, Madame de Stael, Lydia Maria Child, Mrs. Barrett Browning, etc.; but it is to be observed that those who look at the intellect alone, seeking an equality of the sexes, mistake the whole philosophy of the matter. We have no question that the chief and great *practical* disparity observable in the minds of men and women, is owing to circumstance and education; and not to any natural inferiority on either part. Give woman the same advantages, and she would be man's equal, in so far as either could desire, at any time. But in order to do this, and to make it general, the same *time* is necessary — the same number of generations, for her culture and improvement, as have passed in her unequal circumstances and neglect. But the truth is, woman is not to be considered alone, nor man either. The Creator has not designed their entire being thus isolated. The only true philosophy is that which recognizes in these twain, one flesh, one being, in the conjunction of wisdom and love. They are in fact a more perfect and absolute unity together, when perfectly joined, than the most perfect man or woman can be alone. And in heaven they frequently appear, not as two, but as one angel. This is in their more intimate and internal states; ordinarily they appear as two, but with wonderful unity, felt and seen in all the recesses of the mind, and forms and tissues of the body.

"I also spake with the angels concerning conjugial love, or that which exists between two conjugial partners who love one another, that it is the inmost of all loves, and such that partner sees partner in mind (*animus*), and mind (*mens*); so that each partner has the other in himself or herself; that is, that the image — nay, the likeness of the husband is in the mind of the wife, and the image and likeness of the wife is in the mind of the husband, so that one sees the other in himself, and they thus cohabit in their inmosts. This was represented by angelic ideas, which cannot be expressed by words." S. D. 4408.

"And because there was in my thought a desire of knowing what marriages were amongst the most ancient people, I looked by turns on the husband and wife, and observed, as it were, the unity of their souls in their faces; and I said, You two are one: and the man answered, We are one; her life is in me, and mine in her: we are two bodies, but one soul; the union between us is like that of the two tents in the breasts, which are called the heart and lungs; she is my heart, and I am her lungs; but as by heart we here understand love, and by lungs wisdom, she is the love of my wisdom, and I am the wisdom of her love; wherefore, her love from without veils my wisdom, and my wisdom from within is interiorly in her love; hence, as you said, there is an appearance of the unity of our souls in our faces." C. L. 75.

Here it may be understood, also, that, although in single ones as viewed upon earth, the man predominates in the intellect, and the woman in affection, yet, "in marriages in the heavens *there is not any predominance*, for the will of the wife is also that of the husband, and the understanding of the husband is also that of the wife, since one loves to will and think as the other, mutually and reciprocally; hence their conjunction into one." H. H. 369.

The distinction of sex in heaven, then, would seem to be mainly in the *position* of the characterizing principles; man's love being inmost, with a covering of wisdom, and woman's wisdom being inmost, with a covering of love.

In the view of all this, how could there be a greater equality? How shall we dispute any longer the matter? Once for all, the question is killed; and in the light of these transcendent principles, the sexes rise in their own true sublimity as one Man, male and female, whom the Lord God created.

An excellent writer most truthfully says, "The man is endowed with a more powerful intellect, and with strength and courage, because he is appointed to the performance of the more active, difficult, and laborious duties: the sphere of his activities is more extensive, and his powers are consequently more developed and brought into observation; but, remove the inspiring spirit of the ardent affections of the woman, by which she 'applies herself to the will-desires of the man,' and is there no reason to conclude that, deprived of this primary stimulus to exertion, his *will* would languish, and his boasted intellectual and bodily powers lose their activity, and, finally, all manifest existence? And thus it is with all the operations of the intellect; they display themselves while the secret sources of their activity in the will are concealed. The man might, with some degree of justice, lay claim to superiority on account of his strong intellectual and bodily powers, if he *could* confine the exercise of them to himself, and if he *could* resist the influence of the woman over his mind; but the case is otherwise; for the woman 'is gifted with a perception of his affections, and the utmost prudence in moderating them;' and by virtue of the conjugial sphere which she transmits, and which is received by the man, she can bring him into subjection to her will, and render all his powers subservient to her use. Thus beautifully has the Creator balanced the excellencies of each sex. The man is formed by nature as a natural man, to gather goods of the natural world, and knowledges pertaining to them; and as a spiritual and rational man, to gather and deduce truths of a rational and spiritual kind, and to present them to the woman, who is formed, not to investigate and deduce truths, but to perceive and receive them, and to make a return to the man for them, by an accession of satisfaction in their enjoyment; which satisfaction, had it remained with him uncommunicated, would have been of a polluted kind, founded in self-love and self-esteem: for while a man loves to acquire and possess truth, as a means of delighting the mind of his wife, (which is always the case when he desires truth for the sake of good,) it is a generous affection; but if he loves it merely as a means of feeding his own self-conceit, it is a mean and defiled affection: in the one case it is of heavenly extraction, in the other it is from beneath."*

A similar observation may be made of the woman; *viz.*, that were it not for the influence of the man, by the presence and display of his intellectual powers, and the thought of the woman that she is to be united with him, she would be without that impulse which she now has to expand and elevate her understanding, and thus fit herself for a true marriage with him.

But we should fail to derive a full understanding of this connection between the sexes, without a still more expanded view of their interior relationship. This, also, is derived from the Divine Word. It shows not only the *nature* of the relationship, but more particularly the *reason* of it, or why it is necessary for the sexes to be thus constituted. It is a reason founded deeply in the wants and liabilities of poor human nature, and is alike reflective of the beauty and wisdom of the Creator's plan, and his regard for his imperfect creatures.

We find it recorded in Genesis 2, that the Lord created woman *from* man, — that the rib which was taken from Adam was made into a woman, and she was brought to the man,

---

* Old New Jerusalem Magazine.

"And Adam said, this is now bone of my bone, and flesh of my flesh: she shall be called Woman, because she was taken out of man."

Here in this allegory is a deep spiritual truth; and that truth is, as it first presents itself, that the feminine principle, whatever it is, is derived from the masculine; or that feminine love is derived from masculine wisdom. Let us look at this in the light of that genuine philosophy which must forever appear, when once seen, to be the very truth of God and glory of man. It is known, then, that one great object of the creation of man is that he may perfect himself by all that wisdom which is to be derived from a study of the works of God, assisted by his Word, in every department of material and spiritual nature. He is to become more and more God's image, and filled with more and more of his happiness, in proportion as he receives of this wisdom, united with his love, and this he is to do by the use of those varied faculties which have been conferred upon him for the purpose. Here, then, we are to recognize a fundamental love in the character of man. It is the love of growing wise. This is the *primary* love. It is the foundation of endless progression. But it will at once be seen, that this love cannot be exercised without giving rise to another, *viz.*, the love of wisdom. For when man, by the love of growing wise, comes into possession more or less of the wisdom he has sought for, then he must necessarily love that wisdom. The two fundamental loves of man, then, are first, the love of growing wise; and second, the love of that wisdom. And when it is considered to be, as appropriate to man's state in the regeneration, not merely *natural* wisdom, but the knowledge and perception of those vast arcana which pertain to the *spiritual* universe, by which his soul is refreshed, and his whole being lifted up in the contemplation of a myriad beauties, and divine and angelic connections; and when too we contemplate the spiritual world where he is finally to dwell, and where these wonders are more fully opened to him, we have a faint idea of how great that wisdom is which the mind of man is capable of receiving, and how it must delight him through the ages of eternity.

But now observe, if this transcendent wisdom should be left to him *alone*, for him to love *in himself*, and himself for it, it would inevitably tend to pride and self-conceit. The more so, in proportion to its amount. The very greatness of the divine bounty would thus be converted into the greater curse. Thence it would become an evil love, the like of which is now so manifest in many men who are puffed up with their own attainments, enjoying them too exclusively alone, in the most perverted examples of a vain and solitary self-intelligence. And if such a thing could remain, and perfect itself *wholly* in this way, as would be the case were no provision made for its prevention, it would become a *destroying* love, reacting against humility and the love of God, till it finally destroyed the very sources of wisdom with himself. For the influx of the Divine Wisdom is not into receptacles of this kind, but only into those which diffuse and multiply it.

Behold, then, the beauty and the love of God. It was to prevent such a catastrophe, and to secure a more divinely beautiful result, that this second love was taken out of man, and transcribed into woman; or that woman was created with a soul appreciative of the wisdom of the man, who in all the softness and delicacy of her feminine nature, could love that wisdom better than her own self. And the man also, being delivered from self-conceit, or the destroying influence of the love of his own intelligence, can now love that very wisdom in another who most dearly loves him for *it*. The love which man has for his own wisdom in himself is designated by the "rib," or intellectual *proprium*, or self-hood, which was taken out of him and made into a woman, and she became "bone of his bone, and flesh of his flesh." By this divine and beautiful act of creation, it is also still provided that man shall be kept in his own proper and fundamental love—the love of growing wise, but that the *woman*, rather than the man, shall be gifted with the love of wisdom, which she perceives in her man, so that from these two nicely balanced loves in different persons, there shall be a perpetual tendency and inclination to unite, and to become in male and female, one perfect Man!

But here I anticipate an objection. I have heard it several times put, even by woman. There is something in her nature which *objects* to the mere love of wisdom. "What!" says she, "do I love a man for his wisdom alone? Am I only enamored of his intellect, or of spiritual truth? Do I not rather love him for his love? These dry metaphysics may do for Swedenborgians, and for the dryest kind of them; but what is simpler than to love another for his love to you? — to love love, and not mere wisdom?"

To this it may be replied, and I *beg* not as mere metaphysics, that to love a man for his wisdom, or to love his wisdom, *is* to love his love. For his love takes that *form;* truth is nothing but the *form of good* — the way in which it puts itself forth. The spirit of man going forth to the spirit of woman, if it could be seen as it is in the spiritual world, presents itself in the beautiful form of his own love, which is wisdom or truth. And the spirit of woman going forth to man, presents itself in the form of *her* own love, which is likewise wisdom or truth. These forms vary with every variety of beauty, according to the nature of the intelligence so presented. And if a man *does* manifest true wisdom, it is invariably the wisdom of love; that is, which has grown and culminated from his very deepest love, and is characterized by all that tender regard and affection for the welfare of another, which properly belongs to it. Cannot a woman love that? Nay, *does* she not love it, with all the strength of her most ardent affection? Is there any thing else that she *can* love? For love without its form is nothing — not any thing perceivable. It cannot exist without its form. Man, then, is the wisdom of love, and woman is the love of *that* wisdom. And oh, how great — when it embraces the universe, as far as it can reach, and is enriched with all variety of knowledge, which shines upon his person, and glows in his face, and glitters in his garments, and is all consecrated to her most devoted service, to rejoice her heart, to illumine her beauty, and cement and lift them both up in mutual, ever-growing affection!

From the whole, then, we find unmistakably the ground and foundation of sex *in the spirit.* Must it not, therefore, be eternal? Can any earthly circumstances put an end to a love like this, or can death interrupt it? "What God," in his own nature and eternity, "hath joined together, let not man put asunder." Let him not for a moment think of it.

Here may occur, perhaps, as an objection to this theory of marriage, the words of the Saviour to the Sadducees. "They which shall be accounted worthy to obtain that world, and the resurrection from the dead, neither marry nor are given in marriage." (*Luke,* 20: 35.) And they do *not,* in that carnal, natural sense, which the Sadducees had contemplated; nor in a sense which is too applicable to the dealings of men in this world — form the merest external motives, mercenary expedients, and vain considerations: but is there any thing said here against that truly spiritual marriage which pertains to concordant souls? It is plainly implied here that some spiritual *worthiness* is necessary to attain that higher world. All could not obtain it. And what can that worthiness be but that very union or marriage of good and truth in the soul, which alone fits us for the angelic world? It is the whole object of the regeneration to effect that marriage? Hence so much is said in the Word of the marriage state as applicable to salvation, and of the church as a bride and wife, and of the marriage supper of the Lamb. Nothing indeed is more conspicuous than the well-recognized soul-marriage which appears throughout the Old and New Testaments. From the union of Adam and Eve in the Garden of Eden, to the grand apocalyptic vision of the New Jerusalem coming down from God out of heaven, prepared as a bride adorned for her husband, there stands out continually the remarkable and "mystical *marriage*" of the followers of Christ. It is inwrought into several of the Saviour's parables, and was significantly embodied in his first miracle in Cana of Galilee. But it has not been fully understood, especially not in its sublime relation to the sex of the spirit, and the conjugial union of two souls in one. The world has not been prepared for it. These arcana of the Divine Word, as also many others, will break out in precise proportion as there is preparation on the part of men to profit by them. But by the true and divine philosophy which already appears in regard to this subject, it must be recognized by many as self-evident truth, that a *perfect* soul-marriage cannot take place, even in the regeneration, without the union of good and truth in two individuals who may constitute such a one: for in such a union only is their entireness of manhood. "Male and female created he them, and blessed them, and called *their* name Adam," or Man. (*Gen.* 5: 2.) And now, whence is the further significancy of the Saviour's words to the Sadducees? The truth is, this marriage of good and truth in the soul must be effected in *this world*, to be fully established in heaven. Here in this rudimentary and probationary state, is the foundation to be laid, the great salvation to be determined, in the very ultimates of the natural mind. If it is not secured here, it cannot, *as to this individual organism*, be effected after death. They who have immersed themselves in evil, and have thus "unworthily" passed into that world beyond, "neither marry nor are given in marriage." They have effectually divorced themselves from the divine good and truth. Such is the further spiritual meaning of the text, and it conflicts not in the least with the genuine truth which is here set forth, but is rather indispensable to the fullest perfection of it; *viz.*, the conjugial and eternal union of two souls in one.

Another distinction must be noted in this marriage. It is the distinction between the love of the sex, and the love of one of the sex. The first is more properly a natural love, the second a spiritual. The love of the sex in general is an affection common to all animals; but the pure and chaste love of *one* of the sex, is a spiritual affection peculiar to man, and is only acquired by regeneration. That is to say, he is not *born into it*, as into other loves, but he comes into it when he is "born again" of the Holy Spirit. It is not indeed meant to say that the love of the sex in general is necessarily an impure love; for if it is friendship, or a sincere love of their good qualities, their feminine graces, and a delight of their society, it may be "chaste as ice, and pure as snow:" or it may be warm and glowing with the most rapturous affection: how many such loves must there be in heaven, and intimacies dear and sacred, which stand in the closest proximity to conjugial love, but cannot touch it! Into the holy relation of conjugial partners, only two *can* enter, nor is it desirable. It is a love distinct and separate from all others, which cannot by any possibility be shared by a third. Before man is regenerated in some degree, he is so in love with the evil and the false, and has so mixed these in his own mind, that he cannot ascend even to the conception of a legitimate and holy union for eternity with one only of the female sex: but as he is interiorly in spiritual adultery, so he is interiorly in natural or sexual adultery.

Let us now observe the *effects* of this pure love, as it may exist on earth, and as it exists in heaven. On earth, it is the fountain of all joys and delights, from first to last. It is necessarily so, because it is the fundamental of all loves, and the very origin of the highest uses. The higher the use is, the more interior and intense the delight. And if *natural* marriage is so sweet, — if the joys attendant upon merely natural affections and earthly uses are so high and ennobling, what must it be when natural marriage is exalted to the spiritual, — when spiritual affections and thoughts have directed it upwards to its divine source, and under the influence of this source it has become admissive of heavenly blessedness as far superior to all natural enjoyments as heaven itself is superior to earth? Let it ever be remembered that this marriage primarily proceeds from the Marriage of Love and Wisdom, or Goodness and Truth, in the Divine Mind. And it first passes into the celestial heaven, uniting the angels there; next into the spiritual heaven; next into the spiritual-natural; and lastly to men on earth. And inasmuch as it is the *first* and *primary* union, so it is the principle which unites all particulars and varieties among the angels, in their life, experience, occupations, and uses. In each and all, as an all-pervading, assimilating element, it exists in an infinity of conjugial ties, making life happy, and filling heaven with beauties and wonders. The very air itself is sweet and pure with its divine chemistry, and the blessed birds make music from its joys. Not a flower exists, or a fruit is ripened, without its harmonizing and perfecting influences; the whole creation teems with its truth, and is redolent with its good. It is, in fact, the conjugial sphere which flows forth from the Lord and fills the universe. As God is married, so nature is married; and as one rejoices, so the other, in proportion as this element prevails, is fruitful and rejoices.

In man on earth, its great use is to propagate the human race, and thence to extend the angelic heaven. And inasmuch as true marriage is the conjunction of two minds in love and wisdom, so it is by the mutual reciprocation of these two minds that all that is delightful and heavenly in affection and thought, words and works, have birth between them. To what extent this may exist, is as yet but little known upon the earth. Indeed, it is not in the power of man to know of this love at all, unless he is principled in the life of religion. For it is not given to merely natural love, and the natural man must forever be a stranger to it. It is the love of the *sex* only, that is the uniting principle of most marriages, and not of *one* of the sex, although, from prudence and custom, that love may be mainly restricted to one. But inasmuch as there can be but one truth for one good, and every truth must have its *appropriate* and *equal* good, and these exist in an infinite variety, so there can, truly and spiritually, exist but one man for one woman. It is the recognition of this truth that introduces to spiritual wisdom. It is the practice of it which confers perfection of character. Wherever such a union exists, there are derivations, fructifications, and multiplications of delights from the Great Fountain of Love and Wisdom, which perfect and rejoice the souls so related, and more and more perpetually unite them.

I need not speak at length of the *children* born from such a love. How can it be otherwise than that they will partake of the spirituality of their parentage, be delivered from a large share of hereditary evil, inheriting the divine harmonies even from the mother's womb? Children born of this love, and not of lust, inherit from birth a tendency to perceive the things which are of wisdom, and to love the things which wisdom teaches. And they grow up with a far greater facility into the form and order of heaven.

And how is it in eternity? Natural children are not indeed born there, but the offspring of such marriage among the angels exists in the most beautiful manner. It is by union from this love, that pairs of angels are continually receiving of each other's life, and are strengthened by each other's strength, all from the Divine received first into their own minds, while they rejoice and progress eternally together, drawing nearer and nearer to the Lord who keeps them. In every thing pertaining to thought and affection, they are thereby greatly quickened and enlarged, so that the most glorious mental creations are continually being produced as the offspring of such a marriage, and thus they wend their happy way through the upward paths of glory and of beauty.

"They who are in love truly conjugial, after death, when they become angels, return into youth and adolescence; the males, however worn out with age, become young men; and the wives, however worn out with age, become young women:

each conjugial partner returns into the flower and joys of the age in which this love begins to exalt the life with new delights, and to inspire sportiveness for the sake of prolification: into this state, first exteriorly, afterwards more and more interiorly to eternity, comes the man who had fled adulteries as sins, and was inaugurated into that love whilst he lived in the world. * * * The reason why man thus grows young in heaven, is, because he then enters into the marriage of good and truth, and there is in good an effort of continually loving truth, and in truth there is an effort of continually loving good, and then the wife is good in its form, and the man is truth in its form: from that effort man puts off all the severity, sadness and dryness appertaining to age, and puts on the liveliness, gladness, and freshness of youth, from which the effort lives and becomes joy. It has been told me from heaven, that they have then a life of love which cannot otherwise be described than as being the life of joy itself." A. E. 1000.

"From conjugial love the angels also derive all their beauty: thus each angel is beautiful according to that love: for all the angels are born of their own affections, inasmuch as in heaven it is not allowed to feign with the face things which are not of the affection, wherefore the face of the angels is a type of their mind: whilst therefore they have conjugial love, they have love to the Lord, mutual love, the love of good and the love of truth, and the love of wisdom: these loves with them form their faces; and present themselves as fires of life in their eyes, to which moreover innocence and peace are added, which complete their beauty. Such forms are the forms of the inmost angelic heaven, and are forms truly human." 1001.

Such, we are compelled to believe, is true marriage. And now, what shall we say for its realization on the earth? What is the Divine Providence concerning it? It is manifest from several considerations that such a marriage once was, more generally than now. If the race has fallen, this love has fallen. It is the testimony of Swedenborg that such a marriage was universal, or nearly so, in the most ancient times—in the Golden Age of the First Church, and that it gradually declined as men grew sensual, but that nevertheless it may be raised up again by the God of heaven, and will be so raised in the New Jerusalem.

But, at present, how dark is the prospect! How gross are the conceptions of men and women! How little does the world in general know about such a love! And yet there has always been an instinct, more or less faint, of the "right one," the "only one," and that "matches are made in heaven." These are the remnants of a more sacred truth, which have survived the ruins of the Fall, and which have lived on through all ages, glowing in the hearts of humanity like embers in the ashes. But sad, sad indeed, is the common faith and practice. Marriage is entered into by young men and maidens, old men and women, with scarcely any reference to equality of interior principles — scarcely *any* knowledge of the divine, philosophical unity that exists between the sexes; and chiefly for mere outward considerations — for situation in life, for respectable equality in circumstance, for beauty, for mere fancy or caprice, to say nothing of the baser bribes of wealth and sense, by which the most heterogeneous and opposite materials are brought together; and under these circumstances the acquaintance is made, the bargain struck, the law applied, and the marriage effected. Then comes the trial of this treachery with the eternal laws. It soon begins to be perceived, even by those who are not remarkable for great spirituality and sensitiveness of soul, that the internal affinities are somewhat of a higher order, — that the State and the church, externally so considered, have little or nothing to do with the reality of marriage, — that what of love and what of wisdom have been exercised in the case, will neither assimilate in quality nor proportion, — that, in fact, the union is the greatest outrage against the divine principles, and some other parties have only been defrauded of their proper partners, which doubles the confusion, and doubles the misfortunes of earth. Let it indeed be acknowledged that there is a Divine Providence in or over all this; so there is in murders, robberies, and all other evil work. We must be serious here, or we shall not write to the purpose. We know how this subject is prostituted. We would, if possible, utter a voice which shall be heard round the world. We believe that society is in the midst of a gradual revolution on this subject; but in the realization of the evils of impure and ill-assorted marriages, it has not, generally, any radical cure for them. Hence the vagaries of "Free Love," and all the legitimate abominations connected with it. Oh, *how* shocking, and how terribly re-active must this experience yet continue to prove to many!

But let us learn wisdom, ere it be too late. Let us remember that love has its arguments as well as its flames, and that *true* love is of the spirit, and thence of the body; and not of the body, and thence of the spirit. External, sensual love, is only the symbol, expression, or ultimation, (at least, in true union it is,) of internal affections and principles. If there is no marriage of the mind, there *can* be none of the body. And hence it is that these bodily enjoyments so often die out, or become insipid, having nothing at all of the spirit to sustain them. And if young men and maidens do not consult these mental, moral, and spiritual characteristics, they may prepare for themselves a more direful punishment than is possible to conceive of in the whole range of disobedience. There is *nothing*, NOTHING so utterly tiresome, and the cause of so many and so bitter regrets, — nothing that so wears upon the very soul itself, and if the nature be at all sensitive, so curses and torments it, as the compelled experience of a legal tie which death only can annul, with one with whom is no interior unity, no love grounded in a mutual reciprocation of soul-affections and soul-thoughts, and who only exists as a sham and a semblance of what ought to be, but, alas, cannot be! "Bonds of iron and steel cannot unite two inharmonious substances, and the heart is never so lonely as when mocked by the semblance of unreal union." The parties are not only, by these false views of marriage, laying the foundation of their own misery, but cursing themselves in their children's children, to the third and fourth generation. They are peopling the world with deformities and inharmonies, and eternity itself with imperfections to be outgrown there.

I have no words to express my horror of the haste, and lightness, and frivolous manner with which this subject is treated in the community. There is more cause to rejoice in death, and to make merry and sing at the spirit's departure from this bondage of corruption, than in a large proportion of the marriages of earth. And the false delicacy which refuses to speak on this subject is not to be tolerated for a moment. If we could see the world uncapped — if we could view the secrets of all the marriages and all the deaths, we might have less cause to rejoice at one and weep over the other.

This whole marriage institution is undoubtedly, in these latter days, to be re-explored by the light of interior truth, and undergo a gradual and thorough change. It is the one great subject which lies at the foundation of all others. The church itself begins in the family — in the marriage of two souls who receive of the divine goodness and truth in their most interior relations, and exemplify it in their lives. From thence it proceeds to the neighborhood and the world.

But this subject *perverted* as it is, is the one great *sore* which festers and corrodes upon the corrupted body of humanity. It is the most delicate of all subjects, to be touched even by skillful hands. But the truth must be told; the times are ripe for it. The truth is, society is reeking and rotting, and exuding corruption from all its pores, by the abominable evils and falsities which have profaned this holy of holies. There is no soundness, no security anywhere but in a return to first principles. We are a nation of corrupters. Not only a nation, but the whole Christian world is probably more corrupt in this respect than is scarcely ever suspected. It is the testimony of Swedenborg, (we know not how much restricted to locality and time,) that "those who are out of the church, and are called Gentiles, live a much more moral life than they who are in the church, and far more easily embrace the doctrine of true faith. This is very evident from the state of souls in another life; for the worst of all are those who come from the so-called Christian world, bearing a mortal hatred against their neighbor and the Lord, and being more addicted to adultery than any other people on the face of the earth." A. C. 1032. The reason of this is, that true and pure marriage is from the conjunction of good and truth; but Christians having separated these principles, and exalted the principle of faith alone, and so *mixed* the goods and truths of the church with abominable evils and falsities, the result is *spiritual adultery.* And this is what is referred to many times in the Word, where whoredoms and adulteries are spoken of. It is this spiritual adultery which becomes ultimated into *natural* adultery, and fornication, and all uncleanness. One is the effect and outbirth of the other.

Now, therefore, there is no deliverance from this, but in a return to first principles, — to the perfect marriage of good and truth in the mind, and to the recognition and practice of the conjugial relationship between individuals. But here let us be careful. It by no means follows, because false marriages have been entered into, and true principles afterwards begin clearly to be seen, that any hasty steps are to be taken to disannul or to disrespect the former marriage. There are many who would be so tempted. The re-action of so much truth against so much mal-practice is sometimes terrible. None but the sufferer can know the anguish of spirit, or realize, in some of the unhappy cases, how the soul is wrung through all its fibres, when once it has realized its solitary misery. But it must be submitted to. This is the penalty of tampering with the highest laws of God. Divorces in such cases would only increase the evil. They would cause that marriages be entered into all the more lightly, looking to the expedient of a ready divorce in case of a blunder; they would also operate badly in respect to families of children; they would lead to multiplications and repetitions of evils of this kind; and in short, unloose the gates of hell for the inflowing of a worse confusion than now exists. Besides, where could be drawn the line between such marriages as should be legally recognized as binding, and those which should not? "The heart knoweth his own bitterness, and a stranger doth not intermeddle with his joy." It is very evident that a general, or any laxity, of the laws pertaining to divorce, would only increase the evil. And besides, there are many spiritual reasons which might be given, why such separations should not be permitted.* Therefore, what the statute-book, and the clergyman, and the Justice of the Peace so often sanction and confirm, be it as pitiable as folly can make it, be it even like Socrates and Xantippe, or honey and wormwood, is made, by the present state of sinful humanity, the fastnesses of nature and fate.† Because truer marriages might have been made, or because human beings are destined to be eventually united in pairs for eternity, that is no reason why society should be outraged with licentiousness and disorder. Besides, it is impossible to tell now who *are* our true partners. God has wisely veiled that fact from our present imperfect state, and ordained that a *conservative semblance* of conjugial love, many times truly happy, should exist as a substitute. It is by the continuance of this semblance, or approximation to the spiritual reality, that the conjugial principle is providentially kept alive in human bosoms, without which it would experience more violence than it now does, and eventually die out of the heart of humanity. By living, therefore, faithfully with one wife, and discharging from principle all the duties of the marriage tie, we are best preparing ourselves for that higher union in the heavens, with our true spiritual companions. But by rebelling against this union, because of its uncongeniality, we thereby dishonor the Divine Providence

* For an excellent and truthful article on "Marriage and Divorce," from an interior standpoint, by Rev. T. L. Harris, see the "Herald of Light" for June, 1858.

† The usual cases of adultery and desertion are of course here excepted.

which has so permitted, and are in danger of destroying the conjugial principle altogether. Besides, the state of mankind at present does not admit of true conjugial relationships. It would even be an evil, sometimes, to allow two *true* partners to dwell together, before being suitably prepared in the regeneration; for the evils of one or both might be so great, and still the love attraction so strong, that they would be loving and overlooking each other's *evils*, and forming the most intimate alliances with them: thus the infernal marriage of the evil and the false might be going on between them, and the beautiful union which is really hastened by a temporary separation, and by preparatory states with other connections, is not only postponed, but greatly injured, by a premature attempt at spiritual nuptials. And often too it may be the case, when one partner is in heaven and the other on earth, that the heavenly angel will still look down, not with jealousy, but with complacent joy, to see its own dear companion united with another, and so enjoying the most it can, in a state which so approximates the heavenly union. It would grieve at any act of unfaithfulness. For it is known in the heavens, that thus the best possible preparations are making for the fulness and ultimation of the perfect joy.

Finally, is not this a subject of the very greatest earthly and heavenly importance? Can it be possible that the utmost carefulness of the Divine Providence is not exercised over such a matter as this? When we consider the deeps of human misery, the horrible soul-agonies, the suffering, mal-formed children, and all the dreadful accumulation of sins and diseases entailed upon the corrupted body of humanity by the so called *marriages* of the world; and on the other hand, the bliss serene and heavenly, the ineffable delight, and the high, immortal uses of the true soul-connection, we have no words to express our horror of the one, and approbation of the other. But how shall such a marriage be promoted? We have only room to say — Be convinced, in the first place, that there *is* such a thing as a true soul-marriage. If our young people only *knew* of such a truth, what wonders would it accomplish! For then, though they might not and could not, find their real partners, they would many times come much nearer to it than they do now. At present they have nothing to guide them, — nothing higher than earth and its conveniences, and the dissolution of the holiest of all ties at death, to govern them in their choice of persons. If they only knew, therefore, that there *was* such a thing as spiritual and eternal marriage, how would they pause, frequently, before this sacred temple of the soul, before they entered with desecrating hands into its holy of holies! They would not rush as they now do, with passion and dread strife, and from a thousand external motives, into a union so momentous, but they would gradually approximate the true and heavenly reality. Let no principles, then, be tolerated, as fundamental and governing, but those of the true and philosophical unity, and oneness of the sexes. Let this be the bright and polar star in all our outfits for this great voyage of matrimonial life, or else prepare for disasters more terrible than can possibly exist in any other adventure. Because this union is the *highest* of all the connections of the divine principles, so, when perverted, it becomes the *lowest*, and attended with worst evils. And oh, *how* low, and how debasing may it become! Soon, after marriage, is this love of the externals quenched in the night of its own darkness, and the spirit which has been so outraged asserts with over-mastering authority its terrible remonstrance! It is its own Judge, and Executioner of Justice. Marry, I say, as far as possible, for equals, and for eternal ends. Wait not for perfect equality; it is not attainable in this world. But make the best approaches to it. To the young and unmarried I would more particularly speak, and I say, obey God's laws which are written in Nature and the open Word, and bring not, for yourselves nor for your children, an inheritance of suffering into this world. Marry for earth, and marry for heaven. Consider this Institution as the highest of all God's institutions on the earth or in the heavens,

— the initial Church, the most absolute State, the Holy of Holies in the Great Temple of Humanity.

And after all, do I hear a note of discouragement? Is it said that much cannot be done, the world is so wilful, sensual, and corrupt? I have only space to say, for this as for all other subjects, they that have grace must be the salt of the earth. Every true man and every true woman, who, by principle and life, will see, acknowledge, and uphold such a marriage, may do *much* to shame this wretched trafficking in human hearts, and throw a glory and a grandeur over the most sacred of all unions — the most divine of all God's gifts and blessings.

CHAPTER XXIV.

DIVINE PROVIDENCE IN THE TIME OF ONE'S DEATH.

"A Christian cannot die before his time,
The Lord's appointment is the servant's hour."

"I took them away as I saw good."—*Ezekiel,* 16 : 50.

THERE are three distinctly marked and most important periods in the life of every one: the time of one's birth, the time of his decision for heaven or for hell, and the time of his death. From one point of view it might seem that the time of one's *birth* was the most important; for it is then that he is ushered from comparative unconsciousness into this living and breathing world, an immortal and wonderfully endowed creature; and, whatever destiny he may now choose for himself, he has clearly commenced an eternal existence. The very thought is enough to overwhelm the mind with issues of unspeakable importance. But in so far as the man himself has any thing to do with his destiny, the time of his decision for heaven or for hell is by far the most important. And though it be impossible for any one to tell, precisely, when that time of great decision is, yet it must be admitted that there is such a time; and I think it will also be admitted in general, by those who are accustomed to think seriously and deeply upon the subject, that there is, commonly, a point in a man's lifetime when, if he has not already made the heavenly choice, he will not be likely to make it. It is true, it may be with some that they will make this choice very late in life; almost the last thing, perhaps, that they seriously set about; but these cases rarely exist, if ever; we do not *know* what may be the Divine

Providence in such cases, nor is it any part of our business to try to decide: we know the general law and the general fact, that it is not what a person's character or appearance of character may be in the last hours, by any influences which then altogether operate, but what it is in consequence of a *whole previous life*, the result and end of which may manifest itself in the last hours, and may not, very distinctly; it is *this* which decides a person's destiny. And if goodness begins to appear then, and to predominate, after a whole life of impenitence and sin, it is not because the man then wills it independently of his past course, but because that course itself, and all that pertained to it, was taken into view by the Divine Providence, and so ruled and regulated as to bring out the final result. So that, while we never know what is being wrought within a man, and he *may* turn about very late in life, seeking heaven as his chief good; yet all our rational calculations are to be based upon the whole course of a man's probation. And we say that there is very likely to exist a point in a man's lifetime, when, if he has not yet made the heavenly choice, he will not be likely to make it. This may result from the steady perseverance which he has made in sin, and the forms of evil which he has thereby organically established in his mind. He may weave for himself a spiritual body so distorted and perverted, that he not only has no desire to change it here, but which he will find it impossible and alike undesirable to unweave, when he passes out of the world where it was done. For it is here, as has been said before — here in this world of nature, that the foundation is laid, the ultimates acquired, upon which the interiors of the mind must rest as a house upon its basis. One may make some *external* improvements beyond the grave; may come temporarily into less and less actual evil, and into some sort of natural, external good; but he cannot, while in this position, change his motives, or be led to good from the love of good.

"The experiment was made whether they were able to resist

evils whilst the punishments of hell were announced to them, yea, while they were seen and likewise felt; but still it was vain, for they hardened their minds, saying, come what will, provided only that we are in the delight and joys of our hearts so long as we are here; we know things present, what is to come we are not concerned about; we shall not suffer more evil than many others; but after a stated time they are cast into hell, where they are compelled by punishments *not to do evil;* but punishments do not take away the *will*, the *intention*, and consequent *thought* of evil, *they only take away the act*." A. E. 1165. "The evil remains within, and recurs when the fear ceases." 1164.

But note carefully that there must have been a time — a turning moment — a choice amid all other choices — (fearful and momentous consideration it is,) when the first decisive inclination to that evil life — the one which turned the scale, and kept it ever after that way, commenced in that man's history. *He* did not know it; no mortal, and perhaps no angel knew it; but God saw it, and was working in reference to it. But the man must be held in freedom. Then it was that he made the fatal choice! It determined all other choices, and involved a destiny of unimaginable horror.

Here, then, is the *second* great period of a man's life. It is when he makes his decision for heaven or for hell.

"Once to every man and nation comes the moment to decide,
In the strife of truth with falsehood, for the good or evil side:
Some great cause, God's new Messiah, offering each the bloom or blight,
Parts the goats upon the left hand, and the sheep upon the right,
And the choice goes by forever, 'twixt that darkness and that light."

Observe, we are not saying that any man can know when that time is; we only say that such a time there must be; and to doubt that the Divine Providence is most particularly concerned in it — that even the time of our death is wisely ordered in reference to it, would be to doubt one of the most reasonable and evident things in all theology. Religious writers have often spoken of this time as one of *unusual struggle*, and of more or less sensible surrender, either to good or evil. And why may we not suppose the angels who watch over a man's destiny, to be particularly active and anxious at such a time? Swedenborg also speaks of the particular leading of the good and evil through this world, and of a similar decision. His language, too, is remarkably discriminative.

"There are in the world men-angels and men-devils. [That is, human beings who will people heaven, and who will people hell.] With a man-angel all the degrees of his life are open even to the Lord; but with a man-devil only the ultimate degree is open, and the superior degrees are closed. A man-angel is led of the Lord, both within and without; but a man-devil is led of himself from within, and of the Lord from without. A man-angel is continually withdrawn from evil by the Lord, and led to good; but a man-devil is continually, also, withdrawn by the Lord from evil, but from a more grievous to a less one, for he cannot be led to good. A man-angel is continually withdrawn from hell by the Lord, and is led into heaven more and more interiorly; but a man-devil is continually, also, withdrawn from hell, but from a more grievous to a milder one, for he cannot be led into heaven. A man-angel, because he is led of the Lord, is led by civil law, by moral law, and by spiritual law, on account of the Divine [principle] which is in them; a man-devil is led by the same law, but on account of what is of himself in them. * * * A man-angel and a man-devil appear like to each other as to externals, but they are altogether unlike as to internals; wherefore, when external things are laid aside by death, they are manifestly unlike; the one is taken away into heaven, and the other is conveyed down to hell." A. E. 1145.

Again, touching the changes and determinations of life to which we have referred, we find this language in the work on Divine Providence.

"Man [in the world] is not [in hell or heaven] as a spirit who is inscribed in the society, for man is continually in a state of reformation; wherefore, according to his life and its changes, he is transferred by the Lord from one society of hell into another, if he is evil; but if he suffers himself to be reformed, he is led out of hell, and is led away into heaven, and is also transferred there from one society to another, and this until death; after which he is no longer carried from society to society there; because he is then no longer in a state of reformation, but remains in that in which he is according to life: wherefore, when man dies, he is inscribed in his place." D. P. 307.

From the whole, then, it is evident how much the Divine Providence must have to do with the time of a man's death. However we may settle the eternity of this most sorrowful of all questions, there is enough in the *temporary* features of it — in the unimaginable ages of sin and its consequences — and the awful uncertainty which hangs around the whole theme, to convince one of the infinite importance of the results determined by this great change of worlds.

Now, whichever side a man may decide for, be it heaven or be it hell, it is the *state of his life here in the world*, the quality of his spirit, and what can be made of him in the spiritual world; nay, it is really what he is making of himself now, and what the Lord is doing for him, both in his own soul and in the world beyond, which decides to a *moment* the time of his death, which is the third great period in the life of man.

This event is ordered, therefore, with the utmost precision. So is every other event; but this assumes to our minds a greater importance, being so full of eternal consequences. It is alike important to the good and to the evil. In the passage of the Word at the head of this chapter, it is said — "I took them away as I saw good." This is said of the evil Sodomites. And it is taught here, even of the wicked, and the most wicked, that the time of their death is ordered with a no less particular reference to the utmost amount of good which can be done for them. If they cannot be regenerated, they may be reformed; and if they cannot be in the highest sense reformed, they are capable of more or less external improvement; at all events, it is seen exactly what and how much *can* be done for them, and their life in the world is not permitted a moment longer than, all things considered, is for their best good throughout eternity. Sometimes they are cut off to prevent their wickedness increasing, which would make it still worse for them in the spiritual world. Sometimes they are spared for a length of time, because it is seen that they will reform and improve their condition before leaving this world. Sometimes it is seen that they will not do it here, and it is better that they should be removed, and come under the instruction and discipline of angels. In many ways, and by many secret connections, is the exactitude of Providence accomplished with them, and with the good also; so that this mystery of death, in all its forms, whether premature, as we say of it, or occurring at a ripe old age, or sudden, or accidental, with a lingering sickness or without it, is performed at the best possible time, and solely with reference to the soul's condition in eternity. "I took them away as I saw good." It is the divine announcement for the whole method of the Lord's working, "with whom is the fountain of life," and to whom also "belong the issues from death."

That there is "a time to die," — that this, in fact, may be considered in the light of exact truth, — that no accidents can interfere with it, but must be subordinated to it, so that all apparent accident shall be merged into the great system of a connected and universal providence, may be seen from the Lord's own life upon the earth. It is, in fact, a fundamental characteristic of the true theology, that every point of correct faith may be seen in the great *central* doctrine of the incarnation, glorification, resurrection and ascension of the Lord. They ray out from this Centre, as distinct beams from the great orb of day. Thus, regeneration is best illustrated by the Lord's glorification; the infinite personality by his finite personality; the infinite love by his love; the sight, the hearing, the intimate relationship, and all the divinely human attributes and qualities which endear and attach us to the infinite Father, by this exhibition of Himself in a finite form. So, also, the varied experience of man is best known as to its character and tendency by the Lord's experience when he dwelt among men as one of them. It is one of the great excellencies of this doctrine of the Lord, as unfolded by Swedenborg, that it accommodates *every* truth, which otherwise would lose itself in the vagueness of the infinite, to the receptive capacity of the creature. And so also this truth of the time of a man's departure from the natural world.

To borrow the language of a Christian brother, "Christ always spake as if He had an appointed time to remain on earth, a fixed work to accomplish, during the progress of which He must continue incarnate; and until 'His hour was come,' the Jews had no power over His physical life. Twice He was delivered out of their hands in a mysterious way. But when 'He knew that His hour had come,' and that 'the Father had delivered all things into His hands,' He was given up unresistingly to the malice of His enemies. It was not that some blind fate had fixed the time of His death; not that He had accomplished every thing possible in gaining converts, or in imparting truth to His disciples. His converts were very few, and His disciples, at the moment of His death, understood very little as to who and what He was. He might have lived on half a century more, under the Divine protection, teaching the truth, and gaining followers, and exhibiting to the world the charms and graces of His character; and then He would only have lived through the common period of human existence. But the time came, at thirty years of age, when He could say, 'It is finished,' since the work for which He came into the world was done. What was it? Evidently the very thing we have been describing. It was His glorification. It was when the material had served its end as the basis of the spiritual, and within its continents the divine organism was completed whose processions of power were to come in Pentecostal gales, and sweep down our human nature till they woke from it new tongues of utterance, and drew lyric praises from all its strings." *

And so it is in the corresponding work of our regeneration, and in the removal of the good and evil from this world. It is no more blind fate than the time of our Lord's crucifixion. It is when the utmost of that work is done which can be done in the human spirit, to fit it for eternity. This, and this alone, is the signal for the flight to the unseen world. No matter if a man goes from the gallows; if Providence so orders, it is best he should be off; and, indeed, when a man has come to that pass that he can be guilty of the crime of murder, it may be that he has filled up the measure of his iniquity, and indicated such a state as is more hopeless for him in this world than it is in the next. The angels and good spirits may there do for him what man in the world cannot. Or he may be saved from going to a still lower hell. It may, therefore, in some instances, be the better charity—though I do not pretend to decide this awful question of punishment by death.

This event of death, however or whenever it may occur, is too vastly important not to be under the most particular supervision, as to all its connections. When we reflect that "as the tree falls, so it remains," as to all its prominent characteristics; that the very degrees of a man's mind, which are the great distinguishing marks of his character in eternity, are opened or kept closed, by his conduct in the world; that though he may progress indefinitely after death, it must be upon the plane of life which he has acquired to himself here; that the ruling love remains in some sense to eternity; that with the good, the progression must be immense, according to every faculty and facility they have procured to themselves here; and with the evil, even their evils and falsities must in many cases increase, for a while, at least, until they have acted out all the evil that

* "Sears' Foregleams of Immortality," pp. 230, 231.

lay inwardly concealed in them; and when we consider that though this life is short, and extremely uncertain, it is still long enough to decide eternal destinies; then we may receive from this whole subject a most solemn impression, and an admonition worthy of its greatness. Death is truly a grand and finishing point, by which, in this first sphere of conscious existence, a work for eternity is decided with wonderful precision. Not *the* finishing point of all our destiny, but a grand and finishing stroke in every man's history.

But it cannot be understood fully without a more perfect philosophy.

"It is the concordance of the internal or spiritual man with the external or natural man, which remains where it falls; man has both the external and the internal in the other life, but the internal or spiritual is terminated in his external or natural principle as in its ultimate. The internal or spiritual man is perfected in the other life, but only so far as it has concordance in the external or natural; but this latter cannot be perfected in the other life, since it remains such as it was acquired in the life of the body; and in this life it is perfected in proportion as the love of self and of the world is removed, and consequently in proportion as the good of charity and the truth of faith are received from the Lord; *hence is the concordance or non-concordance, which is the tree with its root, which after death remains where it falls.*" S. D. 4646.

The lesson which we would derive from this whole subject is, *carefulness* and *watchfulness*, *assiduity*, and *practical determinateness.* The object of a knowledge of the truth, or of a new impression of it, is to make good use of it. We can do much to *affect* and *influence* our last hours. What is it, in short, but to prepare for eternity? And we know not how near, or how distant, may be our time. It is wisely provided that we should not. If we saw it very near, we should be overwhelmed with too much consternation and alarm; if we saw it very distant, we should lapse into indifference. But not knowing any thing about it, except that it is likely to occur at *any* time, we have the advantage of continual presence, without bewildering fear or supine indifference. But the reflection that the *Lord* knows it—knows it to a certainty, and to a moment, and is ordering things with reference to it, with as much directness and system as we would arrange for the departure of a son for a distant country—it should make us better co-operators with the Divine Providence, and produce a deeper interest in the mighty change.

How affecting, too, are many of the connections and dependencies of death, as they relate to others with whom we are associated—both as to time and circumstance. To quote again a very instructive passage from Swedenborg,—

"If some die in infancy, others in childhood, others in youth, others in riper years, and others in the latest old age, there are four reasons for all this. The first regards man's use in this world in reference to his fellow-creatures; the second regards his use in this world in reference to spirits and angels with whom man is in communication as to his interiors, so long as he lives in this world, which is the general ultimate and basis of all things; the third regards man's use in this world in reference to himself, either in order that he may be regenerated, or that he may be immersed in his own evils, lest they should be dormant, and should break out in another world, which would tend only to his eternal detriment; the fourth regards also his use in another life, and onward to eternity." S. D. 5002–3.

Thus we see, that it is not for ourselves alone, but for others, even with reference to the spirits and angels with whom we are in association, who may, by this connection, be advanced with us. For the great Orb of being is One, embracing all in heaven, and all in hell, and all in the world between; and the onward stream of life bears us all forward to the ever-swelling ocean of eternity. Nor can we tell what forms of use we may be filling out for the invisible company with which we are connected. Often, very often, it may be, that the silent ones gather around us in our hours of retirement, in our studies, or go with us to more active scenes, and derive a blessing from our labors, from our thoughts and affections — something to lift them up, and to send them onward in their path of being. Yea, how true it is that all heaven is in sympathy with one man! — that our penitence rejoices, our minds assist, in this great abyss of being, above, around, and beneath us!

We shall not die, then, before all *that* work is accomplished.

The usefulness to our fellow-creatures here — to assist and regenerate them, and to fill out all the measure of charity; and to ourselves also, and sometimes even to be plunged in evils, that we may see and correct them ere it is too late — this whole use of living, and this wisest moment of dying — how affecting and practical is the lesson which it teaches!

He takes us away as He sees good. If infants die, we know that they are needed for the heaven of innocence, that they may flow back with their tender influx, and perform some of the most interior works of man's regeneration here. Moreover, they are thus saved from a dangerous and perilous life, and made safe in heaven. It is not orderly for children to die; but in the present state of disorder, the system of God's providence largely requires it. If the children of wicked parents die, we see the good providence of God in so ordering it that the very *sins* which cut off so ruthlessly the offspring of a wicked generation, are turned to an account in peopling heaven. For while by their wickedness they miserably destroy themselves, their children also die off in infancy and youth, infected and corrupted all through with disease, and go to the enlarging of all the heavens. Thus it is again, that even the *wrath* of man is made to praise the Lord, and the remainder of the wrath is always restrained. If accidents occur, and death takes frightful forms, we know that there is a permissive as well as a provisive providence, and that the causes even of these disasters lie frequently concealed in the spiritual world. What is accident to us may be sometimes design and direction in the spiritual world, where is seen more fully the chain of causation, and the personal agents who are permitted to have a part in it. Such things are indeed for the most part disorderly, but they are frequently permitted and overruled in a higher and more definite sense than we ever think of. If the young and the useful are taken by any means, let us call to remembrance how opportunely and quickly a death may occur.

This world is not the only field of usefulness; and "to constitute the Grand Man," says Swedenborg, "there is need of spirits from several earths; those who come from our earth into heaven not being sufficient for this purpose, being respectively few; and it is provided of the Lord, that whenever there is a deficiency in any place, as to the quality or quantity of correspondence, a supply be instantly made from another earth, to fill up the deficiency, that so the proportion may be preserved, and thus heaven kept in due consistency." (E. U. 9.)

Now, cannot the same be done from *our* earth? Should it be any marvel that there are *sudden* and *unexpected* deaths?

"But this is *Nature* operating," says one. In reply, it is merely to be remarked again, how prone are all merely natural minds to stop in second causes. It is the great error of the irreligious philosophy. True it is that nature operates, and operates according to laws; but the Great First has included *all* causes and all effects in His Infinite Mind, and nothing transpires, or can transpire, in the world of nature, but from eternity it was seen to be so, and seen to be best in every particular. If it is wrong or evil, it was permitted as the best that could be, consistently with man's freedom. When, therefore, the thing happens, whether by nature so called, or by some angelic or other interposition in the spiritual world, it happens as it was seen and provided for from eternity; and the *time* of the occurrence is included to a moment!

Here it may be remarked, that we do not always die by natural diseases, even when it appears so. When a person's work on earth is done, or when it is seen that he cannot or will not do any more; when his usefulness, therefore, is brought to its highest possible point in this world, he can easily be made to die, without waiting for the ordinary operation of merely natural laws. We live by influx from God through the heavens. And it is only necessary to cut off that influx, or for the attendant spirits to withdraw a certain distance from the man, and leave him more fully to himself, and he may sicken and die at any time, pining away for the want of that vitality. This may account for many sudden and mysterious deaths, and for many forms of misunderstood diseases. Evil spirits also, with their poisonous and fatal influx, may at any time approach the man who is in evils, being permitted by an all-seeing God.

Thus it is, from all these causes, that death walks round the world. And finally, it is to be observed, that if man had lived in true order, and not fallen into sin, he would *never* have died in infancy, nor prematurely. He would have lived without disease, and have attained a ripe old age; and then, when the body could no longer minister to the internal man, he would have migrated easily and without pain, into the spiritual world.

But now it is not so. And since sin *has* entered into the world, and this kind of death by sin, it is provided that our life be vigilantly guarded and watched; and from the moment of birth, to the point of great decision in every man's destiny, and to the hour of his departure, it is arranged by the Lord with the utmost precision, that we shall come and go under His all-merciful care.

And thus it is that there is "a time to die." The common sense of the world has always recognized it, in that it declares that no one goes till his time has come. And may God in mercy grant that we may live a good and useful life, that when our summons comes for the great departure, we may go,

> ———"Not like the quarry slave at night,
> Scourged to his dungeon, but sustained and soothed
> By an unfaltering trust, approach the grave
> Like one who wraps the drapery of his couch
> About him, and lies down to pleasant dreams."

CHAPTER XXV.

TRUST IN THE DIVINE PROVIDENCE: ITS NATURE AND EFFECTS.

> "The more thou puttest in the Lord thy trust,
> The stronger shall thine arm for service be;
> When thou rememberest that thou art but dust,
> Then first awakes a living soul in thee.
>
> When thou canst say, O Lord, thy will be done,
> Then shall *thy* will grow strong for truth and right;
> When thou despairest, thou hast first begun
> To learn from whence the feeble heart hath might."

We have not written the foregoing chapters without a definite and practical purpose. Our object has been to scatter doubts, to beget a true and rational faith, or confirm and extend it where it is begotten, and to show how reason and revelation, faith and philosophy, unite and harmonize in the well-instructed soul. Thus we have striven to elevate men's minds above the visible and perishing, the unsatisfying and seemingly confused, and fix them rejoicingly in the Everlasting Good: — to bid despair forsake the soul, and sin retire, and a cheerful, hopeful trust and sweet piety take up its abode in the mind. How well or successfully we have done this, must be left to every reader to decide for himself. We do not deem our work by any means perfect, nor even to possess that completeness and finish which we had hoped, in the outset, to have been able to bestow upon it. We honestly confess we have fallen far short of our beloved ideal. But we must crave the privilege of adding one more chapter, and pray heaven to aid us in the writing. If men will not *trust* in the Divine Providence, it is in vain for them to know it. We have, therefore, one last word — trust, *trust*, TRUST.

To rely with humble and unshaken confidence on such a Providence, is, perhaps, the highest privilege of human beings; for it is attended with an inward peace, and a serene, undisturbed happiness, through all life. But in order to this, something more than mere faith is necessary: "Trust in the Lord and do good," is the brief and divine announcement; and it must be at once perceived that the most unremitting activity of goodness is alone consistent with the most perfect trust. In fact, there can be no true trust which is not founded in good, and which is not in some way — either mentally or bodily, or both — constantly active. The Lord is Good itself, and thence Truth itself; and when a man is engaged in this, he is, in fact, working *with* the Lord, and the Lord with him, to accomplish every purpose of the Divine Wisdom, to lighten every difficulty, and to bring to pass every rational desire of the heart.

But this is a matter not attended to and thought of as it should be; nay, it is an error quite prominent, frequently, among those who have the most enlarged views of the Divine Providence, and which springs, perhaps, from a remnant of the old principle of faith alone. A man may be in faith alone with the truth, as well as in falsity. There is no good reason why it should be so; though, undoubtedly, from avoiding one error, they have sometimes lapsed into the opposite extreme. From the manifest folly and uneasiness of men who have hurried and blustered about as though the business of the universe depended upon them, and who, in a state of self-trust, could hardly wait for the slow and orderly movements of Providence, — and, indeed, who seem to have no worthy views of Providence at all, they, in their larger and more spiritual views, have lapsed into a dignified quiet: not only quiet, which, in its true and more appropriate meaning, is a state of harmonious action, — so harmonious, and so perfectly at one with the divine everlasting movement, as not to be felt at all as an exertion; but they have settled into what has not inappropriately been called a "masterly inactivity" — frequently into a do-*nothing* state; and thus this great fact and faith of a divine and all-embracing Providence has been recognized *too exclusively* as a fact and faith; it has not been ultimated, as every thing good and true in principle should be, into *works*, which are the outermost and practical plane of this tangible, every-day existence. Next in enormity to acting from self-trust and self-dependence, is not acting at all; and though this latter state cannot come entirely to exist, for the soul is inmostly and constitutionally active, yet we must all confess to a great liability to negligence and sloth; and where nothing good is done, there is a strong proclivity, and, indeed, a way open for influx, to evil. "Idleness is the devil's pillow, or workshop." "Man was created for uses. While, therefore, he is in any study and business, or in any useful occupation, then his mind is limited and circumscribed as by a circle, within which it is successively co-arranged into a form truly human; from which form, as from a house, he sees various lusts out of himself, and from soundness of reason within, exterminates them. The contrary happens to those who give themselves up to sloth and idleness: the mind of these is unlimited and undetermined, and thence man admits into it every thing vain and ludicrous that flows in from the world and the body, which leads to a love of them. Hence other loves, and especially conjugial love, is cast out into exile. In consequence of sloth and ease, the mind grows stupid and the body torpid, and the whole man becomes insensible to every vital love, especially to conjugial love, from which, as from a fountain, issue all the activities and alacrities of life." C. L. 249.

In teaching the lesson of Providence, it has been fitly observed, "the Lord says—'Behold the fowls of the air; they sow not, neither do they reap, nor gather into barns; yet your heavenly Father feedeth them.' True it is, that God provideth food for them, but they take the pains to seek it out, and to gather it, and provide for their little families; and by being examples of industry in their way, teach us that Providence will do nothing for the sluggard." "Trust in the Lord and do good: so shalt thou dwell in the land, and verily thou shalt be fed." It is not temporal and earthly subsistence which is here primarily referred to, but heavenly and eternal. Both are included, and by trusting in the Lord and doing good, is meant that true and genuine trust which consists in the activity of regenerated affections. To have this is to be almost constantly at work doing something. But are there no moments of rest—no cessation from labor? Here, indeed, we are brought to another consideration concerning the mind which relies upon the Divine Providence. There are times, evidently, when the more active and specific duties of life cannot be at all followed, but where both rest and recreation are necessary. But rest itself is not inaction, death-likeness, but, generally speaking, change from one thing to another. There is indeed such a thing as absolute rest; that is, cessation from all bodily action, when the soul needs to recuperate itself by Divine Influx, and, something as in sleep, to repair its wasted energies in the utmost silence and stillness, preparatory for new and more vigorous action. And such periods, we are assured, exist even in the spiritual world. But generally speaking, rest is only change, or the state brought about by change, from one thing to another. This brings into exercise a new set of faculties and powers, allows the former to rest, and so varies the circulation of divine influx in the soul, that what before produced fatigue, now gives pleasure and excitement. But the truth is, were society in its true order—were the church and world what they ought to be, and what they are destined one day to become, we should not pursue one thing till we get fatigued with it, but change before that condition is induced. Thus, it appears, it is in heaven.

Rest, then, is change. No man is so unhappy as when he is doing nothing, and has nothing to do. The reason is, the thoughts then acquire a corrosive quality, and react upon the soul itself. To be truly happy, and truly at rest, is to be almost constantly engaged in some useful employment, because this is that harmonious activity in which the very essence of happiness consisteth. This is the secret of the *Divine* happiness, if we may speak reverently on so high a subject. What we call recreation, or re-creation, is the creating of ourselves anew by fresh supplies of the divine life, so that we ourselves may in turn become creators; that is, may throw off from the soul in new forms of use, what otherwise would react in misery upon ourselves. The Divine Being does not need re-creation, for He is the uncreated and infinite Source of all life and happiness; but his happiness consists in continual creation—continual impartation of himself to others.

We see, then, what it is to trust in the Lord and do good. It is to partake of the Divine Nature itself. It is, by the almost incessant activity of regenerated affections going forth into old and new forms of use, to dwell continually in the land of the divine Cultivator, and verily to be fed:—to be fed with all that richness which belongs to a true church of the Lord, and with all that temporal prosperity which is the appropriate condition of a well-ordered life.

It is true in both senses. This trusting in the Lord, in a true and genuine way—there is more in it than appears to be. Still, there are many natural men who are sorely bewildered at the prospect of a disordered world, and in view of the many grievous inequalities, the strifes and cruelties that come upon suffering and innocent ones, they are visited with many heart-failings, and life itself, to them, seems little better than a game at hazard.

But now, for the clearer and more systematic understanding of this subject, it may be remarked, that there are two opposite and still connected *spheres* of the Divine Providence, and these spheres are always to be thought of as *substantial*,—as real and tangible to spiritual senses as the system of the material universe, or any connection whatever of human machinery. They are spheres of Order and Disorder. That is, what is in agreement with the Divine Will, as being in accordance with goodness and truth, and what is in disagreement with it, as coming from the free-will of men and spirits, and consisting only of the evil and false. These spheres may indeed be *mixed* with men in the world, and also in the World of Spirits; but for distinction's sake, and as answering all the purposes of our present subject, they may be spoken of as two separate and altogether distinct spheres, the one of Order, the other of Disorder. Now, within the one or the other of these spheres of absolute, substantial, net-and-chain-work, so to speak, is every man in the world predominantly fixed, and his destinies determined by that inevitable power.

Let us now consider it in regard to man's free-will. He goes to work forming his plans, and with much apparent wisdom, and truly a great outlay of thought, to accomplish some definite object; and after a long trial, perhaps, is amazed that his purposes succeed no better. But the simple truth is, he has *not acknowledged the Lord*, not *believed* in Him with any thorough-going faith, but trusted mainly to himself. And if he has looked to the Lord at all, has it been with the saving clause — Trust *and do good?* Has it not been, rather, some worldly speculation pursued too exclusively for himself, without that consecrating power which layeth holy hands on all such objects, communicating to them the quality of good use? If so, then it is but a short story to the secret of his failure. He was a comprehensive man, a talented man, a man perhaps of wondrous activity and energy; it is melancholy to see such a man fail; but all his plans had been laid mostly *without the sphere of Divine Order*. Being an irreligious man, in a sense of that word which applies to all business operations, he *could* not, very largely, bring his plans within the divine sphere of protection. And what is the consequence? The first thing he knows, some unforeseen occurrence turns up, having its cause in that other sphere, which is filled, from centre to circumference, with the disorderly spirits of the evil and the false; and the germ of disorder which originates there, works out with most fatal certainty its ultimation in the natural world. There was no accident, chance, or bad luck about it. It was seen from the beginning how it was coming out, and that such a course must inevitably end in failure.

Sometimes, indeed, such a course is permitted to succeed for a while, perhaps all through the man's lifetime in the world, because it is foreseen that nothing else can be done with him; and so he is permitted to amass worldly goods, even in an unrighteous way, for certain uses to himself and others; but if any thing better can be done with him, be sure he is not permitted to succeed in that way.

Here, then, is making religion practical; — trust in the Lord a matter of mercantile and business-like propriety. Let it not be thought for a moment, that a right disposition towards God has little or nothing to do with our worldly concerns. The truth is, it is the same God who governs our earthly, that governs also our heavenly or spiritual interests; and the two are most intimately connected. Indeed, *all* our *true* interests, whether of a spiritual or material nature, are made to bear upon our heavenly destiny. They are connected with some spiritual discipline of the mind and heart, and reach into eternity. And that eternity is more or less present with us now — stretching out and reaching down its all-enveloping sphere of good or evil, order or disorder, and confirming in every-day life the practical truths of God's Word to man.

But let us look at it again from a different point of view. What, philosophically and psychologically, is this trust in the Lord? The truth is, that by thus submitting the whole matter of our earthly life to Him, we derive, from that very trust, which is no mere abstraction, a distinct, substantial *form* of divine organic life in the soul, and hence a corresponding form of influx from the Lord through the heavens. We turn ourselves to the central Source upwardly, as we do our feet to the centre of gravity downwards, and thus point the soul to the centre of influence. We are thus poised correctly in the spiritual universe, and the trust is astronomical. The great Spiritual Sun then keeps us steadily and securely, and we receive directly of its most copious beams. We derive a higher wisdom for our whole worldly and spiritual life. And we prosecute every undertaking to a more ultimate success, because we have thus attracted into our own souls, and in turn are attracted into, a circle of divine and heavenly influences, which is equivalent to the Lord coming nearer to us, to accomplish by Himself and his angels, the purposes of his wisdom, and to fulfil the desires of them that fear Him.

How different is the case of one who has *not* this form of divine good in the soul! He cannot trust in the Lord, and he knows nothing and feels nothing of that divine sphere of protection which proceeds from this principle of Order. Such a man may fret and fume his whole life away, in the workings of his self-conceited wisdom; and perhaps, in his utter worldliness, cast ridicule upon the idea of trust in God, as having little or nothing to do with our prosperity. He is a man full of self-energy and self-acting,—one who thinks and says what *he* is going to do—what great things *he* will accomplish: and by this very confidence in himself alone, he withdraws from the circle of Divine Providence which is arranged through all the heavens,—cuts himself off from that very influx of the Divinity which constitutes all true wisdom and strength, and invites to his aid a class of spirits who are similar to himself, who are immersed in self-love and self-conceit, and who, together with him, are plotting with all hellish interest against God and against heaven. And when such enterprises are overthrown, suddenly or gradually, then to be told there was no trust in God, and no reference to the Lord's providence, is little better than mockery to such a man. Whereas, it was a sequent in the Divine economy as orderly and regular as the fall of a stone when thrown beyond its place of rest upon the earth. The man fell, and the stone fell, for they had strayed beyond the bounds of order.

Again, sometimes the man who trusts in the Lord is in *perplexity*, and he not only knows not how to act, but *cannot* act, in any way commended to his wisdom. But he is still within the sphere of the Divine Order, and though he may not be able to act outwardly in any given case, yet he acts inwardly, and with great efficiency. He acts involuntarily. For by this acquired *spiritual* activity — this habit of looking to the Lord, and referring every thing to Him, he does, without any labor on his part, attract to himself a class of spirits who are in similar principles, and the influx is given through them, of as sure and certain a character as can possibly be made to operate in the case. A multitude of fit and appropriate thoughts come streaming into his mind, obscurities begin to scatter, and plans are suggested which appear to be all his own, but are given of the Lord by a law as regular as that by which the planets roll, or the winds blow. The only condition is *Trust — active Trust.* "Trust ye in the Lord forever, for in the Lord Jehovah is everlasting strength." (*Isa.* 26 : 4.)

And so with all our worldly and heavenly affairs. The promise to all such is, "So shalt thou dwell in the land, and verily thou shalt be fed." It applies to material, no less than to spiritual support. It cannot fail, for it is the everlasting law of God made prominent in all things. Once let a man give himself entirely up, without reservation, without compromise, and consecrate himself and all his works entirely to God, and he will be cared for supernaturally. It is no mere cant of religion, it is solid philosophy. Such a man may indeed be afflicted, and kept in many straits, for it may be that his salvation yet requires it; it may be the very design of Jehovah to humble him, and make him all the *more* trustful. And it may frequently happen, too, — indeed, it seems to be a well-observed *law* of the Divine Providence, that help is sometimes delayed to the very last moment, in order to teach man that Providence is supremely wise, and does nothing unnecessarily, and so to inspire the soul with a still deeper reliance through all states and in all extremities.

An eminent instance of this kind of provision was in the case of the celebrated Stilling, a German writer and physician, whose works have acquired a well-deserved popularity, and whose history is so touchingly and artlessly given in his Autobiography. And here let me take the opportunity to *recommend the perusal* of the beautiful story of this amiable and devout man, as one of the best, indeed *the* best living exemplification of the subject that we write upon, with which we are acquainted. It is a story which should be circulated everywhere, and rejoice the heart of the most desponding. Every important step of Stilling's eventful life seemed to be under the guidance of a perceptible providence, and directed by promptings, in himself and others, from the unseen world. In the darkest seasons of adversity, when utterly destitute and without credit, and when immediate pecuniary assistance was necessary to save himself and family from ruin, some unforeseen hand was always stretched out to help him, some friend at his side to suggest the needed relief, and almost miraculously, again and again, was the process repeated. He left his early home without definite plans and almost penniless, and wandered forth like Abraham of old, obeying a command which his circumstances seemed to make imperative, and from that time forth led the life of a most remarkable pilgrimage. He was truly a "providential man." So are we all; but it was the beauty of his life that he could see it so well,—that the instances were so marked and wonderful,—that his prayers were so frequently answered,—that his faith and trust were so tried and yet so triumphant, and that he could still in simplicity persist that from first to last, he had contributed nothing whatever to any part of the manner in which he had been so remarkably led. Reader, if you have not read the Autobiography of Heinrich Stilling, I would commend it as a most fitting sequel of practical life, to follow in the train of these poor theorizings. It has all the interest of a thrilling romance, at the same time possessing the advantage of serious reality.

One great part of our wisdom in this matter is to learn to see the Divine Providence in particulars. It is comparatively easy to acknowledge the Providence of God in general, or in universals; scarcely a human being can be found who has not some idea of the government of God over the general course of events; but to stop here, is to stop short almost of the whole truth. There can be no general or universal Providence which does not include *all the particulars;* and to rest in an easy faith merely of such a *general* disposition of events, is to leave out of account, especially, many *disagreeable* things which our self-love or self-conceit finds it hard to ascribe to any particular or necessary providence in our behalf, and which we fain would think might be dispensed with. But what reason have we for such a conclusion as this? Does not the Lord rule throughout, from centre to circumference, and does He not know all our states, both the evil and the good, and has He not seen and arranged for them all? Who are we, that we may select a part, and accept a part as divine treatment, and reject the other part? Now there is *nothing,* perhaps, more needed to perfect the faith of many minds, to complete their piety, and their happiness also, than to recognize the Divine Providence not only in general, but in particulars. Then a thousand things which appear disagreeable and averse will begin to be lighted up with a divine brightness, and be acquiesced in as beautiful to contemplate. By a constant watchfulness, the mind will acquire a *habit* of discerning the Lord's providence in many little things before unnoticed, and the faith which is so beautiful to cherish will descend into the very outermost regions and ultimates of the mind, permeating all the thoughts and influencing the affections, and producing a wisdom and a calm too heavenly to describe. "Whoso is wise, and will *ob-*

serve these things, even they shall understand the loving-kindness of the Lord." (*Psalm*, 107 : 43.)

We must discard, as far as possible, all anxieties and thoughts about the future. This was the overplus of that manna among the Israelites which was reserved till morning. This they were commanded not to do. It was enough that they gathered of it every day, every man according to his eating. But the spirit of fear and distrust came upon them, and they reserved of it till the next day, "and it bred worms and stank." So it is with all such care for the morrow. It is a principle which has corruption dwelling within it, and is the death of all true faith. We have neither right nor reason for such anxieties about the future. We do not know that any such future will be ours. We may die at any moment. To be anxious and solicitous about the future, therefore, is not only uncalled for and vain, but greatly obstructs the happiness and duties of the present. "Sufficient unto the *day* is the evil thereof." The future is God's, and He alone may see to it. Take care of the moments, and God will take care of the years. It is not, of course, prohibited that a reasonable care shall be exercised, and reasonable provision made for what may be the common wants of life; but the spiritual of the Lord's words is, that we should not have that care for the morrow which disposes one to be discontented with his lot, to distrust the Divine Being, and to be more anxious about worldly than about heavenly things. It is well and wisely said, that those who truly trust in the Divine Being "have a care for the morrow, and yet have it not; for they do not think of the morrow with solicitude, still less with anxiety; they are of an equally composed mind whether they obtain what they desire or not; neither do they grieve at its loss, but are of a contented mind. If they become opulent, they do not set the heart on opulence; if exalted to honors, they do not consider themselves more worthy than others; neither are they made sad if they become poor, nor dejected if their condition be humble; they know that, with those who trust in the Divine

Being, all things tend to a happy state to eternity, and that the things which befall them in time, still conduce to that end."

A very visible illustration of the happy effects of trusting calmly in Providence, at all times, may be gathered from a phenomenon of common life, even with the irreligious. How often is it remarked that those persons who have the least care, and are even careless in their adventures in every-day life, seem to get along the best; while those who are full of care and fearfulness lest some danger should befall them, are more commonly found in difficulty! Now, one reason for it is, that such persons invariably attract around them a class of spirits who are in similar fears, in similar uneasiness, which brings them into a fluttering and trembling sphere, and makes every thing go wrong with them. Their very fears, by connection with the spiritual world, introduce them to many and many an accident, and many a blunder; while those of a contrary character, irreligious though they may be, acquire a sphere and company of steadier material, and by driving *dull care* away, drive away, also, all the thousand mishaps which follow from it. This is not saying that such a careless disposition should be cultivated, or that it does not frequently lead into deeper and more serious difficulties; but it illustrates the truth, and shows how a *religious* carelessness — trust in the Divine Providence — in a super-eminent manner makes smooth and felicitous the path of life, and introduces into heaven at last.

Finally, what remains but calmly to review the whole subject; and when we think of its mighty sweep, its stupendous heights and depths, and its all-embracing nature; — when we think of the eternal *necessity* for the Divine Providence, and still its connection with the free human will; — of the origin of evil, and its subserviency to the ultimate good; — of the absoluteness of the Divine Sovereignty; — of the intimate connection of God with Nature, in the inmosts and in the ultimates of all things; — of the sublime philosophy of such a religion; — of all general and all special providences; — of the angelic ministry so active and efficient everywhere; — designs and permissions; — the great heaven for which all is done; — the eternal memory of the human soul, and the whole course of the regenerating life — its struggles, triumphs, fluctuations, final rest; — when we think of the wonderful treatment and moderation of the human will; — the control of human prudence; — the infinite divine foresight; — the admirable regulation of earthly and heavenly riches; — of prayer and its answer; — of fortune, chance, and accidents; — of the ministrations of sorrow; — of the sublime economy in regard to little children; — of the divine beauty of Marriage and its accompaniments; — and then see how the whole train of this grand arrangement rolls onwards with unerring wisdom through all this life, to the hour and moment of the human being's death, and with equal precision to eternity beyond it, — what remains but to receive most fully the spirit of the whole Truth, and by a life of reverent Trust and active doing in all good works, fit and prepare ourselves for what still lies beyond? We would not seek presumptuously to lift the veil which falls before that future; but with the amount of truth we do know, we would look cheerfully upward and heavenward forever, purge out every sin and evil that remaineth, and thus endeavor to *act* that Providence which the Lord Messiah is endeavoring to act through us.

www.ingramcontent.com/pod-product-compliance
Lightning Source LLC
LaVergne TN
LVHW010528100826
845148LV00001B/127

9781425576813